Philosophy of Mathematics and Mathematical Practice in the Seventeenth Century

Philosophy of Mathematics and Mathematical Practice in the Seventeenth Century

PAOLO MANCOSU

New York   Oxford
OXFORD UNIVERSITY PRESS
1996

Oxford University Press

Oxford   New York
Athens   Auckland   Bangkok   Bombay
Calcutta   Cape Town   Dar es Salaam   Delhi
Florence   Hong Kong   Istanbul   Karachi
Kuala Lumpur   Madras   Madrid   Melbourne
Mexico City   Nairobi   Paris   Singapore
Taipei   Tokyo   Toronto

and associated companies in
Berlin   Ibadan

Published by Oxford University Press, Inc.
198 Madison Avenue, New York, NY 10016

Oxford is a registered trademark of Oxford University Press

Library of Congress Cataloging-in-Publication Data

Mancosu, Paolo.
Philosophy of mathematics and mathematical practice in the
seventeenth century / Paolo Mancosu.
p.   cm.
Includes bibliographical references and index.
ISBN 0-19-508463-2
1. Mathematics—Europe—Philosophy—History—17th century.
I. Title.
QA8.4.M36   1996
510′.9′032—dc20   95-47024

1 3 5 7 9 8 6 4 2

Printed in the United States of America
on acid-free paper.

To my parents, Angela and Porfidio

PREFACE

The present book is the result of several years' work in the history of the philosophy of mathematics in the seventeenth century. While doing research for it I have come into contact with several scholars whose help and encouragement it is a pleasure to acknowledge here. I began work on this subject while I was a graduate student at Stanford University. At that time I had the opportunity to talk a great deal with Wilbur Knorr, Nancy Cartwright, and Ezio Vailati. Ezio kindly agreed to my using a joint article in chapter 5 of this book. I also owe a great deal to my Ph.D. advisor, Solomon Feferman. Although we rarely spoke about the seventeenth century (we were too busy discussing theories of operations and classes) his point of view on the foundations of mathematics has greatly influenced my outlook on the subject. And that influence goes far beyond purely technical knowledge; Sol has been a model as a scholar and as a human being.

A great deal of the archival research for the book was made possible by a stipendiary junior research fellowship in the history and philosophy of science and mathematics at Wolfson College, Oxford. During those three years (1989–91) I had access to the treasures of the Bodleian Library. In addition to the joy of being at Oxford, I also experienced the wonderful friendship and intellectual support provided by Daniel Isaacson.

The book was completed in Germany thanks to an Alexander von Humboldt-Stiftung fellowship and a Morse fellowship (from Yale), which allowed me to take time off from my teaching duties at Yale University. During my stay at the Institut für Philosophie, Wissenschaftstheorie, Wissenschafts- und Technikgeschichte of the Technische Universität in Berlin, Eberhard Knobloch has been a most wonderful host and a critical reader of my work.

Other scholars have also helped me with the project or have invited me to give seminars. I will simply list them in alphabetical order, confident that they are aware of my gratitude even if I cannot express their merits individually: Ruth Barcan-Marcus, Philip Beeley, Patricia Blanchette, George Boolos, Fabio Bosinelli, Herbert Breger, Peter Cramer, Lisa Downing, Michael Dummett, Luciano Floridi, Sergio Galvan, Donald Gillies, Giulio Giorello, Anthony Grafton, Karsten Harries, Jonathan Lear, Ernan McMullin, Giuseppe Micheli, Siegmund Probst, Neil Ribe, Carlos Sá.

I want to thank my friend and colleague Gyula Klima for having provided the translation of Biancani's work published in the appendix to the book. I owe very special thanks to Amy Rocha. She has not only discussed with me several parts of this work but has been for years a wonderful companion and friend.

I am grateful to the University of Chicago Press for the permission to use the article "Torricelli's infinitely long solid and its philosophical reception in the seventeenth century" (*Isis*, 82, pp. 50–70, © 1991 by the History of Science Society, Inc. All rights reserved) which I coauthored with Ezio Vailati. It is also a pleasure to acknowledge that Mancosu (1989, 1991, 1992a, 1992b, and 1995) parts of which are used in this book (see notes) have respectively appeared in *Historia Mathematica* (© 1989 by Academic Press, Inc.), *Synthese* (© 1991 by Kluwer Academic Publishers, Inc.), *Studies in History and Philosophy of Science*, Gillies (1992) *Revolutions in Mathematics* (© 1992 by Oxford University Press), and Conway and Kerszberg (1995) *The Sovereignty of Construction: Studies in the Thought of David Lachterman* (© 1995 by Rodopi). The relevant parts are here reprinted by permission of the publishers.

Finally, I want to thank Wolfson College, the Whitney Griswold Faculty Research Fund, the Morse Foundation, and the Alexander von Humboldt-Stiftung for their generous financial support.

Berlin, Germany   P.M.
May 1994

CONTENTS

Philosophy of Mathematics and Mathematical Practice in the Seventeenth Century

Introduction

There are many ways of posing the question of the relationship between philosophy and mathematics during the seventeenth century. A favorite subject of research has been the influence of the mathematical method on other disciplines, such as philosophy, theology, or natural philosophy. It is well known that during the seventeenth century the mathematical method—either in its analytic or in its synthetic form—represented for many authors a guarantee of clarity and order in the development of a discipline. It is this fascination with the mathematical method that is responsible, to name but the most well-known example, for the structure of Spinoza's *Ethica More Geometrico Demonstrata*.[1]

This application of the mathematical method in the areas of philosophy, theology, and the natural sciences must be carefully distinguished from the application of mathematical techniques to specific areas of study. The mathematization of mechanics carried out in Galileo's work is the paradigm of this type of approach, but attempts to extend calculations to several areas of knowledge, such as probabilistic thinking in theology, run deep through the seventeenth century. The philosophical problems generated by the so-called mathematization of physics are still problems of great philosophical importance.[2]

One might also investigate which seventeenth century philosophers were particularly influenced by mathematics in the development of their philosophical systems. We then enter the area of what Brunschvicg calls in a happy expression "la philosophie mathématique," the study of those philosophers whose systems bear the mark of a deep influence of the mathematical disciplines. In the seventeenth century the most important among them are Descartes, Spinoza, Malebranche, and Leibniz.[3]

In none of these areas do we deal directly. As its title indicates, this book is concerned with the relationship between philosophy of mathematics and mathematical practice. By "philosophy of mathematics" I mean the specific set of concepts, categories, and theories employed, implicitly or explicitly, by philosophers and mathematicians in their discourse about mathematics. Understood in this way, philosophy of mathematics would include, among other things, some rather ethereal discussions on the nature of numbers by several hermetic philosophers,[4] and the status of various notions, including number, space, and infinity, according to the philosophers and mathematicians operating in the seventeenth century, as well as several other areas of investigation. Therefore I must introduce the qualification contained in the concept of "mathematical practice." The reader should not take this term in connection with the so-called mathematical practitioners. I use the term as it is used today in mathematical logic and philosophy of mathematics, simply to indicate mathematics as it is done, not as it should be done according to some preconceived philosophical viewpoint. Those familiar with contemporary logic and philosophy of mathematics know very well that, far from eliminating the philosophical questions, an interest in mathematical practice has actually extended their range.

Addressing the issue of mathematical practice requires a detailed knowledge of the mathematical literature of the period. However, from the point of view of the philosophy of mathematics, not every single theory or theorem produced by mathematicians has the same importance. Some specific concepts, theories, or theorems function as catalysts for the wide range of problems they embody in a particularly conspicuous way. For instance, Bolzano's proof of the intermediate value theorem is the classic example used in exemplifying what is central in the process of arithmetization of analysis. However, it is merely a historical fact that *this* very proposition is the one on which attention has been focused. There are other theorems that could be used to exemplify the development in question but they are simply not the theorems around which the foundational reflection has been centered. In this book I attempt to point out which theories, concepts, and theorems were at the center of foundational reflection in the seventeenth century. My emphasis on mathematical practice is justified by the fact that these foundational reflections follow closely the development of mathematics in the seventeenth century.

I attempt to situate my investigation at the crossroads between the history of philosophy and the history of mathematics, and to define a general area that could be called seventeenth-century foundations of mathematics, although the term should be taken with a grain of salt.[5] I try to bridge what I see as two parallel developments in seventeenth-century scholarship on foundational issues. On the one hand, one finds a number of articles concerned with the philosophy of mathematics of individual philosophers (e.g., Descartes, Locke, and Leibniz) and philosophical studies related to the mathematical method in philosophy (mainly in Descartes and Spinoza). On the other hand, historians of mathematics have provided an impressive number of technical studies on seventeenth-century mathematics (e.g., studies on algebra, analytic geometry, the calculus, etc.).

Regrettably, the historians of philosophy tend to emphasize issues in the epistemology and ontology of the philosophers and they do not take into account the dramatic developments of seventeenth-century mathematics or the deep interaction between the mathematics and philosophy. This gives the false impression that the majority of philosophers of the period could only tackle very elementary quesions in geometry and were not aware of the significant transformation mathematics was undergoing. Moreover, this approach blinds us to the significant contribution that many philosophers at that time made to the clarification of foundational issues of central concern to mathematical practice, and it ignores the capacity of the philosophers to take into account the new mathematical results.

Similarly, the historians of mathematics tend to give an image of mathematical development as being independent of philosophical considerations. Sometimes this approach is broadly justified using the argument that many central mathematical concepts had been well clarified by the seventeenth century and that a study in the background philosophical assumptions is therefore unnecessary for an understanding of the mathematical issues in question. But this is ultimately unsound. Even if we grant that certain mathematical concepts had been well clarified, this still does not explain why a certain mathematician might espouse one foundational program as opposed to another. For example, it does not explain why Descartes consciously avoided treating infinitistic mathematics in his *Géométrie* although he had the technical resources to do so. The answer is simple: Descartes had made a foundational choice, which is ultimately justified on philosophical grounds. As will be seen later, Descartes' case is only one among many. Of course, my characterization leaves out many authors who have been working at the intersection of these two traditions; the importance of their contribution for my work is duly noted at the appropriate place.

The general strategy of the book is to provide a substantial number of case studies that show unequivocally how profound was the interaction between these fields. Moreover, they are linked in such a way as to give an overall appraisal of the topic. However, the reader should not expect *completeness* in any sense. Although I have tried to isolate what I found to be the most fascinating and important cases of seventeenth-century foundational reflection, it would have been impossible, and indeed useless, to attempt to take into account all the foundational topics discussed during the period in question. Impossible, given the limitation of my knowledge and the absence of previous works of synthesis on which to base my research; useless, because piling up more and more detailed case studies would have hindered the vision of the central developments.

Another type of incompleteness stems not from the things I have excluded, but from the contents themselves. I have tried to strike a balance between the mathematical details and the philosophical issues. The mathematical details aim to provide just enough of the technical development so that the foundational discussion makes sense to someone having no previous knowledge of the history of mathematics. And I have contained the philosophical discussion within a reasonable limit. Leibniz and his work are already covered by several volumes and still more could be written. It has therefore been impossible to treat Leibniz and many other philosophers with the depth they deserve. In order to remedy this situation, I have tried to indicate in the notes which bibliographic references the reader will find useful in pursuing those topics that could not be fully developed in the text.

However, this book is no mere summary of the existing literature. Each chapter aims to provide new historical facts or new interpretations for known facts. To this end, I have also used my previous articles on the philosophy of mathematics in the seventeenth century. I explicitly indicate in the notes which sections of the book are taken from my previous publications.

A summary of the contents should at this point give the reader a taste of the main topics treated in the book. The seventeenth century saw a dramatic development of the science of mathematics.[6] Indeed, after the recovery and new editions of many of the classical Greek mathematical texts a century or so earlier, not only were new mathematical results added to the preceding body of mathematics, but new techniques were grafted onto the old ones and several new areas of mathematics emerged or were consolidated. Reaching full maturity within a hundred years, algebra, analytic geometry, the geometry of indivisibles, the arithmetic and geometry of infinites, and the calculus are among the most significant. Each new area led inevitably to foundational discussions about its status.

The structure of the book is thus greatly dictated by the historical order in which these areas emerged and became the focus of foundational attention on the part of philosophers and mathematicians. Accordingly, most of the chapters begin with a detailed account of the technical background. This enables the reader to reach a fully informed appreciation of how the philosophical reflections interacted with the technical developments.

In chapter 1 I begin by rooting certain aspects of seventeenth-century philosophy of mathematics in a Renaissance debate on the certainty of mathematics (*Quaestio de Certitudine Mathematicarum*). Here classical mathematics is the focus of attention. The denial of the scientific nature of mathematics by a group of Aristotelian philosophers led to a discussion about the causality of mathematical demonstrations (in the sense of Aristotle's *Posterior Analytics*), which had important developments in the seventeenth century. First, I demonstrate the continuity between the sixteenth and the seventeenth centuries in the treatment of various epistemological issues in mathematics. Second, I elucidate the interaction between the philosophical *Quaestio* and mathematical practice by analyzing proofs by contradiction and proofs by superposition. This sets the stage for the developments to be analyzed in chapters 2–4.

Chapter 2 deals with the emergence and structure of the geometry of indivisibles (Cavalieri). The foundational implications of Cavalieri's work are spelled out through an analysis of the Cavalieri-Guldin debate. Guldin's program is also analyzed with special emphasis on his attempt to develop mathematics without proofs by contradiction.

Chapter 3 is devoted to Descartes' "analytic" geometry. Although analytic geometry did not generate a philosophical debate, I analyze Descartes' restriction of the geometrical universe to the so-called geometrical curves, and argue for a novel interpretation of Descartes' foundational choice by relating his project to Clavius' attempted quadrature of the circle in 1591. The last part of the chapter describes the foundational issues raised by the algebraization of mathematics in the seventeenth century.

Chapter 4 rounds off the issues raised in the first three chapters. After an introductory section on the topic of motion in the mathematics of the period, the discussion on continuity between certain aspects of sixteenth- and seventeenth-century philosophy of mathematics is brought to completion with reference to Arnauld's theory of demonstration. In the second part of chapter 4 I extend these claims of continuity by looking at later authors and, in particular, at the theory of demonstration in Bolzano and the fortunes of the debates on proofs by contradiction in Kant and Bolzano.

Chapter 5 is about paradoxes of the infinite. Paradoxes of various kinds arose both in the geometry of indivisibles as well as in the geometry of infinites (Torricelli). These paradoxes were central in the discussions concerning the foundations of the theory of indivisibles and in the reflections on the nature of the infinite. In particular, Torricelli's determination of the volume of an infinitely long solid brought to the fore the issue of how to account epistemologically for infinitistic theorems of geometry.

Chapter 6 deals with the foundations of the Leibnizian differential calculus and its opponents. The interaction between mathematical practice and the philosophy of mathematics is studied with reference to the debate between Leibniz, Nieuwentijt, and Hermann, and the debate on Cartesian techniques versus differential techniques in the Paris Academy of Sciences (Rolle, Varignon, and Leibniz).

The appendix contains a translation of Biancani's *De Mathematicarum Natura*. At first I had included in the notes the original version of the sources quoted in the text. However, this increased the size of the work so much that I eventually gave up the idea. All translations are mine unless otherwise indicated. The sources quoted in the notes have been left in the original version, unless an English translation is readily available.

1

Philosophy of Mathematics and Mathematical Practice in the Early Seventeenth Century

In the last forty years one of the most active areas of research in the history and philosophy of science has been the study of the Galilean revolution in physics. In particular, scholars have focused their attention on the relationship between the emergence of Galilean science and the scientific developments of the Middle Ages. Already Duhem at the beginning of the century in his ten-volume work *Le Système du Monde* had uncovered the existence of a vital scientific thought in the medieval period. In the English-speaking world, the work that has done most to bring about awareness of the deep links between medieval and seventeenth-century science has been Crombie's *Augustine to Galileo* (1952). In this justly celebrated book, Crombie defends a strong version of the continuity thesis. In the preface to the second edition (1958), he describes his effort as follows: "Especially I have tried to bring out, what I believe to be the most striking result of recent scholarship, the essential continuity of the Western scientific tradition from the Greek times to the seventeenth century and, therefore, to our own day." In his *Robert Grosseteste and the Origins of Experimental Science, 1100–1700* (1953), Crombie singled out Grosseteste's commentary on Aristotle's *Posterior Analytics* as representative of a new conception of scientific methodology.

The other scholars who have argued extensively for the continuity thesis are J. H. Randall in his 1961 work *The school of Padua and the Emergence of Modern Science* and W. Wallace in *Galileo and his Sources: the Heritage of the Collegio Romano in Galileo's Theory of Science* (1984). Consider, for example, Randall's thesis: Randall argues at length that Galileo's conception of science was ultimately dependent on Zabarella's notion of *regressus*,[1] which in turn could be traced back to the medical commentaries on Galen's writings, such as that of Pietro d'Abano. Finally, it is an easy step to show that the latter commentaries rely heavily on distinctions made by Aristotle in the *Posterior Analytics*. Randall could thus conclude that

> Zabarella's version of the Aristotelian logic, though interpreted and colored in terms of each of the three great theories of knowledge inherited and reconstructed by the seventeenth-century thinkers, and though receiving in practice

wide variations of emphasis on its several parts, remained the method and ideal of science for all "natural philosophers" until the fresh criticisms of Locke and Berkeley. For though the language is diverse, the whole great literature on method that fills the scientific writing of the seventeenth century is at bottom a series of footnotes to the *Organon* of Aristotle.[2]

Thus, Randall emphasized the dependence of Galileo's methodology on that elaborated by the school of Padua and in particular by his most famous representative Giacomo Zabarella.

More recently, Wallace has given extensive documentary evidence to show the dependence of some of Galileo's early work on the traditional commentaries on Aristotelian natural philosophy and logic which were elaborated in the Jesuit Collegio Romano.

Such claims have not gone unchallenged. E. McMullin in his article "Medieval and Modern Science: Continuity or Discontinuity" (1965) drastically qualified Crombie's position, N. W. Gilbert in "Galileo and the school of Padua" (1963) questioned Randall's interpretation of the Galilean texts and N. Jardine in his "Galileo's road to truth and the demonstrative regress" (1976) endeavoured to show that Galileo's was very critical of arguments that were based on *regressus*. Since my primary concern here is not the Galilean revolution I must refer the reader for a critical appraisal of these various works to recent surveys by B. S. Eastwood and by E. McMullin.[3]

For the moment I simply want to stress how these authors have tackled the problems of continuity by overcoming the one-sided approach that consists in the search for "predecessors" to specific scientific results; instead they emphasize issues of methodology and conceptions of science. And I, too, am content to claim that, whichever side one chooses, the comparison of Galilean and Aristotelian viewpoints has helped us to picture the emergence of modern science in ways much more sophisticated than we would otherwise have managed.

I would now like to make a comparison between the scholarly endeavours already described and the situation in the history and the philosophy of mathematics of the seventeenth century. Pure mathematics developed at an extremely rapid pace during the seventeenth century. In less than a century, algebra, analytic geometry, projective geometry, probability theory, the calculus, and other highly significant areas of mathematics reached their full maturity. Algebraization and the invasion of infinitistic techniques drastically changed the face of mathematics.[4]

As in the case of physics, there has been much discussion about the continuity or discontinuity between Greek mathematics and seventeenth-century mathematics. Suffice it to recall Milhaud's arguments in *Descartes Savant* (1921) in favor of a continuous development between Greek and Cartesian mathematics and the recent book by Lachterman (1989) *The Ethics of Geometry*, which argues for a radical discontinuity between Greek mathematics and seventeenth-century mathematics.[5]

But unlike the case of physics, almost nothing in this area resembles the kind of work on methodology and conceptions of science that has brought so much light in the history and philosophy of the natural sciences. Although there has been a flurry of research on Renaissance epistemology of mathematics, it has not been related to later seventeenth-century issues in philosophy of mathematics and mathematical practice. In my opinion, this is because those who investigated Renaissance debates on the nature of mathematics did so in an attempt to understand better the Galilean mathematization of physics and were thus not focusing primarily on the development of mathematics itself.

This is the goal I for set myself in this chapter. I will show that the Aristotelian conception of science provided the conceptual categories for an analysis of mathematical discourse in the earlier seventeenth century. Moreover, I will argue that the conception of science in question affected to a great extent the mathematical equivalent of physical methodology, that is, the mathematical practice of many mathematicians. The latter part of the enterprise will unfold gradually for several chapters. In chapter 4 I will also take a stand on the problem of continuity between Renaissance and seventeenth-century conceptions of mathematics as posed in the literature.

My main concern in this chapter is classical mathematics—the classical texts of Euclid, Archimedes, Apollonius, Pappus, and their followers. These works constituted an extremely stable body of results whose absolute certainty had seldom been put into doubt. In the scholastic Aristotelian tradition a long list of commentators argued for this certainty by remarking that mathematics conforms to the specifications for a perfect science set down by Aristotle in his *Posterior Analytics*. However, during the middle of the sixteenth century several objections were raised against such justifications of the certainty of mathematics. The debate that ensued from such criticisms is known as the *Quaestio de Certitudine Mathematicarum*.[6] The main issues raised by this debate were (a) Does mathematics fit the definition of Aristotelian science or does it fall short of it? This problem led in turn to a careful analysis of mathematical demonstrations. And (b) If the certainty of mathematics cannot be argued by appealing to its logical structure on what other grounds can we justify it?

I will begin with a brief overview of the main issues raised by the *Quaestio*, then I will move on to relate it to two types of proofs of central concern for mathematical practice: proofs by contradiction and proofs by superposition.

1.1   The *Quaestio de Certitudine Mathematicarum*

Aristotle had formulated in *Posterior Analytics* an articulate theory of scientific knowledge. Such theory was based on the assumption that in order to possess scientific knowledge we need to know the cause of the results of which we possess knowledge. The opening passages of the *Posterior Analytics* are explicit:

> We suppose ourselves to possess unqualified scientific knowledge of a thing, as opposed to knowing it in the accidental way in which the sophist knows, when

we think that we know the cause on which the fact depends as the cause of the fact and of no other, and, further, that the fact could not be other than it is.[7]

In this context 'cause' means any of the four Aristotelian causes: formal, material, efficient, and final. It is the translation of the Greek *aitia* and the reader should be careful not to superimpose on it a Humean notion of causation. This is why many commentators prefer to translate *aitia* as explanation.[8] I prefer 'cause' as a translation of *aitia* because it simplifies translations from the Latin *causa*.

Scientific knowledge, continues Aristotle, is obtained by demonstration. In order to guarantee a scientific transition from premisses to conclusion a syllogism must not only be valid but premisses and conclusion must stand in a specified relation.

> What I now assert is that at all events we do know by demonstration. By demonstration I mean a syllogism productive of scientific knowledge, a syllogism, that is, the grasp of which is eo ipso such knowledge. Assuming then that my thesis as to the nature of scientific knowledge is correct, the premisses of scientific knowledge must be true, primary, immediate, better known than and prior to the conclusion, which is further related to them as effect to causes.[9]

It is immediately evident that the requirements set down on the premisses-conclusion relation are much stronger than simple logical consequence. In particular, there are several valid forms of inference that do not yield, in Aristotle's theory, scientific knowledge. In *Posterior Analytics* I.13 Aristotle introduced an important distinction between two types of demonstrations— demonstrations *tou hoti* and *tou dioti*—which are translated as demonstration 'of the fact' and demonstration 'of the reasoned fact'. In the later Latin commentaries they were often called *demonstratio quia* and *demonstratio propter quid*. The former proceeds from effects to their causes, whereas the latter explains effects through their causes. Aristotle gives the following examples. Suppose one wants to prove that the planets are near the earth. One could argue as follows:

The planets do not twinkle.
What does not twinkle is near the earth.
Therefore, the planets are near the earth.

This demonstration, says Aristotle, is a demonstration of the fact but not of the reasoned fact. Indeed, he explains, the planets are not near the earth because they do not twinkle, but they do not twinkle because they are near the earth. In this case we can reverse the major and the middle of the proof so as to obtain a proof of the reasoned fact.

What is near the earth does not twinkle.
The planets are near the earth.
Therefore the planets do not twinkle.

The second type of syllogism is superior to the first, according to Aristotle, because in it an affection (not twinkling) is predicated of a subject (the planets) through a middle term (being near the earth) which is the proximate cause of the effect. Of all the syllogistic figures, Aristotle thought the first figure was the most adequate for demonstration of the reasoned fact.

> Of all the figures the most scientific is the first. Thus, it is the vehicle of the demonstrations of all the mathematical sciences, such as arithmetic, geometry, and optics, and practically of all sciences that investigate causes: for the syllogism of the reasoned fact is either exclusively or generally speaking and in most cases in this figure.[10]

The distinction between demonstration of the fact and of the reasoned fact was maintained by the Aristotelian commentators and was further developed by Averroës in his prohemium to Aristotle's *Physics*, where demonstrations are partitioned into three genders: *quia, propter quid* and *potissima*. The *potissima* demonstration was considered to be the most certain type of proof (so a scientific syllogism). I will characterize the *potissima* demonstration more carefully below. The tripartition of demonstration inherited by the Renaissance was further complicated by the distinctions made by the medical scholars in their commentaries of Galen's work. I again refer the reader to Randall (1961), which reconstructs "the gradual elaboration of the Aristotelian method, in the light of the medical tradition, from its first discussions in Pietro d'Abano to its completed statement in the logical controversies of Zabarella, in which it reaches the form familiar to Galileo and the seventeenth century scientists."[11]

The tripartite classification of demonstration is proposed by Alessandro Piccolomini (1508–1578) in a treatise published in 1547 entitled *Commentarium de Certitudine Mathematicarum Disciplinarum*. In this work Piccolomini challenged the traditional argument that mathematical sciences possess the highest degree of certainty because they make use of the highest type of demonstration, the *potissima* demonstration, defined by him as that which gives at once the cause and the effect (*simul et quia et propter quid*). The exact features of a *potissima* demonstration were widely debated. Suffice it to say they had to embody the properties that Aristotle ascribed to the scientific syllogism. Among other things, Piccolomini required a *potissima* demonstration to be a syllogism in the first figure with universal premises that are prior and better known than the conclusion. Its middle must have the form of the definition of a property, it must be unique, and it must function as the proximate cause of the conclusion.

In chapter 11 of his treatise, Piccolomini argued that demonstrations in mathematics do not fit and cannot possibly fit the definition for *potissima* demonstration. However, he argued for the certainty of mathematics by appealing to the conceptual nature of mathematical objects which, being created by the human mind, posses the greatest degree of clarity and certainty. We will come back to some of the arguments used by Piccolomini to reach the conclusion that mathematical demonstrations could not be *potissimae*.

The ensuing debate focused on the more general issue of whether mathematical demonstrations could be causal. As a *potissima* demonstration had to be causal, denying that mathematical demonstrations could be causal was sufficient to reach the conclusion that mathematical demonstrations could not fit the definition for scientific demonstration in the Aristotelian sense, and more generally, that mathematics could not be a science, at least not an Aristotelian one. This position was held, for example, by Piccolomini, by Pereyra, and later by Gassendi. A Jesuit, Pereyra wrote in *De communibus omnium rerum naturalium principiis et affectionibus* ([1562] 1576):

> My opinion is that the mathematical disciplines are not proper sciences.... To have science [*scire*] is to acquire knowledge [*cognoscere*] of a thing through the cause on account of which the thing is; and science [*scientia*] is the effect of demonstration. However, demonstration (I speak of the most perfect kind of demonstration) must depend upon those things which are 'per se' and proper to that which is demonstrated; indeed, those things which are accidental and in common are excluded from perfect demonstrations. But the mathematician neither considers the essence of quantity, nor treats of its affections as they flow from such essence, nor declares them by the proper causes on account of which they are in quantity, nor makes his demonstrations from proper and 'per se' but from common and accidental predicates. Thus mathematical doctrine is not properly science.[12]

However, he believed that in physics one could achieve the perfection of *potissimae* demonstrations, and thus included physics in the realm of Aristotelian science. By contrast, Gassendi went as far as to claim in the second part of his *Exercitationes Paradoxicae adversum Aristoteleos*, written in 1624 but published posthumously in 1658, that no science exists, and in particular no Aristotelian science. In connection with mathematics he simply referred to Pereyra's opinion and concluded that "whatever certainty and evidence there is in mathematics is related to appearance, and in no way related the genuine causes of things."[13]

Understandably, these denials of the scientificalness of mathematics generated a host of reactions. Several scholars, such as Barozzi, Biancani, Barrow, and Wallis, addressed the issues raised by the *Quaestio* in an attempt to reinstate mathematics to the realm of causal sciences.[14] Others, such as Clavius, worked at the institutional level to insure mathematics was given its due share and respect in the school curriculum of the Jesuits (the *ratio studiorum*). Clavius, among the finest mathematicians of the early seventeenth century, taught mathematics in one of the most prestigious learned institutions of the late Renaissance and early seventeenth century, the Collegium Romanum. In a memo written on the topic "the way in which the mathematical disciplines could be promoted in the schools of the society" (1580s) Clavius delineated a program of mathematical studies for the Jesuit scientists and philosophers and addressed what had clearly become a serious internal split between the mathematicians and the (natural) philosophers.

> It will also contribute much to this if the teachers of philosophy abstained from those questions which do not help in the understanding of natural things and very much detract from the authority of the mathematical disciplines in the

eyes of the students, such as those in which they teach that the mathematical sciences are not sciences, do not have demonstrations, abstract from the being and the good, etc.; for experience teaches that these questions are a great hindrance to pupils and of no service to them; especially since teachers can hardly teach them without bringing these sciences into ridicule (which I do not just know from hearsay).[15]

It is easy to individuate behind these skermishes the serious threat posed by the mathematization of physics to the classical Aristotelian approach in natural philosophy. It is not by chance that many of the Aristotelian scholars who attacked the scientificalness of mathematics were teachers of natural philosophy. Pereyra, for example, was a colleague of Clavius in the Collegium Romanum and for many years he ran the course in natural philosophy.[16]

But what exactly were the arguments raised against the scientificalness of mathematics? Of course, I cannot rehearse here in detail the different positions of the individual scholars. Let me just illustrate with a single mathematical example how the issue of causality was raised by Pereyra. The simplest strategy to follow in order to subvert the traditional causal picture was to point to theorems in Euclid that could not easily be interpreted causally. Pereyra considered proposition I.32 in Euclid's *Elements* to the effect that the sum of the internal angles in a triangle equals two right angles. Recall how the proof goes. Let ABC be a triangle (see Fig. 1). Let BC be produced to D. Draw through C a parallel to BA, say CE. Then by appealing to previous theorems we have BAC = ACE and ECD = ABC. Thus ABC + ACB + CAB = ACB + ACE + ECD = two right angles.

The scholastic tradition would have assumed this to be a causal proof by maintaining the triangle must have an essence (given by a definition) that determines, as in a formal cause, the rest of its properties, in particular, the sum of the internal angles is equal to two right angles. However, a closer look at the theorem makes it hard to isolate the cause from which the property is derived, or in syllogistic terms, to isolate what plays the role of the middle term. For Pereyra the middle was the appeal to the auxiliary segments and to the external angle. But, objects Pereyra, this appeal to auxiliary segments shows how the proof is not truly causal, since the result holds even without

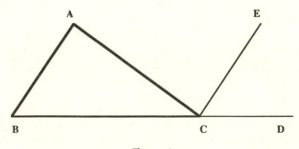

Figure 1

consideration of the external angle and of the external segments. In other words, the external angle and the auxiliary segments cannot be the true cause of the equality.

> The geometer proves that the triangle has three angles equal to two right ones on account of the fact that the external angle which results from extending the side of that triangle is equal to two angles of the same triangle which are opposed to it. Who does not see that this middle is not the cause of the property [*passionis*] which is demonstrated? . . . Besides, such a medium is related in an altogether accidental way to that property. Indeed, whether the side is produced and the external angle is formed or not, or rather even if we imagine [*fingemus*] that the production of the one side and the bringing about [*effectionem*] of the external angle is impossible, nonetheless that property will belong to the triangle; but, what else is the definition of an accident than what may belong or not belong to the thing without [*praeter*] its corruption?[17]

This example was widely discussed at the time. Heralded as a clear counter-example by those who objected to the causal theory of mathematics, it was consistently reanalyzed and brought back to dignity by those who sided for the central role of causality in the mathematical sciences.

1.2   The *Quaestio* in the Seventeenth Century

The reason I began with a Renaissance debate is because I believe there is a close continuity between some aspects of Renaissance and seventeenth-century philosophy of mathematics, and this continuity can be best appreciated through a detailed study of the fortunes of the *Quaestio*. Moreover, several of the questions raised by the participants in the *Quaestio* were motivated by mathematical practice and, conversely, mathematical practice was affected by philosophical positions, maintained during the course of the debate. Accordingly, I will show how the fortunes of the *Quaestio* in the seventeenth century were indeed significant. Then I will argue for the interaction between mathematical practice and the *Quaestio* through looking at proofs by contradiction and proofs by superposition.[18]

1.2.1   Biancani's *De Mathematicarum Natura* (1615)

So far we have dealt with some of the Renaissance participants in the *Quaestio*: Piccolomini, Barozzi, Pereyra, and Catena. To this list we should add the *Coimbran Commentaries* (1594), a course in philosophy written by the Jesuits at Coimbra, who took Pereyra's side on the issue of causal demonstrations. The first text in the seventeenth century to address extensively the issues of the *Quaestio* is *De Mathematicarum Natura* (1615) by Giuseppe Biancani (1566–1624), a Jesuit professor of mathematics at the University of Parma.[19] It was written as an appendix to a lengthy treatise, the *Aristotelis Loca Mathematica*, a collection and commentary of Aristotle's passages related to mathematics. Biancani had studied mathematics in the Collegium Romanum under Clavius and was very well informed on the status of the *Quaestio* because Pereyra had taught natural philosophy in the same institution for many years.

The *De Mathematicarum Natura* is divided into five chapters. The first chapter deals with the subject matter of mathematics. The second chapter is entitled "Of the middle of geometrical demonstrations or, whether they are *potissimae* demonstrations?" The third chapter confutes the mistakes of other authors. The fourth chapter treats of the excellency of mathematics, and the fifth investigates the applied mathematical sciences (e.g., astronomy, optics, mechanics, music). Biancani's treatise embodies the reaction of the traditional Aristotelian scholastic against the innovative thesis of Piccolomini, Pereyra, and the *Coimbran Commentaries*. Although the treatise as a whole is quite interesting, I limit myself to a few of the main points from the first two chapters, points more directly relevant to our topic (the reader will find a translation of Biancani's treatise in the appendix).

The first chapter considers what are the objects of mathematics and whether they exist; it also deals with the nature of definitions in mathematics. According to Biancani, the objects of mathematics are quantities abstracted from sensible matter. Arithmetic and geometry, which together constitute pure mathematics respectively deal with discrete and continuous magnitude. Next Biancani explains how mathematics differs from physics; the mathematician deals with this abstracted matter in so far as it is limited "terminata" whereas the physicist is not restriced to limited quantity. This position is remarkable for the explicit mathematical finitism that goes with it.

> But the geometer and the arithmetician consider [quantity] not absolutely, but insofar as it is delimited, as are the finite straight or curved lines in continuous quantity; and the delimited surfaces from which there result various figures, like circle, triangle, etc.; and, finally, the solids, again delimited, which constitute the various species of solid figures, like pyramid, cube, cone, cylinder, etc., which pertain to the geometer.[20]

One of the mistakes made by those who criticized geometrical proofs, claims Biancani, is that they had not understood how the subject matter of geometry and arithmetic is a limited quantity. According to Biancani, that is why mathematicians are said to consider finite quantities, since "accipit terminatam quae finita est." Indeed, he concludes, what has limits or boundaries is finite. Thus for Biancani the geometrical universe must in principle be limited to figures and solids bounded on every side, and thus finite. Biancani's position could perhaps account for the mathematical practice of his time, but the study of infinitely long figures and solids would soon constitute a serious challenge to this type of finitism. We will return to this issue in connection with the debates raised by Torricelli's infinitely long solid.

Biancani then proceeds to tackle the issue of the existence of mathematical entities against those detractors who had argued that mathematical entities do not exist in reality. This is due, he says, to the crassness and imperfection of sensible matter. However, mathematical entities exist as ideas in the divine and the human mind:

> Therefore, even if these [perfect mathematical figures] do not exist in the nature of things, since in the mind of the Author of Nature, as well as in the human mind, their ideas do exist as the exact archetypes of all things, indeed, as exact mathematical entities, the mathematician investigates their ideas, which are primarily intended per se, and which are [the] real entities.[21]

These remarks and others to be found in Biancani concerning the crassness of matter have been used, first by Galluzzi, to show the existence of Platonistic motives in Biancani's development. However, this interpretation has been challenged by Dear, who claims that Biancani in the passage above "is in fact exploiting the ordinary scholastic interpretation of the 'forms' of things as corresponding to 'ideas in the mind of God.' This was an inseparable and uncontentious part of Christianized Aristotelianism."[22] Although this issue is not quite relevant here, careful analysis of writers such as Biancani is essential to evaluate claims on the importance of Platonism in the emergence of Galilean physics.

Biancani concludes by analyzing definitions in mathematics; he aims to show that definitions in geometry and arithmetic are essential, that is, they give the essence of a thing considered as existent. However, his arguments are vague and inconclusive.

The second chapter is explicitly aimed at Piccolomini, Pereyra, and the *Coimbran Commentaries*, and is designed to show there are mathematical demonstrations that proceed from formal and material causes. Biancani begins with an erudite list of quotations from Aristotle, Plato, Proclus, Averroës, Toletus, Themistius and Zabarella to remark that the tradition has aways attributed to geometrical proofs the features of *potissimae* demonstrations. He then presents some arguments. First of all, Biancani limits the causes employed in geometry and arithmetic to formal and material causes (*intrinseca*) and excludes the use of efficient and final causes (*extrinseca*) . The cause is sometimes formal, as when the middle is the definition of the subject or of the property, and sometimes material, as when "utuntur pro Medio partibus, respectu totius."[23]

Some have claimed that causes could be efficient but they err, says Biancani, since they do not realize that the constructions of lines or divisions of figures, which brings about the result and which they claim to be the middle of the demonstration, are only employed as the middle of discovery "inventionem." This is also proved by the fact that many results derived using constructions could be obtained without them, for example, I.15, I.33, I.34, I.36, and I.42 in Euclid's *Elements*. As for final causes, Biancani does not take them into explicit consideration, and final causes had, in fact, traditionally been excluded from the realm of mathematical demonstrations.

Having excluded the possibility that efficient and final causes could be found in arithmetic and geometry, Biancani finally proceeds to argue that, on the contrary, formal and material causes can be found in pure mathematics. Consider Biancani's analysis of proposition I.1 from Euclid's *Elements* and his claim that it appeals to a formal cause. Proposition I.1 shows how to construct an equilateral triangle over any given segment. Its argument goes as follows. Let AB be a segment (see Fig. 2). Draw two circles with radii of equal length AB and centers in A and B, respectively. Let C be one of the points where the circles intersect. Connect A and C and C and B. Then ABC is an equilateral triangle, since its sides are equal to the radius of the same circle, and thus are equal to each other.

The proof is causal argues Biancani, relying on a previous argument by Proclus, since it shows that the cause of the equality of the sides of the triangle ABC is that they are radii of equal circles. And the argument ultimately rests on the definition of the circle, which thus acts as the formal cause of the proof. Biancani then deals with material causes by arguing that proposition I.32, which we have already analyzed, proceeds by material causes when it infers the equality of the wholes from the equality of the parts.

I do not think it is necessary to follow Biancani further in his detailed treatment of the objections raised by Piccolomini, Pereyra, and others, or in his discussion of the other calumnies that had been raised against mathematics (ch. 3). I will return to some of these issues later on. For the moment it will be enough to remark that, although Biancani's arguments are often unsatisfactory, they do make sense *within* the Aristotelian framework. Moreover, his work is representative of an effort on the part of these late Aristotelians to proceed to a more careful analysis of mathematical practice (as embodied in Euclid's *Elements*) to verify how far the causal model could be applied to mathematics. As we will shortly see, this led the Aristotelians to maintain the causal classification for the majority of demonstrations but to deny it to certain types of proof. Indeed, at the end of the booklet, Biancani lists all the propositions in book I of the *Elements* and classifies them according to whether they are proved through a causal proof or by some other means. These efforts were doomed to be inconclusive because, as we know very well today, the syllogistic structure is not sufficient to recapture adequately the mechanics of an informal mathematical argument, and without such an analysis there was plenty of room for probable conflicting analyses of the same theorems.

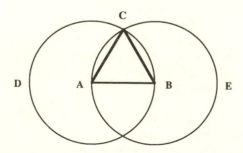

Figure 2

Biancani's work was well received. His text was followed, often verbatim, by Hugh Simple in *De Disciplinis Mathematicarum* (1635) and by Bettini in *Aerarium Philosophiae Mathematicae* (1648), and is quoted with respect by mathematicians and philosophers such as Barrow, Mersenne, and Guldin. Moreover, Bayle (1974) refers constantly to Biancani in his *Dictionnaire Historique et Critique* in the entry Zeno (of Sidon). However, Biancani's work did not stop others from siding with Pereyra on the main issues of the *Quaestio*, as witnessed by M. Smiglecius and P. Vallius, both authors of books called *Logica*, which appeared in 1618 and 1622, respectively (although Vallius' text had been written long before).

1.2.2   Barrow and Gassendi

One might think these developments merely peripheral to the main movement of ideas that shaped the seventeenth century. This is not the case. Peter Dear has put to good use the Renaissance and early seventeenth-century debates on the *Quaestio* to clarify a number of issues related to Mersenne's philosophical outlook on mathematical necessity in his *Mersenne and the Learning of the Schools* (1988). The following passage summarizes his conclusions upon Mersenne and mathematics, neatly reflecting most of our issues:

> This examination of Mersenne's scholastic apologia for mathematics shows both a determined and a selective use of argumentative and conceptual resources. All of his positions, equipped with standard arguments, conspired to justify a high estimation of the mathematical disciplines and the kind of knowledge they produced. Mathematical demonstrations were certain; they were also causal and thus scientific; their objects existed archetypically in the mind of God like those of physics; and their objects were necessarily concomitants of God's creative power. Physics could be made to suffer by comparison, as Clavius had shown: if mathematics fulfilled all these desiderata while physical demonstrations typically failed to achieve that of certainty, a good foundation seemed established for an alternative mathematical natural philosophy to replace essentialist physics.[24]

And in a previous paper I have shown how the fortunes of the *Quaestio* were indeed significant by revealing its seventeenth-century developments, involving scholars such as Smiglecius, Barrow, Gassendi, Hobbes, and Wallis. Then I was unaware of Dear's book. Now it is interesting, although given his connections to Mersenne not surprising, that my conclusions about Hobbes' position on the nature of mathematics parallel Dear's conclusions on Mersenne. Hobbes dealt with the *Quaestio* in his *Examinatio et Emendatio Mathematicae odiernae* (1660) written to confute Wallis's *Mathesis Universalis* (1657). Hobbes defended the thesis that all mathematical proofs are causal and scientific whereas physics, once thought to be the science that could best display causal reasonings, relies on *hoti* reasonings, which Hobbes interprets as fallible reasonings because they rely on induction. Mancosu (1992a) gives a full treatment of the topic.

Now I want to return to Gassendi and Barrow, and their engagement in the *Quaestio*. The reason is that, whereas the Smiglecius-Wallis-Hobbes intervention is easily explainable within the boundaries of the previous debates, Gassendi and Barrow may lead to a broader, and ultimately more interesting, interpretation of the *Quaestio* as an important event in the history of seventeenth-century skepticism. Let us start with Barrow.

Barrow's contribution to the *Quaestio* occurred in his *Lectiones*,[25] especially the fifth and the sixth, which were entitled respectively "Containing answers to the objections which are usually brought against mathematical demonstrations," and "Of the causality of mathematical demonstrations." Barrow was motivated by the aim to show that mathematics is a real science against those who "both have been, and still are so subtle as to deny that the Mathematics are truly Sciences, and that they afford true Demonstrations."[26] Barrow quotes directly from two of the primary sources of the *Quaestio*, Biancani and Pereyra. Barrow's discussion is very extensive consequently I will emphasize only the points most closely related to our issue.

The evidence and truth of mathematical axioms, said Barrow at the beginning of his fifth lecture, were already questioned in Greek times. One of the main skeptical objections usually raised in this connection is that universal axioms are obtained by induction and therefore are fallible. This opens up the problem of certainty and the role that sense and intellect play in science. It suffices here to say that Barrow rejected the theory that all principles of mathematics depend only upon induction from the senses. However, he is ready to add that sensation plays a role in showing the possibility of a mathematical hypothesis. It is in connection with the problem of existence of mathematical entities that Barrow argues a few pages later against Biancani and Vossius, who held that mathematical figures have no real existence outside the mind.[27] By contrast, Barrow wants to put emphasis on the potential actualizability of mathematical entities.[28] In Barrow's organization of the lecture this was simply a digression from the main aim—to show the certainty of mathematical axioms. More relevant for our topic is Barrow's discussion of the claims of "those who study to detract not from the certitude and evidence, but from the dignity and excellence of mathematics." Among these detractors is mentioned Pereyra.

> For they attempt to prove that Mathematical Ratiocinations are not *Scientific*, *Causal* and *Perfect*, because the Science of a Thing signifies to know it by its Cause; according to that Saying of *Aristotle*; "We are supposed to know by Science, when we know the Cause." And to use the Words of *Pererius*, who was no mean Peripatetic; "A Mathematician neither considers the Essence of Quantity, nor treats of its Affections, as they flow from such Essence, nor declares them by the proper causes by which they are in Quantity, nor forms their Demonstrations from proper and essential, but from common and accidental Predicates."[29]

Barrow must have thought Pereyra's objections to represent a challenge. Indeed, he spent part of his fifth lecture and the whole sixth lecture arguing against them. He has no doubts that mathematical ratiocinations satisfy the Aristotelian strictures for scientific ratiocinations: "To which I answer, that those scientific Conditions, which *Aristotle* prefixes to Demonstration, who was most observant of its Laws, do most fitly agree with Mathematical Ratiocinations." He goes on to assert that mathematical ratiocinations in fact use premises that are universal, necessary, primary, and immediate. They are "*More Known* and *More Evident* than the Conclusion inferred." And they are also causal. Barrow's comments on this point are important because he states that at least some mathematical demonstrations are *dioti*,[31] initially argued by appealing to Aristotle. He claims that Aristotle's only examples of causal demonstrations are taken from mathematics, and Barrow's sixth lecture proposes to show that

> Mathematical Demonstrations are eminently *Causal*, from whence, because they only fetch their Conclusions from Axioms which exhibit the principal and most universal Affections of all quantities, and from Definitions which declare the constitutive Generations and essential Passions of particular Magnitudes. From whence the Propositions that arise from such Principles supposed, must needs flow from the intimate *Essences* and *Causes* of the Things.[32]

The main elements to be analyzed in a demonstrative science are the notions of subject, affection of the subject, and common axioms. In demonstrations we usually want to show how certain affections belong to a subject; common axioms are instrumental in allowing us to do so. Barrow does not have much to say about subjects of demonstrations; by contrast, he spends a great deal of time explaining the nature of affections and of axioms.

There are two types of affections, common and proper. Common affections are those "which agree with their Subject *necessarily*, but not *solely*, as being also capable of being truly attributed to other Subjects." For example, it is a common property of an isosceles triangle to have the internal angles equal to two right angles, but this property is also enjoyed by the scalene triangle. By contrast, "proper affections, are such as agree with their Subject both *necessarily* and *solely*, *i.e.* they do so reciprocate with their Subjects, that if they be supposed, it is also supposed of Necessity." Barrow gives the example of the circle. It belongs only to the circle among geometrical figures to have equal radii and every figure which has "*equal Radii* from the *Center* to the *Perimeter* or *Circumference* is a *Circle*." However, proper affections may not be unique. For example, it is a proper affection of the circle "that every two Right Lines that can be drawn from the Extremities of the Diameter to any Point in its Circumference will make a Right Angle." On this issue Barrow admits to disagreeing with Aristotle who thought definitions should be unique. In Barrow's opinion it is only a matter of convenience how to choose a proper affection as a starting point for a demonstrative chain.[33] It is exactly in this feature, adds Barrow, that the causality of mathematical demonstrations consists.

> Such in Reality and no other is the mutual *Causality* and Dependence of the Terms of a *Mathematical Demonstration*, *viz.* a most close and intimate Connection of them one with an other; which yet may be called a *formal*

Causality, because the remaining Affections do result from that one Property, which is first assumed, as from a Form. Nor do I think there is any other *Causality* in the Nature of Things, wherein a necessary Consequence can be founded.[34]

Thus we must add Barrow's name to those who claimed in the debate surrounding the *Quaestio* that mathematical demonstrations are causal, since they make use of syllogisms proceeding from formal causes. But Barrow's requirements are much less stringent; he hardly worries about the unicity of the middle, which had played a major role in the *Quaestio*.

Are there any other types of mathematical causal demonstrations beside those that rely on formal causes? Barrow shows at length how geometry does not admit demonstrations that argue from efficient or final causes.[35] The argument depends on a form of theological voluntarism. God can alter the normal causal course of nature

for every Action of an *efficient Cause*, as well as its consequent *Effect*, depends upon the *Free-Will* and Power of *Almighty God*, who can hinder the Influx and Efficacy of any *Cause* at his Pleasure; neither is there any *Effect* so confined to one *Cause*, but it may be produced by perhaps innumerable others. Hence it is possible that there may be such a *Cause* without a *subsequent Effect*, or such an *Effect* and no peculiar *Cause* to afford any Thing to its *Existence*. There can therefore be no Argumentation from an efficient *Cause* to the *Effect*, or contrarily from an Effect to the Cause, which is lawfully necessary.[36]

However, God cannot modify necessary truths

for necessary Propositions have an universal, immutable and eternal Truth, subject to nothing, nor to be hindered by any Power.[37]

The two claims combined seem to exclude the *hoti* reasonings from mathematics; for they proceed from effects to causes. Barrow applied the same arguments to final causes. He then proceeded to discuss the nature of axioms. His main conclusion is that their use in a demonstration preserves the causal nature of that demonstration. This concludes Barrow's general discussion of the nature of causality in demonstrations.

The last part of the lecture provides an articulate analysis of Euclid's propositions I.1 and I.32, which had played the role of paradigm examples throughout the debate. After discussing I.1 at length Barrow proceeded to discuss I.32: "But as I remember *Pererius*, and others, do produce another Instance, also blaming that celebrated Proposition which is the thirty-second of the first Element, as not scientifically demonstrated."[38] He then went on to summarize the main criticisms by Pereyra and made four replies. In the first reply he invoked the authority of Aristotle who, he claimed, quoted this proposition as an example of causal demonstration; in his second remark he argued that since a triangle is constituted by straight lines then what is essential to lines also pertains to the triangle. "But it is the Property of a Right Line that it may be produced, therefore this Production is not altogether accidental or external to a Triangle." The third point argued that division of the external angle is the most natural way to obtain the sought result. His fourth and last point was that one can give a step-by-step analysis showing how Euclid's proof conforms to his schema for mathematical demonstrations, which as he has already argued, embodies the form of causal, and hence scientific, demonstrations. Barrow could at last conclude by boasting the superiority of mathematical demonstrations:

> It seems to me . . . that Demonstrations, though some do outdo others in Brevity, Elegance, Proximity to their first Principles, and the like Excellencies, yet are all alike in Evidence, Certitude, Necessity, and the essential Connection and mutual Dependence of the Terms one with another. Lastly, that Mathematical Ratiocinations are the most perfect Demonstrations.[39]

Although Barrow still appears willing to frame his arguments in the context of the Aristotelian logical terminology, he begins with the basic presupposition that mathematics is the science par excellence. Nothing can be more remote from his perspective than the subtle scholastic distinctions that had characterized the Renaissance contribution to the *Quaestio*. When Barrow was writing, Aristotelian logic had already lost its battle to be the universal language of science.

So why was it necessary to reiterate the scientific nature of mathematics? There does not seem to be any reason why Barrow would want to spend so many pages arguing against an author like Pereyra, who was far from being an authority. Barrow himself gives us a clue when he says that "some both have been, and *still are so subtle* as to deny that the mathematics are truly sciences, and that they afford true demonstrations." I believe that Barrow is addressing not Pereyra but Gassendi.

It was in 1665 that Barrow delivered the lectures I analyzed. Only a few years before, in 1658, Gassendi's *Opera Omnia* had been published. The third volume contained a work written by Gassendi in 1624 but never published, the second part of the *Exercitationes Paradoxicae adversus Aristoteleos*. In the sixth *Exercitatio* "That no science exists, and especially no Aristotelian science" Gassendi argued that none of the so-called sciences could be said to provide Aristotelian knowledge, that is, causal knowledge from the essences of the subjects. Of course, he could not leave unanswered the challenge that mathematical sciences represented for such a position. He himself acknowledged it was general opinion that nobody, *nisi is sit furiosus*, could deny the certainty and evidence of mathematics.

Gassendi's only weapon was to quote the opinion of Pereyra who, he claimed, was a Peripatetic and nevertheless denied that mathematics was a science. Gassendi quoted at length from Pereyra (see note 12). This is not the place to give a complete account of what Gassendi was trying to achieve in the more general context of his work.[40] Suffice it to say that Pereyra's position was used to support his general attempt to show that all our knowledge is from appearances: "Therefore, I conclude that whatever certainty and evidence there is in mathematics is related to appearances, and in no way related to the genuine causes of things."[41] Thus, Barrow had in mind not an obscure Jesuit from the previous century but an adversary of the caliber of Gassendi, whose influence on the philosophical world had already proved to be immense and therefore deserved an extensive confutation.[42]

Gassendi's appeal to the *Quaestio* to support his skeptical position as to the nature of our knowledge raises the further issue of the relationship between skepticism in the seventeenth century and the *Quaestio*. *De Veritatibus Geometricis* by Wilhelm Langius (1656) contains references to the *Quaestio* in the context of a defence of geometry against the skeptical attacks on the certitude of mathematics. Langius shows awareness of the primary literature concerning the *Quaestio* and, against a skeptical use of the debates on the nature of mathematical demonstrations, he appeals to Barozzi who "with arguments, derived both from authority and from various certain reasons very learnedly and firmly established that mathematical demonstrations not only are to be called true and proper demonstrations, differently from what some thought, but also that they are the highest of all and very certain."[43] Moreover, Pierre Bayle in the entry Zeno (of Sidon) in his *Dictionnaire Historique et Critique* (1974) provided a list of (by then) standard arguments pointing to the incertitude of mathematics. Biancani, Barrow, and Gassendi figure most preeminently in Bayle's discussion. It is thus evident from the assertions of Barrow, Gassendi, Langius, and Bayle that there is an important connection between skepticism in the seventeenth century and the *Quaestio*. It may be worthwhile to investigate this problem further.

1.3   The *Quaestio* and Mathematical Practice

1.3.1   Proofs by Contradiction

Proofs by contradiction are ubiquitous in mathematical practice. In ancient mathematics they constituted the logical scaffolding of proofs by exhaustion, and their use appears very early in Euclid's *Elements*. Consider, for example, proposition I.6 to the effect that if in a triangle two angles are equal to one another, the sides which subtend the equal angles will also be equal to one another. Let ABC be the given triangle and ABC = ACB (see Fig. 3). We want

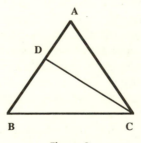

Figure 3

to show that AB = AC. We begin by assuming exactly the opposite (i.e., AB ≠ AC) and proceed to show that this leads to a contradiction. Thus, let AB ≠ AC. Assume, without loss of generality, that AB > AC. Take D on AB such that BD = AC. Join C and D. Consider now the two triangles BDC and BAC. We have DB = AC and BC is in common. Moreover, DBC = ACB. Therefore, DC = AB. Thus the two triangles BDC and BAC are equal. But this cannot be, since clearly BDC < BAC. Thus we reject the assumption AB ≠ AC, and we conclude that AB = AC.

Proofs by contradiction are often needed to prove geometrical converses of theorems. For example, I.6 is the geometrical converse of the first part of proposition I.5, which asserts that in an isosceles triangle the equal sides subtend equal angles. It is exactly the issue of converse propositions that focused attention within the *Quaestio* on proofs by contradiction.

Piccolomini in chapter 11 of his *Commentarium* had given several arguments aimed at showing that mathematical propositions could not be proven by causal proofs. One of the arguments appealed to the authority of Proclus, who had remarked that in geometry there are propositions of equal value and dignity that can be proved from each other. Although Piccolomini did not specify the passage from Proclus, he probably had in mind a remark Proclus made when commenting on Euclid's propositions I.35 and I.36, which are the converse of each other. In Piccolomini's opinion this argues for the noncausality of such theorems. Were they causal, Piccolomini said, the same proposition would be the cause of itself. But this is a contradiction since nothing can be its own cause. The problem that Piccolomini is addressing here is the following. In mathematics one can often prove that A implies B and that B implies A—that A and B are equivalent. However, if we read 'implication' as being more than just logical consequence, and we demand the antecedent acts as the 'cause' of the conclusion then we run into trouble in trying to make sense of those theorems in which antecedents and consequences can be reversed, since in the intuitive reading of the relation of causality if A 'causes' B then B cannot 'cause' A. For, were the latter allowed, one could infer that A 'causes' A. But this goes against the intuitive reading of causality since, as Piccolomini remarks, nothing can be its own cause.[44]

Piccolomini's arguments were addressed by Barozzi (1537–1604) in his *Oratio* (1560), the prolusion he gave on occasion of his election to lecturer of mathematics at the University of Padua. The *Oratio* is a detailed reply to Piccolomini's *Commentarium* aimed at showing that the mathematical sciences fit the Aristotelian model of science. Concerning Piccolomini's argument for converse propositions, Barozzi granted to Piccolomini that although the phenomenon described in Piccolomini's argument on converse propositions does manifest itself in mathematics, this gives however no ground to conclude that causal proofs are never to be found in mathematics. In arguing for his thesis, Barozzi made the interesting remark that most of the converse theorems are not proved using direct proofs *which proceed by true causes* but using proofs by contradiction.[45] Thus both parties seem to find a common ground in the exclusion of proofs by contradiction from the realm of causal proofs. This was true of two other opponents in the *Quaestio*, Pereyra and Biancani. Pereyra in *De communibus* refers to proofs by contradiction in the course of his argument that causal proofs cannot be given in mathematics:

> In the mathematical sciences are found several demonstrations leading to impossibility, which are not the highest demonstrations [*simpliciter*; this is synonymous of *potissima*] but from the effect [*secundum quid*], as Aristotle says in Metaphysics 4, ch. 9.[46]

Biancani, while defending the causal nature of mathematical demonstrations, granted that proofs by contradiction do not qualify as causal proofs

> as in demonstration from a cause, as are almost always in geometry and arithmetic, except for proofs by impossibility.[47]

There was thus a consensus on the part of these scholars that proofs by contradiction were inferior to direct proofs, on account of their lack of causality. The consequences to be drawn from this position are of relevance to the foundations of classical mathematics. One could simply state that some parts of mathematics are more scientific than others, or worse, that only some parts are scientific and not others. One could try to reinterpret talk of causality to include all types of proofs, and thus also proofs by contradiction. Finally, one could try to eliminate proofs by contradiction from the development of classical mathematics. The appeal of the *Quaestio* as an issue in philosophy of mathematics is that all three possibilities had their proponents.

The first possibility was represented by scholars such as Barozzi and Biancani, who argued that most mathematical demonstrations are causal and thus 'scientific' but that some do not qualify as such, for example, proofs by contradiction.

The second possibility was represented by Barrow, as we have seen, and with different arguments by the Archimedean commentator, Rivaltus, who addressed the issue of proofs by contradiction in his influential commentary on Archimedes' work, written in 1615. As many proofs in Archimedes are proved by exhaustion, and hence by contradiction, Rivaltus found himself forced to take up the issue when arguing against Scaliger's attacks on Archimedes contained in his *Cyclometrica* (1594). Scaliger had attacked Archimedes' methods of proof, especially proofs by exhaustion, in which one needs a double reduction to absurdity. Rivaltus' reply to Scaliger occurred in his *Prolegomena* to the book *On the Sphere and the Cylinder* by Archimedes. There he argued that, in particular, direct proofs and proofs by contradiction have the same degree of perfection: "Ostensive demonstrations in mathematics are not considered more perfect than the ones by contradiction, since in these disciplines it is not made use of the cause of the thing, but of the cause of the knowledge of the thing."[48]

As an example Rivaltus mentioned the proposition of the book *On the Sphere and the Cylinder* where Archimedes shows that the surface of the sphere is four times the great circle of the sphere. The Archimedean proof proceeds by inscribing and circumscribing auxiliary solids to the sphere.

Through the use of these auxiliary solids one proves, by the usual exhaustion method, that the surface of the sphere can be neither smaller nor greater than four times the great circle, and thus it must be equal. It is concerning the use of the auxiliary figures in the proof that Rivaltus makes the following observation:

> The figures drawn are not truly the causes of that equality but are reasons from which we know it. From whence it follows that whatever is more fit to knowledge is more appropriate to the mathematician. But we know more easily that absurdities are impossible, false and repugnant by reason than we know the true things. Indeed the truths are concealed and conversely the errors are obvious everywhere.[49]

Rivaltus reiterated his main point in the scholium at the beginning of the *Quadrature of the Parabola*: "Again it is to be observed that the Geometers do not make use of the cause of a thing, but of the cause from which the thing is known. Indeed it is sufficient to them to show the thing to be so and they do not enquire by which means it is so."[50]

Although framed in a causal language, since it appeals to *causas cognoscendi*, Rivaltus' position is at the opposite extreme from an orthodox Aristotelian position. Aristotle had explicitly distinguished between "what is prior and better known in the order of being and what is prior and better known to men." Moreover, Aristotle had explicitly asserted in *Posterior Analytics* I.7 that direct proofs are superior to proofs by contradiction. For these reasons Rivaltus faced an outspoken opponent in an able mathematician, Paul Guldin, a Jesuit whose position represents the third of our possibilities.

Guldin is the best example of the interaction between philosophy of mathematics and mathematical practice that the *Quaestio* brought about. Indeed, his philosophical training familiarized him with the main texts of the *Quaestio* and he had the mathematical ability to devise a suitable mathematical program to vindicate his philosophical standpoint. Guldin took up the philosophical issue of the status of proofs by contradiction against Rivaltus in his *Centrobaryca*, published between 1635 and 1641. In Guldin's opinion, direct proofs are clearly superior to proofs by contradiction: "Indeed, ostensive demonstrations have always had the applause and the victory over negatives and those reducing to absurdity or impossibility, whatever at last Rivaltus says."[51] He also believed that causal proofs could be given in mathematics and argued for this by appealing to the authority of Biancani.

> I do not dispute that proofs by contradiction, or leading to impossibility, from effects and from the cognition of the cause are very common among them [the geometers]. There are, however, also plenty of others which proceed by material, efficient and even by formal causes, to which geometers have always granted pride of place. But whoever reads the very learned dissertations "On the Nature of Mathematics" by our Josephus Blancanus will easily confute David's [Rivaltus's] opinion.[52]

But Guldin was more ambitious. He set out to show that proofs by contradiction could be eliminated from the development of Euclidian and

Archimedean mathematics. His technical program will be analyzed in chapter 2. I will come back several times to the issue of proofs by contradiction. I will argue in later chapters that the practice of Descartes, Cavalieri, Guldin, Wallis, and many other mathematicians reflects a deep concern with the issues I have been raising. What we have achieved in this initial part is to have shown how the *Quaestio de Certitudine Mathematicarum* played a significant role in focusing attention upon the logical peculiarities of proofs by contradiction.

1.3.2 Proofs by Superposition

Alongside proofs by contradiction, proofs by superposition also underwent scrutiny in the earlier seventeenth century; a typical example of such proof is Euclid I.4.[53]

PROPOSITION 4. *If two triangles have the two sides equal to two sides respectively, and have the angles contained by the equal straight lines equal, they will also have the base equal to the base, the triangle will be equal to the triangle and the remaining angles will be equal to the remaining angles respectively, namely those which the equal sides subtend* (see Fig. 4).

PROOF. Let ABC, DEF be two triangles with AB = DE, AC = DF, and the angle BAC equal the angle EDF. We want to show that BC = EF, the triangle ABC is equal to the triangle DEF, the angle ABC is equal to the angle DEF, and the angle ACB is equal to the angle DFE. Now Euclid applies superposition:

> For, if the triangle ABC be applied to the triangle DEF, and if the point A be placed on the point D and the straight line AB on DE, then the point B will also coincide with E, because AB is equal to DE. Again, AB coinciding with DE, the straight line AC will also coincide with DF, because the angle BAC is equal to the angle EDF; hence the point C will also coincide with the point F because AC is again equal to DF. But B also coincided with E; hence the base BC will also coincide with the base EF. For if, when B coincides with E and C with F, the base BC does not coincide with the base EF, two straight lines will enclose a space: which is impossible. Therefore the base BC will coincide with EF and will be equal to it.[54]

The last step of the proof appeals to Euclid's common notion 4, known also as the *congruency axiom*: "Things which coincide with one another τὰ ἐφαρμόζοντα ἐπ᾿ ἄλληλα) are equal to one another." For the axiom to

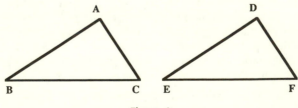

Figure 4

become effective, as in the above proof, it is necessary that figures or lines be applied or superposed to each other. Three basic theorems are proved according to this strategy; I.4, I.8, and III.24. The proofs show the equality of two figures by *applying* one figure to the other and then, after noticing their coincidence, appealing to common notion 4 to conclude their equality.

It has often been noted that the distinction between coincidence and application is subtly expressed in Greek by appealing to two different forms of the same verb, ἐφαρμόζειν. In common notion 4 the verb appears as an active participle (ἐφαρμόζοντα), whereas in the proof of I.4 we find a middle passive form (ἐφαρμόζεσθαι). The former conveys the meaning of a *coincidence with* or *fitting with*, whereas the latter conveys the meaning of *applying* or *superposing*. The notion of congruency is not peripheral to Greek mathematical development. On the contrary, it is used not only by Euclid but also by Archimedes in *The Equilibrium of Planes* and *On Conoids and Spheroids*. Euclid seems to have used the axiom only when he could not avoid it, but according to Heath, there does not seem to have been any explicit criticism of the method in ancient times. Murdoch came to the same conclusion about medieval times.[55] But by the middle of the seventeenth century, we find Barrow forced to defend congruency and superposition, which he deems as the "bulkward of mathematics." He confirms that congruency had become central to foundational reflections on geometry: "They therefore who despise and reject it in mathematical Demonstrations, as favouring too much of mechanical Bungling do endeavour to overthrow the very Basis of geometry; but without either Wisdom or Success."[56] In what follows I shall clarify how congruency and superposition had suddenly become of such concern.

While commenting on the well-known nineteenth-century criticisms concerning the use of motion in geometry raised by Veronese and others, Heath (Euclid 1956, vol. I, p. 249) remarked that these objections were raised already as early as the middle of the sixteenth century by Jacques Peletier in the long note appended to proposition I.4 of his *In Euclidis Elementa Geometrica Demonstrationum Libri XV*, published in 1557. However, Heath says nothing more about discussions on congruency in the late Renaissance and in the seventeenth century. I think Heath was right in singling out Peletier as one of the earliest critics of superposition. Peletier had two objections to superposition as a method of proof. The first was that if superposition were allowed then many proofs of geometry would simply be redundant. For example, one could do without the proof of proposition I.2.—to place at a given point (as an extremity) a straight line equal to a given straight line—and simply take the line and superpose one of its endpoints on the given point. The second objection was that the method of superposition does not suit the dignity of geometry because it has something mechanical about it (*figuras figuris superponere, mechanicum quippiam esse*). This is mainly because superposition implies a displacement or a motion of the objects being superposed and, although this can be allowed in applications, it cannot be accepted as a geometrical operation.[57]

Peletier's solution to the problem of superposition was rather drastic. He claimed that theorems such as I.4 should be taken as principles and that one should not attempt to derive them from simpler properties. He did, however, provide an alternative proof of I.4.

Peletier was not the only Euclidian commentator in the late Renaissance to raise doubts about congruency, especially the status of Euclid I.4. Only a few years after Peletier's commentary, the Euclidian commentator, Flussas Candalla, in his *Euclidis Megarensis Mathematici Clarissimi Elementa Geometrica* (1566) attempted to give an alternative demonstration that would avoid its mechanical features.

> We are compelled to provide another demonstration of this fourth proposition, so that we do not have recourse to the use of any mechanical instrument in a demonstration. For Campanus and Theon, when demonstrating this proposition, superimposed the triangle to the triangle, the angle to the angle, and the side on the side, groping for a demonstration by instruments, rather than firming it by reason. But rejecting this as alien after all to the true cultivation of our discipline, we offered another demonstration, without the transposition of lines or figures, which is elucidated by reason.[58]

It is quite possible that such rejection of motion from geometry had Platonist overtones, although the Aristotelian tradition contains explicit statements to the effect that geometry abstracts from motion and matter.[59] Peletier's and Candalla's remarks were felt as a foundational threat to the basic principles of geometry and they had to be addressed. Peletier's rejection of superposition was attacked by Clavius in the context of the debate on the angle of contact,[60] and Candalla found a resolute rebuker in Sir Henri Savile.

Clavius devoted a long section to the problem of congruency in the second edition of his *Euclidis Elementorum Libri XV* (1589) against the positions held by Peletier. After having summarized Peletier's objections, Clavius accused him of not having understood in which sense geometers use superposition.

> For he does not seem to have understood in a satisfactory manner how Geometers use that superposition. For they do not want that superposition to be carried out in reality (for that would be something mechanical), but only in thought and in the mind, which is the task of reason and of intellect.[61]

Thus in geometry we deal with an intellectual superposition, not a mechanical one. Moreover, giving up superposition would be crazy since it would subvert the whole body of geometry.

> Peletarius saw (and indeed he could not fail to see a thing so manifest), that if he discarded this kind of proof, then he would totally subvert the whole of geometry, for many propositions, important in geometry, are proved from the fourth proposition and the eighth in the first book, and from the twenty-fourth in the third book, which cannot be otherwise demonstrated, but by that superposition of figures; though not by a real superposition, but by one conceived only in thought, as I said. So where could he have turned? What should he have done? He invented that thing, completely alien to geometry, which is that superposition of figures.[62]

The last part of Clavius' section was devoted to showing that Peletier's alternative proof involved a *petitio principii*. The same concern over the foundations of geometry was voiced by Sir Henri Savile in his *Praelectiones Tresdecim in Principium Elementorum Euclidis* (1621). His tenth lecture was devoted to a detailed commentary of Euclid I.4 "which is the basis and the foundation of all geometry" (p. 182). He starts by recalling Candalla's objections against I.4.

> Furthermore, many people rejected this demonstration as being hardly geo-
> metrical, for the reason that it seems to involve something mechanical,
> assuming a triangle together with motion, as if it were removed from its place
> and transferred to another position; and this hardly seems to accord with
> geometry, which considers things without motion and matter; and this was the
> opinion of Flussas Candalla, a nobleman of Gallia, an otherwise learned
> gentleman.[63]

Savile granted, as had Clavius, that superposition should not be used in problems, although it is absolutely necessary in theorems "praesertim in ijs propositionibus quae proximae sunt principijs, & paucas habent praemissas."[64] Most of the section was spent in analyzing Candalla's alternative demonstration to I.4 to conclude, perhaps justifiably, that "in totâ hac demonstratione nihil est sanum, nihil solidum, nihil tanto viro dignum."

I have intentionally omitted the details of these alternative proofs to I.4 because I do not believe they are very interesting. Although Peletier and Candalla were unsuccessful in their attempts to get by without superposition, their criticisms highlighted the role played by motion and superposition in geometry. It was not until Bolzano's *Betrachtungen über einige Gegenstände der Elementargeometrie* (1804) that a serious mathematical attempt to remove superposition from geometry was to take place.[65]

The issue of superposition was not, however, limited to discussions among the mathematicians. As a matter of fact, it became an issue of concern for those involved in the *Quaestio*. In *De Mathematicarum Natura* Biancani, summarizing in chapter 3 the arguments that were raised against the dignity of mathematics, mentioned how the method of proof by superposition is considered by some as "valde imperfectus, ac penè ridiculus." Biancani answers these objectors by remarking that only three propositions in the *Elements* are actually proved by superposition. Moreover, and this connects superposition with the issue of causality, it is erroneous to claim that superposition functions as the middle of a demonstration. Indeed, proofs by superposition are as evident as the others, and superposition plays the role of a construction. Superposition, he adds, is not the middle of the demonstration—it is not true that the bases are equal because they are superposed—superposition is only a construction allowing us to infer that the bases are equal without superposing them.

> Secondly, that they are as perfect and as evident as are the others, for they are
> mistaken who think that the superposition here is the medium of the
> demonstration, for it is there in place of a construction. And what are to be
> proved to be equal are not even the superposed things, as they think, for this

would be a reason of no moment, and not even a geometrical, but rather a physical one, for it would rely on the senses; but some things which are equal are superposed here, so that from their superposition there will be apparent the equality of those that are not superposed. Consider 4. of bk. 1. and you will see that here two equal sides of two triangles are superposed, and then their bases, which are not superposed, are inferred to be equal. And the reason by which they are proved to be equal is their congruence, and not that they are superposed, as our opponents think, not understanding what is the medium of this demonstration.[66]

Does it follow that I.4 is a causal proof? That depends, says Biancani (see appendix), on the definition of equality. If the definition of equality is given in terms of congruency then the proof proceeds by appeal to a formal cause. If the congruency is only a sign of equality then the proof is *à signo* and *a posteriori* (i.e, from effects to causes).

I conclude this section with a passage from 1680 that provides further support for my historical reconstruction, Pierre Daniel Huet's *Demonstratio Evangelica* a significant theological work in the history of Spinozism and the application of the mathematical method in philosophy and theology. The *Demonstratio Evangelica* is in fact an axiomatic treatment of the scriptures and was written to show the pious use one could make of the mathematical method in theology, thereby showing that the impious Spinoza had simply misused it. Against this background Huet's introduction tackles the issues of mathematical method, particularly whether there be more disagreements "altercationes" in theology than in geometry; his main examples of problematic geometrical procedures are superposition and proof by contradiction.

> As we said, it is from this axiom, namely, that what are congruent are known to be equal, that the demonstration of the fourth proposition of the first book of Euclid proceeds; and when some renowned geometers reject this proposition, they also have to reject those which depend on it. And these are quite a few, so that this error infects the whole of geometry. Josephus Scaliger repudiated as paralogistikon [fallacious] the kind of proof which consists in deductio ad absurdum, and which was used by Archimedes.... I could bring up even more points for this argument, but lack of time prevents me from collecting them all. And, at any rate, these are sufficient for this discussion.[67]

That these arguments appear in a theological text confirms their fairly wide knowledge throughout the philosophical community. In particular, the *Demonstratio Evangelica* itself enjoyed a considerable success, being referred to approvingly by Bayle in his *Dictionnaire Historique et Critique* under Zeno (of Sidon).

During the latter part of the Renaissance and the early part of the seventeenth century, we have seen the emergence of several problems concerning proofs by contradiction and proofs by superposition, both of them centrally important to mathematical practice. Emerging in mathematical and in philosophical circles, they were later to influence foundational discussions. Proofs by superposition became central to debates over foundations of the geometry of indivisibles; and proofs by contradiction spurred some mathematicians in an attempt to eliminate them from the development of geometry. These topics will be considered in the next few chapters.

2

Cavalieri's Geometry of Indivisibles and Guldin's Centers of Gravity

The passage from classical Greek mathematics to seventeenth-century mathematics is marked by two dramatic events: the widespread use of infinitary techniques in geometry and the algebraization of geometry. At first independent, they show a close interaction later in the century. In this chapter I shall begin the analysis of the relevance of the use of infinitistic techniques for the philosophy of mathematics, and in later chapters I shall deal with the issue of analytic techniques.

It is often said that the Greeks avoided recourse to the infinite in their mathematics. However, one should be careful here. The remark is correct only if referred to the formal expositions found in Greek mathematical texts. Indeed, it is quite well known that heuristically the Greeks appealed to infinitistic techniques, as witnessed by Archimedes' *Method*, a short treatise rediscovered in 1906 which contains, in the form of a letter from Archimedes to Eratosthenes, an explanation of Archimedes' heuristic strategies for the discovery of theorems in geometry concerning areas, volumes, and centers of gravity. Archimedes explains in his *Method* how to exploit in geometrical investigations mechanical considerations and indivisibilist techniques, where the latter denomination refers to the idea of considering a plane figure (or a solid) as being "constituted" by lines (or planes).

Starting from the *Method*, W. Knorr in his "Before and after Cavalieri: the method of indivisibles in ancient geometry" has given intriguing evidence to support the claim that the use of indivisibilist techniques in ancient times must have been a widespread heuristic tool for the geométers.

> The indivisibilist technique in geometry was not an isolated and idiosyncratic whim of Archimedes, published in only a single work the *Method*; but rather ... it was a technique already familiar to Archimedes from his own technical sources, whose tradition could still be drawn upon by later commentators like Hero and Theon.[1]

Thus, in which sense is the widespread use of infinitesimalist techniques such a novelty in the seventeenth century? There are three orders of reason that

34

justify this claim. The first is historical; the sources of Greek mathematics which made use of indivisibilist concepts, such as Archimedes' *Method* and Theon's *Commentary on Ptolemy's Book I,* were unknown to the seventeenth-century geometers. Thus, Knorr rightly speaks of a seventeenth-century "rediscovery" of the indivisibilist method. The second reason brings into play the distinction between heuristics and formal validity. For the Greeks there was no doubt that infinitary techniques, like the ones employed in the indivisibilist method, could not be formally accepted and had only heuristic value. What is new in the seventeenth century is the effort on the part of several first-rate mathematicians to grant these heuristic techniques a formal validity. It was this attempt to provide the indivisibilist method with the credibility of a rigorous theory that led to many discussions about the nature of the method.

Thirdly, the seventeenth century engaged in types of infinitistic mathematics that do not seem to have any precedents in the Greeks, as for example, the infinitary congruence procedures found in Cavalieri, or the study of solids of infinite length and/or width, pioneered by Torricelli.

The above remarks about Greek mathematics were made in order to dispel the widespread belief of an *horror infiniti* dominating classical Greek mathematics. But seventeenth-century geometers only inherited the formal developments of Greek mathematics, not their heuristic underpinnings. It follows that an understanding of the new techniques emerging in the seventeenth century can only take place against the background of the formal developments of classical Greek mathematics. Most important for this chapter are the concepts of magnitude and ratio, and the method of exhaustion. The next section spells out some of their main features in the Greek setting.

2.1 Magnitudes, Ratios, and the Method of Exhaustion

It is not easy to determine what exactly the Greeks meant by magnitude. Paradigms of magnitude are numbers, lines, plane figures, and solid figures. However, the Greeks never gave an explicit axiomatization of the properties that magnitudes should satisfy. But their work implicitly assumes certain properties for magnitudes, including

> Homogeneous magnitudes can be ordered by a relation $<$ which determines a total ordering, that is, given A and B in the same class of magnitudes either $A < B$ or $A = B$ or $A > B$.

> Homogeneous magnitudes A and B can be added to and subtracted from each other; subtraction can only be performed when the second quantity is greater than the first. We write $A + B$ and $B - A$.

> Homogeneous magnitudes A and B can have a ratio to each other denoted by $A : B$.

It has been the merit of Andersen (1985) and Giusti (1980), from whose articles the above characterization is drawn, to show how Cavalieri's work depends on these notions.[2] But before discussing Cavalieri, we must say a few more things about ratios and the method of exhaustion.

The theory of ratios and the method of exhaustion are both associated with Eudoxus, whose contributions to mathematics are embodied in books V and XII of Euclid's *Elements*. After the Pythagorean discovery of incommensurable lines, Eudoxus' work on ratio was motivated by the need to provide a proportion theory that would apply to them as well as to commensurable lines. We need not delve into this theory, which has already been the object of detailed studies, but it is essential to give definitions 3 and 4 of book V of the *Elements*.

DEFINITION 3. *A ratio is a sort of relation in respect of size between two magnitudes of the same kind.*

DEFINITION 4. *Magnitudes are said to have a ratio to one another which are capable, when multiplied, of exceeding one another.*[3]

Definition 3 calls for homogeneity between the magnitudes under consideration. Moreover, a ratio is clearly not a new object but a relation. Many seventeenth-century debates on the nature of proportion theory were motivated by the systematic misreading of ratios as numbers (fractions) that the analytic techniques allowed with respect to the proper definition of ratio; see Sasaki (1985) and section 3.2. More important here is definition 4, sometimes called the axiom of Eudoxus–Archimedes: Given any two magnitudes A and B of the same kind, if $A < B$ then there is a natural number n such that $A + \ldots + A > B$ (n A's).

This definition excludes, among other things, the possibility of a ratio between a finite magnitude and an infinitely great or infinitely small magnitude. Indeed, if there could be a ratio between a finite quantity and an infinitely large quantity then there would be a natural number n such that the finite quantity added to itself n times would become greater than an infinitely great quantity, which contradicts a basic property of finite magnitudes. Similarly, if an infinitely small magnitude had a ratio to a finite one there would be an n such that the infinitely small quantity added to itself n times would be greater than a finite quantity; another contradiction. In the seventeenth century this state of affairs was denoted by the slogan: There is no proportion between the finite and the infinite.

Definition 4 also puts into motion the machinery required for proofs by exhaustion. Suppose we want to compare the areas of two figures. Sometimes this can be done directly by finitely decomposing the figures involved (say, when we are dealing with polygons or triangles) but usually when one of the two figures to be compared is a curved figure, a direct approach would involve us in infinitistic arguments whose logical reliability could be put into doubt. In their formal expositions the Greeks therefore preferred a logically rigorous method that would exclude recourse to dubious infinite processes. Instead of proving directly that $A = B$ they would use a double reductio ad absurdum to exclude the possibility that A < B and A > B. Let us see how this works in a concrete case.

We need to start with a general lemma about magnitudes which, given two unequal magnitudes A and B, allows us to subdivide the greater into 2^n parts, for some n, such that each of the 2^n parts is less than the smaller given magnitude. In Euclid's words:

PROPOSITION 1. *Two unequal magnitudes being set out, if from the greater there be subtracted a magnitude greater than its half, and from that which is left a magnitude greater than its half, and if this process be repeated continually, there will be left some magnitude which will be less than the lesser magnitude set out.*

As an example of proof by exhaustion we will consider proposition 10 of book XII of the *Elements*.

PROPOSITION 10. *Every cone is the third part of the cylinder that has the same base and equal height.*

PROOF. We take for granted that any pyramid is a third part of the prism which has the same base with it and equal height (*Elements* XII. Porism to proposition 7). There are three steps in the proof.

Step 1. Given a cylinder it is always possible to inscribe in it a prism, with a sufficiently large number of sides such that the difference between the cylinder and the prism is less than any arbitrarily chosen magnitude. Consider, in fact, inscribed in the cylinder a square-prism; it is bigger than half the cylinder (because it is half the square-prism circumscribed to the cylinder and bigger than this). Therefore the remainder R_1 between the cylinder and the prism is less than half the cylinder.

If we divide in half the arc subtended by the side of the square (see Fig. 5) and denote the resulting point by C, the triangle ACB will be bigger than half the segment ACB; therefore every triangular prism built on the triangle and inscribed in the cylinder is bigger than half the portion of the cylinder on ABC. So subtracting from the cylinder the octagonal prism, we get a difference

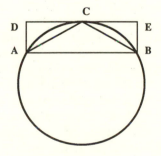

Figure 5

$R_2 < R_1$. And continuing in this fashion, inscribing prisms with polygonal bases having $4 \cdot 2^2, 4 \cdot 2^3, \ldots$ sides, by proposition 1 we get a prism such that the difference with the cylinder is smaller than any preassigned magnitude, however small.

Step 2. Similarly, given a cone it is always possible to inscribe in it a pyramid with a sufficiently large number of sides such that the difference between it and the cone is less than any preassigned magnitude, however small.

Step 3. This is the double reductio ad absurdum. Let O, V be the volume of the cylinder and of the cone respectively. If $O \neq 3V$ then either $O > 3V$ or $O < 3V$. We show that both cases lead to a contradiction.

Case I: $O > 3V$. Inscribe in the cylinder successive prisms so that we get a prism P such that the difference from the cylinder is less than the difference $O - 3V$, that is, $O > P > 3V$. But P is the triple of the pyramid with the same base and height, inscribed in the cone, and this pyramid is less than V. Thus, $P < 3V$. But this cannot be, because by construction $P > 3V$. Thus, it is not the case that $O > 3V$.

Case II: $O < 3V$. Thus we have $V > O/3$. Let us inscribe in the cone successive pyramids until we get a pyramid P' that differs from the cone by less than $V - (O/3)$. So $V > P' > O/3$. Now P' is one-third of a prism with the same base and height, and this prism is less than the cylinder. So $P' < O/3$ (since $3P' < O$). But this cannot be, because $P' > O/3$. Thus, it is not the case that $O < 3V$.

The conclusion from both cases is that O can only be equal to 3V.

We will see how Cavalieri's indivisibles and Guldin's centers of gravity allow us, among other things, a more direct approach to the proof of theorems that the Greeks had proved by exhaustion.

2.2   Cavalieri's Two Methods of Indivisibles

The exhaustion method of the Greeks was logically very rigorous but it had the defect of not giving a sense to the working mathematicians of the way in which the result had been obtained. The mathematicians of the sixteenth and seventeenth centuries often voiced their dissatisfaction with proofs by exhaustion, claiming that the ancients had hidden their methods of discovery. This led several mathematicians to attempt the development of new methods that would, so to speak, bridge the gap between the context of discovery and the context of justification, or in other words between the heuristics and the formal techniques. Some, such as Valerio in *De Centro Gravitatis Solidorum* (1604), attempted a streamlining of the exhaustion method[4] that would still satisfy the logical rigour of the Greeks and yet would avoid the double reductio ad absurdum involved in the exhaustion method. Others, such as Kepler in *Stereometria Doliorum* (1615), decided to modify the procedures of Euclid and Archimedes by appealing to infinitary techniques. This recourse to infinitary techniques, in the form of infinitesimals, was well beyond the formal bounds within which the Greek tradition had operated. It led Anderson, the Scottish mathematician, to use his *Vindiciae Archimedis* (1616) for an attack on Kepler's lack of rigour. Thus, already at the beginning of the century, several attempts had been made to develop geometry in more direct ways that would overcome the complexity and limitations imposed by the exhaustion method. However, it was Cavalieri's geometry of indivisibles that commanded most of the mathematical and philosophical attention.

Cavalieri's geometry of indivisibles was elaborated in the 1620s and expounded by Cavalieri in *Geometria Indivisibilibus Continuorum Nova Quadam Ratione Promota* (1635) and in *Exercitationes Geometricae Sex* (1647). Both works are very long and not easy to read. Today the task of studying Cavalieri is made easier by two excellent works, Andersen (1985) and Giusti (1980), which give a thorough analysis of Cavalieri's work. I will limit myself to the essential technical points that will allow me to introduce the philosophical discussion.

Cavalieri had two methods of indivisibles. To one of them he devoted the initial six books of the *Geometria*; the other he covered in the seventh book. He also gave an exposition of both methods in the first and second investigation of the *Exercitationes*, written as a defence of his indivisibilist approach against the attacks it had received. I will mainly concentrate on the *Geometria* since that is the development against which Guldin raises most of his objections, described in detail later on. Let me begin with Cavalieri's first method.[5]

2.2.1   The First Method of Indivisibles

In the preface to the *Geometria*, Cavalieri recounts that he had been led to his method of indivisibles by reflecting on the surprising fact that solids generated around an axis from plane figures did not have the ratio of the generating figures. Consider a square and a right triangle whose legs are the base and the height of the square and whose hypotenuse is the diagonal of the square. The triangle is to the square as 1 is to 2. However, if we rotate the triangle and the square around the height of the square, we obtain a cone and a cylinder whose ratio is 1 to 3. After some wrong attempts at investigating this phenomenon, Cavalieri hit on the key idea of his method:

> Having thus considered the above mentioned cylinder and cone as being intersected . . . parallel to the basis, I found that what I call in book II all the planes of the cylinder have the same ratio to all the planes of the cone as that of the cylinder to the cone.[6]

The notion of "all the lines" of a plane figure, and "all the planes" of a given solid correspondingly, are the central concepts in Cavalieri's method. Here is how Cavalieri explained the first of these notions (see Fig. 6):

> Let ABC be any plane figure, and EO and BC two opposite tangents of the given figure, however drawn. Consider then two mutually parallel planes, indefinitely extended, drawn through EO, BC of which the one that, for example, passes through EO is moved toward the plane passing through BC, always keeping parallel to it until it coincides with it. Thus, the intersections of this moving plane, or fluent, and the figure ABC, which are produced in the

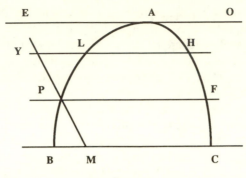

Figure 6

overall motion, taken all together, I call: all the lines of the figure ABC
(some of which are the LH, PF, BC) taken with reference to one of
those, such as BC: of rectilinear transit, when the parallel planes intersect the
figure ABC at right angles; of oblique transit when they intersect it obliquely.[7]

If ABC is a solid then the motion of the plane, as above, characterizes all the
planes of that solid. Cavalieri calls BC the 'regula', and I will refer to it either
as the regula or as the reference line.

We follow Anderson (1985) in using the notation $O_F(l)_{BC}$ to denote the
Cavalierian concept of "all the lines" of the figure F with reference to the regula
BC (O stands for *omnes*). For the moment we will deal only with rectilinear
transits; the notion of oblique transit will be referred to in chapter 5.

Cavalieri wants to exploit the collection of all the lines of the figure to
obtain information about the original figures. In general, given two figures F_1,
F_2 the aim is to determine the ratio between their areas by appealing to the
ratio between their associated collections of lines;

$$F_1 : F_2 = O_{F_1}(l) : O_{F_2}(l)$$

where we have assumed the collection of lines is taken with respect to the
same regula. Indeed, the result appears as the statement of theorem II.3 of
the *Geometria*. The above innocent-looking proportion is, however, quite
problematic. Even assuming that the concept of "all the lines" is a well-defined
concept, the further problem arises as to what is implicit in posing a ratio
between two collections of lines. We have seen that Euclid's theory of
proportion stated that two magnitudes A and B have a ratio A : B, if there
exists an *n* such that A + ... + A > B (*n* A's). Thus it must be verified that the
collections of lines can be compared relative to size and that in fact given $O_{F_1}(l)$
and $O_{F_2}(l)$ it makes sense to say that, for some *n*,

$$\underbrace{O_{F_1}(l) + \cdots + O_{F_1}(l)}_{n\text{-times}} > O_{F_2}(l)$$

In short, Cavalieri must show that the O's are magnitudes in the Greek sense. Cavalieri does not evade the task and, indeed, in the second book of the *Geometria* he proves theorem II.1.

THEOREM II.1. *All the lines of rectilinear transit of arbitrary plane figures, and all the planes of arbitrary solids, are magnitudes which have a ratio among each other.*[8]

The only explicit postulate about collection of lines presented by Cavalieri is that all the lines of congruent plane figures are congruent. But the *Geometria* does not explain what is meant by congruent collection of lines. Indeed, it is not even explicitly stated what is meant by saying that two collections of lines are equal. Cavalieri assumes without explicit justification that collections of lines satisfy, among other things,[9] the first two properties about magnitudes listed above. How two collections of lines may be added and compared in this sense is something which can only be gathered from the proofs, and as remarked by Giusti, Cavalieri "not only fails to produce explicitly the rules of the operations [between collection of lines] but from time to time uses different methods himself."[10] The outline of the proof will help us in determining some of the main features of Cavalieri's use of the concept of "all the lines." Let us consider two figures ABC and A'B'C' (see Fig. 7).

Assume without loss of generality that the regulae of the figures be the bases of the two figures BC and B'C'. Let RA and R'A' be the heights of the two figures. Cavalieri distinguishes two cases, RA = R'A' and RA ≠ R'A'. When RA = R'A' he argues as follows. Consider a point I on RA and a parallel to BC, and thus to B'C', passing through I. This parallel determines a segment LM in the figure ABC, a corresponding segment L'M' in A'B'C', and a point I' corresponding to I. Thus, all the segments LM are the indivisibles of the first figure and all the segments L'M' the indivisibles of the second figure. Cavalieri's idea is to compare the class of indivisibles by operating on each one individually. Thus, given an arbitrary l in O$_{A'B'C'}$(l), say L'M', and assuming without loss of generality that L'M' < LM, Cavalieri extends L'M', in the direction of LM, by adding it to itself until it covers all of LM and therefore producing a line TM' such that LM is a part of TM'. Since this can be done for an arbitrary indivisible of the figure A'B'C' he concludes that, as all indivisibles of A'B'C' have been

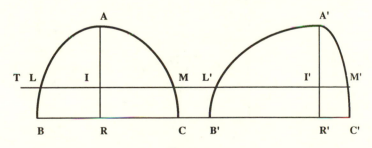

Figure 7

extended to contain, as a part, all the indivisibles of ABC, that the indivisibles of A'B'C' have been shown to be comparable to those of ABC. A symmetrical argument shows that the indivisibles of ABC are comparable to those of A'B'C'.

The proof for the case $RA \neq R'A'$ is obtained by reducing it to the previous case. Assume $RA > R'A'$. Cavalieri decomposes the figure ABC in such a way that the height of the component parts is less than or equal to $R'A'$. These component parts are then juxtaposed to each other. The figures are then compared as in the previous case. However, in order to conclude, Cavalieri is forced to assume implicitly that if a figure F is congruent to two figures F_1 and F_2, then $O_F = O_{F_1}(l) + O_{F_2}(l)$. The proof is interesting in that it shows that the implicit criterion for adding collections of indivisibles is to add the indivisibles individually. Then one collection of lines can be said to be greater than another when each of the indivisibles of the figure is greater than the corresponding indivisible of the second figure.

Theorem II.2 states that all the lines of equal plane figures are equal, that is, if $F_1 = F_2$, then $O_{F_1}(l) = O_{F_2}(l)$. The proof employs a process of decomposition and congruency of the figures. Let ADC and AEB be two equal plane figures with regulae AB and AC respectively (see Fig. 8). Cavalieri superposes the two figures. If AEB is congruent to ADC then, by postualte 1, $O_{AEB}(l)$ is congruent to $O_{ADC}(l)$ and thus equal (the last step is actually never explicitly postulated by Cavalieri). If the two figures only partially superpose, as in the figure, then one superposes the figure AED on the figure BDC, making sure that all the lines are still compared with respect to the same regula. One then proceeds in the same fashion until AEB is decomposed in parts that totally cover ADC. But congruent figures have congruent collection of lines, and once again Cavalieri infers that the collection of lines must be equal, on account of their congruency. The weak point in the above proof is that the process of superposition might never terminate, an issue to which I shall return more thoroughly when analyzing theorem VII.1, the basis of the second method of indivisibles.

In theorem II.3 Cavalieri shows that figures A and B (and solid figures S and T) are to each other as their collections of lines, respectively planes;

$$A : B = O_A(l) : O_B(l)$$

$$S : T = O_S(p) : O_T(p).$$

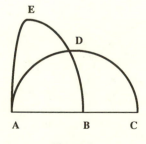

Figure 8

The theorem is proved in the usual Euclidian fashion (see *Elements* V.5 in note 1) by showing that for all *m, n,*

$$\underbrace{A + \cdots + A}_{m\text{-times}} \gtreqqless \underbrace{B + \cdots + B}_{n\text{-times}} \quad \text{iff} \quad \underbrace{O_A(l) + \cdots + O_A(l)}_{m\text{-times}} \gtreqqless \underbrace{O_B(l) + \cdots + O_B(l)}_{n\text{-times}}.$$

An analogous proof is also given for solids.

The proofs of theorems II.2 and II.3 show, as remarked by Giusti, a tension in Cavalieri's conception of "all the lines," in that the criterion for comparing collections of lines turns out to be formally indistinguishable from that used to compare the figures themselves—decomposition and inclusion.

> We are therefore led to the conclusion that all the lines of plane figures ... are magnitudes that are added together and compared exactly with the sames rules as the figures themselves, and then, at least as long as the fundamental Theorems II and III of the second book are involved, these two classes of magnitudes are in fact indistinguishable from each other. In plain language, Theorems II and III are nothing but tautologies.[11]

In order to use the result of theorem II.3 effectively, Cavalieri must show how to obtain a ratio between collections of lines. This is done in theorem II.4 as follows. Consider two figures ACM and MCE (see Fig. 9) having bases situated on the same line, equal height, and such that for any parallel to the base that intersects the figure, the segments BR and RD determined in the figure stand always in the same ratio as AM to ME. Then ACM:CME is as AM:ME.

The proof relies on a principle that from the constancy of the ratios between the BR's and RD's, now considered as corresponding indivisibles of the two figures, concludes that the collections $O_{ACM}(l)$ and $O_{MCE}(l)$ also stand in that ratio. And thus, by theorem II.3, we obtain that AM:ME = ACM:MCE. The principle used in the proof is often referred to in the literature as the *ut unum* principle, from Cavalieri's own wording, which refers to this inference mode as *ut unum ad unum, sic omnia ad omnia.* The wording betrays, as emphasized by Giusti, an origin of the principle in proportion theory where from $a_1:b_1 = \cdots = a_n:b_n$ one can conclude $(a_1 + \cdots + a_n):(b_1 + \cdots + b_n) = a_1:b_1$. Cavalieri thus proceeds by "a twofold extrapolation: the first when passing

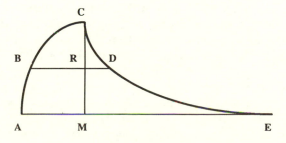

Figure 9

from a finite to an infinite number of proportions, and the second identifying *omnia antecedentia*, an abridgment for *summa omnium antecedentium* with *omnes lineae.*"[12] This ambiguity certainly opened the way for the systematic misreading of collections of lines as sums, which was typical of many seventeenth-century geometers. This concludes the foundational theorems associated with the first method of indivisibles. In the next section I will show how Cavalieri proved the classical result that a cone and a cylinder with the same base and height are to each other as 1 is to 3, so that the reader will better be able to appreciate Cavalieri's manipulations with indivisibles and how Cavalieri's methods of proof are radically different from the exhaustion method.

2.2.2 Computations with Indivisibles

In the theorems immediately following proposition II.4, Cavalieri uses his previous theorems on collections of lines to prove several results about parallelograms already found in Euclid. In the process he also develops a number of theorems about collections of squares, by generalizing the concept of all lines. If for each l in $O_F(l)$ we consider the square built on l we obtain the concept of all the squares of the figure F, which we denote by $O_F(\Box l)$. For example, in theorem II.9 he proves that all the squares of parallelograms with the same height, with references the bases from which the height is considered, are to each other as the square of the bases. Moreover, in theorem II.13 he proves that the collection of all squares of two similar parallelograms, say A and B, taken with reference to two homologous sides, have the same ratio as that of the cubes of the homologous sides. And in theorem II.22 Cavalieri proves by a reductio ad absurdum that given two parallelograms, A and B, and any one of the triangles individuated by their diagonals, say A_1 and B_1, then the collection of squares of the first parallelogram is to the collection of squares of one of the triangles individuated by its diagonal as the collection of squares of the second parallelogram is to the collection of squares of one of the triangles individuated by its diagonal:

$$O_A(\Box l) : O_{A_1}(\Box l) = O_B(\Box l) : O_{B_1}(\Box l).$$

We can outline how one can obtain through the first method of indivisibles the result that a cylinder and a cone with same base and equal height are to each other as 3 is to 1. Before looking at the case of the cone and the cylinder we will first establish a lemma about triangles and parallelograms, whose proof uses results established in the earlier part of book II (II.13, II.22, and II.23).

THEOREM 24. *Given any parallelogram and a diagonal in it, all the squares of the parallelogram are three times the squares of any of the triangles formed by the above mentioned diagonal, with a common reference one of the sides of the parallelogram.*[13]

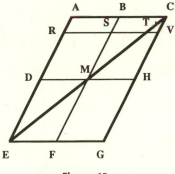

Figure 10

PROOF. Let ACGE be a parallelogram with diagonal CE (see Fig. 10). The claim is that, with reference EG

$$O_{ACGE}(\square l)_{EG} = 3O_{CGE}(\square l)_{EG}$$

where the triangle CGE can be replaced by the triangle AEC. Let B and F be the midpoints of AC and EG, respectively. Similarly let D and H be the midpoints of AE and CG, respectively. Cavalieri notices that, for an arbitrary RV parallel to EG and intersecting BF and CE in the points S and T, the following relation holds:

$$\square RT + \square TV = 2\square RS + 2\square TS,$$

where $\square$ denotes the square on the side. Cavalieri then proceeds to infer using theorem II.23, the generalization to squares of the *ut unum* principle, that

$$O_{ACE}(\square l) + O_{CEG}(\square l) = 2O_{ABFE}(\square l) + 2[O_{BCM}(\square l) + O_{MEF}(\square l)] \quad (2.1)$$

By using the assumption that congruent figures have equal collection of squares we have

$$O_{ACE}(\square l) = O_{CEG}(\square l) \quad \text{and} \quad O_{MEF}(\square l) = O_{BCM}(\square l).$$

Moreover, Cavalieri proved, by appealing to II.13 and II.22, that

$$O_{CEG}(\square l) : O_{MEF}(\square l) = EG^3 : EF^3 = 8 : 1.$$

Or equivalently

$$O_{CEG}(\square l) : [O_{MEF}(\square l) + O_{BCM}(\square l)] = 4 : 1. \quad (2.2)$$

But from (2.1) we have

$$O_{CEG}(\square l) = O_{ABFE}(\square l) + O_{BCM}(\square l) + O_{MEF}(\square l). \quad (2.3)$$

And by (2.2)

$$[O_{ABFE}(\square l) + O_{BCM}(\square l) + O_{MEF}(\square l)] : [O_{MEF}(\square l) + O_{BCM}(\square l)] = 4 : 1.$$

From the above it follows that

$$O_{ABFE}(\square l) = 3[O_{BCM}(\square l) + O_{MEF}(\square l)].$$

Moreover, by II.9 we have

$$O_{ACGE}(\square l) : O_{ABFE}(\square l) = EG^2 : EF^2 = 4 : 1 = 12 : 3.$$

Thus

$$O_{ACGE}(\square l) : \{3[O_{BCM}(\square l) + O_{MEF}(\square l)]\} = 12 : 3.$$

And

$$O_{ACGE}(\square l) = 12[O_{BCM}(\square l) + O_{MEF}(\square l)].$$

It follows that

$$O_{ACGE}(\square l) : \{O_{ABFE}(\square l) + [O_{BCM}(\square l) + O_{MEF}(\square l)]\} = 12 : 4.$$

But by (2.3)

$$O_{ACGE}(\square l) : O_{CGE}(\square l) = 12 : 4 = 3 : 1, \quad \text{i.e.,} \quad O_{ACGE}(\square l) = 3O_{CGE}(\square l).$$

Let us now rotate ACGE around the axis CG. ACGE will generate a cylinder and CGE a cone. We now appeal to theorem 33.

THEOREM 33. *Given any two plane figures, and taking an arbitrary regula in each one of them, arbitrary solids mutually similar generated by the same figures according to the same references will be to each other as all the squares of the same figures taken with respect to the common referents.*[14]

This theorem can be seen as the central result in Cavalieri's theory. It allows Cavalieri to generalize and extend several results concerning cubatures that the ancients had proved only for specific cases. A solid is said to be similar when all its cross sections taken with respect to the same regula (i.e., a plane figure) are all similar figures. Standard examples are pyramids, cones, and cylinders. We can think of these solids as generated by two figures, P and B. Each solid is considered as being obtained by taking all the cross sections of P to be similar to B. In the case of the cone, P is a triangle and B is a circle. When, as in the case of a cone and a cylinder with the same base, two similar solids S_1 and S_2 are generated by two figures P_1 and P_2 by means of the same B, then the two solids are said to be mutually similar. In essence, theorem 33 shows that in the case of two mutually similar solids the ratio between the solids is only a function of the squares of P_1 and P_2; it does not depend on B;

$$S_1 : S_2 = O_{P_1}(\square l) : O_{P_2}(\square l).$$

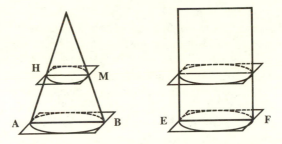

Figure 11

The result is established by making use of theorem II.15 to the effect that similar plane figures are to each other as the square of homologous lines (special cases of this result are already in Euclid.) We thus prove theorem 33 with reference to a cone and a cylinder, keeping in mind that Cavalieri proves the results for arbitrary figures. In this case P_1 and P_2 are a triangle and a parallelogram, respectively, and B is a circle in both cases (see Fig. 11). Let AB and EF be the regulae. First we consider the figures independently. Let HM be an arbitrary parallel to AB. Consider the square on AB, $\square AB$, and the square on HM, $\square HM$. Now, $AB^2 : HM^2 = \square AB : \square HM$. Consider now the similar circles C_1 and C_2 on AB and HM. By II.15 they stand in the ratio of the squares of the homologous sides, that is, as AB^2 is to HM^2. Thus

$$C_1 : C_2 = \square AB : \square HM \quad \text{and} \quad C_1 : \square AB = C_2 : \square HM.$$

As HM was arbitrary we now use the *ut unum* principle to infer that all the squares of the triangle stand to all the circles of the triangle as the square on AB stands to the circle on AB. But this holds also for the second solid, the cylinder. Thus the collection of all the circles on the triangle P_1—the collection of all the planes of the cone—is to the collection of all the circles on the parallelogram P_2—the collection of all the planes of the cylinder—as $O_{P_1}(\square l)$ is to $O_{P_2}(\square l)$. But from II.24 we know that the last ratio is 1 to 3, and by II.3 that the cone and the cylinder have the same proportion as their collection of planes. We conclude that a cylinder and a cone with same base and height are to each other as 3 is to 1.

The proof is extremely general in that it applies to solids generated by arbitrary figures, so that theorem 33 represent a very fruitful theorem from which Cavalieri was able to prove with surprising generality, many results unknown to the Greeks. Moreover, most applications in the *Geometria* rely on this theorem. Let us now move on to the second method.

2.2.3   The Second Method of Indivisibles

In the preface to the seventh book of the *Geometria*, which contains the second approach to the geometry of indivisibiles, Cavalieri lists a number of objections that might be raised against the foundations of the first method. Its main concepts ("all the lines" and "all the planes") might be considered to be incomprehensible. Or some might suspect that he has fallen into composing the continuum out of indivisibles; or finally it might be objected to the fact that the concept of infinity is at the basis of his *Geometria*: "Or finally, because I dared put as a most solid foundation of the *Geometria* an infinite greater than the high seas." Concerning the first objection, Cavalieri refers the reader back to the things said in book II proposition 1, which we will analyze later. In reference to the problem of the composition of the continuum, Cavalieri points out that his position does not commit him to compose the continuum out of indivisibles. Finally, the aggregates of indivisibles are not compared with respect to their "infinite" character (i.e., possessing infinitely many indivisibles) but on account of their finite features. Since all three objections will actually be raised by Guldin, I shall save them for later. I now concentrate on the technical solution offered by Cavalieri in the seventh book.

The new approach consists, according to Cavalieri, in providing a new foundation "free from the concept of infinity." What Cavalieri means here is that the notion of comparison of infinite aggregates will not be used in the new approach. But we will have to assess whether this second approach is really free from the concept of infinity. Cavalieri's main idea consists in comparing the indivisibles of two figures "distributively" but not "collectively," that is, he will refrain from using the notion of aggregate of indivisibles. The cornerstone of the new approach is the so-called Cavalieri principle, which is theorem 1 of the seventh book.

THEOREM 1. *If between the same parallels any two plane figures are constructed, and if in them, any straight line being drawn equidistant from the parallels, the included portions of any one of these lines are equal, the plane figures are also equal to one another; and if between the same parallel planes any solid figures are constructed, and if in them, any planes being drawn equidistant from the parallel planes, the included plane figures out of any one of the planes so drawn are equal, the solid figures are likewise equal to one another. The figures so compared let us call equally analogue.*[15]

The proof has been entirely translated in Struik and analyzed in several places (Struik 1969; Cellini 1966a, 1966b). I will limit myself to give the gist of it. Consider the two equally analogue figures ABC and XYZ shown in Figure 12. By assumption, the two figures are equally analogue, that is, ABC and XYZ are constructed between the same parallels, PQ and RS. We also know that for any parallel to RS, say OU, the segments intercepted in ABC and XYZ must be equal, EF + GH = TV. (Note that the first figure is hollow.) Similarly for the parallel DN we have JK = LM. The proof now proceeds by superposition. Keeping ABC parallel to itself superpose it to XYZ. There are two possible cases. Either ABC is completely congruent to XYZ in which case by postulate 4 of Euclid's *Elements* they are equal. Or there will be a partial superposition of ABC on XYZ.

After the superposition, ABC and XYZ will have a common part, say XMC'YThL. Consider now the parts not in common, LB'YTF' in ABC and

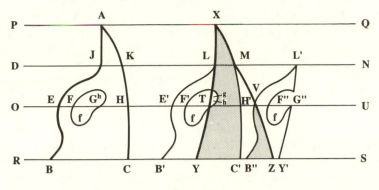

Figure 12

MC'Z in XYZ. The superposition is such that "whatever straight lines (included in the figures) are in line remain in line" so it follows that the residual lines in the figures, LB'YTF' and MC'Z, satisfy the original assumption of the theorem —they are equally analogue (with respect to new parallels DN and RS in Fig. 12) and each parallel intersects in the two figures equal segments, for example, E'F' = H'V. Now we simply reiterate the procedure.

> If now we superpose these residua again, but so that the parallels between which they lie be always superposed respectively, and this is supposed to be done continually, until the whole figure ABC shall have been superposed, I say the whole of it must coincide with XYZ; otherwise if there were any residuum of the figure XYZ upon which no thing is superposed, there would be also some residuum of the figure ABC which would not have been superposed, as we have shown above to be unavoidable; but it is granted that the whole of ABC is superposed upon XYZ. Thus they are so superposed upon each other that they coincide, and therefore the figures ABC, XYZ are equal to each other.[16]

Cavalieri felt that the above proof could still be found unsatisfactory and thus added a proof by reductio ad absurdum. We will come back to these proofs in connection with Guldin's criticisms. Theorem 1 is thus the basis of Cavalieri's reconstruction of the results contained in the first six books of the *Geometria*. Theorem VII.2 extends the above result to deal with plane figures contained between parallel lines and in which the corresponding indivisibles of the two figures stand in a constant ratio. It goes on to state that the two figures also stand in that ratio. Theorem VII.3 gives the analogue result for solids. Starting from these results, which correspond to the content of theorem II.4 in the first method, Cavalieri proceeds to show how to reconstruct most of the theorems contained in the first six books of the *Geometria* with these new foundations. For example, the proposition that gives the ratio between cylinders and cones with the same base and height is regained in theorem VII.8. The proof appeals to theorem 7 of book XII of Euclid's *Elements*, proved without recourse to exhaustion; any pyramid is a third part of the prism that has the same base with it and equal height.

Given the cone and the cylinder with common bases B and height h, one looks at an arbitrary cylindrical solid with triangular base T, which is indeed a prism, and height h. Using this theorem the prism is three times the corresponding pyramid with same base and height h. But this pyramid is indeed a cylindrical solid. However, by making use of the result that two cylindrical solids with the same height have a ratio to each other equal to the ratio of the bases (theorem VII.5) and the equivalent result for conic solids (theorem VII.7), one can infer that the cone and the cylinder have the same ratio as the corresponding pyramid and prism, 1 to 3. Compared with the first method, notice how this second approach avoids the calculations involving collection of planes, such as those contained in II.4, II.24, and II.33. Theorem II.4 is replaced, as already noticed, by theorems VII.2 and VII.3. Moreover, the results on squares contained in theorems II.24 and II.33 are replaced by appealing to Euclid XII.7 and to theorem VII.7 of the *Geometria*, which depends on the result that similar plane figures are to each other as the squares of homologous lines.

The second method is less general than the first because it can only be applied to figures of the same height. But in Cavalieri's eyes, this loss of generality was compensated by a foundational superiority. However, both approaches were found defective by the Jesuit mathematician, Paul Guldin, who engaged in an extensive attack on Cavalieri's two methods.

2.3   Guldin's Objections to Cavalieri's Geometry of Indivisibles

Cavalieri was well aware of the possible objections that could be raised against his geometry. Indeed, for years he had hoped, alas in vain, to receive Galileo's approval of the principles on which his *Geometria* was based, only to discover that Galileo did not mention the *Geometria* in the *Two New Sciences* (1638). Moreover, Galileo argued there against the possibility that two aggregates of indivisibles could be said to have a proportion. The correspondence with Galileo[17] shows that Cavalieri was extremely concerned about the foundations of his methods. The scant exchange with Galileo had already acquainted him with the two kinds of objections he would have to face. On the one hand, technical objections raising the possibilities of the emergence of paradoxes. On the other hand, philosophical objections related to the notion of infinity and the continuum. This explains the variety of foundational approaches contained in the *Geometria* and analyzed in the previous section.

The most challenging objections to appear in print were raised by two Jesuit mathematicians, Paul Guldin and André Tacquet. Guldin attacked the *Geometria* of Cavalieri in his *Centrobaryca* (1635–41) and Tacquet proposed some technical difficulties in his *Annularia et Cylindrica* (1651). To these criticisms one should add those of Bettini in the *Aerarium Philosophiae Mathematicae* (1648) whose contents, however, add nothing to Guldin's attack.[18]

The debate between Cavalieri and Guldin is usually mentioned in connection with the objections made by Guldin to Cavalieri's use of indivisibles.

Although that is probably the main issue between Cavalieri and Guldin, a more careful reading of the debate will allow us to indicate the existence of other interesting issues, which so far have not received the attention they deserve.

As its title suggests, Guldin's *Centrobaryca* is a work devoted to the study of centers of gravity and their use in establishing quadratures and cubatures of geometrical objects obtained by the revolution of a generating line or figure around an external axis. In it we find Guldin's rule, which we now call the theorem of Guldin and Pappus, concerning the dimension of geometrical objects generated by revolution of a geometrical object of lower dimension around a fixed axis. The dimension of the generated object depends on the dimension of the generating object and on the path traversed by the generating object's center of gravity during its revolution around the axis. Later in the book I will return to the technical content of Guldin's *Centrobaryca*.

Guldin attacked Cavalieri's *Geometria* on several grounds. In books II and III of the *Centrobaryca* he accuses Cavalieri of having plagiarized Kepler and Sover. The real foundational objections occur in book IV, which criticizes the foundations of both methods of indivisibles. Cavalieri replied to Guldin in the third *Exercitatio* of his *Exercitationes Geometricae Sex* (1647), which contains a step-by-step commentary of Guldin's objections. Cavalieri had at first planned a reply to Guldin in the form of a dialogue, following the style of Galileo's *Two New Sciences*, but the project was abandoned.[19] However, in describing the projected dialogue to Torricelli in 1643, Cavalieri describes a two-pronged reply to Guldin. One of the dialogues was to be a defence of his own principles against Guldin's objections. Another dialogue was to be the offensive—a thorough examination of Guldin's own program and work. One should keep this in mind when reading the third *Exercitatio*. Indeed, chapters I–XIII of the *Exercitatio* correspond to the defensive part, whereas chapters XIV–XV focus on the foundation of Guldin's method. Thus, the *Exercitatio* has a double interest. On the one hand it contains Cavalieri's attempt to defend his own method of indivisibles against criticism; on the other it draws attention to Guldin's important mathematical program and its foundations. Accordingly, I divide my treatment into two separate sections. I begin by looking at Guldin's attack on the geometry of indivisibles and at Cavalieri's replies. Then I describe the general program of the *Centrobaryca* and Cavalieri's criticisms.

Let us begin with a quick overview of the accusations of plagiarism. Guldin claimed that the main ideas of the *Geometria* were borrowed from Kepler's *Stereometria Doliorum* (1615) and Sover's *Curvi ac Recti Proportio* (1630).

Kepler had resorted to infinitesimal considerations in the *Stereometria Doliorum*. For example, he gave an alternative proof of the quadrature of the circle whereby its circumference "is cut into very small arcs which appear to be equal to straight lines." This allows him to regard the circle as an infinitary polygon constituted by an infinity of infinitesimal triangles whose bases are the infinitesimal sides of the polygon and the sides radii from the center of the circle to the extreme points of the bases. In this conception the circle is composed of infinitesimal figures of the same dimension. Thus Cavalieri objects to Guldin that his indivisibles are very different from Kepler's infinitesimals, and emphasizes that "whereas Kepler ... composes greater bodies from extremely small bodies ... I only say that two plane figures are to each other as the aggregates of all the parallel lines to a given one."[20] Cavalieri is certainly right in stressing the difference between Kepler's infinitesimals and his own indivisibles, although as noticed by Boyer (1959, 109) one should recall that Kepler himself sometimes "lapsed into the language of indivisibles." However, there is no trace in Kepler of the elaborate structure concocted by Cavalieri for comparing aggregates of indivisibles. Thus, Cavalieri's defence appears very convincing.

Guldin also mentioned Sover in an attempt to cast doubt on the originality of the second approach to indivisibles presented by Cavalieri, and claimed that the notion of analogue figure, central to book VII of the *Geometria*, is already to be found in Sover's book. Cavalieri defended himself against these accusations by remarking that the *Geometria* had already been completed before Sover's book was published and thus he could not have had the opportunity to borrow from it.[21]

Before providing an extensive criticism of the foundations of the two Cavalierian methods, Guldin criticizes the first proposition of book I of the *Geometria*. Although neither the theorem nor the objection directly relate to the issue of indivisibles, I think it is worthwhile mentioning it because it will give us a sense of the distance separating Guldin, a follower of the ancients, and Cavalieri, who is attempting to break new ground. Problem 1, proposition 1 of book I reads as follows (see Fig. 13):

> *To find the vertex of any plane figure whatsoever, or a solid one, with respect to a straight line in the case of a plane figure, and with respect to a given plane in the case of a solid figure.*[22]

The proof in the case of a plane figure is as follows:

> Let ABC be an arbitrary plane figure, and let it be drawn through it a straight line BC: one has to find a vertex of the figure ABC with respect to BC. In the plane of the figure ABC, indefinitely extended, consider an arbitrary point N

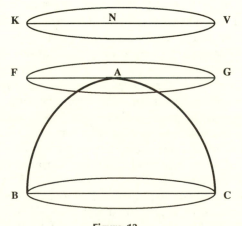

Figure 13

and let the parallel KV be drawn through N to BC itself, extended indefinitely on both sides. Thus: either KV touches the figure BAC, and then we have what is sought, or it does not touch it, and thus KV will be either inside or outside the figure. Whatever the case let KV be moved, keeping always in the same plane of the figure and parallel to BC, away from BC itself, if it was within the figure, and towards BC, if it was outside, until it touches the figure ABC. Let the figure be touched in the position of FG, in the point A. A will thus be a vertex of the figure ABC found with respect to line BC, which was sought in the first part of this problem.[23]

What is striking about this result is the extreme generality of the statement. It is not a question of finding a tangent to a specific curve, say a cissoid or a parabola, as would have been the case with a Greek geometrical work. Rather, we are aiming at a general solution of the problem. But the increase in generality creates a loss in constructivity. In other words, the theorem functions more as an existence theorem than as a constructive rule for drawing a tangent to an arbitrary curve. Indeed, how would Cavalieri's theorem help to draw, say, the tangent to the cissoid?

Guldin shows his attachment to the classical approach to geometry by raising several objections against Cavalieri's general approach, which he deems to be more appropriate to a "land-surveyor" than a geometer. What is the criterion, he asks, that will tell us where and when figure is touched by the line? The request for a criterion is equivalent to the request that a well-specified rule be given for drawing the tangent. But, of course, this cannot be delivered by Cavalieri's "existence" theorem. Thus, Cavalieri emphasizes the notion of *possibility* involved in such general theorems. The existence theorem shows that it is possible to find a line like the one sought after:

> I observe first of all that from the demonstration of the proposition in question one concludes with perfect certainty that it is possible to draw a line, or a plane, that touches any given figure. If in fact the said line, or plane, during the motion, which is always supposed to be parallel, is at times internal and at times external to the figure, then it is without doubt necessary that at a certain time it will touch it.[24]

Thus for Cavalieri's goals it is enough that such a line can be found. However, Guldin is not willing to grant any geometrical interest to such a generalized approach; he remains within the bounds of the special figures constructed by the ancients, and then of special constructions for their tangents, and so on. His objections highlight an important aspect of the characteristic trend of seventeenth-century geometry—the passage from special constructions to general theorems. Guldin himself, despite his criticism, is an important player in this tendency towards generalization, as we will see when analyzing his work.

Let us now consider Guldin's objections against the first method of indivisibles. Guldin begins the foundational criticism of the first theory of indivisibles by criticizing the notions of "all the lines" of a figure and "all the planes" of a solid. In essence his position is as follows. He accepts that the movement of a generating line gives rise to a figure, a generating plane to a solid, but he refuses to call the generated figures or solids the "set of all the lines" or "the set of all the planes."

> In my opinion no geometer will grant him [Cavalieri] that the surface is and could in geometrical language be called "all the lines of such figure"; never in fact can several lines, or all the lines, be called surfaces; for, the multitude of lines, however great that might be, cannot compose even the smallest surface.[25]

It is quite clear that Guldin is taking Cavalieri to be composing the continuum out of indivisibles, a position rejected by the Aristotelian orthodoxy as having atomistic implications. Cavalieri replies by stressing that his position does not commit him to any particular position on the problem of the continuum.

> Actually, for those who claim that the continuum is composed by indivisibles the description of the said indivisibles will be the description of the surface. On the contrary for those that, in addition to the said indivisibles, put something else in the continuum, one will have to say that that something else is described during the motion.[26]

Strictly related to these objections concerning the composition of the continuum are Guldin's objections concerning the use of infinite collections involved in Cavalieri's approach. Against Cavalieri's proposition that "all the lines" and "all the planes" are magnitudes—they admit of ratios—Guldin argues that "all the lines ... of both figures are infinite; but an infinite has no proportion or ratio to another infinite."[27] Cavalieri replies to this objection by distinguishing two notions of infinity, absolute and relative. Something is infinite in the absolute sense if it is infinite everywhere, "*simpliciter* and *undequaque*." Something is infinite in a relative sense if it is not infinite everywhere but only relative to something. In the case of absolute infinity Cavalieri grants that there cannot be a ratio between two infinites, but he denies the same claim when it is a question of relative infinity. However, the collections of "all the lines" and "all the planes" are relative infinites and thus we can investigate their ratios.

> Now, all the mentioned lines and the planes are infinite relative to something; although they are infinite with respect to number, they are not such with respect to magnitude, since the individual lines and planes are finite and their aggregates are delimited everywhere by sides. For this reason the intellect will recognize that one can perform on them additions and subtractions, whatever might be the number of indivisibles that can be imagined to be added or subtracted. Thus these aggregates can be compared.[28]

Cavalieri goes on to compare the collections (of all the lines and planes) to irrational square roots used by the algebraists who "not knowing what is what they call the root, the side, or the cosa, i.e. what are the ineffable roots, nonetheless by multiplying and dividing them etc., arrive in the end to the solution of the problem by passing, as it were, through these obscure detours [*obscuras ambages*]."[29]

We conclude this section by stressing the radical opposition between Guldin and Cavalieri on this issue. For Guldin the concepts of "all the lines" and "all the planes" are inconsistent.

> Since the collections of all the lines or of all the possible parts are not given, nor could they be given, there cannot be a ratio of the lines to the lines, or of the parts to the parts; indeed, things which do not exist, nor could they exist, cannot be compared. We add nothing else to this question, which is clear for all geometers.[30]

By contrast, Cavalieri insists on the legitimacy of his intellectual abstraction. We have here another example of Cavalieri's intellectual boldness in opposition to Guldin's classical standpoint.

Chapters X to XII of Cavalieri's third *Exercitatio* are devoted to replying to Guldin's objections against the distributive method and its foundation as presented in book VII of the *Geometria*. Guldin's objections can be summarized as follows. First, he objects again to the possibility of proving theorems about arbitrary figures that are not previously constructed. We have already dealt with this criticism and Cavalieri simply reiterates the general nature of the result. Second, Guldin tries to argue that Cavalieri's procedure in proposition 2 of book VII involves him in a decomposition of the continuum into indivisibles. However, the objection is unwarranted, and Cavalieri makes a number of interesting remarks about the very same proposition, remarks much more interesting than Guldin's objection. Indeed, it was Cavalieri, not Guldin, who realized that a serious objection to his procedure had to do with the termination of the superposition process.

> I do not ignore, however, that the preceding demonstration could be objected to, that the superposition in question, which must always be made piecewise, could in some figures perhaps never end; in fact we do not know which, and how big, is the part of the underlying figure. The same point could have been made in connection to the first proposition of the second book, in which this superposition is carried out piecewise. If it has to take place by means of acts continually repeated perhaps in some figures it would never end; for from this infinitely repeated superposition it seems that infinitely many pieces might arise: but Guldin neither sees nor makes this objection.[31]

We see therefore that Cavalieri's foundation of the method of indivisibles free from the concept of infinity turns out to invoke infinity at least in the form of the acceptance of a nonfinitistic procedure: the equality of two figures by superposition may not be a process that terminates in a finite number of steps, but Cavalieri's defence of his theorem shows that he was willing to extend the field of geometrical operations to allow such nonfinitistic procedures.

A third set of objections by Guldin has to do with the use of superposition in the proof of VII.1 and more generally with the use of superposition in general. The issue is related to our discussion in chapter 1 of the validity of superposition as a method of proof. Cavalieri is aware of the several objections to super-position raised, among others, by Peletier, and his line on the issue is exactly that of Clavius, whom he quotes approvingly, against Peletier. First of all, superposition for the geometer is an intellectual operation; moreover, giving up superposition would mean subverting the whole foundation of geometry.

We can thus see the importance of superposition for the foundations of mathematics in the early part of the seventeenth century. Superposition acts as a foundational tool not only in Euclidian geometry but also in Cavalieri's *Geometria*. That is why Barrow in his *Lectiones Mathematicae*, quoted here in chapter 1, stresses the centrality of congruency and superposition to the fabric of Euclidian and Cavalierian geometry. Cavalieri then went on to distinguish and classify several types of superposition procedures (by simple motion, by inflexion, and by fluxion), which suffice it to say clearly influenced an analogous treatment found in lecture XI of Barrow's *Lectiones Mathematicae*.

To summarize, Guldin was a "classicist" geometer, steeped in the idea of explicit construction, skeptical of considerations of infinity in the domain of geometry, and wary of the risk of ending up with an atomistic theory of the continuum. Whereas Cavalieri took a new approach, reliant on the classical theory of ratios but departing from traditional geometry in its generality and boldness. Cavalieri used indivisibles, collections of infinite lines and planes, and nonfinitistic procedures. The interest of the debate lies in the explicit thematization of these topics. We have to discuss two more sections of Cavalieri's answer to Guldin: section XIV is Cavalieri's analysis of Guldin's program; section XV deals with a number of paradoxes that might seem to discredit the viability of the method of indivisibles. First, I will describe Guldin's project, then I will deal with section XIV. I will leave section XV until chapter 5, on paradoxes of the infinite.

2.4   Guldin's *Centrobaryca* and Cavalieri's Objections

Guldin's *Centrobaryca*, unlike Cavalieri's *Geometria*, has not been the subject of a detailed historical investigation. In the major histories of mathematics, references to Guldin mainly consider whether or not he had plagiarized Pappus' *Collections*; two recent articles have satisfactorily clarified the situation.[32] Unfortunately, I will not be able to fill this gap in the literature, but I will try to raise a number of issues about Guldin's *Centrobaryca* and claim that the work has much to offer any readers interested in foundational issues. I will begin with an overview of its contents.

The first volume of the *Centrobaryca* was published in Vienna in 1635. The book is prefaced by a description of the mathematical sciences, being the content of a lecture delivered by Guldin in 1622. The preface defines mathematics according to the Aristotelian classification, as that part of philosophy lying between physics and metaphysics. Mathematics is the science that considers quantity abstracted from sensible matter. Concerning pure mathematics, arithmetic is described as the science of discrete quantity, and geometry as the science of continuous quantity. It is interesting to note the addition of algebra to the traditional disciplines of pure mathematics; of course, Guldin's conception of algebra depends in large part on the work of Viète.[33]

The real treatise on centers of gravity begins after the preface. Guldin starts by discussing the definitions of center, center of a figure, and center of magnitude. However, the central definition is that of center of gravity. In order to insure that the definition be general enough to allow for the possibility of considering the center of gravity not only of a plane or solid, but also of a line, Guldin modifies the definition given by Commandino in *Liber de Centro Gravitatis Solidorum* (1565) to read as follows:

> The center of gravity of any finite quantity is that point placed either inside that quantity, or in its boundary, or outside it, around which on all sides are parts of equal moment. For either the center itself, or the straight line, or a plane however drawn through the center, will always cut the proposed figure in parts of equal weight.[34]

The mention of moments and *partes aequeponderantes* puts Guldin's approach squarely within the tradition emerging from Archimedes' *On the Equilibrium of Planes* and passing through Commandino, Guido-Ubaldo, Valerio, and Stevin, all of whom are quoted by Guldin. Indeed, in chapter II Guldin begins with a number of postulates and axioms following, or closely dependent on the works of Archimedes and Guido-Ubaldo. Guldin then proceeded to investigate the centers of gravity of a set of points and a set of lines (ch. III), of the perimeter of rectilinear figures (ch. IV), and of curves and mixed figures (chs. V, VI, and VII). In chapter VIII he moved on to the centers of gravity of plane figures bounded by straight lines, such as triangles and parallelograms. In chapter IX he studied the centers of gravity of plane figures bounded by curvilinear or mixed lines, such as semicircles and elliptical segments. Chapters X and XI introduce centers of gravity of solid bodies, the subject of books II and III.

Book II was published in 1640 and contains the celebrated rule on centers of gravity. After several chapters devoted to the detailed treatment of, among other things, spiral lines and conic sections, Guldin turned to the central part of his work in chapter VIII. This chapter deals with the genesis of circular quantities "quantitatum rotundarum" and is presented by Guldin as the reason and the culmination not only of the things he has thus far presented but of all the previous works on centers of gravity. He intends to show how to use the center of gravity in a new way—by exploiting the genesis of circular quantities and the determination of their dimensions.

In the preface to the second book Guldin had distinguished between geometric and algebraic powers "potestates." Whereas in algebra there are infinite powers, in geometry there are as many powers as dimensions, namely, three. The line is the power of the point; the surface is the power of the line; and the body is the power of the surface. These distinctions are expanded upon in proposition 1 of chapter VIII, where we find the additional distinction between direct and circular powers. Objects that are generated by a rectilinear motion of a point, a line, or a plane are called direct powers. Those that originate from the circular motion of a point, a line, or a plane are called circular powers. The simplest examples of circular powers are the circle, being obtained by the rotation of a line around one of its endpoints, and the sphere, being obtained by the rotation of a semicircle around its diameter. Circular powers are the main subject of Guldin's interest. To present his main result we need a few definitions:

> A rotation [*rotatio*] is a simple and perfectly circular motion, around a fixed center, or an unmoved axis, which is called the *axis of rotation*, turning around either a point, or a line, or a plane surface, which, almost as leaving a trace behind it, describes or generates a circular quantity, either a line, or a surface, or a body.[35]

The generating point, line, or surface is called the quantity to be rotated "rotanda" or the quantity rotated "rotata." The object generated by such rotations is called the circular quantity "rotundum." The path of rotation is the circumference of the circle described by the center of gravity of the rotated quantity. We are now ready to state Guldin's rule: "A quantity to be rotated drawn along [*ducta*] the path of rotation produces a circular power of one degree higher than the rotated power or quantity."[36] Guldin stressed the simplicity, unversality, and generality of his rule, which can be easily modified to deal with direct powers as well as circular powers. In his subsequent corollaries, Guldin specified how to use the rule to compute the dimensions of the generated quantities by noticing that the dimensions of the generated quantity simply depends on the dimensions of the generating object and on the path traversed by its center of gravity.

Guldin presented his rule without proof. He was satisfied that a wide variety of cases demonstrated how the rule produced the right results.[37] The remaining part of book II was then devoted to investigating, by application of the rule, the centers of gravity of lines and surfaces. Book III extended the development to the case of solids, thereby showing what Guldin called "the fruit of the center of gravity."

The fourth book of the *Centrobaryca*, published in 1641, is the most interesting from the foundational point of view because Guldin attempts a reconstruction of a great part of the mathematics of his time (e.g., Euclid, Archimedes, Pappus, and Kepler) without recourse to proofs by contradiction. Guldin's rule is exploited to provide the means for a reformulation of the structure of proofs and theorems which the tradition had handed down in apagogical form. At the same time, the philosophical assumptions behind the foundational and revisionistic reconstruction of mathematics propounded by Guldin show what he calls "the Glory of the center of gravity," and are thus used to argue implicitly for the superiority of a certain form of mathematical practice (based on centers of gravity as opposed to exhaustion, Cavalierian indivisibles, or Keplerian infinitesimals). Indeed, the full title of book IV is *De Centro Gravitatis, liber quartus, de gloria, ab usu centri gravitatis binarum specierum Quantitatis continuae parta. Sive Archimedes Illustratus.* Let us move to the programmatic statements contained in the preface to book IV. The book is called *Archimedes Illustratus* "because we substitute for the obscure Archimedean demonstrations clear and evident ones."[38] Guldin expressed his admiration for the theorem that the surface of the sphere is equal to four times the great circle, a theorem proved apagogically by Archimedes. However, the proof provided by Archimedes does not proceed from causes or intrinsic principles.

> A great desire therefore kindles men's minds to know on the basis of what intrinsic causes and principles he established this equality. But after sharp eyes and minds had examined the entire matter, the naked assertion, so to speak, imposed itself, that is, that this plane can be neither less nor greater than the convex surface. He thought that this assertion would be supported by this one argument, as if by a strong pillar, if he showed that some things in other respects absurd and foreign to mathematics are nonetheless to be admitted.[39]

This is why, Guldin continues, Scaliger had attacked in his *Cyclometrica* the procedures by reductio ad absurdum by which Archimedes "adeo creber est, ut non regnum in Geometria obtinere, sed tyrannidem exercere videatur." After having recalled Rivaltus' objections to Scaliger (see ch. 1) he objected to Rivaltus that ostensive proofs are indeed superior to negative and apagogical proofs: "Indeed, ostensive demonstrations have always had the applause and the victory over negatives and those reducing to absurdity or impossibility, whatever at last Rivaltus says."[40] Against Rivaltus, who had claimed that proofs in mathematics proceed from the cognition of the cause and thus are never truly "causal" or from intrinsic principles, Guldin objected by proposing to show how to demonstrate a great part of the body of classical mathematics from intrinsic principles, by means of ostensive proofs—proofs that produce certain and eternal science.

> We will therefore prove ostensively, in this fourth book, through our principles from rotation and originating from the center of gravity, the main propositions proved by Archimedes on the Sphere and the Cylinder and similarly on Conoids and Spheroids, which he himself had established by contradiction. Whether indeed the demonstrations originating from our first principles proceed from a formal cause, or an efficient one, etc., the careful and learned reader will determine. I do not put an end to this dispute. However, I strongly claim that they proceed from intrinsic principles and are ostensive, which is so far the thing most desired from the Archimedean demonstrations.[41]

In the first four chapters of book IV Guldin then proceeded to reformulate classical mathematical theorems in an attempt to vindicate the programmatic statements made in the preface. Chapter I deals with theorems taken from the Archimedean treatise *On the Dimension of the Circle* and from the first book of *On the Sphere and the Cylinder*. Chapter II deals with theorems taken from Archimedes' work *On Conoids and Spheroids*. Chapter III tackled a number of propositions from book XII of Euclid's *Elements*, and chapter IV extended the treatment to deal with Kepler's additions to Archimedes' work. Guldin warns the reader that he has not dealt with Pappus' work for lack of time, although he sees no obstacle to extend his treatment to account for the main theorems of the *Collections*.

Let us now look at two examples to get a sense of the simplification introduced by the use of the center of gravity. First we look at the ostensive proof of the quadrature of the circle; then we look at the ostensive proof that the cone is one-third of the cylinder with same base and height (Euclid, book XII, prop. 10).

THEOREM. *The area of a circle C is equal to the area of a right triangle T whose legs are equal to the radius and the circumference of the circle.*[42]

GULDIN'S PROOF (BOOK IV, CH. I, PROP. I). Consider a segment AB with middle point C (see Fig. 14). C is the center of gravity of AB. Rotate AB around A. AB will produce, according to Guldin's rule, a surface, indeed a circle, say BFG. And AC will at the same time produce a smaller circle, say CDE. Now by Pappus, book V of the *Collections*, proposition 11, the peripheries of the circles have the same ratio to each other as their diameters. But the circumference CDE is the path traversed by the center of gravity of AB, and thus the area of the circle BFG is equal to that of a rectangle, one of whose sides is the radius AB and the other the circumference CDE (which is equal to half the circumference of BFG); or, equivalently, to the area of the triangle whose sides are the radius AB and twice CDE, that is, the circumference BFG.

We can now move on to the proof of Euclid's XII.10 given by Guldin (book IV, ch. III, prop. II). We think of the cone and the cylinder as generated by the rotation of the triangle CAD, and the rectangle FADC, respectively, around the axis CD (see Fig. 15). Guldin uses some results about the centers of gravity of triangles and parallelograms, already known to Archimedes, and stated in book I, chapter VIII of the *Centrobaryca*.[43]

In particular, the center of gravity I of the triangle is such that, after drawing BE passing through it and parallel to AD, we have 2AB = BC, 2ED = EC, and BI = IE. Moreover, if M is the center of gravity of the parallelogram FADC then the parallel to AD, say GH, passing through M divides FA and CD in equal parts, and is such that GM = MH. In order to compute the ratio between the cylinder and the cone, Guldin's theorem requires us to know the ratio between the areas of the generating figures and the ratio between the circumferences generated by the center of gravities of the two figures after they have been rotated around CD. The ratio between the rectangle FADC and the

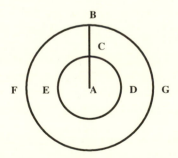

Figure 14

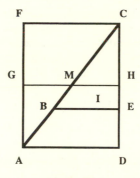

Figure 15

triangle CAD is as 2 to 1. As for the ratio between the radii MH and IE, we know that 2ED = EC, that is, CD : EC = 3 : 2. Since BCE and ADC are similar triangles we have AD : BE = 3 : 2. Since GH = AD we have GH : BE = 3 : 2. But GH = 2GM and BE = 2IE. Thus MH : IE = 3 : 2. By composing the ratios we obtain that the cylinder is to the cone as (FACD : CAD)·(MH : IE), that is, as 3 is to 1.

Both examples make essential use of the result that circumferences of circles are to each other as the radii, a fact which is of relevance to the assessment of the viability of Guldin's program. The above examples suffice to illustrate the nature of the technical simplification introduced by the employment of the center of gravity, vis-à-vis the double reductio ad absurdum. However, this simplification depends on the assumption of the validity of Guldin's rule, and the result about the radii and the circumferences, a result proved by exhaustion.

Let us now address the specifics of Cavalieri's criticisms. In section XIV of the third *Exercitatio* Cavalieri employs a more aggressive strategy against his opponent, Guldin, by criticizing the central tenets of the *Centrobaryca*— Guldin's rule and his foundational ostensive programme.

Concerning Guldin's rule, Cavalieri objects to Guldin for not having established apodictically the validity of the rule, relying instead on probable and inductive arguments. And thus to vindicate his indivisibles he provided a proof of Guldin's rule for solids based on indivisibilist considerations, found by G. A. Rocca, an Italian mathematician close to Cavalieri and Torricelli. The proof need not be presented here.[44] Suffice it to say that, by this astute move, Cavalieri implies the geometry of indivisibles can provide a foundation for Guldin's approach. And, indeed, this line of attack receives more strength when one considers the issue of the elimination of proofs by contradiction, so dear to Guldin. In fact, one could perhaps give a classical reductio proof for Guldin's rule. However, only the geometry of indivisibles seems to be able to give an ostensive proof of it.

Moreover, I know that all the mentioned things can be reduced to Archimedes' style. This, shown to Guldin by the Indivisibles, could have at least served him, even if he had rejected them, and precisely by transforming the proof by indivisibles into an Archimedean one, as can be done in all demonstrations which are obtained by indivisibles. And he, who everywhere praises the excellence of the direct demonstration, should not have avoided them [the Indivisibles] since in this case the direct demonstration could be given to him only by the Indivisibles. In vain then he would have restored, in his fourth book, propositions from Euclid and Archimedes proved by reductio to impossibility so that they would acquire the said excellency of direct demonstrations, unless the general rule had been proved directly too.[45]

We thus see how Cavalieri is aware that ostensive demonstrations can sometimes be obtained only at the cost of stronger ontological assumptions on infinity (i.e., the use of indivisibles). Moreover, the dilemma he puts to his adversary is logically justified. The search for direct proofs is relevant only if the theorems used in the demonstration are themselves proved by direct proofs. Guldin should not have abhorred, in Cavalieri's lucid analysis, the use of indivisibles because only through indivisibles could he have avoided the reductio ad absurdum and proved his results by truly ostensive demonstrations. At the end of the section Cavalieri reiterated the point.

> Nor perhaps would he have so much despised the Indivisibles, from which he could have obtained a big benefit, once having obtained the direct demonstration that he so much praised, had he not preferred to follow the Archimedean style that he criticized for the *reductio ad absurdum*, and by which method through inscription and circumscription etc. ....[46]

On a critical note, the proof of Rocca's theorem appeals to several classical theorems proved by contradiction, and thus Cavalieri here does not carry his analysis far enough.

Cavalieri's emphasis on proofs by contradiction not only confirms that he had seen their centrality to Guldin's program, but it also highlights an important feature of Cavalieri's work. Indeed, a very interesting fact about the first six books of the *Geometria*—those containing the first method of indivisibles—is that Cavalieri used the proof by contradiction only once. Moreover, Cavalieri worked hard and finally succeeded in finding a direct proof of that proposition. He presented the new proof several years later in the *Exercitationes Geometricae Sex*.

> Seeing that only proposition 22 [of book II] ... in the whole of the *Geometria Indivisibilium* was shown by the first method by a demonstration reducing to impossibility, I added (to make evident to the reader that by the said first method everything can be directly demonstrated) the above proposition so that prop. 22 as well as prop. 24, which depend from it, and all those derived from there, are proved directly.[47]

In Lombardo Radice's opinion it was on logical grounds that Cavalieri preferred direct proofs over proofs by contradiction. If this is meant to imply that Cavalieri had qualms about the logical validity of reductio ad absurdum, I think there is no evidence for this. However, if "logical" is taken broadly to imply epistemological and methodological, I agree that Cavalieri favored ostensive proofs on heuristic and epistemological grounds. Although Cavalieri and Guldin disagreed on many issues, it is quite interesting to see how they agreed in their preference for ostensive proofs as opposed to reductio proofs. For Cavalieri such proofs are the welcome outcome of his use of indivisibles; for Guldin they can be obtained by exploiting the theory of centers of gravity.

A number of questions come to mind concerning this part of the exchange between Cavalieri and Guldin. Perhaps the most pressing for us is, how are we to explain the marked preference for direct proofs in two different mathematicians, traditional and "unorthodox"? I offer two reasons, which I call mathematical and logico-epistemological.

The mathematical reason lies in the often mentioned dissatisfaction of the mathematicians of the sixteenth and the seventeenth centuries with Archimedean proofs that suffered from being extremely tedious and never disclosed how the result had been found. There are plenty of complaints from seventeenth-century mathematicians accusing the ancients of deliberately hiding their methods of discovery. Consider the following judgment by Wallis:

> But this, their Art of Invention, they seem very studiously to have concealed: contenting themselves to demonstrate by Apagogical Demonstrations, (or reducing to Absurdity, if denied,) without shewing us the method, by which they first found out those Propositions, which they thus demonstrate by other ways.[48]

This dissatisfaction had very positive consequences in that it forced classical mathematicians (e.g., Valerio and Guldin) and "unorthodox" ones (e.g., Wallis, Cavalieri, and Torricelli) to look for proofs that would be more direct than the Archimedean ones. Torricelli is very explicit about this when he defines the method of indivisibles as a "truly scientific method of demonstration which is direct, and so to say, natural."[49]

We can conclude that the attempt to overcome the opposition between *methods of proof* and *methods of discovery* was probably one of the main factors that led many mathematicians to think seriously about the status of reductio ad absurdum in mathematics.

As for the logical and epistemological reasons, I have already introduced them by an analysis of the *Quaestio* in the first chapter. We have seen that the requirement for a scientific demonstration to be more than a logically compelling proof led to a hiatus between the notions of certainty and evidence. Although all forms of logical reasoning are certain, not all of them provide the "causal" evidence required by scientific demonstration. This distinction, to which I will return in the next chapters, is also explicitly thematized by G. Nardi, perhaps the most philosophically sensitive mathematician in Cavalieri's circle. In a work that he never published, preserved in manuscript form at the Biblioteca Nazionale in Florence,[50] Nardi claims it is certain that

> Archimedes' admirers need to excuse his oblique procedure; both because it is long and complicated in the constructions and the proofs and because it is not completely satisfactory, since it produces certainty but not evidence. I am of the opinion that everything evident is certain but not everything certain is evident.[51]

And again:

> As for Archimedes and his oblique procedure one has to conclude that such
> procedure can be improved, for it does not generate scientia (as Proclus says)
> if not by accident, and it assumes situations which are impossible, as well as
> false.[52]

Finally:

> From what we have assumed it will be clear that the oblique demonstrations
> with two false assumptions, and constructions, can be reduced to the simple
> and direct procedure; and this fact, either because it was so far not well known,
> or because it was not rightly put into practice, has much hindered progress in
> the comparison of straight and curve. Indeed, many have though that by
> following the usual Euclidian procedure this task can hardly be accomplished.
> But our principles, which are still drawn from Euclid's bowels, not only suffice
> to accomplish this task but will also establish the most ingenious principles of
> the indivisibles which in our days begin to spring up with wonderful success.[53]

I think these quotes by Nardi beautifully wrap up the issues raised in this
chapter. Let me summarize the main results. The important mathematical
programs of Cavalieri and Guldin have been shown to rest on a number of
epistemological assumptions that ultimately derive from Aristotle's methodological pronouncements in the *Posterior Analytics*. This Aristotelian position
introduces a distinction between the class of logically cogent arguments
(generating certainty) and its subclass containing scientific arguments or
syllogisms, which are not only certain but also evident. The desire to develop
mathematics according to the strictest criteria for scientific demonstration
brings about an attempt to base mathematics upon ostensive proofs and to
eliminate proofs by contradiction. Despite their attempts to develop mathematics using only ostensive proofs, the programs of Guldin and Cavalieri seem
to suffer shipwreck because at crucial points they appeal to theorems proved
by contradiction without providing an ostensive alternative. In the next chapter
we will see how Descartes' *Géométrie* is also related to these developments. And
in chapter 4, almost as a pendant to section 1.3, I will investigate the
mathematical and philosophical importance of proofs by contradiction beyond
the seventeenth century. In the process I will strengthen my claims about the
deep influence of the Aristotelian epistemological framework in the seventeenth
century and beyond.

3

Descartes' *Géométrie*

Earlier I claimed that the development of mathematics, and therefore of the philosophy of mathematics, in the seventeenth century is marked by the invasion of infinitary techniques and by the widespread use of analytic techniques. In Chapter 2 I dealt with the issue of Cavalieri's appeal to infinitary techniques, now I shall analyze one of the most important texts in the complex development of the algebraization of geometry, Descartes' *Géométrie*.

First, I shall present some of the most important results contained in the *Géométrie* and investigate the foundational assumptions on which the Cartesian project is founded. I hope to acquaint the reader with some important critical contributions. And I give a detailed analysis of Descartes' most important foundational move—the exclusion of the mechanical curves from the geometrical realm. Secondly, I shall investigate the foundational problems raised by the algebraization of mathematics.

3.1 Descartes' *Géométrie*

The *Géométrie* was first published in 1637 as an appendix to the *Discours de la Méthode*. The work was translated from French into Latin in 1649 by F. van Schooten, who published it with notes by him and F. de Beaune (Descartes 1649). A second Latin edition (Descartes 1659–61) also contained, in addition to the 1649 edition, contributions by De Witt, Hudde, Van Heuraet, Bartholinus, and van Schooten. These scientists can rightly be considered the first active group of "Cartesian" mathematicians; see Lenoir (1974, ch. 4) for an analysis of this second Latin edition.

Although the *Géométrie* is a short work (116 pages in the original French edition), its interpretation has given rise to several contrasting positions. However, before we venture on to the delicate subject of its interpretations, it is better to go over its contents. The work is divided into three books: Problems the construction of which requires only straight lines and circles; On the nature of curved lines; and On the construction of solid and supersolid problems.

65

The first book contains a geometrical interpretation of the arithmetical calculus and a solution to Pappus' problem for four lines by a ruler-and-compass construction. The basic strategies of Cartesian analysis ('analytic geometry') occur for the first time in the solution to Pappus' problem.

The second book can be divided into four main sections. The first one has to do with a new classification of curves; it spells out the epistemological and ontological boundaries of the *Géométrie*. The second section contains a complete analysis of the curves required to solve Pappus' problem for four lines, and a special case for Pappus' problem for five lines. The third section presents the celebrated method of tangents (or better, of normals), and the fourth shows the utility of abstract geometrical considerations when applied to the "ovals," a class of curves extremely useful for solving problems in dioptrics.

The third book contains an algebraic analysis of roots of equations. Here we find, among other things, Descartes' rule of signs, the construction of all problems of third and fourth degree through the intersection of a circle and a parabola, and a reduction of all such problems to trisection of an angle or to finding two mean proportionals.

Of course, I cannot rehearse in detail the entire contents of the *Géométrie*, so I shall concentrate on certain parts and refer the reader to the literature mentioned in the bibliography. My discussion is divided into five sections. Section 3.1.1 presents Descartes' algebra of segments. Section 3.1.2. deals with Descartes' solution to Pappus' problem for four lines and shows how Cartesian "analytic geometry" is embedded in such a solution. Section 3.1.3 discusses Descartes' classification of curves and the foundational problems involved in the rejection of the mechanical curves from the domain of Cartesian geometry. Section 3.1.4 is about Descartes' method of tangents. And section 3.1.5 summarizes some of the main features of Descartes' program. Admittedly, I devote little attention to book III, which is in many ways less innovative with respect to the previous algebraic tradition.

3.1.1 Descartes' Algebra of Segments

The first book of the *Géométrie* opens with a bold claim: "Any problem in geometry can easily be reduced to such terms that a knowledge of the lengths of certain straight lines is sufficient for its construction."[1] It exemplifies how all the problems of *ordinary* geometry (i.e., those amenable to construction by ruler and compass) can be constructed. In particular, constructing any such problem will turn out to be equivalent to the construction of the root of a second-degree equation. In order to show how this can be achieved, Descartes proceeds to explain "how the arithmetical calculus is related to the operations of geometry."[2]

Arithmetical operations are addition, subtraction, multiplication, division, and extraction of root. Let a and b be line segments. Addition and subtraction of line segments are unproblematic. To explain multiplication, division, and extraction of root, Descartes makes use of proportion theory through the introduction of a line segment that functions as unity. Then ab, a/b are $\sqrt{a}$ are line segments which satisfy respectively the following proportions:

$$1 : a = b : ab,$$

$$a/b : 1 = a : b,$$

$$1 : \sqrt{a} = \sqrt{a} : a.$$

The construction of ab is as follows (see Fig. 16). Let $AB = 1$ be the unit segment, and assume we want to multiply the segment BD (denoted by a) by BC (denoted by b). This is done by joining A and C and drawing the line DE parallel to AC. Then $BE = BD \cdot BC = ab$. The claim is easily verified by exploiting the proportionality between the triangles ABC and DBE. Similar constructions are given for a/b and $\sqrt{a}$. Descartes also introduces the notation a^2, a^3, and so on, for powers of a.

The main point of the geometrical interpretation of the arithmetical operations is to overcome the problem of dimensionality, which limited to a great extent the previous geometrical work. Indeed, in ancient geometry as well as in Viète,[3] the multiplication of two lines is interpreted as an area, and the multiplication of three lines gives rise to a volume. But there is no corresponding interpretation for the product of more than three lines. We shall see how the new interpretation allows Descartes to solve in one fell swoop the extension of Pappus' problem to an arbitrary number of lines.

What follows now is nothing less than the general strategy for solving all geometrical problems. It can be roughly divided into three steps: naming, equating, and constructing.

Naming. One assumes the problem at hand to be already solved, and gives names to all the lines that seem to be needed to solve the problem.

Equating. Ignoring the difference between known and unknown lines, one analyzes the problem by finding the relationship that holds between the lines in the most natural way. One then arrives at an equation (or several equations)—an expression in which the same quantity is expressed in two different ways. (Descartes knows, of course, that for a problem to be determinate there must be as many equations as there are unknowns.)

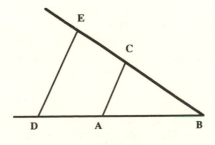

Figure 16

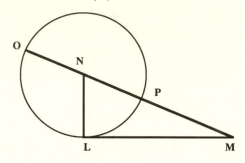

Figure 17

Constructing. The equation must then be constructed: its roots must be found (geometrically). If we now consider only those problems that can be constructed by ruler and compass, then the second step, Descartes claims, will lead to a second-degree equation, and all that is left to do is to construct the roots of such an equation. Let us consider, for example, the construction of the positive root in the equation $z^2 = az + b^2$ with a and b positive quantities. To construct z we consider the right triangle NLM with legs $LM = b$ and $LN = a/2$ (see Fig. 17). Now we produce MN to O so that $NO = LN$. Then OM is the root z we are looking for. Indeed, by Pythagoras' theorem, $MN^2 - NL^2 = LM^2$, and since $MN = OM - NL$, by substitution $(OM - NL)^2 - NL^2 = LM^2$, that is, $OM(OM - 2NL) = LM^2$. But $2NL = a$ and $LM^2 = b^2$. Thus, letting $z = OM$, we have $z(z - a) = b^2$, or $z^2 = az + b^2$.

Descartes concludes the section by mentioning that all the problems of *ordinary* geometry can be constructed this way, something he believes could not have been known to the ancient geometers because the length and order of their work shows how they proceeded at random rather than by method. Had they had a method, they would have been able to solve Pappus' problem, which neither Euclid nor Apollonius nor Pappus were able to solve in full generality. I now turn to Pappus' problem and to its solution in the *Géométrie*.

3.1.2 Pappus' Problem for Four Lines and Its Solution

Descartes' claim to a unique mathematical achievement rests on his solution to a problem stated by Pappus and left unsolved by ancients and moderns alike. The solution to this problem plays the role of a paradigm example of how to solve all geometrical problems.

Statement of Pappus' problem for four lines.[4] Suppose we are given four lines in position, say AB, AD, EF, GH (see Fig. 18). It is required to find a point C such that, given angles α, β, γ, δ, lines can be drawn from C to the lines AB, AD, EF, GH making angles α, β, γ, δ, respectively, such that $CB \cdot CF = CD \cdot CH$. Moreover, it is required to find the locus of all such points C, that is, "to know and to trace the curve containing all such points."[5]

The solution given by Descartes proceeds as follows. From the various lines, AB and BC are chosen as principal lines in terms of which all the other

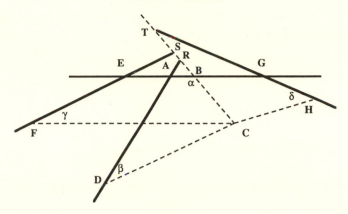

Figure 18

lines are expressed. In other words, CB, CF, CD, and CH will be expressed in terms of AB, BC, and other data of the problem. According to the general strategy presented in section 3.1.1 we begin by naming. Let the segments AB and BC be denoted respectively by x and y. Also let EA $= k$ and AG $= l$. The segments k and l are known, since the four lines are specified. For the same reason we know all the angles of the triangles ARB, DRC, ESB, FSC, BGT, TCH; or, which is the same, we know all the ratios of the sides of these triangles. We now set up the equations. Let

$$AB/BR = z/b, \tag{3.1}$$

$$CR/CD = z/c, \tag{3.2}$$

$$BE/BS = z/d, \tag{3.3}$$

$$CS/CF = z/e, \tag{3.4}$$

$$BG/BT = z/f, \tag{3.5}$$

$$TC/CH = z/g, \tag{3.6}$$

where z, b, c, d, e, f, g are all constants.

Since AB $= x$, (3.1) becomes $x/BR = z/b$ and thus BR $= bx/z$. Consequently,

$$CR = CB + BR = y + (bx/z). \tag{3.7}$$

By (3.2), we can write CD $= c \cdot CR/z$ and, by (3.7),

$$CD = (cy/z) + (cbx/z^2).$$

Since $EA = k$ we have $BE = EA + AB = k + x$. By (3.3) $(k + x)/BS = z/d$. Thus $BS = (dk + dx)/z$, and

$$CS = BS + CB = [(dk + dx)/z] + y = (dk + dx + yz)/z. \qquad (3.8)$$

By (3.4) $CF = CS \cdot e/z$ and by (3.8) we get

$$CF = (ezy + dek + dex)/z^2.$$

Since $AG = l$ and $BG = l - x$ by (3.5) we obtain $BT = (f(l - x))/z$. Thus

$$CT = BC + BT = y + ((fl - fx)/z) = (yz + fl - fx)/z. \qquad (3.9)$$

By (3.6) $CH = g \cdot CT/z$. Thus, by (3.9),

$$CH = (gzy + gfl - gfx)/z^2.$$

We have therefore expressed CB $(= y)$, CD, CF, and CH in terms of the principal lines and the other data of the problem. If we now set, according to the problem, $CB \cdot CF = CD \cdot CH$ we obtain an equation of degree 2 in x and of degree 2 in y. This completes the second step of the solution. The final step in the solution is constructing the problem. To this end we assign an arbitrary value to y, and thus we obtain an equation that is quadratic in x. The construction of the solution of a quadratic equation is not a problem as it has already been shown how to carry it out. The locus of points is then constructed by taking arbitrary values for y and constructing the corresponding values for x.

> If then we should take successively an infinite number of different values for the line y, we should obtain an infinite number of values for the line x, and therefore an infinity of different points, such as C, by means of which the required curve could be drawn.[6]

Pappus' problem can be generalized to an arbitrary number n of lines ($n \geq 3$). The case for three lines is simply the case for four lines with the third and fourth lines coinciding, namely, $CB \cdot CF = CD^2$. Let $n \geq 4$. Assume that $l_1, \ldots, l_n$ are lines given in position, and $\beta_1, \ldots, \beta_n$ fixed angles. Let s denote an arbitrary line segment. The problem of Pappus for n lines consists of finding the locus of points C such that if $d_1, \ldots, d_n$ are the segments drawn from C to $l_1, \ldots, l_n$ making angles $\beta_1, \ldots, \beta_n$ then

$$\begin{cases} d_1 \cdot \ldots \cdot d_k = d_{k+1} \cdot \ldots \cdot d_n & \text{if } n = 2k \\ d_1 \cdot \ldots \cdot d_k = d_{k+1} \cdot \ldots \cdot d_{2k-1} \cdot s & \text{if } n = 2k - 1. \end{cases}$$

The solution for four lines easily generalizes to n lines. Indeed, each distance d_i from $C(x, y)$ to the line l_i making an angle β_i is expressed by $\pm A_i x \pm B_i y \pm C_i$. Thus the equation of the general locus is

$$\prod_{i=1}^{k} (\pm A_i x \pm B_i y \pm C_i) = \prod_{i=k+1}^{2k} (\pm A_i x \pm B_i y \pm C_i) \qquad \text{if} \quad n = 2k$$

$$\prod_{i=1}^{k} (\pm A_i x \pm B_i y \pm C_i) = \left[\prod_{i=k+1}^{2k-1} (\pm A_i x \pm B_i y \pm C_i)\right] \cdot s \qquad \text{if} \quad n = 2k - 1$$

Thus for $2k - 1$ and $2k$ lines, we end up with an equation of degree k in x and degree k in y.

The generalization of the problem to an arbitrary number of lines was already in Pappus, but the ancients could not make much sense of it because they could not make geometrical sense of the product of four or more lines.[7] Descartes' new calculus, by interpreting products of line segments as yielding line segments, allows him to bypass the issue with finesse.

3.1.3   Descartes' Classification of Curves

In the opening part of book II, Descartes recalls approvingly[8] Pappus' distinction between plane, solid, and linear problems. Plane problems are those that can be constructed by means of straight lines and circles; solid problems those that can be constructed by making use of conics, and linear problems those that require more composite lines. This last category of problems is called linear "for lines other than those mentioned are used in the construction, which have a varied and more intricate genesis, such as the spirals, the quadratices, the conchoids and the cissoids, which have many marvellous properties."[9] But Descartes is "surprised, however, that they did not go further, and distinguish between different degrees of these more complex curves." And he wonders "why they called the latter mechanical, rather than geometrical."[10]

Descartes then endeavours to explain why the ancients distinguished between mechanical and geometrical curves, claiming they had misgivings about whether to accept the conic sections as fully geometrical. In any case, he suggests they grouped together spirals, quadratices, conchoids, and cissoids[11] because in their inquiries they encountered the spiral and the quadratix, curves that are truly mechanical, before the conchoid and the cissoid, curves that Descartes considers acceptable.

> Perhaps what stopped the ancient geometers from admitting curves more complex than the conic sections is that the first curves to which their attention was attracted happened to be the spiral, the quadratrix, and similar curves, which really belong only to mechanics, and are not among those that I think should be included here, since they must be conceived of as described by two separate movements whose relation does not admit of exact determination.

Yet they afterwards examined the conchoid, the cissoid, and a few others which should be accepted; but not knowing much about their properties they took no more account of these than of the others.[12]

This section of Descartes' text was analyzed very carefully by Molland, who concluded that his exposition was "a misconstrual of the ancient distinction between geometrical and instrumental." In connection with the passage quoted above, Molland considers Descartes' third attempted explanation to be that

The spiral and quadratix, which were not geometrical, were discovered first and only afterwards the acceptable conchoid and cissoid. But, as we have seen, there was no ancient compunction about admitting the spiral and little about the quadratrix, and there could well have been more doubt about the geneses of the conchoid and cissoid.[13]

However, the misconstrual was instrumental, concludes Molland, in that "his faulty exegeses allowed him [Descartes] to introduce more naturally his own basis for geometry." What Molland's analysis leaves unanswered is whether Descartes is completely responsible for the misconstrual or whether he is sharing a reading of the ancients that was commonplace in the contemporary mathematical literature. I shall have something to say about this when I comment upon several passages from Clavius. For now, two questions await us. Which curves did Descartes admit? And why did he reject others?

Geometrical and Mechanical Curves

Descartes' proposal is that by 'geometrical' should be understood what is precise and exact, and by 'mechanical' what is not so. The curves to be admitted in geometry are given by a kinematical criterion.

Nevertheless, it seems very clear to me that if we make the usual assumption that geometry is precise and exact, while mechanics is not; and if we think of geometry as the science which furnishes a general knowledge of the measurements of all bodies, then we have no more right to exclude the more complex curves than the simpler ones, provided they can be conceived of as described by a continuous motion or by several successive motions, each motion being completely determined by those which precede; for in this way an exact knowledge of the magnitude of each is always obtainable.[14]

The kind of regulated continuous motions that Descartes has in mind are illustrated by the generation of curves provided by the machine shown in Figure 19. It consists of several rulers linked together. YZ is fixed, and Y is a pivot so that YX can rotate. Perpendicular to YX we have a fixed ruler BC and sliding rulers DE, FG (the machine could be extended indefinitely). Perpendicular to YZ are the sliding rulers CD, EF, GH, and so on. In the initial position YX coincides with YZ. As YX rotates counterclockwise, the fixed ruler BC pushes the sliding ruler CD which, in turn, pushes the sliding ruler DE, and so on. All the curves described by the (moving) points B, D, F, H, and so on, are admissible and are called geometrical. This is by no means the only

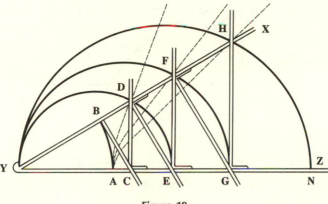

Figure 19

type of machine considered by Descartes; in fact, he adds that many similar types of machine could be considered. However, a unifying feature of all the curves generated by such instruments is that they have an algebraic equation.

> I could give here several other ways of tracing and conceiving a series of curved lines, which would be more and more complex by degrees to infinity, but I think the best way to group together all such curves and then classify them in order, is by recognizing the fact that all points of those curves which we may call 'geometric', that is, those which admit of precise and exact measurement, must bear a definite relation to all points of a straight line, and that this relation must be expressed by means of a single equation.[15]

This allows Descartes to classify curves by making use of the degree of their equation. Descartes classifies curves by gender, curves of gender 1 are the circle and the conics, curves of gender 2 have equations of degree 3 or 4, curves of gender 3 have equations of degree 5 or 6, and so forth; see Grosholz (1991a, ch. 2) for an analysis of the notion of gender. Descartes never says explicitly that all the algebraic equations define a geometrical curve although, as Bos (1981) has argued, he implicitly assumed this.

We have already encountered two different types of curve construction: by points, as in the solution to Pappus' problem, and by regulated motions. However, not all motions or all pointwise constructions are to be allowed in geometry. Let us begin with the unacceptable motions. I have already quoted a passage where Descartes claims that the quadratix and the spiral should be rejected because they are generated by two different motions "between which there is no relation (*raport*) that can be measured exactly." This is exactly the same criticism that was raised, according to Pappus, by Sporus (third century A.D.) against the use of the quadratix in the squaring of the circle.

The quadratix is a curve generated by the intersection of two segments, one moving with uniform rectilinear motion and the other with uniform circular motion. Let ABCD be a square, and BED the quadrant of a circle with center

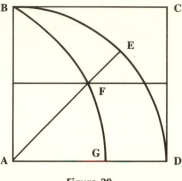

Figure 20

A (see Fig. 20). Let AB rotate uniformly clockwise towards AD, and let BC move with uniform rectlinear motion towards AD, keeping parallel to AD, in such a way that the two lines AB and BC start moving at the same time and end their motion coinciding with AD at the same time. The locus of points described by the intersection of the two moving segments is the quadratrix.

Sometimes employed to trisect an angle, the quadratrix was principally used in attempts to square the circle, but this was severely criticized even in ancient times. Pappus approves of Sporus' objections that, in order to adjust the speed of the motions as required and to determine the point G on the quadratrix, one already needs to know what is sought—the quadrature of the circle.[16] And Pappus concludes by consigning the construction to mechanics.

One possible way out of the situation could have been to attempt a construction of the quadratrix that required no independent motions and that could be considered more geometrical.[17] This attempt was made by Clavius in his *Commentaria in Euclidis Elementa*, in an appendix to book VI entitled "De mirabili natura lineae cuiusdam inflexae, per quam et in circulo figura quotlibet laterum aequalium inscribitur, & circulus quadratur, & plura alia scitu iucundissima perficiuntur" ([1589] 1591, 296).[18] I claim this text to be the source of the reflections on pointwise constructions contained in the *Géométrie*. In it Clavius proposes a pointwise construction of the quadratrix similar to those given for the conic sections, which is therefore, Clavius claims, geometric.

> And although the said authors endeavoured to describe such line [the quadratrix] by two imaginary motions of two straight lines, in which thing they beg the principle, so that on that account the line is rejected by Pappus as useless and not describable; however, we will describe it *geometrically* through the determination of however many of its points through which it must be drawn, just as it is commonly done in the description of the conic sections.[19]

The construction given by Clavius can be summarized as follows. Divide the arc DB and the sides AD and BC into 2^n equal parts for n as large as you please (the larger the n the more accurate the description). Figure 21 shows the situation for $n = 3$. Thus we have seven points on DB, AD, and BC. Connect by dashed lines the corresponding points on AD and BC, and the point A to

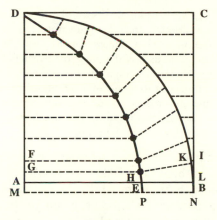

Figure 21

the eight points on the arc DB. The points of intersection are points on the quadratrix. By refining the partition on the arc and on the sides, Clavius claims to approximate the quadratrix more and more precisely. Moreover, he implicitly assumes that he will be able, with the single exception of the point E, to obtain in this fashion all the points on the quadratrix. He continues by noticing that E cannot be found in such a way (i.e., geometrically) since, when the two motions are completed, the two segments no longer intersect. In order to take care of this case, he resorts to a trick.[20]

Consider the segment AF on AD, and bisect it continually until we reach a very small part of it, say AG. Similarly, bisect the arc BI in the same number of parts, and let BK be the arc thus obtained. Now, construct BL, BN, AM equal to AG. Connect G and L, M and N, A and K by dashed lines. The segment AK intersects GL at H. If MP is taken to be equal to GH, and the quadratrix is extended unformly to P, then the curve must pass through E. Indeed, Clavius argues that one need only "squeeze" E between H and P to an arbitrary degree of accuracy.

Clavius also offers a different construction in which the approximation does not require the curve to be extended below the side AB, and in which all the lines in the construction meet at right angles (whereas in the previous construction the radii originating from A intersected the segments originating on AD at different angles).

Clavius does not realize there is an (uncountable) infinity of points (not just E) that can only be approximated, since his construction will produce a (countably) dense set of points, but not all the points on the quadratrix. However, Clavius believes to have given a geometric construction that uniformly yields all the points on the curve.

> This is therefore the description of the quadratrix, which in a certain sense can be called geometrical, just as the description of the conic sections, which are also made by points, as are handed down by Apollonius, are called geometrical, although in truth they are more liable to error than is our description. This is

a consequence of the determination of several proportional lines which are necessary for their description and which are not an issue in the description of the quadratrix. On this account, unless someone wanted to reject the whole doctrine of conic sections as useless and not geometrical (which I think nobody will do since the best Geometers employed the conic sections in their demonstrations)... he is compelled to admit that our description of the quadratrix is in a certain sense geometrical. Add that the conchoid, through which Nicomedes sharply searches two mean proportional lines, is also decribed by points, as we say in the book of mensurations.[21]

It is hard to overestimate the above passage for an understanding of what Descartes is up to in book II of the *Géométrie*: (1) Clavius claims his construction by points to be geometrical; (2) Clavius claims it to be more geometrical than the construction by points given for the conics, which is more liable to error than his construction; (3) Clavius proposes that constructions of conic sections are to be considered geometrical; and (4) Clavius stresses the similarity between his construction and that given for the conchoid.[22] Notice that Clavius, following Pappus, rejects the construction by double motion as mechanical, and that by arguing for the geometrical nature of constructions involving conic sections he unwittingly acknowledges that the point might be challenged. This is in line with Descartes' rejection of the quadratrix and his doubts as to whether the ancients accepted as geometrical the solutions obtained by means of conic sections.

A consequence of points (1) to (4) is that, in a certain sense, the quadrature of the circle can be effected geometrically. However, as I shall argue in the next section, Descartes could not accept this consequence. In the following passage, although not mentioning Clavius, Descartes claims there is a difference between the construction by points for the geometrical curves (such as the conics and the conchoid) and that used for the spiral and similar curves (e.g., the quadratrix). Only special points can be constructed on the latter curves.

> It is worthy of note that there is a great difference between this method in which the curve is traced by finding several points upon it, and that used for the spiral and similar curves. In the latter not any point of the required curve may be found at pleasure, but only such points as can be determined by a process simpler than that required for the composition of the curve. Therefore, strictly speaking, we do not find any one of its points, that is, not any one of those which are so peculiarly points of this curve that they cannot be found except by means of it. On the other hand, there is no point on these curves which supplies a solution for the proposed problem that cannot be determined by the method I have given. And since this way of tracing a curved line by determining several of its points at random, applies only to those curves which can also be described by a regular and continuous motion, we should not reject it entirely from geometry.[23]

Thus Descartes accepts (3) but rejects claims (1), (2), and (4) of Clavius' argument. Of course, the reader might still question whether Descartes had in mind Clavius' text when writing the previous passage. I shall show this to be the case in the next section.

Similar to Bos, I conclude by remarking how Descartes maintains the extensional equivalence of the following three classes of curves: (1) curves generated by regulated continuous motions; (2) curves generated by (uniform) pointwise construction; and (3) curves given by an algebraic equation. Although some of the implications are only implicit in the *Géométrie*.

Mechanical Curves and the Quadrature of the Circle

The extent of mechanical curves known to Descartes at the time of the publication of the *Géométrie* was very limited. Indeed, in the *Géométrie* he explicitly mentions only the quadratrix and the spiral as examples of mechanical curves. We have seen that Descartes rejects them because "they are considered as described by two separate movements, between which there is no relation (*raport*) that can be measured exactly." Moreover, he mentions that only special points can be constructed on the mechanical curves. Bos remarks: "There is no evidence that Descartes before 1637 actively studied transcendental curves other than the quadratrix and the spiral."[24] However, this is not correct. Descartes studied at least one other transcendental curve before 1637, the cylindrical helix, and explicitly rejected it as mechanical.

In addition to these two criteria for rejecting mechanical curves from geometry, Descartes invokes another criterion when discussing construction by strings:

> For although one cannot admit [in geometry] lines which are like strings, that is, which are sometimes straight and sometimes curved, because the proportion between straight lines and curved lines is not known and I also believe it cannot be known by men, so one cannot conclude anything exact and certain from it.[25]

The idea that there is no proportion between curved and straight lines, or motions, goes back at least to Aristotle's *Physics*. In Bos' opinion, the Aristotelian dogma is the very foundation of Descartes' distinction between geometrical and mechanical curves:

> Thus the separation between the geometrical and non-geometrical curves, which was fundamental in Descartes's vision of geometry, rested ultimately on his conviction that proportions between curved and straight lengths cannot be found exactly. This, in fact, was an old doctrine, going back to Aristotle. The central role of the incomparability of straight and curved in Descartes's geometry explains why the first rectifications of algebraic (i.e. for Descartes geometrical) curves in the late 1650s were so revolutionary: they undermined a cornerstone of the edifice of Descartes's geometry.[26]

I do not deny that Descartes (and many of his contemporaries) believed in the Aristotelian dogma,[27] but I am puzzled by the fact that, although the algebraic rectification of algebraic curves was essential in destroying the Aristotelian dogma, it did not really undermine the foundations of Descartes' *Géométrie* nor, to my knowledge, did anybody at that time claim this to be the case. This suggests that the real motivation and foundation for Descartes' exclusion of the spiral, quadratrix, "and the like," may be based on something else. I suggest this something else to be Descartes' parti pris—that the quadrature of the circle is impossible geometrically. The following passage, taken from a letter to Mersenne dated 13 November 1629, points to the likelihood of my hypothesis:

> Mr. Gaudey's invention is very good and very exact in practice. However, so that you will not think that I was mistaken when I claimed that it could not be geometric, I will tell you that it is not the cylinder which is the cause of the effect, as you had me understand and which plays the same role as the circle and the straight line. The effect depends on the helix which you had not mentioned to me, which is a line that is not accepted in geometry any more than that which is called quadratrix, since the former can be used to square the circle and to divide the angle in all sorts of equal parts as precisely as the latter can, and has many other uses as you will be able to see in Clavius' commentary to Euclid's *Elements*. For although one could find an infinity of points through which the helix or the quadratrix must pass by, however, one cannot find geometrically any one of those points which are necessary for the desired effects of the former as well as of the latter. Moreover, they cannot be traced completely except by the intersection of two movements which do not depend on each other, or better the helix by means of a thread [*filet*] for revolving a thread obliquely around the cylinder it describes exactly this line; but one can square the circle with the same thread, so precisely that this will not give us anything new in geometry.[28]

In this long and dense passage, which leaves no doubt as to Descartes' knowledge of Clavius' work on the quadratrix, Descartes considers explicitly the cylindrical helix, which he does not mention in the *Géométrie*. Moreover, he gives several reasons for excluding curves like the quadratrix and the helix. We are already familiar with some of them. Both curves are such that only special points can be constructed on them. The quadratrix is excluded on account of its being generated by two independent motions and the helix is excluded because it is generated by a *filet* 'thread'. Descartes *ultimately* excludes them because both curves allow us to square the circle, "pource qu'elle sert a quarrer le cercle"; he also mentions once the division of an angle into arbitrary parts. He adds that these curves do not give us anything new in geometry. In a sense they beg the question. This is simply Pappus' criticism.

If we now consider, in addition to the points already made, that the curves which had been used in antiquity (and which passed down to the seventeenth century) in attempts to square the circle were the spiral, the quadratrix, and the cylindrical helix, as Iamblichus reports (quoted in Heath 1921, vol. I, p. 225), I think one can confidently claim that one of the unifying criteria at work in Descartes' mind when he excludes the mechanical curves, is that they can be used to square the circle.

The point about the impossibility of squaring the circle is reiterated in Descartes' letter to Mersenne dated 31 March 1638: "For, in the first place, it is against the geometers' style to put forward problems that they cannot solve themselves. Moreover, some problems are impossible, like the quadrature of the circle, etc."[29] How could Descartes have been so confident? It is not until 1882 that Lindemann was able to prove there is no algebraic quadrature of the circle. Moreover, the discussion on whether the quadrature of the circle was possible was still very lively in Descartes' period. For example, Mersenne devotes Question XVI of his *Questions Théologiques* (1634) to the topic, "La quadrature du cercle est-elle impossible?" He remarks how deeply split is the mathematical world over this very question: "This problem is extremely difficult, for one can find excellent geometers who claim that it is not possible to find a square whose surface is equal to that of the circle, and others who claim the opposite."[30]

Mathematicians have often been divided over the status of various mathematical proposition (just think of the problem of the independence of the axiom of choice, or the continuum hypothesis from Zermelo-Fraenkel set theory). But what is surprising is to find Descartes basing his whole "foundational" enterprise on the assumption that the circle cannot be squared. How did he arrive at such a conclusion?

We have evidence that Descartes worked on the problem of squaring the circle. A fragment in the tenth volume of the Adam-Tannery edition (number 6, dated 1628 or earlier) purports to give the best way to effect the quadrature of the circle. Interestingly, it is obtained by constructing an infinite sequence of points that converges towards a certain point. We have an *approximation argument* akin to the determination of the point E in Clavius' argument for the pointwise construction of the quadratrix.[31] Since the fragment claims to have provided the best possible quadrature of the circle, it is quite likely Descartes convinced himself that no quadrature of the circle was possible unless it involved infinite approximations of the type we have considered.

How does the criterion that there is no exact relation between curved and straight lines relate to the impossibility of the quadrature of the circle being effected geometrically? The quadrature of the circle is equivalent (by Archimedes' proof) to the rectification of the circumference. Thus what suffices for exclusion of the mechanical curves mentioned by Descartes before 1637 and in the *Géométrie*, is the lack of an exact proportion between the circumference and the radius—the circumference cannot be algebraically rectified. A correct guess, but an unproven one at that. However, this is why the algebraic rectification of curves leaves unthreatened the Cartesian distinction stated in the *Géométrie* between geometrical and mechanical curves. Only an algebraic rectification of the circumference would have destroyed the rationale for Descartes' position.[32]

3.1.4 Descartes' Tangent Method

The class of curves that Descartes called geometrical turned out to be an extremely natural and fruitful one to isolate. Moreover, the fact that each curve can be described by an algebraic equation allows Descartes to solve in all its generality the problem of drawing a tangent to an arbitrary point on each one, which is the same as drawing a normal to each point. Let us follow Descartes' example. Suppose we are given an ellipse having the equation

$$x^2 = ry - (ry^2/q) \tag{3.10}$$

where r is the latus rectum and q the major axis.

We wish to draw a normal at an arbitrary point C on the curve (see Fig. 22). According to the general strategy for solving problems described in section 3.1.1, we begin by considering the problem solved and by naming the lines in question. Let AM $= y$, CM $= x$; the normal PC $= s$, PA $= v$ and PM $= v - y$. We now look for the relevant equations. Since CMP is a right triangle we have

$$s^2 = x^2 + v^2 - 2vy + y^2. \tag{3.11}$$

We impose the condition that the point C must lie on the curve. From (3.10) and (3.11), we obtain

$$ry - (ry^2/q) = s^2 - v^2 + 2vy - y^2,$$

and by simple algebraic manipulations

$$y^2 = [q(2v - r)/(q - r)]y + [q(s^2 - v^2)]/(q - r). \tag{3.12}$$

From (3.12) we proceed to determine r or s. We must exploit the other piece of information at our disposal, that CP must be normal. If CP is not normal then the circle with radius PC will cut the curve in C as well as in another point E different from C. The condition of normality is thus equivalent to the condition that the two points C and E must coincide in one point or, algebraically, there is a double root of equation (3.12). If (31.2) has a double root, say e, then it is of the form $(y - e)^2 = 0$, that is,

$$y^2 = 2ye - e^2. \tag{3.13}$$

By equating coefficients in (3.12) and (3.13) we obtain $(2qv - qr)/(q - r) = 2e$, and solving for v we obtain $v = [2e(q - r) + qr]/2q$, and since $e = y$, $v = [y(q - r)/q] + (r/2)$. The third step of the solution is constructing v. However,

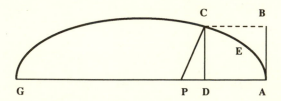

Figure 22

the construction is routine and Descartes leaves it out. Notice the extreme generality of the method—it applies to any algebraic curve; the essential role played by the equation of the curve; and the absence of infinitesimal considerations in the solution to the problem.[33]

3.1.5 Some General Features of the *Géométrie*

Descartes' Program

The first book of the *Géométrie* has shown through the paradigmatic solution of Pappus' problem for four lines the main strategy for solving problems. What problems can be solved? Those that admit a geometrical solution, a solution that makes use only of geometrical curves. The class of geometrical curves is described (by no means univocally) in book II, which delimits the ontological domain of the *Géométrie*. But the problems treated in book I were plane problems, ones which could be solved by the intersection of straight lines and circumferences. It is in book III that Descartes shows how the approach is to be generalized, not only to solid problems but also to arbitrary problems. An acceptable solution is obtained only when we employ the simplest curve that can be used to solve the problem. Descartes is explicit about this:

> While it is true that every curve which can be described by a continuous motion should be accepted in geometry, this does not mean that we should use at random the first one that we meet in the construction of a given problem. We should always choose with care the simplest curve that can be used in the solution of a problem.[34]

The criterion of simplicity is purely algebraic. The complexity of the curve is measured by the degree of the equation by which they can be expressed. Thus in book III Descartes shows how solid and supersolid problems (i.e., of degree 3 or 4) can be solved through the intersections of a circle and a parabola (a curve of degree 2), and in general how problems of degree $2n - 1$ and $2n$ can be solved through the intersection of a circle and a curve of degree n. The grand vision of Descartes consists of a classification of all geometrical problems by means of the simplest curves that can be used to solve them.[35] This, in turn, allows Descartes to claim his method is better than any other that has been proposed, and that his work marks, if I am allowed the expression, the "end of geometry." Writing to Mersenne in December 1637, he says:

> Moreover, having determined as I have done in every type of question all that can be done, and shown the means to do it, I claim that one should not only believe that I have done something more than those who have preceded me but also one should be convinced that our descendants will never find anything in this subject that I could not have found as well as they, if I only bothered to look for it.[36]

Algebra and Geometry

The relationship between analytic objects (equations) and geometrical objects (curves) is crucial for evaluating the *Géométrie* and has given rise to two different interpretative positions in the literature. Bos, Boyer, Grosholz, Lachterman, and Lenoir have claimed that algebra is simply a tool in the economy of the *Géométrie*. For example, Bos has argued at length that the equation of a curve is not allowable for Descartes as a genuine representation of a curve.

> The conclusion from these facts must be that for Descartes the equation of a curve was primarily a tool and not a means of definition or representation. It was part of a whole collection of algebraic tools which in the *Géométrie* he showed to be useful for the study of geometrical problems. The most important use of the equation was in classifying curves into classes and in determining normals to curves. Here the equation must actually be written out. In many other cases Descartes could get through his calculations about problems without writing the equation of the curve explicitly.[37]

Moreover, once the equation is found we must always construct the roots geometrically, that is, the equation is never the last step of the solution.

Bos' position has been challenged by Giusti, who claims that for Descartes "the curve is the equation" and speaks in this connection about a "revolutionary position." Giusti emphasizes the algebraic component of the *Géométrie* which allows Descartes to give general and uniform solutions to a variety of problems central to his program. Giusti grants the presence in the *Géométrie* of more "constructive" strands, but claims that the identification of the curve with its algebraic equation is at the core of the Cartesian program. He then claims that the constructive elements (e.g., the appeal to machines for generating curves, or the geometric construction of roots) play a role more rhetorical than scientific in the economy of the *Géométrie*.

> By contrast, our thesis is that from the mathematical point of view these [constructive] representations have a secondary role with respect to the algebraic equation. Thus one needs to justify their presence in Descartes's work, and their role in the economy of the *Géométrie*. In our opinion, their role is more rhetorical than scientific.[38]

The *Géométrie* is a striking work in which old geometrical paradigms and new algebraic strands intermingle at the same time. Determining the exact balance between the two will prove to be one of the long-standing interpretative issues on Descartes' contribution to mathematics. I shall return to the issue of the foundational significance of the algebraization of geometry in section 3.3.

Finitism

Generations of scholars[39] have remarked on Descartes' finitism, and we have seen some explicit examples. His rejection of the mechanical curves is grounded in the idea that their construction involves us in infinite processes of approximation which cannot be exact (geometrical). His method of tangents also exemplifies his careful avoidance of infinitesimal arguments. However, one should not make the mistake of believing that Descartes simply does not have the techniques to engage in "infinitistic" mathematics. His letters show how well versed he was in infinitesimalist techniques, as his solutions to problems involving the cycloid and Debeaune's problem abundantly show.[40] What is difficult to evaluate is how the limitation to finitary mathematics in the *Géométrie* fits into the Cartesian project. Some interpretations seem to imply that infinitistic mathematics will never be granted *droit de cité* because they involve procedures "que sa [Descartes'] méthode récuse."[41] Recently, Costabel suggested that the elaboration of an incontestable finitary mathematics is only a first step towards the more complex goal of developing "infinitary" mathematics. Descartes' restriction to finitary mathematics in the *Géométrie* is only a sign that he did not want to engage prematurely in infinitary mathematics.[42]

In Descartes' refusal to admit infinitary mathematics in the *Géométrie*, Belaval sees the clearest sign of how "l'esprit de la méthode cartésienne ... s'oppose à celui de la méthode leibnizienne."[43] I shall come back to the problem of Cartesian finitism in chapter 5.

Direct Proofs and Proofs by Contradiction

The *Géométrie* is a work of its time. For example, the "constructive" representations of curves contained in it are in direct line of succession of a long tradition of treatises on the construction of curves by the use of strings and other mechanical means (Ulivi 1990). I have emphasized how the discussion of pointwise constructions is motivated by Clavius' pointwise construction of the quadratrix. I wish to remark here on another feature of the *Géométrie* that joins it, and the analytic method in general, to Cavalieri's *Geometria* and Guldin's *Centrobaryca*, major works of the 1630s. In the previous chapter I have shown that both Cavalieri and Guldin aimed at a development of geometry by means of direct proofs, and that they explicitly avoided proofs by contradiction whenever possible. Cavalieri welcomed direct proofs as the outcome of his use of indivisibles, and Guldin provided an ostensive development of geometry by means of his fundamental theorem about centers of gravity.

We have seen that the emphasis on direct proofs was not just for purely mathematical reasons, but was connected with, and ultimately relied upon, more global epistemological positions that can be traced back to Aristotle's distinction between demonstrations of the "fact" and of the "reasoned fact". Recall that the two types of demonstration were often identified with the resolutive and compositive method of the mathematicians (i.e., analysis and synthesis). Of the two types of proof, synthesis was considered to be superior because it proceeds from causes to effects (a priori), whereas analysis starts from the effects to reach the causes (a posteriori).

My claim is that Descartes is heavily influenced by these developments. Lachterman (1989, 158–159) has observed that Descartes reverses the traditional distinction connecting analytic proofs with a posteriori proofs (from effects to causes) and synthetic proofs with a priori proofs (from causes to effects). Descartes claims that analytic methods, by showing how a result is obtained, also show why the result holds, and therefore analysis deserves to be considered as the paradigmatic form of a priori proof.[44] Moreover, Descartes claims the superiority of the analytic method comes from the fact that the proofs obtained by applying it are causal, ostensive, and therefore superior to proofs by contradiction. The most explicit statements by Descartes in this connection are to be found in the letters exchanged between Descartes and Mersenne on the subject of Fermat's method of tangents. Descartes defended his own method against Fermat's claims to superiority, claims backed by Roberval. One of the arguments used by Descartes draws a sharp contrast between proofs by contradiction and a priori proofs:

> For, in the first place, his method is such that without intelligence and by chance, one can easily fall upon the path that one has to follow in order to find it, which is nothing else than a false position, based on the way of demonstrating which reduces to absurdity, and which is the least esteemed and the least ingenious of all those of which use is made in mathematics. By contrast, mine originates from a knowledge of the nature of equations which, to my knowledge, has never been explained as thoroughly as in the third book of my Geometry. So that it could not have been invented by a person who ignored the depths of algebra. Moreover, my method follows the noblest way of demonstrating that can exist, i.e. the one that is called a priori.[45]

And again, against Roberval (July 1638), on the issue of proofs by contradiction:

> And I do not find anything reasonable in what he says, as when he claims the way of concluding ad absurdum to be more subtle than the other. It is absurd and this way has been used by Apollonius and Archimedes only when they could not find a better way.[46]

The appeal to a priori proofs against proofs by contradiction places Descartes' project for an ostensive development of mathematics in the same category as those of Cavalieri and Guldin. Of course, the methods on which Cavalieri, Descartes, and Guldin relied to carry through the project were quite different. However, they agreed on the "metamathematical" preference for direct proofs over proofs by contradiction. Moreover, their position is deeply embedded in the epistemological issues that characterized the Renaissance and early seventeenth-century debates on the nature of proofs.

3.2   The Algebraization of Mathematics

In the previous sections I have analyzed Descartes' *Géométrie* and its foundations. I introduced the topic by claiming that the algebraization of geometry developed in Descartes' work, together with the entrance of the infinite, represents the most important event in seventeenth-century mathematics. Mahoney defines the passage from a geometrical mode of thought to an algebraic one as "the most important and basic achievement of mathematics at the time."[47] In "The beginning of algebraic thought in the seventeenth century" he characterizes the algebraic mode of thought as presenting three main characteristics: (1) the presence of an operatory symbolism; (2) an emphasis on the relations rather than the objects; and (3) a freedom from ontological commitment. It almost goes without saying that these aspects are found in a variety of degrees in seventeenth-century mathematicians; indeed, not all mathematicians of the period are instances of the "algebraization" of mathematics. We have already encountered some notable exceptions, such as Cavalieri and Guldin. However, the existence of an "algebraization of mathematics" in the seventeenth century is a fact, consequently, I will remark on the foundational problems it poses.

The algebraic mode of thought raised at least three sorts of foundational problems. First, what kind of thought is associated with the algebraical symbolism—what is the nature of symbolic thought as opposed to, say, the classical geometrical thought, and is it indeed thought at all? Second, by concentrating on the structures, as opposed to the objects, algebraic thought identifies what perhaps ought to be kept apart. This turns out to be particularly evident in the case of the sytematic "confusion" between the classical theory of ratios and the arithmetic of fractions, typical of the algebraic practice of the period. Third, the freedom from ontological commitment raised the issue of the status of objects that are introduced without an explicit geometrical justification, such as the imaginary numbers.

These problems were very much present in the mind of seventeenth-century mathematicians and philosophers. The endless discussions as to the status of algebra—Is it an art or a science?—and as to the relationship between algebra, arithmetic, and geometry, bears witness to the effort with which the problems of the foundations of algebra were addressed in the seventeenth century.[48] It is however, important to remark on the character of these seventeenth-century debates with regard to the role of algebra and its relationship to geometry and arithmetic. With very few exceptions, the problems posed by the algebraic mathematical practice were different from the problems posed, say, by the geometry of indivisibles.

First, the practice was through and through consistent. Computations with negative and imaginary numbers showed themselves to be as trustworthy as those with natural numbers. Consequently, the foundational discussions never really called for a revision of the algebraic methematical practice, except perhaps in the most radical sense—its abandonment altogether. In this sense these discussions are, as it were, more global than those we have encountered in the domain of geometry and those we will encounter in the domain of analysis. Finally, it is not accidental that the topics treated in the following two sections correspond to foundational discussions that took place after the 1660s especially in England and France and involving Leibniz. On the one hand, we ought to take into consideration that it took rather a long time for the algebraic mode of thought to spread. Indeed, mathematicians like Cavalieri and Torricelli never really mastered this thought in a profound way. In fact, after the death of these two heroes, the Italian school lost ground with the major trends of European mathematics. This also helps to explain the absence in Italy of important foundational discussions similar to those in England and France.

In section 3.2.1 I shall draw attention to the controversy between Hobbes, Wallis, and Barrow as to the status of geometry, algebra, and arithmetic. In section 3.2.2. I shall then analyze how the algebraic mathematical practice found itself in conflict with the classical understanding of the notion of ratio, and how the extension of such a notion to negative numbers was particularly problematical. The following two sections are not intended to give a detailed appraisal of the situation, but rather to indicate the main problems and refer the reader to the already existing literature on the subject. I also take the opportunity to emphasize some aspects of the issue that have hitherto received no attention.

3.2.1   The Controversy between Hobbes, Wallis, and Barrow

Foundational issues were discussed with particular vehemence in the exchanges between Hobbes, Wallis, and Barrow.[49] John Wallis[50] was the Savilian Professor of geometry at Oxford University. From the very start of his mathematical career, marked by the publication of his treatise on conic sections in 1655 and by the *Arithmetica Infinitorum* (1655b), he espoused the analytic and algebraic procedures delivered by Viète, Descartes, Oughtred, and Harriot. His new method for studying conics considered them as plane curves, unlike the ancients, who saw them as generated by cutting the cone. Wallis also made bold use of infinitistic arithmetical processes in the study of indivisibilist geometry. His preference for the algebraic mode of thought led him to a revision of the traditional classification of the disciplines belonging to pure mathematics. Biancani divided pure mathematics into arithmetic and geometry. Arithmetic dealt with discrete quantities, geometry with continuous quantities. In Euclid's *Elements* geometry is foundationally prior in that the arithmetical theorems are proved by appealing to geometrical consideration. In the late sixteenth and early seventeenth centuries we start seeing signs of the need for a reclassification of the disciplines of pure mathematics. In the late sixteenth century we witness the attempt to define a new mathematical discipline, a *mathesis universalis*, prior to geometry and arithmetic, such as in van Roomen, Dasypodius and Alsted,[51] and already Guldin classifies algebra as a science, alongside geometry and arithmetic. In the meanwhile, arithmetic develops more and more into a generalized arithmetic by relying on algebraic techniques and extending the field of numbers to include rationals and irrationals as well as the discrete series of natural numbers.[52] The process is accompanied by a deep mutation in the concept of number, now seen as a symbolic entity as opposed to "pure" units whose mode of being may be subject to dispute."[53]

John Wallis plays a central role in all these developments. In his *Mathesis Universalis* he reversed the received classification of the mathematical science to give priority to algebra and arithmetic over geometry. He claimed, following an ancient tradition, that "the objects of arithmetic are of a higher and more abstract nature that those of geometry" and thus that arithmetic is prior to geometry. For instance, in classifying equations one should give priority to the notion of arithmetical degree as opposed to geometrical dimension. Wallis' extensive use of algebra and his new classification of the territory of pure mathematics were strongly rejected by Barrow and Hobbes. For Barrow,[54] who in his work also proceeds according to the classical geometrical style, geometry is fundamental and arithmetic is founded on geometrical thought. This is a consequence of his definition of quantity as the object of mathematics. Numbers are acceptable only when they are grounded in geometrical reality.

> Whence by the by we may know how to judge concerning the Opinion of that great Man we have sometimes mentioned [Wallis], who to shew that Arithmetic is much more extensive than Geometry, entirely transfers the whole of *Algebra* from Geometry to Arithmetic, determining Algebraical Equations to ascend higher than Geometrical ones, and denying that Geometry affords as many *Dimensions* as Arithmetic exhibit *Degrees*; with more to the same Purpose. All which Things notwithstanding may be very easily discussed, by saying that by these Algebraical Equations or Dimensions, or Arithmetical Degrees, either nothing at all is understood and really signified, but all are imaginary Chimeras and mere Monsters; or else they have something answering to them in Geometry, which they do signify and represent. As in Reality there is no Number, no Algebraical Power, no Arithmetical Degree, to which innumerable Magnitudes may not answer in every Kind; such Magnitudes being appositely represented and expressed by these Numbers.[55]

Hobbes, whose lifelong polemic with Wallis is well known[56] and who dubbed his treatise on conic sections as a scab of symbols, also rejected this algebraization of mathematics, even in the most basic aspects. In *De Principiis* Hobbes attacked the symbolical geometry of his time by claiming that it had infected the geometers of the age, and was a pest of the true geometry.[57]

Two different styles of mathematical practice face each other in these foundational skirmishes. The algebraical mode of thought raised for many the issue of how it was possible to reason about symbols, especially when they seemed to lack a geometrical referent, as in the case of imaginary numbers. For Hobbes the symbolic writing only introduces extra labour of the mind:

> I shall also add, that symbols, though they shorten the writing, yet they do not make the reader understand it sooner than if it were written in words. For the conception of the lines and figures (without which a man learneth nothing) must proceed from words either spoken or thought upon. So that there is a double labour of the mind, one to reduce your symbols to words, which are also symbols, another to attend to the ideas which they signify.[58]

The algebraic mode of thought also identifies what ought to be distinguished. This was particularly clear in the case of the theory of ratios. Wallis had shown in the *Mathesis Universalis* that the theory of ratios could be treated purely arithmetically. However, an arithmetical treatment easily allows one to think of ratios as fractions—as entities that could be added, multiplied, and so on. Barrow found this confusion unacceptable and therefore devoted an entire chapter of his *Lectiones* (lecture XX) to argue that ratios are not quantities:

> For neither in my Opinion are *Reasons* [ratios] Quantities, nor capable of Quantity (as hereafter I shall endeavour to evince in its proper Place) but are *mere Relations* founded in Quantity; and Numbers I account only as the Names and Symbols of Quantities, which we have already shewn more than once.[59]

The systematic misreading of ratios as fractions was also at the source of a number of amusing paradoxes involving the use of negative numbers and discussed, among others, by Arnauld and Leibniz.

3.2.2   Arnauld, Prestet, Gottignies, and Leibniz on Negative Numbers

Perhaps one of the most interesting discussions on the foundation of algebra concerns the nature of negative numbers. Also called fictitious, false, imaginary, chimerical, or quantities less than nothing, their status remained unclarified in the seventeenth century.[60] Arnauld in the *Nouveaux Elémens de Géométrie* had expressed doubts about the intelligibility of the rule that minus times minus is plus: "it would seem rather strange that minus times minus is plus; indeed one should not think that this could happen but by chance: for, by itself minus times minus can only yield minus."[61] The passages in Arnauld's work spurred a discussion between Prestet and Arnauld on the nature of negative numbers. The contents of this discussion were published in epistolary form in the second volume of the second edition of Prestet's *Elémens des Mathématiques* ([1675] 1689, 366–371).[62] Arnauld raised two issues about negative numbers. First, how it is possible to subtract a greater quantity from a smaller one. Second, the rules that $-$ times $-$ is $+$ seems to lead to paradoxical statements. The paradox arises because the rule seems to be in conflict with the intuitive understanding of ratio.

> It is for this reason that I cannot understand that the square of -5 can be the same thing as the square of $+5$, and that both of them are $+25$. Moreover, I do not know how to fit this with the fundamental property of multiplication, that is that the unity is to one of the magnitudes that are multiplied as the other is to the product. Which thing is true of the integers and of the fractions as well. For 1 is to 3 as 4 is to 12. ... But I cannot fit this to the multiplications of two minuses. For shall one say that $+1$ is to -4 as -5 is to $+20$? I do not see this. For $+1$ is greater than -4. On the contrary -5 is less than $+20$. Whereas in all the other proportions if the first term is greater than the second then the third must be greater than the fourth.[63]

Arnauld took a rather strict stand on these issues. Negative numbers are fictions unless they are used in the context of a subtraction of a smaller quantity from a greater one.[64] Consequently, he concluded that, when used without reference to positive quantities, "minus times minus is plus," is a fiction.[65] Prestet replied that quantities exist only as positive quantities and that therefore one should not, properly speaking, talk about defective, negative, or false quantities. He then explained the use of negative quantities to indicate the quantity that must be added to a smaller one to make a greater quantity. Whereas it would be a contradiction to think that 7 toises can be subtracted from 5 toises, there is no contradiction in thinking that it is by two toises that 7 toises cannot be subtracted from 5 toises. Finally, concerning the paradox that 1 is to -4 as -5 is to $+20$, Prestet claimed that one should simply not consider the signs when dealing with geometrical ratios. Two points deserve emphasis. First, Prestet's theory of negative numbers, as remarked by Schrecker, represents a step in the right direction. However, it was only in the nineteenth century that a satisfactory theory of negative numbers was offered, in particular, by Hankel. Second, and for my purposes more interesting. Arnauld's claim—the ratios in which negative numbers appear are fictional—bears a strong resemblance to the solution that Leibniz will propose in 1712 and to which I will return below.

Arnauld was not the only person who raised doubts about negative numbers. The work of Gilles François de Gottignies (1630–1689) is related to Prestet's *Elémens* and to Leibniz's attitude towards discussions on the foundations of algebra, which up to now seems to have escaped attention. Leibniz mentions Gottignies in a letter to Varignon in 1702:

> I ... think that in order solidly to establish the foundations of sciences it is very important that there be such critics; it is in this way that the Skeptics fought the principles of geometry with much reason; that Father Gottignes, a learned Jesuit, wanted to provide better foundations for Algebra, and that Clüver and Nieuwentijt have recently fought, although in different ways, our infinitesimal Analysis. ... We must not regret the effort which is needed to justify our Analysis against all kinds of persons capable of understanding it.[66]

Gottignies, professor of mathematics at the *Collegium Romanum* from 1662 to 1689, had been a student of André Tacquet. In the *Arithmétique théorique et practique* (1656) Tacquet attempted to provide better foundations for arithmetic by means of algebra.[67] Gottignies' work is rooted in Tacquet's, in particular, it belongs to the tradition of thought that postulates a universal science of mathematics, a *mathesis universalis*, prior to arithmetic and geometry.[68] Gottignies named this science *logistica universalis* and refused to identify it with algebra in that he rejected the use of quantities less than nothing. In the third book of his *Logistica Universalis* (1687) he attacked Prestet's conception of negative quantities, illustrated by the following definitions:

> XVII. Null or zero serves as a middle for comparing magnitudes and for judging their ratios.
> XVIII. Magnitudes have more reality the more their being takes them away from zero, and they have less reality the more their non-being takes them away from this same zero.
> XIX. It is usual to call *positive* or *true* any magnitude that adds to zero, and *negative* or *false* any quantity that subtracts from zero.[69]

Gottignies' attack was quite radical. The first twenty-one pages of his third book are a detailed criticism of the first twenty-two definitions of Prestet's book. Gottignies allows the use of these "false" quantities in practical algebra but not in his *Logistica Universalis*. However, one can speak of negative numbers in his *Logistica*. Commenting on Prestet's definition XIX, he says:

> To the words "it is usual" it is to be added "among all and only the doctors of Algebra": this usage is not common, neither to ancient mathesis nor to our logistics. In the latter some quantities are indeed called positive and others in truth negative: but no quantities less than zero are considered or admitted, or something subtracting from zero; on the contrary the quantities of our logistica, the positive as well as the negative, are each greater than zero and known to the ancient Mathesis. Did ancient Mathesis by chance ignore what is not ignored by any grammarian? that is, what ten degrees of merit and ten degrees of demerit mean. And the numbers which count ten degrees of merit are not equally true, and properly so called, and greater than zero as those that count ten degrees of demerit?[70]

Their disagreement rests mainly on how to interpret the nature of negative numbers. On pp. 22–40 of the same book Gottignies provides a list of seven paradoxes that follow from the notions commonly admitted in algebra. They are not very different from those noticed by Arnauld in the *Nouveau Elémens de Géometrie*. The third paradox reads as follows: "Given two numbers of the same species it is possible that one be greater than the other and not greater than the other."[71] For example $7:5 = -7:-5$, so that the greater is to the smaller as the smaller is to the greater. In 1712 Leibniz, recalling that Arnauld had found it surprising how 1 is to -1 as -1 is to 1, solves the puzzle by claiming that when the antecedent of a ratio is a "quantity less than zero" there is no real ratio but only an imaginary one. "Indeed, -1 being smaller than zero, the ratio of 1 to -1 will be that of the greater to the smaller; on the contrary, the ratio of -1 to 1 will be that of the smaller to the greater. How then will we have the same ratio in both cases? But both are imaginary ratios."[72]

Leibniz also added a "mathematical" proof for his claim based on the reasoning that a ratio to which no logarithm corresponds cannot be a real ratio but only an imaginary one. Finally, he compared this situation to that of the infinitesimal calculus and declared that expressions like '-1 is less than zero' can be allowed, provided one knows what they mean. Using an expression coined by Jungius, he said they are "toleranter verae." Leibniz was very critical of Gottignies' project. Already in his *Responsio ad nonnullas difficultates* (1695) he had reproached Gottignies and some of his disciples on this issue:

> I recognize that I myself attach great importance to those who endeavour to bring carefully all the demonstrations back to their first principles and to have constantly devoted to this all my efforts. But for all that I do not say to hinder the art of invention on account of too many scruples, nor to reject under this pretext the best discoveries, by depriving ourselves of their advantages; and of this I have in the past tried to convince Father Gottignies and his disciples who were punctilious on the principles of Algebra.[73]

It should now be clear that the possibilities offered by an algebraic approach favored a mathematical practice in which the extension of the fractional calculus to negative numbers seemed to conflate with the intuitive under-standing of the notion of ratio. By calling for linguistic reform, Gottignies seems willing to sacrifice the notion of negative numbers as quantities less than zero. But Leibniz insists that one requires only the right conceptual distinctions, and he classifies these ratios as imaginary quantities. Within the domains of computational practice, Leibniz takes advantage of the algebraic mode of thought to unify what ought to be kept distinguished only at the foundational level. A good illustration comes from Leibniz's review of Prestet's *Elémens de Mathématiques*:

> I admit that I have always calculated [with] the [ratios] analogies [as with the fractions] by fractions. For to what use should one introduce a new sort of characters, as if the analogy y . a : a . x [so common by fractio] was something new whose calculus were not subsumed in the common precepts of arithmetic or algebra. Nonetheless, I have not yet dared say that [the] ratio and fraction are the same thing.[74]

In conclusion, the algebraization of mathematics brought about the need to redraw the disciplinary boundaries of the mathematical sciences and to account for a new mathematical practice whose meaning was sometimes at odds with the understanding of the classical theories, as in the extension of the notion of ratio to negative numbers.

4

The Problem of Continuity

In chapter 1 I mentioned that one important issue in the historiography of mathematics is whether there is a continuity or a discontinuity between the mathematics practiced by seventeenth-century mathematicians and the previous developments. In particular, the issue has been dealt with extensively in connection with Descartes' achievements vis-à-vis the Greek mathematical tradition. By bringing into the picture the epistemology of mathematics two further problems can be raised. In the introduction to chapter 1 I have already pointed out the connection of such problems to the debates on continuity and discontinuity in the history and epistemology of physics.

The first problem, which has already been raised in the literature,[1] is that of the continuity between the Renaissance epistemology of mathematics and later, especially seventeenth-century, epistemologies of mathematics. Since we have established that the *Quaestio* enjoyed considerable success in the seventeenth-century we are now in a position to deal with the problem of continuity between Renaissance and seventeenth-century epistemologies of mathematics. The most basic level at which continuity can be claimed is simply by remarking that many seventeenth-century scholars involved in debates on the nature of mathematics did so within the framework provided by the Renaissance *Quaestio*. Passages from Gassendi and Barrow on the nature of mathematics are incomprehensible without referring back to the *Quaestio*. But at a deeper level, I would like to claim that the Aristotelian epistemological framework was pervasive in the seventeenth century and very influential indeed in later centuries. I will argue in this chapter that several of the epistemological features that I take to be central in the Aristotelian theory of science, such as the appeal to causes and effects, still played a central role in the theories of science and mathematics of philosophers like Arnauld, Kant, Bolzano, and Frege.

The second problem is the relationship between philosophy of mathematics and mathematical practice. It is important because it represents the analogue for the field of mathematics of a thesis that has proved so controversial in the case of Galileo—the attempt to use, for instance in Randall, similarities at the level of the conception of science as proofs of a continuous development at the level of methodology. This thesis has been strongly objected to. For example, McMullin says sharply:

> Randall had conflated logic and methodology. It was one thing to say that Galileo's logic (more exactly, his conception of science, his view of what kind of knowledge-claim *scienza* makes) had some affinities with that of the Paduan tradition. But it was quite another to claim that his methodology, the methodology that laid such a distinctive stamp on the natural science of those who followed him, also derived from Padua.[2]

We must translate talk of methodology into talk of mathematical practice. Thus the problem is whether the Aristotelian conception of science influenced the mathematical practice of seventeenth-century mathematicians. In the previous chapters I have shown that the mathematical programs of Cavalieri, Guldin, and Descartes are to be understood in the light of such an influence. We have here a very interesting situation. The attachment to the Aristotelian conception of science provides these mathematicians with a further stimulus to develop new and more direct approaches to mathematics, and to argue at the foundational level for their superiority in comparison to other approaches.

In the case of mathematics we see how similarities at the level of conceptions of science cannot be used to argue for continuity at the level of mathematical practice. On the contrary, I have attempted to show that, unlike physics, we must appeal to the same conception of what kind of knowledge constitutes science in order to explain the shift in the mathematical practice of, among others, Cavalieri, Guldin, and Descartes with respect to the previous Greek tradition. As I have already pointed out, there was also a purely mathematical incentive to develop such programs—the need to overcome the intrinsic limitations of the Greek approach to geometry. And yet the Aristotelian conception of science played a great role in providing the foundational stimulus for carrying out these programs.

Our main goal is to address the first type of continuity problem. First, I will complete my analysis of the "causality" of mathematics in the seventeenth century, by looking at the causality of definitions and demonstrations in Arnauld, Barrow, Hobbes, and Spinoza, accompanied by the role of motion in the foundations of mathematics. Then I will leap to the nineteenth century and analyze the epistemology of Bernard Bolzano. In Bolzano's case I will show that we have a theory of science and mathematics based on the notions of "cause" and "effect," a direct descendant from Aristotle. Bolzano is particularly interesting because of his great achievements in analysis. As he often remarks, his proof of the intermediate value theorem, his definition of a continuous function, and his proof of the binomial theorem depend essentially upon his epistemology and philosophy of mathematics.

Finally, I will show, as I did in chapter 1, that this type of epistemology generated serious misgivings about proofs by contradiction and I will thus investigate the issue of proofs by contradiction from Kant to the present. In this section we will achieve, among other things, a much better picture than hitherto available of some aspects of Bolzano's philosophy of mathematics vis-à-vis the Kantian one. Although these last sections will take us beyond the formal boundaries of the main theme of the book, I believe it is essential to show how the insights we have gained on the seventeenth century can throw light on later developments.

4.1   Motion and Genetic Definitions

Around the 1660s the notion of generation of geometrical magnitudes by motion was related to the epistemological discussions on the nature of definitions.[3] Definitions that appealed to the generation of a magnitude, called genetic definitions, were given pride of place by, among others, Barrow, Hobbes, and Spinoza. In order to appreciate better the background for these theories, it is essential to raise here, albeit briefly, the issue of motion in seventeenth-century mathematics.

4.1.1   Motion and the Foundations of Mathematics

The use of motion in defining and investigating geometrical objects is already found in the ancients. We have already seen how proofs by superposition appeal to motion, in the sense of a displacement. In Euclid's *Elements* we also find an appeal to motion in the generation of certain figures. For example, in book XI, definition 14, a sphere is defined as being generated by the rotation of a semicircle. Similarly, in definitions 18 and 21 of the same book, the cone and the cylinder are obtained by rotating a triangle and a parallelogram, respectively, around a side taken as axis.[4] Sophisticated uses of motion in geometry are also found in Archimedes and later Greek mathematicians. For example, Archimedes defines the spiral by appealing to the movement of a point subjected to different motions at the same time:

> If a straight line one extremity of which remains fixed be made to revolve at
> a uniform rate in a plane until it returns to the position from which it started,
> and if, at the same time as the straight line is revolving a point moves at a
> uniform rate along the straight line, starting from the fixed extremity, the point
> will describe a spiral in the plane.[5]

The quadratrix is another curve defined by appeal to motion; its properties are amply studied in Pappus' *Collections*. We have already dealt extensively with these curves in relation to Descartes' *Géométrie*.

Certainly, the use of motion to generate geometrical figures predates Euclid, as is witnessed by Aristotle's remark in *On the Soul*: "They say that the movement of the line produces a surface, and the point the line" (A4, 409a 4–5). This conception of generation is of Pythagorean origin and has twofold significance for the foundations of mathematics. It is found throughout the history of philosophy and mathematics, passing through Cusa, Bruno, Clavius, Cavalieri, and Newton, and is related to the vexed issue of the generation and the composition of the continuum.[6] In the seventeenth century, it was turned into an effective mathematical tool for the computation of volumes or tangents (see below).

What in ancient mathematics had represented only a peripheral part of the mathematical activity became a pervasive practice in the seventeenth century. In a recent article *Der mechanistische Denkstil in der Mathematik des 17. Jahrhunderts* H. Breger (1991) rightly points out the connection between the widespread use of motion in mathematics during the seventeenth century and the emergence and flourishing of the mechanistic viewpoint. In section 2.2 "Der Bewegungsbegriff in der Mathematik" he lists, among others, Napier, Kepler, Descartes, Fermat, Torricelli, Roberval, de Witt, Wallis, Fabri, Gregorius à S. Vincentio, Gregory, Barrow, and Newton as mathematicians who had appealed to the concept of motion in their geometrical investigations. In the previous chapters we have already seen various seventeenth-century examples of the connection between motion in mathematics and the foundations of mathematics. In particular, we have seen the centrality of motion to Cavalieri's definition of "all the lines" and "all the planes," and thus to the issue of the constitution of the continuum as it emerged in the Guldin-Cavalieri debate. Moreover, we have seen that in Descartes the appeal to motion plays a deep foundational role in being instrumental to his distinction between geometrical and mechanical curves. I will add to these cases Barrow's new grounding of geometry on the concept of motion.

One of the heuristic advantages of accepting motion as basic in the definition of curves is that for geometrical curves, such as the conic sections, and for mechanical curves, such as the spiral and the cycloid, one obtains a global representation of the curve instead of just a set of its points. This heuristic advantage was exploited masterfully in the determination of tangents to curves, such as the cycloid, by Torricelli, Roberval and others. In his *Histoire de la Roulette* (1658) Pascal attributed to Roberval the solution of the tangent problem for the cycloid by a method that appealed to the composition of motions.[7] Although Roverval had found his results in 1635, his method was only published in 1693 in his "Observations sur la composition des mouvements et sur le moyen de trouver les touchantes des lignes courbes." The main observation of Roberval is that "the direction of the motion of a point which describes a curved line is the tangent to the curved line at each position of that point."[8] From there he went on to define a tangent method that relied on the consideration of the component motions which determine the motion of the generating point of the curve:

> By means of the specific properties of the curved line (which will be given to you) examine the different motions which the point which describes the curve possesses at the place where you want to draw the tangent: of all these motions composed in a single one, draw the line of direction of the composed motion and you will have the tangent to the curved line.[9]

A very similar method was published by Torricelli in 1644 and as a result a priority debate ensued between the two mathematicians.[10] In a short essay, not published during his lifetime, Torricelli exploited the kinematic method of tangents to provide a new demonstration of the eighteenth proposition of Archimedes' treatise *On Spiral Lines*. Unlike Roberval, who seems to have had qualms about the rigour of geometrical proofs that appealed to motion, Torricelli emphasizes the connection between motion and causality.[11] Torricelli remarks that, when one starts from the definition of a curve given by motion, one should also prove its properties by relying on the appropriate means—the Galilean theory *de motu*—in order to generate real science, namely, "causal" explanations. However, we do not yet find in Torricelli the stronger statement that in all cases the best definitions for a geometrical curve are those given by motion, a position espoused by Isaac Barrow.

The use of motion in geometry became in Isaac Barrow's *Geometrical Lectures* (1670) the key for a new grounding of geometry. Since the *Geometrical Lectures* have been described in excellent fashion in Mahoney (1990) I will limit myself to the central notions. Barrow begins by stating that, of all the possible ways of generating a magnitude, the most important is the method of local movements.[12] The appeal to motion forces him also to consider time as a basic concept on setting up his geometrical work. There are three possible ways of generating magnitudes: by simple motions, by composition of motions, and by concurrence of motions.

The simple motions are translations and rotations. For example, one can generate a parallelogram by letting a segment move along another line with one of its points, keeping parallel to itself. The same idea can be applied to the generation of solids. By using circular motion we can generate a circle through a rotation of a straight segment around one of its endpoints. In lecture 3 Barrow introduces composite and concurrent motions. The distinction is given through examples. Child summarizes Barrow's distinction as follows:

> Thus, suppose the straight line AB, is carried along the straight line AC by a uniform parallel motion, and at the same time a point M descends uniformly

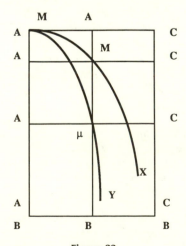

Figure 23

in AB; or suppose that, while AC descends with a uniform parallel motion, it cuts AB also moving uniformly and to the right. From motions of this kind, *composite* in the former case, and *concurrent* in the latter, the straight line AM may be produced.[13] (See Fig. 23.)

Of course, Barrow knows that by imparting different velocities or accelerated motions to the point M or to the baseline AB one obtains an infinite variety of curves. A standard example of a curve generated by composition is Archimedes' spiral; a standard example of generation by concurrence is the quadratrix.

We need not follow the detailed development of Barrow's work but let us examine a specific case to show how Barrow studies the properties of a curve using generation by motion. Let AMO be a curve generated by the motion of a point "descending" on AZ as AZ moves with uniform motion parallel to itself (see Fig. 24):

> Let us suppose that a straight line TMS touches a given curve at a point M (*i.e.* it does not cut the curve); and let the tangent meet AZ in T, and through M let PMG be drawn parallel to AY. I may say that the velocity of the descending point, describing the curve by its motion, which it has at the point of contact M, is equal to the velocity by which the straight line TP would be described uniformly in the same time as the straight line AZ is carried along AC or PM.[14]

Restating his claim, Barrow asserts that the velocity of the descending point at M is to the velocity of the motion of AZ as TP (the subtangent) is to the segment PM. As remarked by Mahoney, the proof is interesting because it takes for granted a form of the intermediate value theorem for motions.[15]

In conclusion, Barrow's use of motion as a fundamental concept in his geometrical work,[16] as opposed to a heuristic tool or an unwelcomed but necessary detour, shows how the epistemological climate had witnessed some serious changes. We will find a proof of this by examining how the appeal to motion had also become a central issue in philosophy.

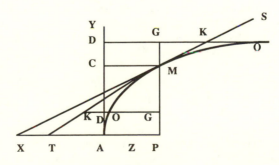

Figure 24

4.1.2   Barrow, Hobbes, and Spinoza on the Causal Theory of Definition

Let us begin by quoting Barrow's *Mathematical Lectures* (delivered in 1665–67). After recalling the different generations by motion of circles, spheres, parallelograms, spirals, quadratrices, and parabolas, he adds:

> Now no body, who will but attend a little can deny, or in the least doubt, but such Motions may be performed; and that such Effects necessarily result from them. Our understandings cannot but clearly perceive what will follow from supposing such Generations. Therefore the Properties of Magnitudes may be easily drawn and demonstrated from such Causes.[17]

Here the terminology of causes and effects is used in connection with mathematical definitions by generation (or genetic definitions). Barrow says the generation acts as a cause that allows us to derive or explain the ensuing effects. We have already seen that Barrow employs this 'causal' terminology extensively in his *Mathematical Lectures*, where he is engaged in defining the 'causality' of mathematical reasoning. While emphasizing the value of genetic definition, Barrow does not believe, unlike Aristotle, that definitions must be unique and he is willing to allow the existence of many 'causal' definitions alongside each other, all of equal value and dignity. Thus we may define a circle by generation or by some alternative equivalent property as, for example, that of being 'a figure endowed with such a property that if a certain right line be assumed in it; and any perpendicular be erected from that to the perimeter of the figure, the square of such perpendicular will equal the rectangle of the segments of that right line'.

Although some properties might be simpler and more evident than others, in the end, whichever property is chosen will play the role of a 'cause' in the mathematical demonstration. However, we find a certain tension in Barrow's account. Sometimes he appears not to give pride of place to genetic definitions; sometimes he argues for their superiority:

> Nevertheless no Geometrician refuses to define Figures by any Motion by which they can be generated with Ease. … Which Definitions are not only the most lawful, but the best: For they not only explain the Nature of the Magnitude defined, but, at the same time, shew its possible Existence, and evidently discover the Method of its Construction: They not only describe what it is, but prove by Experiment, that it is capable of being such; and do put it beyond doubt how it becomes such.[18]

Thus the claim that mathematics argues 'causally' rests on the presence of such definitions at the start of an argumentative chain:

> Mathematical Demonstrations are eminently Causal, from whence, because they only fetch their Conclusions from Axioms which exhibit the principal and most universal Affections of all Quantities, and from Definitions which declare the constitutive Generations and essential Passions of particular Magnitudes.

From whence the Propositions that arise from such Principles supposed, must
needs flow from the intimate Essences and Causes of the Things.[19]

Whereas Barrow had espoused a somewhat ambiguous position on the issue
of definitions, thereby accommodating a variety of equivalent definitions used
in mathematical practice, Hobbes and Spinoza emphasized the role of genetic
definitions as the only causal definitions, thereby excluding the nongenetic
definitions from the realm of science. This forced them, particularly Hobbes, to
call for a revisionist philosophy of geometry in which motion would play a
pivotal role. Indeed, Hobbes claimed to have been the first one to provide a
foundation for geometry. Replying to Wallis, who had objected[20] to his use of
motion in the redefinition of many Euclidian concepts—proportion theory—
Hobbes defiantly asserted it was through the use of motion that he had made
the grounds of geometry coherent.[21] In *De Corpore* Hobbes argued that the
notion of science requires an appeal to genetic definitions:

> To return, therefore, to definitions; the reason why I say that the cause and
> generation of such things, as have any cause or generation, ought to enter into
> their definitions, is this. The end of the science is the demonstration of the
> causes and generations of things; which if they be not in the definitions, they
> cannot be found in the conclusion of the first syllogism, that is made from
> those definitions; and if they be not in the first conclusion, they will not be
> found in any other conclusion deduced from that; and, therefore, by proceeding
> in this manner, we shall never come to science; which is against the scope and
> intention of demonstration.[22]

The conception of geometrical objects arising from these premises has been
analysed by Sacksteder (1980, 1981) and Medina (1985).

Hobbes' emphasis on genetic definitions was also shared by Spinoza. For
example, in *De Intellectus Emendatione* (1661) Spinoza criticizes the definition
of the circle as "a figure, such that all straight lines drawn from the center to
the circumference are equal" on account of the fact that it does not give the
cause or essence of the circle. Thus he espouses the genetic definition of the
circle because "this definition clearly comprehends the proximate cause." Again,
I must here restrict myself to a few quotations and refer the reader to Gueroult's
book on Spinoza for a detailed comparison of the similarities between Hobbes'
theory of geometry and Spinoza's theory of geometry. Gueroult argues for a
direct influence of Hobbes on Spinoza and lists an impressive number of
similarities between their conceptions of geometry.[23]

Before bringing this section to a close, I want immediately to clarify
a possible misunderstanding. Although the seventeenth century saw an
increasingly widespread use of motion in mathematics and in the epistemology
of mathematics, I am far from claiming that this was a universal phenomenon.
In the field of epistemology, we find that authors such as Pascal or Arnauld
(in the *Port-Royal Logic*) do not seem to put any emphasis on genetic
definitions. We have also seen that Wallis was very critical of Hobbes' tampering
with the classical definitions. The picture is very complex and defies easy
characterization. Appeals to motion in authors such as Descartes and Hobbes

(or Spinoza) have very different meanings. Descartes believes that motion is central to analytic geometry; he makes no claim about Euclidian geometry. Not so, say Hobbes and Spinoza; it is exactly Euclidian geometry that is up on trial, an observation recorded by Gueroult.

4.2   The "Causal" Theories in Arnauld and Bolzano

4.2.1   Arnauld's Theory of Demonstration

La Logique ou l'Art de Penser (1662) written by Arnauld and Nicole[24] can rightly be claimed to be one of the most complete expressions of a Cartesian epistemology. In the fourth section of the *Logique* entitled "Of method," written mainly by Arnauld, a number of Cartesian principles were used as a basis for a theory of the method of science. And since demonstrations are used to obtain science, Arnauld provides an analysis of demonstrations. One can reduce all types of demonstrations to two different types: demonstrations a priori, which prove the effect from the causes, and demonstrations a posteriori, which infer causes from the effects. Two general methods are associated with these types of demonstrations. Arnauld borrows from geometry the opposition, analysis/synthesis, and tries to abstract from it a more general epistemological theory. The resolutive or analytical method is used to discover truths and for this reason it may be called the method of discovery "invention." The synthetical or compositive method is used to communicate a truth that has already been discovered; thus, it may be called the method of doctrine.

In Arnauld's opinion there is perfect reversability between the two methods. The synthetical method consists in "beginning with the more general and simple things to then pass to the less general and more complex things." In order to provide a concrete example of this general method, Arnauld considers the method of the geometers. There are several positive features of this method. The geometers do not leave any ambiguity in the terms they employ, and they start their reasonings from clear and evident principles. Moreover, every claim they put forward is proved demonstratively.[25] Demonstrations must satisfy two general constraints: the subject matter of the demonstration must be certain and the reasoning must be sound. The geometers' demonstrations satisfy both criteria because they take as axioms only clear and distinct truths or definitions. Or they proceed from already demonstrated propositions which, by virtue of having been demonstrated, are clear and evident.

But as it stands, several defects can be found in the edifice of geometry. The main defect, upon which all others depend, is that geometers aim at *certainty* at the expense of *evidence*; moreover, proofs are often concocted in a way that compels assent but fails to spread enlightenment.

FIRST DEFECT. *Paying more attention to certainty than to evidence, and to the conviction of the mind than to its enlightenment.*
The geometers are worthy of all praise in seeking to advance only what is convincing: but it would appear that they have not sufficiently observed, that

it does not suffice for the establishment of a perfect knowledge of any truth to be convinced that it is true, unless beyond this, we penetrate into the reasons, derived from the nature of the thing itself, why it is true. For until we arrive at this point, our mind is not fully satisfied, and still seeks greater knowledge than this, which marks that it has not yet true knowledge. We may say that this defect is the source of all others which we shall notice; and thus it is not necessary to explain further here, since we shall speak of it sufficiently in what follows.[26]

Arnauld thus claims that a perfect science must be causal, at least in the sense that it must give a reason why a certain proposition is true. In section X, which gives an answer to possible criticisms by the geometers against his position, the terminology is explicitly causal:

For the geometers may say, if they please, that they do not care about the true order, or whether they prove by near or distant ways, provided that they accomplish what they seek, which is to convince; but they cannot change, in this way, the nature of our mind, nor prevent us from having a knowledge much more accurate, more entire and complete, of things which we know through their causes and principles, than of those which are proved by us only through foreign and indirect ways.[27]

In particular, proofs by contradiction embody the defects Arnauld and Nicole have in mind: they aim more at compelling assent than at "eclaircir la raison," they subvert the natural order of knowledge, and they do not give us the reasons for the truth of geometric facts.

THIRD DEFECT. *Demonstration by impossibility.*
Those kind of demonstrations which show that a thing is such, not by its principles, but by some absurdity which would follow if it were not so, are very common in Euclid. It is clear, however, that while they may convince the mind, they do not enlighten it, which ought to be the chief result of knowledge; for our mind is not satisfied unless it knows not only that a thing is, but why it is, which cannot be learnt from a demonstration which reduces it to the impossible.[28]

Arnauld believes these defects can be taken care of by providing an alternative development of geometry. However, he realizes that in some cases only proofs by contradiction are going to prove the sought theorems, as in the case of negative statements.

Not that these demonstrations are to be altogether rejected, for we may oftentimes employ them to prove negatives, which are properly only corollaries from other propositions, either clear of themselves or demonstrated before in another way; and then that kind of demonstration, by reducing them to the impossible, occupies the place rather of an explanation than a new demonstration. We may say, in fine, that these demonstrations are allowable only when we are unable to furnish others, and that it is a fault to employ them in proving what may be proved positively. Now there are many propositions in Euclid which he has only proved in this way which may be otherwise proved without any great difficulty.[29]

These programmatic statements were also put into practice in the *Nouveaux Elémens de Géométrie* (1667) which, however, developed only a very elementary part of geometry.[30] Arnauld's *Elements* were not an isolated occurrence. I know of two other texts that share some of its goals: the *Elementa Geometriae Planae* (1669) by Gilles François de Gottignies and the *Synopsis Geometrica* (1669) by H. Fabri. Published in the same year, their introductions contain extensive statements of their goals. A review in *Philosophical Transactions* shows just how many scholars were acquainted with the methodological issues I cover in this chapter. Concerning Fabri's work it says:

> This Author [Fabri] in this Geometrical Synopsis hath endevour'd, as M. *Gottignies,* (just now taken notice of,) promiseth to do in his *New Euclid,* to render *Geometry* clearer and easier by delivering such Demonstrations, as prove the thing in hand by *direct* and *intrinsick* Principles, not such as are indirect, and leading ad *absurdum & impossibile,* whereby 'tis only concluded, that the thing cannot be false, but not shewn, why it is and must be true.[31]

It is evident how close is the Arnauldian theory of demonstration and science to the Aristotelian one. With this I conclude the treatment of the issue of continuity between the Aristotelian theory of science and the epistemologies of mathematics in the seventeenth century. I am confident that the evidence provided and the wide spectrum of authors considered are sufficient to establish what I have been claiming all along: a great part of the philosophy of mathematics in the seventeenth century was shaped by the Aristotelian notion of science. But, as I said, I want to claim more. The Aristotelian theory of science was very influential far beyond the seventeenth century. It would be beyond the scope of this book to attempt a detailed analysis of such a problem. So I will only establish the claim in detail for the philosophy of mathematics of Bolzano. The choice of Bolzano is instrumental for the development contained in the second part of this chapter.

4.2.2   Bolzano's Theory of Demonstration

In this section I would like to show that Bolzano's theory of demonstration is very close to that of Arnauld and of the Aristotelians. In sections 512–537 of his *Wissenschaftslehre* (1837) Bolzano presented an elaborate theory of demonstration based on the notion of ground and consequence. Some of the ideas presented therein were already found in his earliest works. In *Betrachtungen* (1804), his first published work, he spoke of the "endeavour of unfolding all truths of mathematics to their ultimate grounds."[32] In "Contributions to a more well-founded presentation of mathematics" (1810) he made the notion of ground "Grund" and consequence "Folge" central to his treatment:

> Now the further question arises, what should properly be understood by the *proof* of a truth? One often calls every sequence of judgments and inferences by which the truth of a certain proposition is made generally *recognizable and*

clear, a *proof of the proposition*. In this *widest* sense, all true propositions, of whatever kind they may be, can be proved. We must therefore take the word in a *narrower* sense and by the *scientific proof* of a truth we understand the representation of the *objective dependence* of it on *other truths*, i.e. the derivation of it from such truths which are to be considered as *the ground for it*—not fortuitously [*nicht Zufälliger Weise*]—but in *themselves and necessarily*, while the truth itself must be considered as their *consequence*.[33]

As in the case of Aristotle and Arnauld, Bolzano requires that a scientific demonstration should prove more than just logical consequences. The relationship between antecendent and consequent is spelled out in terms of a relationship that is stronger than logical consequence, namely, the relationship of ground to consequence. The reader will not be surprised to hear that Bolzano has a serious problem with proofs by contradiction and converse propositions. Indeed, how could the negation of the statement to be proved be the ground of that consequence? Moreover, in the case of converse propositions, which is the ground and which is the consequence? Bolzano gives an extensive treatment of both issues in several of his works. And the nature of the problem is exactly identical to that which had troubled his predecessors. I will return in section 4.3.2 to the technical details of how Bolzano dealt with converse propositions and proof by contradiction.

But how is the *Grund/Folge* distinction related to the Aristotelian distinction between proofs 'of the fact' and proofs 'of the reasoned fact'? The following passage, from *Selbstanzeige der Wissenschaftslehre* (1837), provides Bolzano's own description of one of the achievements of the *Wissenschaftslehre*:

> The distinction between proof of the mere hoti (establishing certainty [*Gewißmachungen*] and of the dioti (grounding [*Begründungen*]) whereby is shown with a striking example from Euclid 1.1 that most proofs in geometry are not grounding proofs.[34]

The paragraph that corresponds to the above description in the *Wissenschaftslehre* is §525 entitled "Erklärung des objectiven Grundes der Wahrheit." In it Bolzano distinguishes between proofs that give the ground and proofs that merely give certainty:

> Not infrequently we can carry out a proof, that something is, directly by making noticeable the ground of why the same holds. Now since the establishment of the objective ground is something so useful that we should communicate it in our scientific texts in general as often as it is possible, then there is no doubt that it must be seen as a virtue of a proof if the truth to be established derives from its own objective ground. To separate them from others, proofs of this sort could be called grounding [*Begründungen*] and the remaining, which aim only at certainty, certain [*Gewißmachungen*].[35]

Bolzano continued by claiming that in the conceptual sciences "Begriffswissenschaften" and in moral philosophy "Sittenlehre" almost every proposition could be proved from its grounds, but that this was rarely the case in empirical disciplines, such as chemistry, medicine, and history. Of great interest is the *Anmerkung*, where Bolzano clearly characterizes his project as reviving the Aristotelian distinction between proofs of the 'fact' and of the 'reasoned fact':

> Since one so far does not always distinguish clearly the objective ground of a truth from its subjective means of knowledge [*Erkenntnismitteln*] so it follows automatically that also the grounding proofs cannot always be distinguished exactly from the purely certain proofs. Indeed Aristotle (An. Post. I,2 and I,13) and the Scholastics very diligently advanced the division of proofs into those which only show that (hoti) something is, and the ones which also show why (dioti) something is. They also maintained, with some exaggeration, that only the latter produce a genuine science. However, the new logicians seem to observe these distinctions very little.[36]

Bolzano states that it is an exaggeration to think that only a grounded proposition gives science because he does not want, as is clear from the rest of the *Anmerkung*, to draw the conclusion that most of geometry is not a science. Indeed, he concludes the *Anmerkung* with the claim that the proof of Euclid. I.1, although direct, does not give the ground for the result. Reinhold had claimed that all direct proofs, unlike apagogical proofs, proceed from the grounds of the result to be obtained, an idea to which Bolzano offers the following objection:

> However, I think that if we want to call direct any proof which does not set forth the truth of its proposition from the falsehood of its opposite, then in no way can it be maintained that all direct proofs show the objective ground of the truth to be demonstrated. So, for example, the proof of the first proposition of Euclid's *Elements* (of the possibility of an equilateral triangle), according to the opinion of all mathematicians, is not apagogical but direct. However, does it show the ground of the truth to be established? Is an equilateral triangle possible only on account of the intersection of those circles, or is it not, on the contrary, rather that the circles intersect because there is an equilateral triangle? What should I say of so many such other proofs, for example, the empirical ones?[37]

In addition to proving the Aristotelian origin of Bolzano's theory of demonstration, the remarks contained in the *Anmerkung* also show how the topic of a priori/a posteriori proof and direct/indirect proof was quite lively in the eighteenth century, too. The identification of the *dioti* proof with grounding proofs and the mention of Euclid I.1 brings us back immediately to the seventeenth-century debates on the causality of that proposition. There is no doubt that the Bolzanian distinctions followed closely the Aristotelian theory of demonstration. Bolzano's case is also interesting because Frege's project has a striking resemblance to Bolzano's. In his recent book *Frege: Philosophy of Mathematics* (1991) Michael Dummett remarked on this resemblance.:

> That was indeed Frege's central concern: not to arrive at certainty concerning the truths of arithmetic, but to establish the *ground* for our acceptance of them, and, in particular, to refute the belief that intuition was among those grounds; and in this regard, he was following the footsteps of Bolzano.[38]

In the next section I will provide a more articulate analysis of how the issue of proof by contradiction allows us, among other things, to clarify a number of interesting issues related to the philosophies of mathematics of Kant, Bolzano, and Frege.

4.3   Proofs by Contradiction from Kant to the Present

In the present section I analyze the debate on whether proofs by contradiction are necessary or whether they are dispensable from the development of the formal sciences, such as logic and mathematics. The time span selected goes approximately from Kant to the present, but references are provided for earlier periods. I will treat the topic of proofs by contradiction as an issue both in philosophy and mathematics. One of the payoffs of considering both fields simultaneously is that a number of technical investigations receive their true sense against the background of the philosophical reflections that prompted them. In particular, I show that Bolzano's attempt to reduce every proof by contradiction to a direct proof has its roots in his opposition to some specific tenets of Kant's philosophy of mathematics. Moreover, this section shows that the apparently queer pronouncements of Bolzano and Frege about proofs by contradiction, and ultimately reasoning under hypothesis, can be understood by taking a wider look at their theories of science; these theories, it will be argued, are in a direct line of tradition with some of the main tenets of Aristotle's theory of scientific demonstration. The final part of the section will outline the fortunes of the debate on proofs by contradiction in the nineteenth and the twentieth centuries.

One of the greatest problems in assessing the debate from the technical point of view is that most of the articles related to this debate were not written against a background of formal logic, and thus it is very difficult to ascertain in each single case what kinds of inferences the author wants to consider direct as opposed to apagogic. Indeed, even the meaning of proof by contradiction (apagogical proof, reductio ad absurdum, reductio ad impossibile, reductio ad incommodum, will be used as synonyms) is not quite clear. Minimally, it means a proof that starts from assuming as a premiss the negation of the proposition to be proved. From this premiss we then derive a falsity or, equivalently, a contradiction. We are then allowed to infer the proposition that had to be proved. Formulated in this way, it seems clear that a formalization of this mode of proof can be most conveniently given in a natural deduction calculus. Let us define a proof to be direct (ostensive) if it is not apagogic—it makes no assumption that is later to be denied. Then an axiomatic calculus à la Frege, Russell, Hilbert, which proceeds from truths to truths, would seem to embody the feature that every proof is direct, despite the fact that everything that can be derived by reductio in natural deduction can also be derived in the axiomatic calculus. These two alternative formalizations of classical logic will be used to attempt a technical characterization of the debate at the end of the section.

4.3.1 Kant on Proofs by Contradiction

The history of the mathematical method in philosophy and of the relationship between philosophy and mathematics in the pre-Kantian and Kantian period has been extensively investigated.[39] However, commentators seem to have ignored one important aspect of Kant's theory, namely, his use of proofs by contradiction as a watershed between philosophy and mathematics. Kant dealt with proofs by contradiction in the section of the *Critique of Pure Reason* entitled "Transcendental Doctrine of the Method." Kant is at this point engaged in a frontal attack against the Leibnizian-Wolffian thesis that the method of philosophy is mathematical. It is well known that Kant believed mathematics and philosophy to have two different methods: "Philosophical knowledge is the knowledge gained by reason from concepts; mathematical knowledge is the knowledge gained by reason from the construction of concepts."[40].

In "The Discipline of Pure Reason in Regard to its Proofs" Kant compares mathematical and transcendental proofs, and sets down rules for the appropriate use of pure reason in its proofs. We are concerned here with the third rule:

> The third rule peculiar to pure reason, in so far as it is to be subjected to a discipline in respect of transcendental proofs, is that its proofs must never be *apagogical*, but always *ostensive*. The direct or ostensive proof, in every kind of knowledge, is that which combines with the conviction of its truth insight into the sources of its truth; the apagogical proof, on the other hand, while it can indeed yield certainty, cannot enable us to comprehend truth in its connection with the grounds of its possibility. The latter is therefore to be regarded rather as a last resort than as a mode of procedure which satisfies all the requirement of reason.[41]

This distinction between apagogical and direct proofs follows closely the distinctions we found in the Aristotelian tradition, in Arnauld, and in numerous other eighteenth-century scholars.[42] What is new in Kant is the exploitation of the distinction between ostensive and apagogical proofs as a separating feature between philosophy and mathematics. Kant proceeds by explaining why it is that apagogical proofs are often employed in various sciences: "When the grounds from which this or that knowledge has to be derived are too numerous or too deeply concealed, we try whether we may not arrive at the knowledge in question through its consequences."[43]

This takes two possible forms. Either we proceed hypothetically—we postulate a proposition whose consequences turn out to account for all the truths we want to account for—or we start by negating the truth we want to prove and we show from there that this assumption leads to a contradiction. The shortcoming of the first approach is that we cannot discover all possible consequences of any proposition, and thus this way of proceeding is not apodeictic. The problem with the second alternative is expressed by Kant as follows:

> Instead, then, as in an ostensive proof, of reviewing the whole series of grounds that can lead us to the truth of a proposition, by means of a complete insight

into its possibility, we require only to show that a single one of the consequences resulting from its opposite is false, and that the proposition which we had to prove is therefore true.[44]

The latter type of procedure, Kant continues, is only admissible in those sciences in which it is not possible "mistakenly to substitute what is subjective in our representations for what is objective, that is, for the knowledge of that which is in the object." Kant is here reflecting on the results of the transcendental dialectic, where is was shown how two contradictory positions could be held, for instance, 'the world is finite' and 'the world is infinite'. Moreover, the reduction of one of the two disjuncts to absurdity would not allow us to infer the truth of the other disjunct. This is because the transcendental activity of pure reason operates within the realm of the subjective, but which "forces itself upon reason, as being objective." So in the case of the infinity of the world, both parties are deceived in their attempt to talk about an objective entity, such as the world:

> In that case we can apply the rule: *non entis nulla sunt praedicata*; that is, all that is asserted of the object, whether affirmatively or negatively is erroneous, and consequently we cannot arrive apagogically at knowledge of the truth through refutation of the opposite. If, for instance, it be assumed that the sensible world is given *in itself* in its totality, it is *false* that it must be *either* infinite in space *or* finite and limited. Both contensions are false. For appearances (as mere representations) which yet are to be given *in themselves* (as objects) are something impossible; and though the infinitude of this imaginary whole would indeed be unconditioned, it would contradict (since everything in appearances is conditioned) the unconditioned determination of magnitude [that is, of totality], which is presupposed in the concept.[45]

In mathematics, however, Kant claims that this confusion between the subjective and the objective cannot take place, and thus in this branch of knowledge apagogical proofs have their real home.

The section is concluded with another blow against the delusion of the dogmatic philosophers who, proceeding by contradiction, thought they were establishing new knowledge: "Everyone must defend his position directly, by a legitimate proof that carries with it a transcendental deduction of the grounds upon which it is itself made to rest."[46]

Kant's main point is that, since mathematics constructs its own concepts in intuition, the law of the excluded middle, which underlies every application of reductio, holds of the constructed entity, whereas in the case of philosophy we might end up predicating properties of a nonentity, and this would subvert the preconditions for a correct application of a proof by reductio. Kant's position grounds the correctness of reductio on the constructivist assumptions of his theory of mathematics.[47]

By stating the inadequacy of the proofs by contradiction, in providing us with insight into the grounds for accepting a certain proposition, Kant joins a long tradition critical of their use and determined to limit their role as a last resort. Moreover, proofs by contradiction might misfire at a more basic level, for example, when they are used to argue about *non entia*, as in the dogmatic philosophy. Thus proofs by contradiction as they are used in precritical philosophy present a double inadequacy. Not only do they give no insight into the grounds of a truth, but also there is no respect for the logical precondition of their use. However, by allowing the use of proofs by contradiction in mathematics and insisting on the use of ostensive proofs in trascendental philosophy, Kant seems to be giving pride of place to philosophy, at least in its critical version, vis-à-vis the mathematical and natural sciences, since the development of the natural sciences also relies on proofs that might give certainty but not evidence. And since there is no suggestion in Kant that such proofs can be eliminated from the development of mathematics and science, it has to be concluded that mathematics is inferior to critical philosophy, at least in so far as it is considered "grounded" knowledge. Kant's main reason for drawing the distinction between the two sciences, philosophy and mathematics, by appealing to proofs by contradiction is that the logical preconditions for applying proofs by reductio are not respected in philosophy but they are always satisfied in mathematics. This last claim hinges upon Kant's constructivist philosophy of mathematics. We will see in the next section that Bolzano strongly reacts to these tenets of the Kantian theory.

Before moving on to Bolzano, I want to raise the following question about Kant's theory: Is it true that in mathematics we cannot have situations analogous to that described by Kant in the case of the antinomies of pure reason? A negative answer to this question would cast serious doubt on the distinction between philosophy and mathematics according to the types of proof they employ. We are not discussing the adequacy of Kant's theory to the mathematical practice of his time (but see below), so let us analyze just one concrete example that shows how mathematics can present us with a situation analogous to Kant's description of the antinomies of pure reason. In order to keep the parallel as compelling as possible, let us then consider the antinomies of set theory, which were plaguing the foundations of mathematics in the early part of this century. In particular, I want to consider Schoenflies' article *Die Logischen Paradoxien der Mengenlehre* (1906) and Frege's review of it (published in the *Posthumous Writings*) dating from approximately the same period. The issue at hand was the status of the Russellian, "the set of all sets which do not contain themselves as elements." Schoenflies was engaged in an analysis of some of the set theoretical paradoxes. He began by asserting the centrality of the law of contradiction to logical thinking. On that is based "the most important mathematical inferential procedure that we know, namely indirect proof." He then identified the source of the logical paradoxes in reasoning about contradictory concepts:

> Up to now we made of course the tacit assumption that the concepts **A**, **B**, . . .
> with which we operate are *consistent* [*widerspruchsfreie*] concepts. This was just
> as natural as necessary. On the contrary, if we operate with concepts that are *not*
> consistent, then the above comments fail [*versagen*]. In particular, the principle
> of contradiction, and the inferential procedure of indirect proof, fails for them
> too. And *this is*, to say it already here, *the source of our logical paradoxes.*[48]

As an example, Schoenflies mentioned the concept **A** of a right-angled equilateral pentagon. If one thought this concept was denoting an object one could, for any property **B**, obtain a contradiction from any of the following two sentences:

(1) This **A** has property **B**;

(2) This **A** does not have property **B**.

But in such a case the method of indirect proof

> cannot lead to a positive result; that is, if any one of the two above propositions is used as starting point [*Ausgangssatz*], then from the falsity of the consequent S, it cannot be inferred that the contradictory contrary to **A** should be true.[49]

However, one positive result that can be obtained from such a situation is to conclude that the concept **A** is not consistent:

> *Concepts for which the principle of contradiction, the method of indirect proof respectively, fails, are not consistent.*[50]

Schoenflies then proceeded to apply his methodological reflections to analyse the paradoxes that had emerged in set theory.

Frege begins his review by remarking on the lack of distinction between concept and object in Schoenflies' article. Replying to Schoenflies' claim that one cannot work with contradictory concepts, Frege tackles the topic of what happens when we take a property A then construct a term like 'the A' (or 'this A'). This is a very common situation in mathematics, where one uses definitions like 'the smallest x such that $A(x)$'. In order to keep out of trouble, Frege insists we have to insure the new term denotes an object:

> In logic it must be presupposed that every proper name is meaningful; that is, that it serves its purpose of designating an object. For a sentence containing a meaningless proper name either expresses no thought at all, or it expresses a thought that belongs to myth or fiction. In either case it falls outside the domain governed by the laws of logic.[51]

Although we might work with contradictory concepts—concepts having an empty extension in Schoenflies' sense—it is a requirement of meaningful logical work, continues Frege, that the concept has sharp boundaries. It is thus necessary as a precondition of a meaningful application of the excluded middle and of proofs by contradiction that proper names and concept-words correspond, respectively, to objects and concepts with sharp boundaries. Thus Frege corrects Schoenflies' analysis by remarking how the problem is not so much in concepts that might have an empty extension, but in the creation of terms from such concepts, which do not refer to anything. Later I will return to some other interesting aspects of Frege's review, in particular, to the thesis that an inference must proceed by appealing to true premises; a statement that, prima facie, seems to exclude outright proof by contradiction from the realm of inferences.

Given that mathematicians do sometimes proceed by defining their concepts without constructing them (e.g., Russell's class), according to Frege and Schoenflies, there is a risk that things might go wrong, that we might witness failings of the law of contradiction or of the proof by contradiction in a manner exactly analogous to the antinomies of reason. So on this account I do not see the reasonableness of Kant's distinction between philosophy and mathematics based on the types of proof they use. Of course, one could object that Kant could not have foreseen the problems related to the antinomies of set theory. Since I take Kant to be proposing a phenomenologically adequate philosophy of mathematics, and thus not a normative one, this raises the issue of the "phenomenological" adequacy of Kant's philosophy of mathematics to the mathematical practice of his time. I claim that Kant's philosophy of mathematics could be shown to be inadequate to account for the mathematical practice of his time. In which sense could we say that complex numbers, Cavalieri's "collection of all the lines," or Lebniz's infinitesimals are constructed in intuition? In particular, the use of Leibnizian differentials (see chapter 6) presents problems for the Kantian theory, both on the issue of constructivity and, consequently, because they seem to defy application of the excluded middle in the form of $dx = 0$ or $dx \neq 0$. Kant relied too much on Euclid's *Elements* to address these issues properly. His position can only be argued by appealing to his claim, ultimately unjustified, that mathematicians proceed by constructing the objects of their investigations in intuition before they study their properties, a claim that also aroused objections for the elementary mathematics Kant had in mind. In the next section I shall investigate Bolzano's objections to the Kantian position.

4.3.2　Bolzano on Kant's Philosophy of Mathematics

Bolzano's disagreement with the basic tenets of Kant's philosophy of mathematics was already evident in one of his earliest works, the 1810 *Contributions to a More Well-founded Presentation of Mathematics*. Section II "On Mathematical Method" begins with Bolzano's allegiance to the Leibniz–Wolff program of treating philosophy mathematically:

> The method which mathematicians employ for the exposition of their science has always been praised on account of its high degree of perfection and it has also been believed up to the time of Kant that its essential features can be applied to every scientific subject. I personally still firmly adhere to this opinion.[52]

Bolzano also attacked Kant's theory that mathematics proceeds by construction of concepts in intuition. In the appendix to the 1810 work "On the Kantian theory of the construction of concepts through intuitions" he states:

> Several people have of course already taken exception to these *a priori intuitions* of the *critical* philosophy. For my part, I readily admit that there is to be a certain basis, quite different from the law of contradiction, by which the understanding connects the predicate of a synthetic judgment with the concept

of the subject. But how this basis *intuition*, and indeed with *a priori* judgments how a *pure* intuition, can exist and be meaningful, I do not find clear. Indeed, if I am to be really honest, all this seems to me to rest on a distinction which is not thought out clearly enough, between that which is empirical, and that which is a priori in our cognitions. The *Kritik der reinen Vernunft* begins with this distinction, but it gives no proper *definition* of these things, and I found this unsatisfactory on my first acquaintance with this book.[53]

The detail of Bolzano's criticisms need not detain us here (for a thorough analysis see Laz 1993). Bolzano wants to give up the Kantian distinction between mathematics and philosophy according to their methods.

It is well known that Kant wanted to draw a most important distinction between the proofs used by the mathematician and the philosopher, in that only the first "proceed by intuition of his object" while the second "can only be carried out by mere words (concepts)." What pernicious influence such claims had on philosophy was already mentioned elsewhere.[54]

Indeed, Bolzano claims that mathematics, like philosophy, proceeds by analysis of pure concepts ("On my part, since I believe that also mathematical proofs can be, and must be, carried out from mere concepts . . ."[55])

Finally, Bolzano challenges the distinction between ostensive and apagogical proofs, one of the pillars of Kant's distinction between mathematics and philosophy. In an entry entitled "Apagogische Beweise" of the *Zusätze oder Verbesserungen zur Logik* (1832–37) we read:

Apagogical proofs. It is a well known remark by Kant that these proofs are not applicable in philosophy because here there are some concepts which necessarily contradict one another. In my opinion, this reason comes to nothing. On the contrary, I believe that apagogical proofs in general can also be dispensed with in mathematics.[56]

The last passage confirms that Bolzano's formal engagement in the *Wissenschaftslehre* with the technical problem of reducing indirect proofs to direct proofs was in the service of a wider philosophical commitment. Showing the inessentiality of proofs by contradiction in mathematics would have also shown the untenability of one of the major distinctions made by Kant between philosophy and mathematics. The rest of this section will analyze Bolzano's stand on proofs by contradiction and his radical challenge to the Kantian distinction.

The topic of proofs by contradiction is already addressed in the 1810 work, where it is evident that Bolzano's main concern is how to allow proofs by contradiction in the light of his theory of the objective connection between truths, a theory I have analyzed at length in section 4.2.2. Apagogical proofs pose a threat to such a conception because the starting point of the proof (i.e., the negation of what has to be proved) cannot clearly be the ground of the conclusion. Are we forced to say that statements proved by apagogical proofs are not scientifically proved? These very issues are treated in §530 of the *Wissenschaftslehre*, where Bolzano argues that proofs by contradiction should be eliminated from the scientific (grounded) development of science, especially mathematics. However, Bolzano makes a concerted effort to show that this elimination of proof procedures does not mutilate the body of mathematics:

> We have already seen in §329 that a very good method of persuading ourselves of the truth of a given proposition is to assume its negation, and to try to deduce from it an obviously false proposition. For, if this can be done, then this negation is obviously false and the negated proposition itself true. Proofs which employ such a procedure are usually called proofs by reduction to absurdity, also apagogical, or indirect proofs. The question here is whether the use of indirect proof should be avoided in a treatise.[57]

Bolzano remarks that proofs by contradiction can be accepted if we are aiming at persuasion. However, he makes the following criticism:

> If the opinions voiced in §221 about the inner connection between truths is not in error, it follows that the propositions upon which a given proposition rests in an apagogical proof can never be its objective ground in its pure form.[58]

The reason why proof by contradiction is not allowable in Bolzano's opinion is because it subverts the right order of truths—the relation of ground and consequence. Bolzano proceeds by claiming that every proof by contradiction can be eliminated.

> I am of the opinion that every apagogical proof, if it contains no other error, can easily be changed so as to avoid the disagreeable consideration of false propositions. I thus want to show this in a general way, and I should like to suggest, as a rule, that we use apagogical proof only with propositions whose predicate idea is negative [i.e. Every A is a non-B].[59]

After having presented his reduction strategy he concludes:

> From this it follows that the apagogical mode of proof should never be used where a clear understanding of the grounds (if only the subjective grounds) of a given truth is intended. For it obviously does not meet this purpose, and through a few alterations in the propositions, which are actually simplifications and which reduce the number of inferences, it is always possible to generate a proof which does not include a reduction to impossibility. But I do not wish to say that it is not permissible to proceed in the apagogical manner where the point is not so much to generate a clear insight into the ground, but to produce conviction in a familiar and succinct manner.[60]

Let us then analyze Bolzano's strategy of reduction of every indirect proof into a direct proof. Bolzano begins by giving the general outline of the reduction in an abstract form then he explicates it by means of an analysis of Euclid's proposition I.19 to the effect that in each triangle acb the longer side ($cb > ca$) is opposite the larger angle ($a > b$), proved by Euclid using two apagogical proofs (see Fig. 25). It has long been known that the general proof is inconclusive (see Berg 1962; Hölder 1929) so we can dispense with a detailed analysis and concentrate on the Euclidian example.

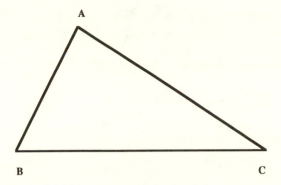

Figure 25

The Euclidian proof appeals to trichotomy for the sides cb and ca; either $cb > ca$ or $cb < ca$ or $cb = ca$. Assume not ($cb > ca$). The either $cb < ca$ or $cb = ca$. By assumption $a > b$. Thus if $cb = ca$ we can appeal to Euclid's I.5 and obtain $b = a$, which contradicts $a > b$ (first reductio). If $cb < ca$ then by Euclid's I.18 $a < b$, which is also contradictory (second reductio). Thus $cb = ca$.

Let us now follow Bolzano in the reworking of this indirect proof. First of all Bolzano exploits the fact that $cb > ca$ implies $cb \neq ca$ to state:

In a triangle acb in which $a > b$ it is false that $cb = ca$.   (4.1)

This statement has the canonical form of a proposition with a negative predicate, where **A** is the concept of triangle in which $a > b$ and **B** is the idea of triangle in which $cb = ca$. The apagogical proof thus starts by assuming:

There exists a triangle in which $a > b$ and $cb = ca$.   (4.2)

From (4.2) we obtain:

There exists a triangle in which $a \neq b$ and $cb = ca$.   (4.2*)

By Euclid I.5,

In every triangle acb in which $cb = ca$, $a = b$.   (4.3)

Thus,

A triangle acb, in which $cb = ca$, but $a \neq b$, has $a = b$;   (4.4)
A triangle acb, in which $cb = ca$, but $a \neq b$, does not have $cb = ca$.   (4.5)

Thus (4.4) and (4.5) are the explicit contradictions that conclude the proof by reductio. A contradiction could be similarly obtained under the assumption that there is triangle acb, in which $a > b$, and $cb < ca$.

Here is Bolzano's direct proof:
By Euclid I.5,

A triangle acb in which $ca = cb$ has $a = b$.

By contraposition,

A triangle acb in which $a \neq b$ does not have $ca = cb$.

But $a > b$ implies $a \neq b$, therefore

In a triangle acb in which $a > b$, $ca \neq cb$.   (4.6)

The second part of the proof would look as follows:
By Euclid I.18,

In a triangle acb in which $cb < ca$, $a < b$.

By trichotomy of $>$,

$a > b$ implies not $(a < b)$

Moreover, by converse of I.18,

not $(a < b)$ implies not $(cb < ca)$.

Thus,

In a triangle acb, in which $a > b$, it is false that $cb < ca$.   (4.7)

Thus (4.6) and (4.7) are the direct proofs of the propositions which were proved by reductio on Euclid's original proof. Actually, one more step is needed to complete the proof, an application of an inference in *modus tollens*; since

either $cb < ca$ or $cb = ca$ or $ca < cb$,

and

not $(cb < ca)$ and not $(cb = ca)$,

then

$cb < ca$.

The reader might think this the most incredible game of mirrors we have played so far. After all, inferences by contraposition and *modus tollens* are normally proved by contradiction, so what's the big deal? Let us first of all eliminate the possibility that Bolzano might have been incredibly confused on this issue. Indeed, he was not. In two notes appended to §530 of the *Wissenschaftslehre* he discusses the opinion of those who claim that contraposition and *modus tollens* are to be considered forms of proof by contradiction. In the first remark, he discusses *modus tollens* with reference to the opinion of the logician, Calker, who in his 1822 *Denklehre* (§190) had classified *modus tollens* as a type of apagogical proof. Bolzano grants that if the concept of agagogical proof is extended in such a sense then "not every apagogical proof can be avoided in our proofs. Indeed, I claim that there are truths that we objectively ground by means of such considerations."[61]

Moreover, in note 2 Bolzano remarks on the kinship of his project with that of Aristotle's in *Prior Analytics* II.14, where Aristotle seeks to show that every proof by contradiction can be recast into an ostensive proof. And although Bolzano does not find the Aristotelian proof conclusive, he sees himself as defending the same claim against logicians such as Reinhold and Leibniz (on Leibniz's position see chapter 5), who had doubted that this could be done. In the same note he argued that contraposition is also a form of direct proof.[62] We might think that assuming contraposition or *modus tollens* as forms of direct inference simply makes the game trivial. However, we cannot stop Bolzano from stipulating the conditions under which he presents his claim.

Hölder had at first thought it was possible to give examples of indirect proofs that could not be reduced to direct ones, even granting (something he was not willing to do) that one could consider proofs obtained by appealing to *modus tollens* and contraposition as direct. He attempted to prove his claim in Hölder (1929) by giving two examples of indirect proofs which, he claimed, could not be turned into direct proofs, even allowing *modus tollens* and contraposition. However, in Hölder (1930) he had to admit that if one allowed *modus tollens* then perhaps it could be possible to transform every indirect proof into a direct one.[63] But Hölder insisted that the transformed (direct) proof would in many cases, be more complex than the indirect one.

4.3.3 Further Developments

The issue of proofs by contradiction was a lively one in the nineteenth century. Besides Bolzano's work one could simply point to the literature quoted in Knabe's dissertation on *Die Formen des indirecten Beweises* (1885), which mentions the contributions of Lotze, Wundt, and Trendelenburg (see also Krähe 1874). The problems that seem to have occupied the attention of philosophers and logicians during this period are mainly those of classifying the forms of indirect proofs and of arguing for their role in establishing principles. For example, Knabe classifies indirect proofs in three classes (disjunctive, contradictory, and contrary) and Trendelenburg and Überweg argue for the use of indirect proofs in establishing principles in a scientific way.[64]

Interest in the topic did not diminish in the early part of this century, in mathematical and in philosophical circles. As an example of mathematical concern with such proofs I shall recall here Hessenberg's *Transzendenz von e und* π (1912), an exposition of the transcendence of e and π from the elementary standpoint. The first part of the book is devoted to the methodological aspects of the proof, and section 3 deals with indirect proofs. Previous to Hessenberg, all the standard proofs of the transcendence of e and π were carried out by contradiction. One would start with the assumption that there was a polynomial with rational coefficients and rational exponents:

$$C_1 x^{c_1} + C_2 x^{c_2} + \cdots + C_n x^{c_n}$$

such that

$$E = C_1 e^{c_1} + C_2 e^{c_2} + \cdots + C_n e^{c_n} = 0.$$

From the assumption $E = 0$ one would then go on to infer a contradiction. Hessenberg provided a new and direct proof.[65]

The reader may be curious to know why I have not quoted from the intuitionistic literature. Contrary to widespread belief, intuitionists are not against proofs by contradiction per se, but only against proofs that involve as an essential step the law of double negation. In other words, an intuitionist accepts that if from the assumption A one derives a falsity or a contradiction, then one can prove not-A. But if from not-A one derives a falsity or a contradiction, then one can only infer not-not-A; one cannot infer A because that would involve an appeal to the law of double negation, which is not generally available to the intuitionist.[66] By contrast, most people involved in the debate on proofs by contradiction have no problem in accepting classical reasoning; they assume the law of double negation, the excluded middle, contraposition, De Morgan's rules, and so on.

Let me now, in passing, raise a problem about the mathematical reworking of theorems proved by contradiction into theorems proved directly, as in the case of Hessenberg's proof. Hessenberg obtains a direct proof by appealing to a variety of mathematical theorems from analysis and number theory, theorems he does not show to be obtained without appeal to proof by contradiction. So it is not clear that there is more than a psychological advantage to the proof. In other words, if one had qualms about the structure of a proof by contradiction then to obtain a *truly direct* proof would require appeal to lemmas and theorems that were themselves proved directly. Hessenberg does not pursue his investigation in this direction.

The possibility of reducing every indirect proof into a direct proof occupied several twentieth-century logicians.[67] I have already mentioned that proofs by contradiction posed a problem for those such as Frege and Bolzano, who claimed that inferences must proceed from true ground to consequences. According to Dummett (1991):

> Frege ... consistently rejected the legitimacy of deriving a consequence from
> a mere supposition: all inference must be from true premises. This excludes the
> use of reasoning under a hypothesis subsequently to be discharged by a rule

of inference such as *reductio ad absurdum*. In ordinary practice, we apply this rule by first stating a hypothesis, such as 'Suppose 2 has a rational square root'. We then reason under this hypothesis, drawing consequences dependent on it; when we finally derive a contradictory consequence, such as that some integer is both odd and even, we conclude to the falsity of the hypothesis, our conclusion of course being no longer governed by it. According to Frege, however, this is not a correct account of any legitimate inferential procedure. On his view, any step in our reasoning has to be asserted outright: what figured in the foregoing description as the initial enunciation of a hypothesis should be considered as the formulation of the antecedent of each of a series of conditionals forming every step in the argument except the final one. The penultimate step will then be of such a form as 'If 2 has a rational square root, some integer is both odd and even' from which we then derive our conclusion '2 has no rational square root.'[68]

Frege dealt with the issue in a paper contained in *Posthumous Writings* "Logic in Mathematics" dated by the editors as written in 1914. Frege remarks that "in indirect proofs it looks as if consequences are being drawn from something false." Frege then proceeds to claim: "We make far too much of the peculiarity of indirect proof vis-à-vis direct proof. The truth is that the difference between them is not at all important." To illustrate the point he then goes on to show how Euclid I.19, the same proposition used by Bolzano,[69] can be recast into a direct proof that makes no use of any false hypothesis. As the strategy of reduction is similar to Bolzano's, there is no need to repeat the details.

Dummett rightly remarked that this insistence on proceeding from truths to truths determined the axiomatic developments of logic à la Frege, Hilbert, and Russell. Only after Gentzen's work on natural deduction systems, in which one proceeds under hypotheses that are eventually discharged, could one derive all theorems within a system of logic without assuming any axiomatic truths at the start.

Indeed, if we define an indirect proof as one that assumes a false formula, for example the negation of what we want to prove, and define a direct proof as one that makes no appeal to any false premises to be discarded, then one can pose the general problem of reducing indirect proofs to direct proofs in the following terms. Consider a natural deduction calculus, say Gentzen's calculus NK, and an axiomatic calculus LK. In the axiomatic calculus every proof, according to our definition, is direct. Moreover, Gentzen has shown how to transform every proof of a sentence A in NK to a proof in LK by a mechanical procedure, such that if x is the number of steps required to prove A then the new proof has at most x^2 steps (Gentzen 1969). Moreover, no new hypotheses are needed to prove the result. In spirit this vindicates the reductions of Bolzano and Frege, and it shatters the Kantian characterization of the difference between philosophy and mathematics according to an alleged difference between the types of proof they employ.

5

Paradoxes of the Infinite

In the introduction to *Paradoxien des Unendlichen* Bernard Bolzano remarked that most paradoxical results found in mathematics rest on the concept of the infinite.[1] The seventeenth century provided many of the paradoxes of the infinite that constitute the topic of Bolzano's treatise. If one restricts attention only to those paradoxes that generated foundational discussions, two classes emerge from the plethora of surprising results provided by seventeenth-century mathematicians and philosophers. First are the paradoxes having to do with what Bolzano would have called the general theory of magnitudes, especially the composition of continuous quantities. These will be analyzed with reference to the theory of indivisibles (Cavalieri, Galileo, Torricelli, Tacquet, and Leibniz). Second are the paradoxes relating to the theory of space. These will be investigated with reference to Torricelli's cubature of an infinitely long solid and the varied philosophical reactions generated by this result, or plane versions of it. The use of infinity in the Leibnizian calculus is the topic of chapter 6.

The term *paradox* will be taken in its original meaning—a statement that contradicts a previous belief—and in the meaning of an outright logical contradiction. Particularly useful to us, paradoxes often reveal the implicit assumptions and tacit conventions that form the basis of a determinate mathematical or philosophical viewpoint. Their study allows us to appreciate the mental obstacles our predecessors had to overcome before they could make further progress in the development of philosophy and mathematics.

The goal of the chapter is to highlight both the mathematical and the philosophical relevance of the topic of infinity for seventeenth-century philosophy of mathematics. In section 5.1 the analysis of the technical objections to the geometry of indivisibles will show that many mathematicians and philosophers endeavored to justify Cavalieri's theory in terms of homogeneous quantities, also in response to the threat of paradoxes. At the same time, the early exchange between Galileo and Cavalieri on the possibility of a geometry of indivisibles reveals how problematic was the idea of a theory of infinite quantities in the early seventeenth century. Section 5.2 moves on to the topic of the infinitely large, a topic that has been largely ignored in the literature in favor of the debates on the infinitely small. But it is in connection with the infinitely large that I believe the most important foundational reflections are to be found. When measuring "finite" figures, the infinite could always be avoided by using the classical technique of exhaustion instead of the method of indivisibles. Whereas for quadratures and cubatures of geometrical objects with infinite dimensions, the infinite is built into the object itself, independent of the method of proof. In other words, it is the very fact that we are measuring an infinite object that constitutes the main novelty vis-à-vis the Greek tradition. Not only is the infinite a means for measuring the finite but also something that can be measured itself. The extent of the philosophical reactions to results involving the infinitely large will confirm that seventeenth century scholars were well aware of their foundational importance.

5.1   Indivisibles and Infinitely Small Quantities

5.1.1   Galileo, Cavalieri, and Tacquet on Some Paradoxes of the Theory of Indivisibles

Chapter 2 analyzed the debate between Cavalieri and Guldin. One of the main objections of Guldin to Cavalieri was that two infinites cannot have a ratio to each other. In his attack against Cavalieri, Guldin could also claim that "in truth Galileo, discussing in the same Dialogue on local motion the infinite and the properties of finite quantities, concludes against him [Cavalieri] that one cannot apply such properties to infinities."[2] The reference is to Galileo's treatment of the continuum and the infinite contained in the first day of the *Discorsi*. Galileo's position is well known.[3] After having rejected the possibility of the composition of the continuum out of finitely many indivisibles, the problem is how to reconcile the fact that two lines of different length have infinitely many points, and thus that there seems to be an infinite greater than an infinite.

> SIMPLICIO: From this immediately arises a doubt that seems to me unresolvable. It is that we certainly do find lines of which one may say that one is greater than another; whence, if both contained infinitely many points, there would have to be admitted to be found in the same category a thing greater than an infinite, since the infinitude of points of the greater line will exceed the infinitude of points of the lesser. Now, the occurrence of an infinite greater than the infinite seems to me a concept not to be understood in any sense.
> SALVIATI: These are some of those difficulties that derive from reasoning about infinites with our finite understanding, giving to them those attributes that we give finite and bounded things. This, I think, is inconsistent, for I consider that the attributes of greater, lesser, and equal do not suit infinities, of which it cannot be said that one is greater, or less than, or equal to, another.[4]

A similar situation emerges when we compare the natural numbers with the squares of natural numbers. There is a one-to-one correspondence between the natural numbers and the squares, and the squares are also a part of the natural numbers. Therefore, Salviati concludes, one cannot say that the natural numbers are equal, or less than, or greater than their squares. Such relations hold only for finite quantities and not for infinite ones.[5]

In the *Discorsi* Galileo never mentions Cavalieri in this connection, but as Guldin rightly points out, it is clear that the two have very different stands on the problem of the infinite. Cavalieri's theory is an attempt to provide a measure for infinite collections of indivisibles. Galileo believes any such attempt is futile because it is not possible to say that "an infinite be greater than another infinite, and not even that it is greater than a finite." Indeed, Galileo had already raised similar objections in his correspondence with Cavalieri. Although we only possess the reply by Cavalieri, dated 2 October 1634, it is nonetheless clear enough that Galileo had proposed two paradoxes for Cavalieri's theory of indivisibles. The two paradoxes, are the so-called paradox of the bowl (or of the soup dish "scodella") and the paradox of the concentric circles.

The paradox of the bowl. Consider a semicircle AFB, with center C, and a rectangle ADEB circumscribed to it, as in Figure 26. Let us also draw the radius CF, so that it is perpendicular to DE, and the segments CD and CE. If we rotate this figure around the axis CF, the rectangle ADEB will generate a cylinder; the semicircle AFB a semisphere; and the triangle CDE a cone. Consider the cone and the solid obtained by removing from the cylinder the semisphere.

Galileo called this solid a bowl. He then proceeded to claim that the cone and the bowl have equal volumes. Moreover, he noticed that each parallel GN to DE determines a plane parallel to the basis of the cone, or the bowl, which intersects the two solids in such a way that (a) the cone whose profile is the triangle CHL is equal to the portion of the bowl whose profile is represented by the mixtilinear triangles GAI and BON; and (b) the plane figures that constitute the bases of the just described solids, a circle in the case of the cone and a ribbon for the portion of the bowl, are also equal. In other words, each parallel GN to DE determines equal solids and planes in the cone and the bowl. The paradox that follows from this result is that the circumference of a circle—infinitely many points—turns out to be equal to a single point:

> From this follows the marvel previously mentioned; namely, that if we understand the cutting plane to be gradually raised toward the line AB, the parts of the solids it cuts are always equal, as likewise are the surfaces that form their bases. Lifting it more and more, the two always-equal solids, as well

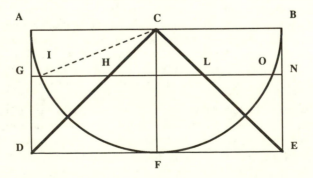

Figure 26

as their always-equal bases, finally vanish—the one pair in the circumference
of a circle, and the other pair in a single point, such being the upper ream of
the soupdish and the summit of the cone. Now, during the diminution of the
two solids, their equality was maintained right up to the end; hence it seems
consistent to say that the highest and last boundaries of the reductions are
still equal, rather than that one is infinitely greater than the other, and so it
appears that the circumference of an immense circle may be called equal to a
single point![6]

Moreover, the above reasoning can also be applied to the plane figures that
constitute the bases of the solids. Finally, since the initial rectangle ADEB was
of arbitrary size it will also turn out that "all the circumferences of all circles,
however unequal [in size], may be called equal to one another, and each of
them [may be called] equal to a single point!"[7]

In the *Discorsi* the paradox was introduced by Salviati to discuss Simplicio's
puzzled reaction to some awkward facts that had emerged in the discussion of
the paradox of the wheel.[8] However, in a letter to Cavalieri, Galileo had used
the example as a difficulty for Cavalieri's theory of indivisibles. What is at stake
here is the preservation of the principle: if $C = A + B_1$ and $C = A + B_2$ then
$B_1 = B_2$; a principle that seems to fail when B_1 and B_2 are taken to be the
"last" indivisibles of the cone and the bowl. In his reply to Galileo, dated 2
October 1634, Cavalieri characterized the difference between the two methods
of indivisibles in the *Geometria* in terms of the use of infinity in the first method,
and the avoidance of it in the second. Then he proceeded to discuss the paradox
of the bowl. He claimed that also in this case one can preserve the principle
that when subtracting equal parts from equal quantities the remaining parts
are also equal. In fact, in the case of the bowl and the cone, the "last"
indivisibles—the circumference and the point—have dimension zero in comparison to the plane indivisibles.[9]

Galileo's objection raises an important issue for the method of indivisibles.
Indeed, there are many cases, such as the cone and the bowl, in which the
comparison of the indivisibles of two figures, or solids, degenerates into the
comparison between objects of different dimensions. In his reply to Galileo,
Cavalieri tries to dispel the paradox by noticing that, in comparison to a plane
figure, a line and a point have the same null dimension. But Cavalieri seems
to have been uneasy about his own reply. Indeed, in a letter to Galileo dated
19 December 1634, he comes back to the paradox of the bowl and claims that
in his definition the indivisibles of a figure or a solid are obtained by considering
the intersections obtained by the motion of a line or a plane, parallel to the
regula, from one tangent to the other. However, the start and finish of this
motion are not motions, and thus the tangents (i.e., the "first" and the "last"
indivisible) should not be counted as being in the aggregate of all the lines (or
planes).

In the letter that contained the objections to Cavalieri's *Geometria*, Galileo
had also raised a different paradox—the paradox of the concentric circles—
related to the so-called paradox of the wheel (see note 8). As in the case of the
paradox of the bowl, we have to rely on Cavalieri's answer to Galileo.[10] From

Cavalieri's reply it is easy to conjecture that Galileo's objection must have been of the following sort. Consider two concentric circles. Each radius of the greater circle determines a point on its circumference and a corresponding point on the circumference of the smaller circle. So there are as many points on the smaller circumference as on the bigger one. But the lines are their collection of indivisibles—their collection of points. And since the two collections have been shown to have the same number of points, the two circumferences have equal length. This paradox was a standard one in the literature.[11]

Galileo proposes it as a difficulty for Cavalieri because Cavalieri always begins by setting up a one-to-one correspondence between the indivisibles of two figures. And since the indivisibles of the two circumferences are the collections of all points, we seem to arrive at a paradox. Cavalieri's reply shows that in his theory he has the resources to block this alleged paradox. The solution is to distinguish between rectilinear and oblique transit in the determination of indivisibles. He does not deny the one-to-one correspondence between the points of the two circumferences, but it is clear to him that this is not enough to account for the size of the two circumferences. Couched in today's language, Cavalieri realizes that the cardinality of a set of points is not enough to give a metric. Moreover, he strongly remarks that his theory does not commit him to the theory of the composition of the continuum out of indivisibles.

Let us then look more closely at the notion of oblique transit. In definition 1 of book II of the *Geometria*, Cavalieri first defines the concept of all the lines of rectilinear transit when the transit is perpendicular to the given figure. But when the planes cut the figure obliquely, we have all the lines of oblique transit. It is essential to Cavalieri's theory that the comparison of two figures be made by taking the indivisibles with respect to the same rectlinear transit. Cavalieri describes the notion in definition 4 of book II.

> If we take all the lines contained between one of the endpoints of the given straight line, and the single points (which, taken all together, are called all the points of rectilinear, or oblique, transit of the said line), then all these lines taken together are called all the abscissae of the given line, which (even if it is not said explicitly) we suppose to be called of rectilinear transit, if the points are of rectilinear transit, or of the same oblique transit if the points of the line are of oblique transit.[12]

Noticed that "all the points of a line" are introduced to allow comparison not of line segments but collections of abscissae. There is no principle in Cavalieri that would allow us to infer from the one-to-one correspondence of points the equality between the collection of points and therefore of the segments. Indeed, such a principle would be contradictory if we did not distinguish between rectilinear and oblique transit, or at best trivial, since it would only allow us to infer that two segments of the same height perpendicular to the same regula have the same ratio as their collection of points. And a similar situation would arise for curves. It is thus not clear how Galileo's objection of the two concentric circles constitutes a problem for Cavalieri's theory. However, it was exactly this type of paradox that led Torricelli to his new theory of indivisibles in which indivisibles are provided with a certain size, "spissitudo."[13] In any case, the distinction between rectilinear and oblique transit was central to Cavalieri's theory and allowed him to block more threatening paradoxes. Moreover, his idea about the density of the indivisibles played a role in his explanations of the basic concepts of his theory and paved the way for a new conception of indivisibles in Torricelli. The distinction between rectilinear and oblique transit, and the idea of the density of the indivisibles also play a role in Cavalieri's treatment of a paradox, contained in the last section of his reply to Guldin.

Consider two triangles HDG and HDA, with same height HD, and bases DG and AD, with AD smaller than DG (see Fig. 27). Every parallel to AG, say IL, determines a point I on AH and a point L on HG. The projections of I and L on AG, say C and E, determine equal segments IC and LE. All segments of the type IC constitute all the lines of the triangle HDA, and all segments of the type LE constitute all the lines of the triangle HDG. And by the above correspondence all the lines of the triangle HDA are equal to all the lines of the triangle HDG with same regula HD. Thus, by proposition 3 of book II of the *Geometria*, the two triangles are equal. But this is impossible since by proposition 1 of book VI of Euclid's *Elements* we know that HDG is greater than HDA.

The example contains many elements of the sorts of paradoxes that were raised against the theory of indivisibles. By a clever one-to-one mapping, one shows that two figures have the same collection of indivisibles and, by Cavalieri's principles, are equal, in contradiction to well-known mathematical results. These paradoxes were taken seriously by the mathematicians who espoused the indivisibilist techniques. For example, Torricelli wrote three small treatises on paradoxes that arise by an incorrect manipulation of the theory of indivisibles.[14] The majority of cases are solved by distinguishing rectilinear and oblique transits. In explaining the alleged paradox, Cavalieri starts by remarking that he has carried out the comparison between indivisibles of two plane figures always with reference to the same transit. This condition is equivalent to the condition that, given any two indivisibles of the first figure, the corresponding indivisibles of the second figure have the same distance as

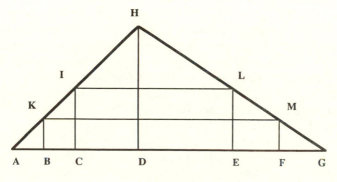

Figure 27

the first two. When this does not happen, he concludes, we are not working under the same transit.

> Thus, when the two lines KB, IC, do not have the same distance as that between MF, LE, which correspond to them, then all the lines of the triangles HDA, HDG, taken in this way, are as if they were constructed under different transits; for which reason they are excluded from the definition I gave of all the lines of a plane figure. Thus, if all the lines of the triangles HDA and HDG have been taken in an erroneous way, one should not be surprised that it is inferred that they are equal when in fact they are unequal.[15]

As de Gandt has remarked, there is an element of novelty in the explanation given by Cavalieri in the *Exercitationes* in comparison to the manipulations of indivisibles contained in the *Geometria*.[16] The novelty lies in Cavalieri's emphasis that the corresponding indivisibles in the two figures be taken equidistant. And since having taken the same regula guarantees the equidistance, as Cavalieri argues in the first *Exercitatio*, he concludes that it is as if the two figures were taken under different transits.

In conclusion, Cavalieri tried to explain the source of the difficulty by remarking on the different density of the indivisibles when they are taken under different transits.

> The solution to this difficulty is very well clarified by a canvas woven with threads, from which we suppose detached the above mentioned triangles. If in fact we suppose that in HAD there are 100 threads parallel to HD, on HA there will be marked 100 points, in the triangle HAG 100 threads parallel to AG will be traced, and consequently 100 more points on HG, and 100 threads likewise in the triangle HDG. But if DG is supposed to be, for instance, twice DA, then on the triangle HDG, when it is imagined as detached from the same canvas, there will be 200 threads. Thus 100 are left: for which reason those left will be sparser than the threads of the triangle HDA. This is the way things are for all the lines of the said triangles taken as we have done; in fact they do not correspond to each other according to an exact rule as it instead happens when all the lines are taken under the same transit.[17]

An alleged paradox for solid figures obtained by the application of Cavalieri's theory was presented by Tacquet in his *Cylindrica et Annularia*. Consider a cone generated by a right triangle VDK (see Fig. 28). Each plane section of the cone parallel to the base determines a circle. For each such circle the ratio between the radius and the circumference is constant. And since the generating triangle VDK can be considered as the collection of all the radii of the form CZ, and the surface of the cone as the collection of all the corresponding circumferences, one can infer that the surface of the cone and the generating triangle are in that constant ratio. But this is evidently false.

Another way of looking at the paradox is to remark that each circumference of the cone corresponds to a circumference, of the same length, of the circle that is the base of the cone. Since the circle is the collection of its concentric circumferences, the surface of the cone and the base circle are equal. Again a contradiction. This apparent paradox was analyzed by Barrow in his *Lectiones*

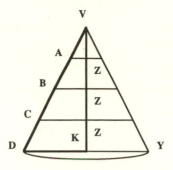

Figure 28

Geometricae. In essence, Barrow remarks that the paradox is obtained because we are working with different transits. So the paradox can be blocked by appealing to the Cavalierian distinction between right and oblique transit.[18]

This would hardly have satisfied Tacquet, whose objections to the theory of indivisibles did not rely on the technical paradoxes but on the basic issue of the generation of geometrical magnitudes. After having presented a result on the equality between a sphere and certain segments of a cylinder Tacquet wrote:

> I do not believe that the method of demonstration by indivisibles, or as I am used to call it by heterogeneous [quantities], can be admitted as proper [*legitima*] and geometrical. This method, which was brought to light by the noble Bonaventura Cavalieri, proceeds from lines to surfaces, and from surface to bodies. It infers the equality or the proportion between surfaces from that found in the lines; and extends those found in the surfaces to bodies. And this form of reasoning, unless it be reduced to homogeneous quantities, proves nothing. For, to show the problem by an example, who is convinced by the following reasoning: all the triangular sections of the cylindrical segment ... are equal to the circular sections of the sphere. ... Therefore the cylindrical segment is equal to the sphere? This is not a rational argument: for, neither is the cylindrical segment composed of triangles, nor is the sphere composed of circles. To be sure, the geometers admit that a line can be generated by the flowing of a point [*ex fluxu puncti*], and a surface by a flowing line, and a body by a [flowing] surface. But it is quite different to say that a quantity is produced by the flowing of an indivisible, and to say that it is composed by indivisibles. The former is an indubitable proposition. The latter is so opposed to geometry that if it does not destroy geometry it must be destroyed by geometry itself. However, it is not my wish to deny a beautiful invention the praise it deserves. I only say that demonstrations by heterogeneous quantities do not compel the assent, unless they be reducible to homogeneous quantities, which is mostly the case. ... But if one proposed a theorem that could only be proved by the method of indivisibles, then one should doubt its truth until it became evident that the argument could be reduced to homogeneous quantities. And to do this is nothing else than exhausting [*exhaurire*] in the way of the ancients the proposed quantities by inscribing homogeneous figures.[19]

The ideas of demonstrating the method of indivisibles by means of the techniques of the ancients was destined to play an important role in the foundations of mathematics.

5.1.2   Leibniz's *De Quadratura Arithmetica*

Bosmans (1923) argued for a direct influence of Tacquet on Pascal. In the letter of Dettonville to Carcavy (1658), where Tacquet is also mentioned, Pascal gives a reading of the geometry of indivisibles in terms of homogeneous quantities. This interpretation of the method of indivisibles is also found, among others, in Roberval and Wallis.[20].

It is within this context that one should analyze one of the most important seventeenth-century works on the foundation of the indivisibilist methods. I am referring to Leibniz's *De Quadratura Arithmetica Circuli Ellipseos et Hyperbolae Cujus Corollarium est Trigonometria Sine Tabulis*. The completion of this treatise can be approximately dated to 1676, Leibniz's last year in Paris.[21] Leibniz had written this work with the hope that it would facilitate a nomination to the Académie des Sciences. Unfortunately, things did not work out, and for various reasons the treatise was not published in Leibniz's lifetime. In 1934 L. Scholtz published a selected part of the work, but it was only in 1993 that, thanks to the efforts of Eberhard Knobloch, the treatise was published in its entirety. The work is very complex and of interest both for its technical results as well as for the philosophical and foundational points of view put forth by Leibniz.[22] Following Knobloch's analysis, its 51 theorems, can be roughly divided into three parts: (1) theorems 1 to 11; (2) theorems 12 to 25; and (3) theorems 26 to 51.

In the first group of special relevance are the first seven theorems, which provide a rigorous foundation of the theory of indivisibles and culminate in the so-called transmutation theorem (theorem 7). The second part consists of a number of preparatory theorems in view of the main result of the third part, the "true numerical quadrature of the circle," where essentially $\pi/4$ is expressed in the form of a convergent sequence of rational numbers, $1 - \frac{1}{3} + \frac{1}{5} - \frac{1}{7} + \frac{1}{9} - \frac{1}{11} \ldots$ (theorem 32).

I will concentrate on two different issues: (1) the foundation of the method of indivisibles and Leibniz's reflection on the issue of proof by contradiction and infinity; and (2) the paradoxes of infinity.

Leibniz prefaced this work with an *index notabiliorum* in which he singled out the first seven theorems as the most important; they provide a rigouous foundation for the method of indivisibles. The emphasis he placed on them should provide sufficient evidence to refute the opinion that, after Toricelli, only figures of secondary importance worried about the foundations of the method of indivisibles, an opinion widespread among historians of mathematics.[23] Since it would take too long to rehearse in detail the content and proofs of these theorems, I will use this *index notabiliorum* to point out the results of interest to us.

The first theorem gives a way of transforming triangles with a common vertex A into rectangles, one of whose sides lies on the same segment AMN.

Theorems 2, 3, 4, and 5 are theorems about absolute differences and are needed for the apagogical demonstrations of the quadratures by means of inscribed figures.

Theorem 6 serves to "lay down rigorously the foundations of the entire method of indivisibles." The proposition is called "spinosissima" ("very thorny" in the meaning of "very subtle") and the proof demonstrates "morose" (i.e., meticulously) that a curvilinear figure can be approximated with an arbitrary degree of accuracy by step-figures, in such a way that the difference between the area under the curve and the area of the step-figures can be made less than any assigned quantity: "Adeoque methodus indivisibilium, quae per summas linearum invenit areas spatiorum, pro demonstrata haberi potest" (p. 29).

Theorem 7, the transformation theorem, is the "fruit" of all that has gone before. It allows one to square any given curve by finding its quadratrix. Here the transformation of triangles in rectangles found in theorem 1, plays a big role. The proof proceeds by contradiction.

In the definitions following the scholium to theorem 7, Leibniz clarifies in which sense the language of indivisibles can be used without dangers. Leibniz allows the use of the expression "the sum of straight lines" only as a way of talking, in reality it should be interpreted as "the sum of all rectangles, each of which has one side equal to one of the straight lines in question, and the other side equal to a constant segment assumed to be indefinitely small [*indefinitae parvitatis assumto*]."

> Indeed, when one makes the interval [i.e., the constant side of the rectangles] arbitrarily small [*utcumque parvum*], all that can be proved of such a sum will also be proved of the curvilinear area ...; for, if one takes the interval sufficiently small then that sum can be so that its difference from the area is smaller than any arbitrarily given one. Thus, if one rejects our claim it will be easy to convince him by showing that the error is smaller than any arbitrarily assignable one, and therefore it is no error at all. He who does not observe these cautions will easily be deceived by the method of indivisibles. We give an example below in the scholium to proposition XXII.[24]

Lebniz interprets the indivisibles in terms of *homogenea* in the way of Tacquet, Pascal, and Roberval, but he goes further by proving his claim in theorem 6. And this allows one to use the language of indivisibles without risk. If these cautions are not observed, he warns, one might easily come across paradoxes. But before turning to the paradoxes, I want to add something about the proofs.

In the scholium to theorem 7, Leibniz remarks on the fact that the proof of this most important result proceeds by a reductio ad absurdum. Leibniz points out that, although the result is not proved directly, it uses only one reductio ad absurdum instead of two, since it is obtained by considering only inscribed figures. And this, according to Leibniz, is the best approximation to a direct proof that one can give in the case of quadratures. Indeed for quadratures, he suspects that no direct proof can be given without the use of infinitely large or infinitely small quantities, quantities he calls fictitious.[25] It is easy to recognize in Leibniz's position a set of concerns we have analyzed at length in chapter 2. Notice how Leibniz reaches the equivalent of Cavalieri's conclusion. Only by allowing infinitesimal quantities can one obtain direct proofs; and Leibniz did allow infinitesimals in his treatise. Starting from proposition 11 he exploits the security offered by his rigorous justification of the method of indivisibles by allowing the use of infinitely small quantities in the proofs.[26]

Knobloch (1990, 38) observes how Leibniz's position on proofs by contradiction presents some serious difficulties. Indeed, Leibniz seems to be involved in a vicious circle. He asserts that the justification for infinitely small or large quantities can only be given using proof by reductio; then claims that only by using infinitely small or large quantities can one give direct proofs. Cavalieri had run into the same type of problem, although he never insisted that indivisibles should be necessarily justified by reductio. However, one possible way out of this circle could be the following. The use of proofs by contradiction to justify the use of the infinitesimal quantities plays the role of a "metatheoretical" justification of a mathematical system in which infinitesimals are used. The "metatheoretical" proof is used to guarantee the certainty and reliability of the system. After that we are free to carry on our practice without fear of running into trouble and by means of direct proofs. Of course, Leibniz does not speak exactly in these terms and one would still have to address the issue of whether this sort of justification for direct proofs also carries an epistemological advantage. I do not think Leibniz had an answer for this problem but he held fast to the point of view that proofs by contradiction cannot be eliminated in the development of mathematics.[27]

Leibniz's justification of the theory of indivisibles was essential to avoid the possibility of the emergence of paradoxes. In the scholium to proposition 22, Leibniz examines the dangers to which one is exposed by an incorrect usage of the concept of indivisibles and shows that "non semper ex partium finitarum perpetuo abscissarum proprietate quadam ad totius infiniti spatii proprietatem posse prosiliri."[28] Consider a hyperbola of equation $xy = 1$ (see Fig. 29).

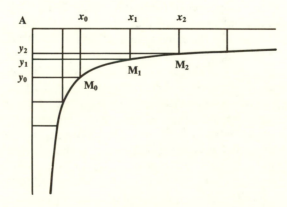

Figure 29

Consider x_0 and x_1. By properties of the hyperbola, the area under the hyperbola between x_0 and x_1 is equal to the corresponding area delimited by y_0 and y_1. Now the infinite area of the segment of hyperbola delimited by $x_0 M_0$ and extending in the direction of $x_1 M_1$, and so on, is given by the segments of the form $x_0 M_0 M_1 x_1$, $x_1 M_1 M_2 x_2$, and so on. Each one of them corresponds to the area $y_0 y_1 M_1 M_0$, $y_1 y_2 M_2 M_1$, and so on. But the infinite area determined by $x_0 M_0$ is a proper part of the sum of all $y_0 y_1 M_1 M_0$, $y_1 y_2 M_2 M_1$, and so on. Thus the whole is equal to the part, an axiom Leibniz was not willing to part with.[29] In a letter to Bernoulli, Leibniz explained that the paradox emerges because one implicitly operates with the "last" abscissa—the infinitely long line, which properly speaking does not exist. The confusion and the paradox can be eliminated only if one carefully distinguishes, following Leibniz's reinterpretation of the method of indivisibles, the infinitely small from the indivisible. Leibniz's clarification eliminates those paradoxical aspects of the theory of indivisibles that appeared in limit cases, such as the equality between the circumference and the point in Galileo's bowl, and at the same time, as we shall soon see, provided him with a framework for interpreting the role of the infinitely large. However, Leibniz simply failed to accept what later will be seen exactly as the central feature of the infinite—when dealing with infinite quantities, in some sense, the part and the whole can be equal. The next section considers, among other things, Leibniz's interpretation of the infinite in connection with Torricelli's result on the infinitely large.

5.2   The Infinitely Large

Cavalieri's *Geometria* was the first worked out attempt to provide a theory that could account for ratios between infinite quantities. No wonder it found opposition from many quarters. The idea there could be no ratio between the finite and the infinite was deeply ingrained and we have found it in Guldin and Galileo. But soon afterwards, in 1641, Torricelli derived a result that showed many people how infinity could be measured using a solid of infinite length but finite volume, an "acute hyperbolic solid." This paradoxical result created considerable interest in mathematical and philosophical circles active around the third quarter of the seventeenth century. It seemed so counterintuitive and astonishing that, at first, some of the leading mathematicians thought it impossible; even eighty years later Bernard de Fontenelle commented: "One apparently expected, and should have expected, to find [Torricelli's solid] infinite [in volume]."[30] Some important philosophers, too, were sufficiently struck by the oddity and the implications of Torricelli's result to comment on it. Of course, not all reacted in the same way, and some were more forthcoming than others. But, by and large, philosophical responses tended to cluster around three main topics, all of considerable importance in the seventeenth century: our knowledge of infinity, the position of geometry in the web of knowledge, and the ontological status of mathematical objects. This section is devoted to the study of Torricelli's result, and results related to it, and the philosophical problems and discussions it generated around the third quarter of the seventeenth century.

5.2.1 Torricelli's Result

In 1642 Torricelli was given the chair of mathematics in Florence, but as Galileo's successor he was virtually unknown to the geometrical community. Two years later, when he came to publish his *Opera Geometrica*, Torricelli had become one of the most acclaimed geometers in Europe.[31] This change of status occurred in 1643, when Torricelli communicated several of his discoveries to the French geometers. The most important discovery had to do with the study of a remarkable geometric solid. If one revolves a branch of the Apollonian hyperbola ($xy = a^2$) around one of the asymptotes (see Fig. 31), one obtains a solid that is infinitely long in the direction of the axis of revolution. Cutting this solid by a plane perpendicular to the axis of revolution, one obtains a solid of infinite length whose volume is finite. This result was to constitute the core of Torricelli's work *De solido hyperbolico acuto*, published in *Opera Geometrica*.

Torricelli's discovery dated back to 1641, when he communicated the result to his friend and patron, Bonaventura Cavalieri. Although Torricelli's letter is lost, we possess Cavalieri's reply.

> I received your letter while in bed with fever and gout ... but in spite of my illness, I enjoyed the savory fruits of your mind, since I found infinitely admirable that infinitely long hyperbolic solid which is equal to a body finite in all the three dimensions. And having spoken about it to some of my philosophy students, they agreed that it seemed truly marvelous and extraordinary that that could be.[32]

In 1643 Torricelli sent a letter to Jean-François Niceron in Paris, attaching a single sheet that communicated the statements of his geometrical discoveries (but not the proofs) to the French mathematicians.[33] Marin Mersenne was immediately informed and he in turn told Roberval, Fermat, and others. Torricelli's celebrity was immediate. Michelangelo Ricci wrote to him:

> Father Niceron writes me that all the excellent men of that kingdom desire to see your works and that the sheet of propositions I sent them is passing through everyone's hands with great praise of your beautiful discoveries [*invenzioni*].[34]

Proposition 14 of Torricelli's letter (on the infinitely long solid) was the most astonishing of all. Even if Torricelli could not claim to have broken new ground in his other results, the cubature of the infinitely long solid brought him to the forefront of European research in geometry.[35] Roberval wrote to Mersenne that he considered Torricelli's result very elegant then added his own proof of the statement.[36]

A complete account of Torricelli's work on the infinitely long solid (which contained much more than the cubature of the solid) was presented in *De solido hyperbolico acuto.*[37] The techniques that led to the determination of the volume were provided by Cavalieri's theory of indivisibles, which Torricelli had recently embraced with the enthusiasm of the neophyte.[38]

Torricelli's commitment to the indivisibilist method is evidenced by the favorable comparison he drew between it and the traditional indirect method of proof:

> As for the method of demonstration, we shall prove a simple notable theorem in two ways, namely, with indivisibles and in the manner of the ancients. And this although, to tell the truth, it has been discovered with the geometry of indivisibles, which is a truly scientific method of demonstration which is direct, and so to say, natural. If feel pity for the ancient Geometry which not knowing or not allowing Indivisibles discovered so few truths in the study of the measure of solids, that a frightening paucity of ideas has continued until our times.[39]

It was important to defend the method of indivisibles because Torricelli's *Opera Geometrica* appeared at a critical moment. As we know, the method of indivisibles, used and explained by Cavalieri in his *Geometria*, had been attacked in 1641 by Guldin in the second volume of his *Centrobaryca* as being non-demonstrative. Torricelli, therefore, emphasized not only the rigor, generality, and directness of the method, but also its productivity, claiming that it made the old geometry look like a poor relation of the new one.

Torricelli did more than cleverly apply Cavalieri's techniques. For one thing, he vastly increased the range of applications of the indivisibilist method by extensively using curved indivisibles.

> Our method, which we are about to use in the aforementioned theorem, will proceed with curved indivisibles without following the example of any predecessor but not without the previous approval of Geometricians. ... Curved indivisibles adequate for these demonstrations are peripheries of circles in plane figures, spherical, cylindrical and conic surfaces in solid figures. They have the advantage of fitting perfectly and having, so to say, a thickness which is always equal and uniform.[40]

Furthermore, Torricelli's curved indivisibles have a thickness. Cavalieri's have none; their dimension is lower than the figure they characterize. Finally, Torricelli substituted for the complexity of Cavalieri's approach (in which the geometric figure and the class of its indivisibles were considered as two separate magnitudes) a simple indentification of the figure with its characterizing indivisibles.[41] This can be illustrated by a simple example that Torricelli presented as a "warm-up" exercise on curved indivisibles before he proved the main theorems of *De solido hyperbolico acuto.* It is a proof of the Archimedean proposition on the measurement of the circle: the area of a circle is equal to the area of a right triangle whose legs are equal to the radius and the circumference of the circle (see Fig. 30).

Draw the circle BDB with radius AB. Consider an arbitrarily chosen point I on AB. Let BC equal the circumference BDB. If one produces a second circle

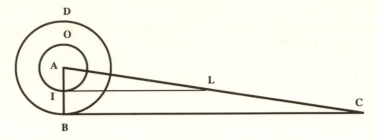

Figure 30

with center A and radius AI, one obtains the following proportions:

circumference BDB: circumference IOI = AB : AI

= BC : IL

Hence,

circumference BDB : BC = circumference IOI : IL.

Consequently, circumference IOI = IL. Since this is true for any arbitrarily chosen point I on AB, Torricelli concluded that "all the peripheries taken together are equal to all the straight lines taken together, that is, the circle BD will be equal to the triangle ABC."[42] In other words, Torricelli identified the circle with the class of its curved indivisibles. In measuring the circle, we dealt with plane curved indivisibles; in the proof of the finite volume of the infinitely long solid, one needs to use solid curved indivisibles.

Before considering Torricelli's proof, we examine his definition of the hyperbolic solid and his statement of the theorem to see how they bring out the infinitistic nature of the result.

DEFINITION. *If one rotates a hyperbola around an asymptote, as around an axis, one generates a solid infinite in length [longitudine infinitum] in the direction of the axis, which we call an acute hyperbolic solid.*[43]

THEOREM. *An acute hyperbolic solid, infinitely long [infinite longum], cut by a plane [perpendicular] to the axis, together with a cylinder of the same base, is equal to that right cylinder of which the base is the latus transversum of the hyperbola (that is, the diameter of the hyperbola), and of which the altitude is equal to the radius of the base of this acute body.*[44]

Thus, we want to show that the solid described in the statement of the theorem composed by the cylinder FEDC (see Fig. 31) and the solid generated by the rotation of the segment of the hyperbola with lowest point D around the axis AB are together equal to the cylinder whose height is CA and whose base is the circle of diameter HA = 2AS.

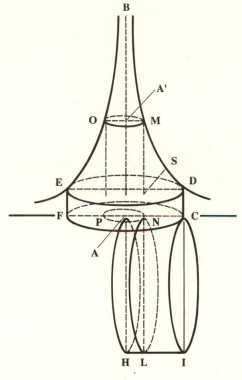

Figure 31

Proof by Indivisibles

The proof is preceded by five preliminary lemmas, demonstrated without the use of indivisibles. The first four build up to lemma 5, used explicitly to prove the theorem. Lemma 5 asserts that the lateral surface of the inscribed cylinder POMN (see Fig. 31), whose axis lies on AB and whose bases are the circles with diameters OM and PN, is equal to the area of a circle whose radius is AS, the semidiameter of the hyperbola, and that this holds for any inscribed cylinder of that form.

   The idea of the proof is very simple. We have to show that the curved indivisibles of the infinitely long solid described in the statement of the theorem are equal to the curved indivisibles of the cylinder ACIH. The infinitely long solid is thought to be made up of all its cylindrical indivisibles, that is, all lateral surfaces of the type POMN. The cylinder ACIH is thought of as being made up of all its circular indivisibles, that is, the cross sections of diameter AH. Some arbitrarily chosen point N determines an indivisible in the infinitely long solid and an associated indivisible in the cylinder ACIH. But each indivisible of the infinitely long solid (i.e., a lateral surface of the type POMN) is equal in area (by lemma 5) to the circle whose radius is AS, that is, to an indivisible of ACIH (since by construction AH = 2AS). Therefore, since the indivisibles of the two figures are equal by the fundamental principle of the theory of indivisibles, the volumes of the two figures will be equal, too. Hence, the infinitely long solid is equal to the finite cylinder whose base is the circle with diameter AH and whose height is AC. This concludes the proof.

In the accompanying scholium, Torricelli made two interesting remarks:

> It may seem incredible that although this solid has an infinite length [*infinitam longitudinem*], nevertheless none of the cylindrical surfaces we considered has an infinite length, but all of them are finite, as will be clear to everyone who is even modestly familiar with the doctrine of Conics.
>
> I consider the previous theorem sufficiently clear in itself, and more than adequately confirmed by the examples proposed at the beginning of the book. However, in order to satisfy also the reader who is scarcely a friend of indivisibles, I shall repeat its demonstration at the end of the work with the usual demonstrative method of ancient Geometers which, although longer, in my opinion is not for that more certain.[45]

The first comment initially seems confusing. In order to fill the solid with the lateral surfaces of the inscribed cylinders, one has to consider the limit case, in which the lateral surface of the innermost cylinder degenerates into an infinitely long line, the axis of the solid. When Torricelli says that none of the lateral surfaces has an infinite length, he means that none of them has an infinite area. This is confirmed in a note published posthumously: "What Galileo says of a point equal to a line is true, and in our hyperbolic solid it is true that the infinitely long axis is equal to a circle [*circolo quanto*]."[46]

Torricelli's proof takes for granted that the equality of the lateral surfaces with a specified circle holds also when N = A, that is, when the lateral surface degenerates into a straight line. This is not, as he implied, a consequence of the theorem but a necessary assumption for the completeness of its proof. To my knowledge none of his contemporaries remarked on this aspect.

The second comment concerns the necessity of proving the result by the method of exhaustion. Torricelli declared himself satisfied by the proof just given, but he added that he would offer a proof by the "usual demonstrative method of ancient geometers" for those who did not like indivisibles. Behind this conciliatory and perhaps condescending attitude we can perceive his cautiousness. Because the method of indivisibiles was under attack, it was safer to publish both proofs. Torricelli's strategy is reminiscent of the caution shown by Archimedes who, in his *Quadrature of the Parabola*, approaching Dositheus for the first time, had sent two proofs of his results, the first mechanical and the second purely geometrical. Although Archimedes expressed no doubts as to the validity of the first proof, he apparently preferred to provide a purely geometrical proof in order to avoid criticism on formal grounds. In introducing the proof by exhaustion, Torricelli remarked that it would seem an impossible task to inscribe in another figure a figure of infinite length, or to circumscribe another figure around such a figure. However, after praising Roberval's proof by exhaustion, he proceeded to give his own.

Proof by Exhaustion

The result to be proved is the same as before, We want to show that (1) the solid described in the statement of the theorem, call it H, composed by the cylinder FEDC (see Fig. 31) and (2) the solid generated by the rotation of the segment of the hyperbola with lowest point D around the axis AB are together equal to the cylinder whose height is CA and whose base is the circle of diameter HA = 2AS. Since the proof is by exhaustion, we will approximate the solids with figures of the same dimension, that is, with finite solids. The two main lemmas needed for Torricelli's theorem are lemmas 6 and 7.

LEMMA 6. *Consider the solid described by the rotation of the mixtilinear figure MNCD around AB. The hollow solid described is equal in volume to the cylinder whose height is NC and whose base is the circle with diameter NL. This is true for any arbitrarily chosen N on AC different from A.*

LEMMA 7. *Consider the cylinder generated by the rotation of the rectangle ANMA' around AB. The volume of this cylinder is half the volume of the cylinder whose height is AN and whose base is the circle with diameter AH. This also holds for any arbitrarily chosen point N on AC different from A.*

We are now ready for the main proof. Let us denote by C the cylinder HACI. To prove V(H) = V(C), where V stands for volume, one proceeds, as usual, by contradiction. Assume V(H) < V(C). Then H is equal to a piece of C, let us say to the cylinder LNCI. Extend NL to meet the hyperbola in M. Then the solid generated by the rotation of the mixtilinear figure MNCD around the axis AB is, by lemma 6, equal to the cylinder LNCI; and this is true for any point N on AC different from A. Thus, since the hollow solid generated is part of H, we have V(C) < V(H), a contradiction. Assume then V(C) < V(H). Since the value of C is finite, it will be equal to some finite segment of H, say FEOMDC. Call this segment W. Thus V(W) = V(C). W is the sum of the hollow solid T, generated by the rotation of the mixtilinear figure MNCD, and the cylinder Z, obtained by the rotation of the rectangle AM. But 2V(Z) = V (cylinder ANLH) (by lemma 7). Hence

$$V(W) = V(Z) + V(T)$$
$$= 1/2V(\text{cyl.ANLH}) + V(T) \qquad \text{(by lemma 7)}$$
$$= 1/2V(\text{cyl.ANLH}) + V(\text{cyl.LNCI}) \qquad \text{(by lemma 6)}$$
$$< V(\text{cyl.ANLH}) + V(\text{cyl.LNCI}) = V(C).$$

Consequently, V(W) ≠ V(C), contrary to the assumption. Hence V(C) cannot be less than V(H). Since both V(H) > V(C) and V(H) < V(C) are false, V(H) = V(C). This concludes the proof.[47]

We are now ready to investigate the philosophical significance of Torricelli's infinitely long solid.

5.2.2   The Philosophical Relevance of Torricelli's Result

To understand the philosophical reactions that Torricelli's result generated, it is important to notice its infinitist nature. The theorem, as it stands, is about the proportion between two figures: an infinitely long solid and a cylinder. Thus, the notion of actually infinite length is present in the very statement of the theorem. Moreover, the proofs themselves, as they stand, make sense only if the hyperbolic solid is given as infinitely long *in actu*. For, we are comparing the volume of a fixed determinate solid to that of a cylinder, and there is no indication that the volume of the hyperbolic solid is thought of as the limit of a succession of volumes converging to that of the cylinder. Furthermore, Torricelli always referred to the hyperbolic solid as being infinitely long, and even Cavalieri, who was otherwise very careful in using the term "indefinite" rather than the term "infinite," referred to it in the same way.[48] The most striking feature of Torricelli's result, then, is that the acute hyperbolic solid, although finite in volume, is not merely potentially, but *actually* infinite in length. This gives rise to three philosophical issues, two of which can be characterized as epistemological, and one as ontological.

The first epistemological issue concerns our knowledge of infinity, or in seventeenth-century jargon, our idea of infinity. Broadly speaking, two positions were prominent around the middle of the century: a negative idea and a positive idea. The negative idea of infinity is traditionally associated with empiricist epistemology (e.g., Gassendi and Hobbes); when we say that something is infinite, all we mean, or ought to mean, is that we are unable to conceive its limits. In other words, we call something "infinite" just when it is epistemically possible that it is boundless. Properly speaking, then, our talk about infinity is nothing but talk about our own inability; it does not involve any sort of knowledge of infinity per se. For example, Gassendi held that mathematical concepts are obtained from sensation through a process of abstraction. Failing to see how we could concoct the idea of infinity out of sensation, he maintained that we have a merely negative notion of infinity, and criticized Descartes' claims in the Third Meditation about our understanding of God as infinite. He pointed out that "we call infinite that thing whose limits we have not perceived, and so by that word we do not signify what we understand about a thing, but rather what we do not understand."[49] Nor does our inability to have a positive notion of infinity involve merely ignorance of the infinite degree to which God possesses his perfections (i.e., what Gassendi called "infinity of perfection"); it also involves ignorance of more mundane sorts of infinity, such as infinite extension. In fact, he told Descartes that "infinitude either of place or of perfection cannot be understood."[50] Gassendi did not address the issue of how to account for the bold infinitistic nature of Torricelli's result in his epistemology. However, as Hobbes' reaction will show, it is clear that Torricelli's cubature is problematic for the view that we have merely a negative idea of infinity, for it certainly seems to provide us with some positive and nontrivial knowledge about infinity. This issue will be addressed in section 5.2.5 in the context of the debate between Hobbes and Wallis.

The positive position holds that we do have some knowledge of infinity per se, however minimal it may be. Descartes, Spinoza, Leibniz, and Malebranche belong to this tradition. However, each one of them presents peculiar differences that are also reflected in their interpretations of the infinitistic results. Section 5.2.4 examines them in connection with Arnauld, Pardies, and Leibniz, and traces back some of their differences to Descartes' stand on the issue of our knowledge of infinity.

The second epistemological issue arises from the combination of the paradoxical nature of the theorem and certain assumptions quite widespread around the third quarter of the seventeenth century. Torricelli himself remarked that his result was both "new and, as it were, paradoxical."[51] The reason is that "if one proposes to consider a solid, or a plane figure, infinitely extended, everybody immediately thinks that such a figure must be of infinite size."[52]

But Torricelli's theorem shows how this intuitive belief is wrong. If we are to judge from the reactions of Torricelli's contemporaries, he was not alone in finding the result paradoxical. Cavalieri was shocked; he wrote to Torricelli:

I thank you for the truly divine demonstration of the acute hyperbolic solid; and I do not know how you fished out its measure so easily in the infinite depth of that solid. For, it seems infinitely long [*lungo*] to me because the plane figure [*spazio*] which generates it appears infinitely long to me, and each of its parts generates part of the solid.[53]

Nor was he the only one to be surprised. In his *Racconto* Torricelli accused Roberval of not having believed the result at first and even of having doubted its feasibility:

Mr. Roberval considered this proposition false and impossible; actually, when Father Mersenne came by here he told me that Roberval, having thought about it for some time wrote I don't know what demonstrations or speeches [*discorsi*] in order to prove that my proposition was absurd and impossible.[54]

And Gassendi, in the *Syntagma philosophicum* (1658) mentions the result by saying that it almost exceeds credibility:

And these are the suppositions from which Mathematicians, within the gates of pure and abstract Geometry and almost constituting a kingdom of their own, weave those famous demonstrations, some so extraordinary that they even exceed credibility [*fidem*], like what the famous Cavalieri and Torricelli showed [*ostenderunt*] of a certain acute solid infinitely long which nevertheless is equal to a parallelepiped or to a finite cylinder. It is clear, therefore, how they protect that kingdom of theirs in which they find [*excogitant*] so many remarkable and pleasurable things and take care not to mix anything with matter.[55]

Many a philosopher held that geometry provides us with indisputable knowledge and that all knowledge involves a set of self-evident truths known by "natural light." But there are good intuitive grounds for holding that an infinitely long solid cannot have a finite volume. Furthermore, such a conclusion seems clearly entailed by the age-old and, according to Barrow, widespread Aristotelian dictum that there is no proportion between the finite and the infinite.[56] We have, then all the ingredients for a contradiction, which can be dispelled by abandoning some of the assumptions, by reinterpreting them, or by reinterpreting Torricelli's result. We shall see that Barrow combined the first and second alternatives and Hobbes took the third. In addition to the two epistemological issues just mentioned, the infinite length of the acute hyperbolic solid highlights the ontological status of geometrical entities. Torricelli himself pointed out that "in school tracts of geometry one finds figures limited in every side, and among all the solids of which ancient and modern authors have determined the measures with much effort, none, as far as I know, has an infinite extension."[57]

He seemed aware that he was opening new vistas for geometry by challenging a number of informal assumptions that ruled and structured geometrical discourse. The notion of an infinitely long solid is perfectly consistent with the definition of a solid given in Euclid—a solid is that which has length, breadth, and depth—but it was apparently at odds with the intuitive universe of geometrical entities constituting the background of the early seventeenth-century geometer.[58] Evidence that this was so is provided by Mersenne's remark in the introduction to his *Universae geometriae mixtaeque mathematicae synopsis* (1644). Commenting on Torricelli's result, he expressed serious concern regarding the propriety of using the word "space" to denote that "which is not closed [*clauditur*] on every side if not, perhaps, at infinity."[59] The quotation reveals that we are witnessing the stretching of some basic intuitive geometrical notions: Mersenne is confronting the idea that figures and solids need not be bounded on every side.

But Torricelli's solid, besides generating the conceptual problem of admitting a solid not bounded on every side (also adressed by Hobbes), further dramatizes the issue of the nature of geometrical entities. This topic was touched upon by Torricelli in the introduction to *De dimensione parabolae*, where he addressed at length two objections raised by philosophers of Aristotelian inspiration against the use of mechanical concepts in geometry. After discussing the first objection, that one cannot properly talk of the center of gravity of geometrical figures, Torricelli took up the second, to the effect that in reality the threads of a balance are never parallel but tend toward the center of the earth, by claiming:

> If this same balance, even though corporeal, were considered to be not on the earth's surface but in the highest regions beyond the sun's sphere, then the threads, while still drawn to the centre of the earth, would be very much less convergent to each other, would be quasi-parallel. Let us imagine a mechanical balance transported beyond the starry balance [i.e., the constellation of that name] in the firmament, to an infinite distance. It will be understood by everybody that the suspension threads would no longer be convergent, but would be exactly parallel. . . . The Geometer has the special privilege to carry

out, by abstraction, all constructions [*operationes*] by means of the intellect. Who, then, would wish to prevent me from freely considering figures hanging on a balance imagined to be at an infinite distance beyond the confines of the world?[60]

This passage should be interpreted as a declaration of the intellectual freedom, the "special privilege" granted to the geometer, who is not bound by physical constraints in the definition of his abstractions. Nothing could stop Torricelli from conceiving a figure, like the acute hyperbolic solid, that is so long as to extend "beyond the confines of the world."[61]

Torricelli's claims on the nature of mathematical abstraction and the geometer's freedom to define objects are consistent with various forms of Platonism and conceptualism. But, as we shall see in the discussion of Barrow, the acceptance of Torricelli's solid presents potential difficulties for those philosophies of mathematics that ground geometrical existence in actual physical existence, for an infinitely long solid may turn out to be problematic for one's cosmological views. Section 5.2.3 will address the ontological issue with reference to Barrow's comments on Torricelli's results. Sections 5.2.4 and 5.2.5 will be mainly devoted to the epistemological issues.

5.2.3   Isaac Barrow

Barrow's discussion of Torricelli's result and its implications occurred in lecture 16 of his *Lectiones*, delivered in 1666 and devoted to the topic of proportion. Torricelli's cubature is mentioned alongside the Aristotelian dictum, "there is no proportion between the finite and the infinite,"

> The truth of which statement, a very usual and well known [*pervulgatum*] axiom, seems to have been in part broken by the sagacity of modern geometricians, since they demonstrate a just proportion or even equality of innumerable planes and solids protracted to infinity with other finite planes and solids: which prodigy the very famous geometer Torricelli exhibited first.[62]

The new theorems about infinitely long figures are relevant to Aristotle's maxim because they show that "not everything without limits in extension is *ipso facto* infinite in quantity; or yet more plainly ... [that] from the infinity of one dimension that of a surface or a body does not follow."[63] The fact that Barrow made such an explicit connection between Aristotle's dictum and Torricelli's result is at first a bit surprising. For, although Aristotle's statement had occurred in the middle of his arguments against the possibility of an infinite body, his discussion had been framed within a context that was much more physical than geometrical.[64] Furthermore, one would be hard pressed to find Aristotle's claim among the explicit principles of the classical mathematical tradition with which Barrow was well acquainted.

However, Barrow's readiness to discuss Aristotle's claim in the light of Torricelli's result is understandable once we comprehend that he, like many of his contemporaries (e.g., Hobbes) embraced the traditional Aristotelian view of mathematics not as an isolated and self-contained discipline, but as embedded in a web of other branches of knowledge with which it shared fundamental assumptions.[65] Indeed, he went so far as to claim that geometrical axioms "are to be drawn from some higher and universal science, as first philosophy."[66] Since Barrow claimed that Aristotle's dictum had been refuted only "in part," he proceeded to explain what had to be retained, namely, that "there is no proportion between a finite magnitude or quantity and an infinite quantity or magnitude of the same genus. But we are not to understand that in general there is no ratio between a limited figure and an unlimited magnitude."[67]

In Barrow's eyes, Torricelli's cubature has the effect of disambiguating Aristotle's saying by rendering clear that it holds not indiscriminately, but only for magnitudes of the same genus, for example, lengths with lengths, areas with areas, and volumes with volumes. Accepting this proviso, Aristotle's dictum can be maintained because it does not allow the intuitive, widespread, and erroneous inference from infinite length to infinite volume or area.

If Torricelli's cubature provided Barrow with an opportunity to clarify an important philosophical statement, it also presented him with serious problems concerning the nature of geometrical entities. He was opposed to any sort of view that posited the existence of mathematical entities only in the human, or even the divine, mind, for otherwise they would be mere "dreams or idols of things nowhere existing."[68] Consequently, he adopted the strong position that

> all imaginable geometrical figures are really inherent in every particle of matter; I say really inherent in fact [actu] and to the utmost perfection, though not apparent to the senses, just as the effigy of Caesar lies under unhewn marble. ... So, if the hand of an Angel (at least the power of God) should think to polish any particle of matter without vacuity, a spherical surface of a figure exactly round would appear to the eyes.[69]

Barrow's view that the reality of geometrical entities is grounded in their material existence is compatible with the mathematical existence of the infinite solid only if that solid is actually instantiated in some piece of matter. By making a link similar to Aristotle's, perhaps unwittingly, Barrow had raised the issue of whether cosmology has sufficient resources to handle geometry. Since he held that space is "really eternal and infinite," Barrow's cosmology certainly has room for Torricelli's solid.[70] But his belief that the amount of matter in the universe is finite would seem to present a problem.[71] Except that this criticism applies Aristotle's dictum in the very indiscriminate fashion Barrow had condemned so convincingly. For although Torricelli's solid is infinitely long, it has a finite volume and hence can be embedded, as it were, in a finite amount of matter. However, an infinitely long solid such as Torricelli's requires an infinitely long piece of matter in which to be instantiated, and although Barrow, unlike Aristotle, has the cosmological resources to build such a chunk of matter, there can hardly be independent reason for holding that it really exists. Although the mathematical existence of Torricelli's solid is compatible with this aspect of Barrow's view of geometrical existence, one must conclude it strains it almost to the point of rupture.

Yet, as well as holding that geometrical entities must actually be instantiated, and possibly instead, Barrow apparently took a weaker view, gauged from what he said about demonstrations. All demonstrations, he claimed, proceed from true hypotheses.[72] But in a circuitous way, as we shall see, he de facto equated the truth of a hypothesis with its self-consistency.[73] This is why "demonstrations may be made of things which never had existence anywhere, nor will ever exist; for, it is sufficient for a demonstration to assume a true hypothesis, i.e. such as to imply no inconsistence in themselves."[74]

It is important to understand that for Barrow the requirement of self-consistency is not a self-contained logical point with no further purpose, but the logical prerequisite for a metaphysical step that confirms the strict ties between the various branches of knowledge and their final subordination to metaphysics and theology. For Barrow claimed that "the truth of a hypothesis intimates the possible existence of the thing supposed; this possibility denotes the efficient cause of the thing (since otherwise it would be impossible for it to exist), and the efficient cause of all things is God."[75] Since logical consistency is viewed as a mere prerequisite for possible instantiation, which conceptually involves the notion of divine production, Barrow could conclude, albeit fallaciously, that every demonstration supposes the existence of God as the creator not only of the knowing subject, but "also of the knowable object."[76]

The consequence of this position is that even if a geometrical item were not actually instantiated, its geometrical existence would be guaranteed if it could be instantiated. This is why "the dominion of reason far extends the limits of nature: the intelligible world is vastly more extended and diffuse than the sensible world and the acuteness of the mind contemplates many more things than the bodily senses."[77] Under this view of geometrical entities, in which their existence if located in possible instantiation, the infinite length of Torricelli's solid poses no problem if one is ready to concede the nontrivial assumption that the very notion of an infinite solid is consistent. For, since space is infinite, God could certainly locate an infinitely long solid therein.

Barrow had a good understanding of Torricelli's result. Moreover, he clearly saw that the theorem can be intuitively explained by the fact that "the infinite diminution of one dimension compensates the infinite increase of the other," and successfully used it to clarify Aristotle's dictum.[78] However, the same cannot be said about his grasp of the problems the hyperbolic solid presented for his philosophy of mathematics. In fact, Torricelli's solid helps to focus attention on an apparently unresolved tension in Barrow's theory. Although he consistently rejected the view that geometrical existence is grounded in human or divine understanding alone, he did not clarify his position as to whether it requires actual or merely possible material instantiation.

5.2.4 French Reactions to Infinitistic Results in Geometry

A group of French thinkers, motivated by apologetics, quickly realized the intimate connection between Torricellian results and the issue of our knowledge of infinity. This, as Itard has noted, is visible in Pascal, who was probably influenced by Torricelli's cubature when he wrote: "Incomprehensible. All that is incomprehensible does not cease to be. The infinite number. An infinite space equal to a finite one."[79] Furthermore, one can reasonably assume that Torricelli's result was known to the group of Port-Royal, especially Arnauld, principally because the French apologetic literature of the 1670s seems to contain plane versions of the paradox: there exists an infinitely long figure with finite area. For example, the Père Pardies used the plane version of the paradox in his *Elemens de la Geometrie* (1671) to argue against the libertines that positive results about the measure of "asymptotic spaces" provide proof for the immateriality of the soul and the existence of God.[80]

Although Pardies' arguments are inconclusive, what is interesting is the explicit connection he drew between the geometrical result and our knowledge of infinity:

> These spaces have an extension which is *actually infinite* [my emphasis] and included between two lines which, being prolonged to infinity, never meet. . . . Nevertheless, one demonstrates that these spaces infinite in length are equal to a circle or to another determinate figure, so that infinity itself, immense and innumerable as it is, is reduced to calculation and to the measure of Geometry, and our spirit, even greater than infinity, is capable of comprehending [*comprendre*] it.[81]

Arnauld, on the other hand, exploited the same type of result in the direction of fideism. He explicitly held that, being finite, we cannot "conceive an infinite object but very imperfectly" and considered an indubitable and axiomatic truth that "it belongs to the nature of a finite mind that it cannot comprehend the infinite."[82] After giving the example of an infinitely long figure with a finite area, he concluded that, far from allowing us to advance towards an adequate idea of infinity, knowledge of this sort shows

> the true limits of our minds and makes us confess, whether we will or no, that there are things which exist although we are not able to comprehend them. Hence it is well for man to weary himself with this sort of subtleties in order to check his presumption, and take away from him the boldness which would lead him to oppose his feeble intelligence to the truths which the church proposes to him, under the pretext that he cannot understand them.[83]

It was just as Pascal had intimated. While Pardies emphasized the positive nature of our knowledge of spaces whose extension is actually infinite, Arnauld dwelled on our alleged inability to comprehend infinity by exploiting the paradoxical nature of those same results. However, in spite of the methodological contrast in the use of the quadratures of infinitely long figures, Pardies and Arnauld shared more than a common apologetic purpose. For, although in different degrees, both owed a good deal to the Cartesian tradition, and it is therefore not surprising that their views on our knowledge of infinity have their roots in the position of Descartes himself.

Descartes had a complex and perhaps ambiguous position on the knowledge of infinity. He constantly denied that we, as finite minds, can have a grasp of infinity, while against Hobbes and Gassendi, he strenuously defended the view that we have an understanding of it.[84] But his references to infinity were generally accompanied by warnings about the futility of our attempts to know it. For example, in 1641 he wrote to Mersenne: "I have never written about the infinite except to submit myself to it, and not to determine what it is or what it is not."[85] And in spite of having known of Torricelli's result since 1643, by the following year, when he published the *Principles*, he was still ready to declare:

> Since we are finite, it would be absurd for us to determine anything concerning the infinite; for this would be to attempt to limit it and grasp it. So we shall not bother to reply to those who ask if half an infinite line would itself be infinite, or whether an infinite number is odd or even, and so on.[86]

Nevertheless, in spite of his claims about infinity, Descartes used infinite series to solve one of Zeno's paradoxes (the Achilles) and employed indivisibles in some mathematical work.[87]

So, the denial of our capacity to grasp infinity led to the fideistic approach of Pascal and Arnauld. But at the same time, Descartes' unwavering insistence that we can understand infinity led to the sort of approach followed by Pardies. In this context, Leibniz's reaction is, as usual, instructive; His comments on *Principles* I, 26 are interestingly close to the views of Pardies.

> Even though we are finite, we can yet know many things about the infinite: for example, about asymptotic lines ... about spaces which are infinite in length but not greater in area than a given finite space, and about the sums of infinite series. Otherwise we should also know nothing with certainty about God. However, it is one thing to know something about a matter and another to comprehend the matter, that is, to have within our power all that is hidden in it.[88]

However, Leibniz did not share Pardies' astonishment about those results. For instance, in 1702 he criticized Bayle by telling Johann I. Bernoulli and de Volder:

> Let me add in passing that not only Cavalieri and Torricelli, of whom Gassendi spoke in the passage cited by Mr. Bayle, but also myself and many others have found figures of infinite length whose areas are finite.
>
> There is nothing more extraordinary about this than about infinite series, where we find that $\frac{1}{2} + \frac{1}{4} + \frac{1}{8} + \frac{1}{16} + \frac{1}{32} +$ etc. $= 1$.[89]

Leibniz's most extensive reaction on these results occurs in a scholium to proposition 11 of his *De Quadratura Arithmetica*. In that work he played down Pardies' enthusiasm and attempted a number of terminological clarifications about the infinite. Against Pardies' claim that infinitistic results provide a proof of the immateriality of the soul, Leibniz remarked that in the case of the infinitely long figures the operations required by the mind are not essentially different from those required for the measurement of finite figures.[90] According to Leibniz, the spirituality of the soul can be argued by simply distinguishing the nature of the soul from the nature of material things. There is nothing extraordinary in the measurement of infinite spaces, says Leibniz, because we make use of a certain fiction; we assume a line that is limited "terminata" and nonetheless infinite.[91]

The juxtaposition of limited and infinite as attribute of the same line might seem paradoxical. One would expect an infinite line also to be unlimited "interminata." However, according to Leibniz, there is as great a difference between the infinite "infinitum" and the unlimited "interminatum" as between the indivisible and the infinitely small "infinite parvum." He maintains that the geometry of indivisibles is liable to error if it is not interpreted in terms of the infinitely small. Points cannot be used as indivisibles. Only infinitely small lines can be used as indivisibles, but because they are lines they are still divisible. In the same way, Leibniz continues, the unlimited quantity differs from the infinite one. As much as the magnitude of the point cannot be the object of geometrical consideration, so cannot the magnitude of the unlimited line. And as it is impossible even for an infinite number of points to constitute or exhaust a limited line, it is just as well impossible for a limited line, however many times repeated, to constitute or exhaust an unlimited line. However, an infinite limited line is constituted by a multitude of finite lines, even if the collection of these lines exceeds every number. And as the infinite limited line is constituted by finite lines, so the finite line is constituted by infinitely small lines. In other words, as the infinitely small line is still divisible, and as such can be the object of geometrical measurement, so the infinite limited line can still be the object of addition, and thus multiplication. By contrast, the point and the unlimited line cannot be the subject of such measurement. Thus, one cannot say that the limited line is the medium between the point, or minimal line, and the unlimited or maximal line. However, one can say, with exactness, that the finite line is the medium between the infinitely small line and the infinite one. In this sense one can say of the hyperbola that the rectangle defined by the infinite line and the corresponding infinitely small abscissa is equal to a finite square. But it would be a mistake, as we have already seen in the explanation of the paradox of the hyperbola, to attempt to work with the unlimited line as ordinate and with the point as abscissa.

Finally, Leibniz introduces the definitions of unlimited "interminatum" and infinite: "Thus I call unlimited that in which no last point can be taken, if not on one side. But by infinite I understand a quantity either limited or unlimited greater than any quantity that can be assigned by us or that can be designated by numbers."[92] Leibniz distinguishes in the general category of the infinite two types of quantities, limited and unlimited. The unlimited quantities cannot be the object of measurement, but the limited quantities can.

In conclusion, how does Leibniz interpret the results about the measure of infinitely long figures? We have seen how Leibniz exploits them to argue that we know something about the infinite. But what kind of infinite? Leibniz claims that we are dealing with a limited infinite. In other passages he gives as an example of such an infinite a straight line with a point at infinity. It would then be interesting to know whether the limited infinite must necessarily be read as an actual infinite. This is a difficult question and, unfortunately, Leibniz does not address the issue directly. But I believe he has the resources to handle these results in terms of potential infinity. His remark that these results are not more surprising than the summation of an infinite series reveals in my opinion, an "analytical" point of view. When interpreting the infinitely long figures, there is a great difference between a geometrical viewpoint and an analytical viewpoint. A geometrical object must be given "all at once," as it were, and must be compared to another given "finite" figure. Analytical reasoning is backed by arithmetical or algebraic theory that allows one to measure the infinitely long figure "directly," by computing piecemeal the numerical value of the area or volume sought. This is exactly what we do nowadays when we solve the problem by means by the integral calculus. This operation can be read in terms of potential infinity. But it requires a different approach to geometry than that which influenced many seventeenth-century geometers. It is thus not surprising that the most interesting debate on Torricelli's infinitely long solid occurred between Hobbes and Wallis, who are almost paradigms for the geometrical and analytical modes of thought.

5.2.5   Thomas Hobbes and John Wallis

The most spirited and philosophically coherent discussion of Torricelli's solid was provided by Hobbes. It is difficult to determine when he was first exposed to Torricelli's result. We know that during his second stay in Paris in the 1640s he renewed his aquaintance with Mersenne and became good friends with Gassendi. Given the interest generated by Torricelli's result, Hobbes probably got wind of it then. However, Hobbes' explicit treatment of the hyperbolic solid occurred much later, in the course of the controversy with Wallis. The phases and various issues of this famous exhange are well known and need not be repeated here.[93] One of its central aspects, concerning the role of infinity in mathematics, does deserve a few lines.

Wallis was a brilliant and outspoken supporter of the new mathematics who suggested that geometry is subordinate to arithmetic and attempted to introduce bold infinitistic considerations in both. In the dedicatory epistle of his most famous work, appropriately entitled *Arithmetica Infinitorum* (1655b), he claimed that he was picking up where Cavalieri (whom he knew only through Torricelli's work) had left off.[94] In the course of the work, he studied infinite series by extending to them results obtained, often perilously, in finite series and he tried to apply the arithmetical results thus obtained to the solution of geometrical problems. As a consequence he dealt, with little in the way of explanation, with infinitely long figures and "proved" some theorems about them. He was therefore able to claim in the scholium to proposition 107, "that famous problem (indeed ingenious and much to be admired) which Torricelli exhibited in one solid figure (that is, construct a cylinder equal to the *Acute Hyperbolic Solid* continued to infinity), we have exhibited in other innumerable figures, both plane and solid."[95]

As much as Wallis was enthusiastically trying to legitimize infinity in mathematics, so much was Hobbes bent on repudiating it. Hobbes' views on infinity originate in his empiricist epistemology. He insisted that we have ideas only of what we sense or of what we can construct out of ideas so sensed; for example, we perceive horses and men, we form ideas of them, and therefore we can conceive a centaur by compounding them.[96] Since the ideas we obtain directly from experience are of finite things, and repeated composition of such ideas cannot produce the idea of an infinite thing, Hobbes claimed that anything we conceive of must have a finite magnitude.[97] Consequently, when we says that something is infinite, all we can justifiably mean is that "we are not able to conceive the ends, and bounds of the thing named; having no conception of the thing, but of our own inability."[98]

Since one of the main sources of error is the use of names for which we have no corresponding conception, it is not surprising that any consideration of infinity, both geometrical and arithmetical, ought to be banished.[99] Hobbes claimed that when mathematicians use the word "infinite," what they usually mean, or ought to mean, is "indefinite," that is, as great, or small, as one pleases.[100] A mathematician who says, "Let a line be extended to infinity," should not be understood as holding that such an operation could be carried out, but rather as allowing the reader to extend the line as long as he pleases.[101] One might object, as Wallis did, that considering an infinite line does not entail extending it, since by hypothesis, such a line cannot be extended by us but merely supposing it extended, and consequently that Hobbes' attack misses the mark.[102] However, such an objection would be unfair, for from Hobbes' standpoint, to suppose an infinite line as given would be begging the question because the only way to gain a conception of an infinite line would be to extend it. Hence, actual infinity being ruled out, in Hobbes' mathematical universe, every figure at every stage of production is finite. Consequently, to talk about a solid

> whose sides are extended out to infinity is absurd. In fact, something is not called a chair before it is finished [*perficitur*]; so neither is something called a space before it is finished. But what is infinite is neither finished, nor can it be finished.[103]

Thus were the battle lines clearly drawn. In 1671 Hobbes wrote three letters to the Royal Society in which he attacked Wallis' contention that there are geometric figures of finite area or volume having no center of gravity. He strongly suggested that, in order to see the falsity of this claim, one needed neither skill in geometry nor knowledge of logic, but merely the common understanding possessed by all humans.[104] As usual, Wallis' reply was quick and caustic; in the same year he commented in the *Philosophical Transactions*:

> A surface, or solid, may be *supposed* so constituted, as to be *Infinitely Long*, but Finitely Great, (the Breadth Continually Decreasing in greater proportion than the Length increaseth) and so as to have no *Center of Gravity*. Such is Torricellio's *Solidum Hyperbolicum acutum*; and others innumerable, discovered by Dr. *Wallis*, Monsieur *Fermat*, and others. But to determine this, requires more *Geometry and Logic* than Mr. Hobs is Master of.[105]

Wallis' reference to Torricelli clearly caught Hobbes by surprise. In his reply he claimed: "I do not remember this of Torricellio, and I think Dr. Wallis does him wrong and Monsieur Fermat too. For, to understand this for sense, it is not required that a man should be a geometrician or a logician, but that he should be mad."[106] Such an answer was hardly satisfying. It looked more like a confession of ignorance than a proper reply to Wallis' sarcasm, and consciousness of the inadequacy of the reply may be what led Hobbes to the rather extensive treatment of Torricelli's solid in his last book-length mathematical work *Principia Et Problemata Aliquot Geometrica Ante Desperata Nunc Breviter Explicata Et Demonstrata*, published in 1672.

In the last chapter of that work, "On Infinity," Hobbes explained that the proper nonmathematical notion of infinity involves the idea of a being greater than any assignable measure.[107] For example, an infinite space would be one that cannot be included by boundaries.

> But it has been demonstrated, they say, by Torricelli that a certain acute hyperbolic solid, in this sense of *infinite*, is equal to a cylinder whose basis has a diameter equal to half the base of the hyperbola and whose height is equal to the latus transversum of the hyperbola [*sic*]. I have read the demonstration of this problem quite often and with attention and have found no paralogism. However, I have found that the distance which Torricelli supposes *infinite* is to be understood as *indefinite*. Nor could it be understood differently by him, who in quite many demonstrations uses Cavalieri's principle of *indivisibles*, which are such that their aggregate can be equated to whatsoever given magnitude. Therefore, a proposition as absurd as this *that the infinite is equal to the finite*, must not be attributed to Torricelli. In fact, as it is clear by the natural light, there cannot be a solid so subtle which does not infinitely exceed every finite solid.[108]

This long passage shows the paradoxical power of Torricelli's result and how the bizarre properties of his solid represent a clear embarassment for Hobbes' position on several counts. The theorem, as Torricelli himself proudly pointed out, is about an apparently infinitely long solid, bitter medicine for Hobbes, who viewed any consideration of infinity in mathematics as wholly pernicious. Moreover, the result was obtained geometrically, both by indivisibles and by exhaustion, according to a demonstrative methodology far removed from what Hobbes considered, not without justification, Wallis' rather cavalier use of infinity and algebraic manipulations. In other words, Torricelli had extended the realm of geometry well beyond the finitistic territory Hobbes was ready to grant it, by employing methods that Hobbes himself could not but accept. Furthermore, Hobbes believed that natural light teaches us that an infinitely long solid, however subtle, must exceed in volume any finite solid. Nor is the reference to natural light merely occasional or at the periphery of Hobbes' mathematical views, for it was his considered opinion that the principles of knowledge include all the propositions known by natural light and that all the principles of mathematics are known to be true by natural light.[109] Since an infinitely long solid must have an infinite volume, he could conclude that interpreting Torricelli's result as saying what it seems to say entails the absurdity that the infinite is equal to the finite. No wonder, then, that he read the demonstration "quite often and with attention," perhaps in the vain hope of finding an error.

But the proof is correct, and the only avenue left open for Hobbes was to try to understand Torricelli's result not as dealing with an infinitely long solid, but with an indefinitely long one, and consequently to reinterpret the theorem in finitistic terms. It is unfortunate that Hobbes did not explain how the finitistic reading of the result is supposed to go, but presumably what he had in mind is this. The hyperbolic solid, viewed as indefinitely long, can be elongated as much as one pleases and, consequently, its volume can be made to differ from that of the cylinder by less than any given quantity. This is certainly true but is hardly satisfactory, for each of the successive hyperbolic solids thus generated is finitely long but not equal in volume to the cylinder. Of course, one could construct an infinite succession of volumes of such solids and claim, by a limit process, that the succession converges to the volume of the cylinder. However, attributing such a view to Hobbes would not only be historically inaccurate, because it would involve forcing on him our own mathematical notions, but would also foist on him conclusions he would hardly tolerate. In fact, although Hobbes would certainly accept the hyperbolic solids whose volumes are elements of the succession, he would have to reject the passage to the limit, since the limit of the succession does not belong to the succession itself, and in order to be equal to the volume of the cylinder, the limit must be equal to the volume of an actually infinitely long solid. In sum, Torricelli's result is boldly infinitistic, and Hobbes' attempts at reducing it to a finitistic framework appear destined to fail.

Not only did Hobbes claim that Torricelli's theorem should be given a finitistic reading; he also claimed that Torricelli himself, who used Cavalieri's methods, must, or should, have understood it so. This is a strange claim indeed. Torricelli certainly interpreted his result in infinitistic terms; furthermore, Cavalieri too, perhaps spurred by Torricelli's cubature, proved by indivisibles that a certain solid of infinite length has finite volume. However, Hobbes' views on Cavalieri's indivisibles may help to dispel some of the bafflement.

In accordance with his empiricist beliefs, Hobbes held that a mathematical line is a body of which we consider only the length and that the very notion of a line without breadth is inconceivable and deleteriously used in geometry.[110] As a consequence, limiting our attention to planes, he considered their indivisibles not as segments, but as very minute parallelograms.[111] Furthermore, given his denial of infinity, he viewed them not as infinitely small (the result of infinite division), but merely as undivided.[112] Since indivisibles are neither one-dimensional nor infinitesimals if added together or multiplied by a finite number, they can exceed any surface.[113] Hobbes views Cavalieri's indivisibles as Archimedean quantities that have a ratio to a given (finite) surface, according to the Eudoxian definition in Euclid's *Elements*.[114] Presumably, mutatis mutandis, the same is true of indivisibles of solid figures, which he must have viewed as very thin solids.[115]

But then, since natural light teaches us that an infinitely long solid cannot have a finite volume, the indivisibles composing it (all of them finite) could not have a Eudoxian ratio to it. Hence Torricelli must, or should, have viewed his solid not as infinitely long, but merely as indefinitely long. Of course, there is a sense in which the argument we have attributed to Hobbes begs the question, since it assumes what Wallis and Torricelli rejected, namely, that an infinitely long solid must have an infinite volume. But Hobbes' assumption is not an unreasonable one, and he can hardly be faulted for adhering to it.

Hobbes' ill repute as a mathematician is even greater than his good repute as a political philosopher; in politics he is held as a genius of the first order, but in mathematics as an ungifted and presumptuous dilettante. There is some truth in this severe judgment. His contributions to mathematical discoveries are limited at best, and his mistakes, which were many, are far from interesting or inspiring. Even his mathematical analysis of Torricelli's cubature is finally ill conceived and fails to do justice to the striking originality of the theorem. However, Hobbes was sufficiently philosophically alert to grapple with issues, such as those arising from Torricelli's result, which were at the forefront of contemporary mathematical debate and come to grips with advanced problems and methods. He saw that Torricelli's cubature could be used to provide support for Wallis' new brand of modern mathematics, a mathematics, he thought, that would lead into the quagmire of infinity, and finally undermine the certainty of geometry, "the only Science it hath pleased God hitherto to bestow on mankind."[116]

5.2.6 Conclusion

The philosophical fortune of Torricelli's result in the third quarter of the seventeenth century revolved around three main themes: our knowledge of infinity, the position of geometry in the web of knowledge, and the ontological status of mathematical objects. Torricelli's hyperbolic solid was the first of a flurry of geometric figures, infinite in one or even two dimensions, that were found and studied by early modern mathematicians. It stretched the intuitive universe of geometrical figures—the background of the seventeenth-century geometer—and consequently it generated problems for views that too tightly connected geometrical and material existence.

Torricelli's cubature of an infinitely long solid called into question traditional philosophical assumptions about infinity, and in so doing it forcefully highlighted the issue of the role of "natural light" in mathematics. Torricelli's result was not the only one to play such a part, but it was the first of its kind. Moreover, it did so not only by employing heuristic or, at least, questionable methods such as indivisibles or Wallisian infinite series, but by using demonstrative procedures that could hardly be rejected.

Finally, the acute hyperbolic solid was the first idea to call into question the empiricist notion of infinity, typified by Hobbes and Gassendi. Further doubts became evident later in the seventeenth century with the work of Locke. After lengthily adopting the empiricist view that we have a negative idea of infinity, his *Essay* concludes with a brief admission that mathematicians might have other ways of obtaining ideas of infinity.[117] Locke effectively intimates that his account does not correspond to the mathematical treatment of infinity. And Torricelli's result appears to deserve a place not only in the history of seventeenth-century mathematics, but also in the history of seventeenth-century philosophy.

6

Leibniz's Differential Calculus and Its Opponents

Of all the mathematical advances of the seventeenth century, the discovery of the calculus is perhaps the most impressive.[1] The techniques of the calculus enabled mathematicians to bridge two of the main areas of mathematical research: the determination of tangents and the computation of areas and volumes. The former is the object of the differential calculus and the latter of the integral calculus. The birth of the calculus coincides with the realization that the problems of determination of tangents and of computation of areas are inverses of each other. Most historians of mathematics agree in assigning to Newton and Leibniz the discovery of this fact.

Everyone has heard something about the fierce priority dispute that surrounded the paternity of the calculus in the early eighteenth century between Newton, Leibniz, and their followers.[2] Today it is generally recognized that the two scholars arrived independently at the discovery of the calculus but that Leibniz published his results first in his 1684 "Nova Methodus pro Maximis et Minimis." Given Newton's slowness in publishing his results, it turns out that the foundational debates on the calculus in the latter part of the seventeenth century are mainly debates centered on the Leibnizian calculus. I should immediately qualify this judgement by noting that in *Principia* (1687) Newton had exposed a method of prime and last ratios that provides in classical garb some results related to the calculus. However, one finds only some sporadic mention of Newton in the foundational debates on the calculus until the first decade of the eighteenth century. Consequently, in this chapter I will only treat of the Leibnizian calculus and the debates that the problem of its foundations gave rise to. The time limit I set to myself is 1705, a date that marks the complete victory of the infinitesimal calculus on the Continent.

The criticism to the Newtonian and Leibnizian calculus raised by Bishop Berkeley in the *Analyst* (1734) are well known.[3] What is less known is that the discussion about the Leibnizian calculus had been raging already four decades before. Moreover, whereas most of the literature in this area concentrates on Leibniz's own attempts to justify his calculus, little attention has been given to the context in which Leibniz operated. The goal of this chapter is to provide an overview of the foundational debates surrounding the Leibnizian calculus. There were three independent sets of debates that involved the foundations of the new Leibnizian analysis. The earliest is the exchange with Clüver; the second is the debate with Nieuwentijt; and the third is the debate within the Paris Academy of Sciences.

I will begin by giving the necessary technical background, and then I will move on to enumerate the main points of the foundational discussions surrounding the calculus in the latter part of the seventeenth century.

6.1   Leibniz's *Nova Methodus* and L'Hôpital's *Analyse des Infiniment Petits*

The 1684 issue of the *Acta Eruditorum* published a short essay by Leibniz entitled "Nova methodus pro maximis et minimis, itemque tangentibus, quae nec fractas nec irrationales quantitates moratur et singulare pro illis calculi genus."[4] This essay represents the official birth of the differential calculus. As the title promised, Leibniz's article contained a new method for the determination of maxima, minima, and tangents together with an associated calculus. The title of this paper also emphasizes the advantage of the new method which, unlike Descartes' or Hudde's, is not severely limited by the presence of fractional or irrational expressions.[5] The paper is remarkable for the paucity of explanations given by Leibniz. He begins by explaining the notion of differential (denoted by d) and then gives, without proof, the rules for the differential of a constant, of sums, differences, products, and quotients.[6] Later on he introduces the rules for the differential of powers and roots. There follow various sorts of applications to, among other things, problems of maxima, minima, tangents, and inverse tangent problems, which exemplify the use and power of the new calculus. Even Johann and Jakob Bernoulli, who acquainted themselves with the new calculus in the years 1687–90, found the article quite difficult to understand. Leibniz does not explain how he arrived at his equations and leaves the reader totally in the dark as to the heuristics and formal proofs of the results therein presented. The paper was also marred by several typos.

In order to gain an easier access to the Leibnizian calculus, it is perhaps then a good idea to turn to the first textbook, the *Analyse des infiniment petits* (1696) by Guillaume de L'Hôpital.[7] We will then be able to go back to the central intuitions lying behind the Leibnizian algorithm. L'Hôpital's text will also be instrumental for the later sections. His first two definitions characterized the basic primitives of the theory:

DEFINITION I. *Variable quantities are those that continually increase or decrease; and constant or standing quantities, are those that continue the same while others vary.*

DEFINITION II. *The infinitely small part whereby a variable quantity is continually increased or decreased, is called the differential of that quantity.*[8]

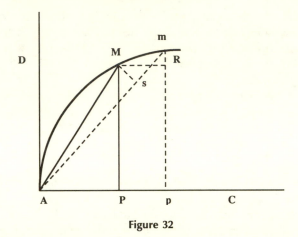

Figure 32

As an example of the first definition consider $y = ax^2$. The parameter a is a constant but the coordinates x and y of the parabola are variable quantities. As an illustration of the second definition, L'Hôpital gave the diagram in Figure 32 (Figs. 32 to 34 are taken from L'Hôpital 1696, 24). Thus, for example, Pp is the differential of AP and Rm the differential of PM and so on. Furthermore the notational convention d is introduced to denote differentials. For example, if AP = x then Pp = dx.

Before I introduce the postulates, I think two remarks are appropriate. Note that definition I presupposes as a primitive of the theory the notion of a continually increasing or decreasing quantity. A constant quantity is merely a specific case of the latter; it is in fact a variable for which the differential is zero. Moreover, definition II postulates dx as an infinitely small quantity. But note that L'Hôpital gave a diagram in which dx must always be represented as a finite increment. As we shall see, the pictorial representation left many in doubt. The postulates of the work were:

POSTULATE I. *Grant that two quantities, whose difference is an infinitely small quantity, may be taken (or used) indifferently for each other: or (which is the same thing) that a quantity, which is increased or decreased only by an infinitely small quantity, may be considered as remaining the same.*

Thus, postulate I says that $x + dx = x$.

POSTULATE II. *Grant that a curve line may be considered as the assemblage of an infinite number of infinitely small right lines: or (which is the same thing) as a polygon of an infinite number of sides, each of an infinitely small length, which determine the curvature of the line by the angles they make with each other (See Fig. 33).*[9]

With respect to the Cartesian tradition, the two postulates of L'Hôpital represented a concept-stretching; he stretched both the notion of equality,

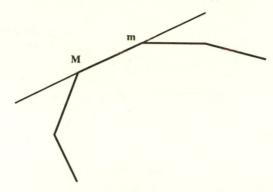

Figure 33

considered now as a relation between two quantities that differ by an infinitely small quantity, and the notion of polygon, extended now to encompass curves.

In 1684 Leibniz had presented without justification the following rules for the calculus:

If a constant, then $da = 0$ and $d(ax) = a\,dx$.

If $v = y$, then $dv = dy$.

If $v = z - y + w + x$, then $dv = d(z - y + w + x) = dz - dy + dw + dx$.

If $y = xv$, then $dy = d(xv) = x\,dv + v\,dx$.

If $z = v/y$, $dz = d(v/y) = [-v\,dy + y\,dv]/yy$.

If $z = x^a$, then $dz = d(x^a) = ax^{a-1}dx$.

If $z = \sqrt[b]{x^a}$, then $dz = d(\sqrt[b]{x^a}) = a/b \cdot dx\sqrt[b]{x^{a-b}}$.

The examples that follow give an idea of the formal manipulations that L'Hôpital's postulates allowed. To compute the differential of a product xy, L'Hôpital wrote:

$$d(xy) = (x + dx)(y + dy) - xy$$
$$= y\,dx + x\,dy + dx\,dy$$
$$= y\,dx + x\,dy,$$

since by postulate I it follows that $dx\,dy$ is of a lower order of magnitude than $y\,dx$ and $x\,dy$.

Let us now see how postulate II is used to compute the length of the subtangent for the parabola. Let $ax = y^2$ be the equation of the parabola (see Fig. 34). The problem of constructing the tangent is equivalent to the problem of finding the subtangent TP. Given postulate II, we can set the following

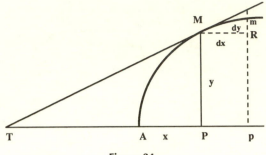

Figure 34

proportion: dy: dx = MP: PT. Hence dy: dx = y: PT. It follows that PT = $y\,dx/dy$. We now use the differential equation for the parabola whose derivation makes use of axiom I: $a\,dx = 2y\,dy$. This yields $dx = 2y\,dy/a$. Using the last equality and substituting in the equation for PT we get PT = $2y^2/a$, and since $y^2 = ax$ it follows that PT = $2x$, which is the length of the subtangent.

L'Hôpital's approach highlights two of the most central ideas of the new calculus. The first, and most central, is to consider a curve as an infinitary polygon. Leibniz often emphasized that this was the key to understanding his calculus. The second is the use of the differential triangle mRM (see Fig. 32). Although Leibniz acknowledges to have found it used in Pascal, it is fair to say that he saw the incredible heuristic potential lying behind its use.

So far I have only spoken of the differential calculus. In 1686 Leibniz published "De geometria recondita et analysi indivisibilium atque infinitorum" an article that gives the foundations of the Leibnizian approach to the integral calculus. As I already mentioned, the central idea of the calculus is that the processes of differentiation and integration are, *grosso modo*, inverses of each other; or, more geometrically, that the determination of tangents to a given curve and the computation of the area between the axis and the curve are inverse problems. Leibniz said explicitly that inspiration for this fundamental discovery came to him by studying differences and sums of number sequences.[10] A simple example will clarify Leibniz's course of thoughts. Consider a finite sequence $a_1, a_2, \ldots, a_n, a_{n+1}$. From this sequence we can construct a new sequence $b_1 = a_1 - a_2$, $b_2 = a_2 - a_3, \ldots b_n = a_n - a_{n+1}$. We can sum the b_i's $(i < n)$ and obtain $b_1 + b_2 + \cdots + b_n = a_1 - a_{n+1}$. Leibniz extrapolates these properties of finite sequences to the infinite. For instance, in 1672 Leibniz managed to sum the series $\frac{1}{1} + \frac{1}{3} + \frac{1}{6} + \frac{1}{10} + \frac{1}{15} \ldots$ by noticing that each term of the sequence,

$$\frac{2}{t(t+1)}$$

for $t > 0$, can be rewritten as a difference,

$$\frac{2}{t} - \frac{2}{t+1}.$$

In the case of a finite sum up to n we have

$$\sum_{t=1}^{n} \frac{2}{t(t+1)} = 2 - \frac{2}{n+1}.$$

If we now extrapolate to the infinite as n grows $2/(n+1)$ becomes infinitely small or null. Thus, the sum is equal to 2. When considered in a geometrical context, these ideas explain how Leibniz sees areas and tangents as inverse problems.

Consider the curve given in Figure 35. We can approximate the area between the curve and the axis by fixing on the axis a sequence of equidistant abscissae, say $x_0, x_1, \ldots, x_{n+1}$, and such that $x_{i+1} - x_i = b$ for a constant b. Corresponding to each abscissa we will have ordinates $y_0, y_1, \ldots, y_{n+1}$. In general the difference of the ordinates will not be constant, and each $y_{i+1} - y_i$ approximates for us the slope of the tangent to the curve between y_i and y_{i+1}. Of course, the smaller the b the better the approximation to the area of the curve, given by the sum $b \cdot \sum y_i (0 < i \le n + 1)$, and to the slope. Extrapolating to the infinite, Leibniz was able to conclude that if b be taken infinitely small then the determination of areas and tangents of the curve in question would have been obtained without error. So b is nothing else than the Leibnizian dx. When dx is infinitely small, the problem of quadrature equates to finding the sum of the ordinates; the problem of finding the tangent equates to finding their difference. Leibniz conjectured that, in analogy with the numerical sequences, problems of integration (determination of areas) and differentiation (tangents) would turn out to be inverses of each other. As is well known, Leibniz used the symbol $\int$ for denoting the integral, a shorthand for *summa* that betrays its origin in the theory of indivisibles.[11] We will seldom need to refer to the integral calculus.

Let us for the moment concentrate on the central notions of differential calculus, and in the first place the notion of differential itself. In 1684 Leibniz explains the concept without any reference to infinitely small quantities. He introduces dx as a fixed finite segment, so dy is a segment satisfying the equation

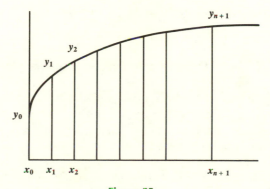

Figure 35

$dy: dx = y: MT$ (see Fig. 34). Leibniz seems to have avoided on purpose the appeal to infinitely small quantities in order to avoid possible foundational objections. As Bos has remarked, this way of introducing the differential was anomalous. In most other articles, Leibniz introduced differentials directly as infinitely small quantities. This oscillation certainly contributed to great confusion and, indeed, the notion of differential was at the center of the foundational discussions concerning the new calculus. However, infinitesimal quantities were not completely absent, even in this article. His definition of tangent appeals to an infinitely small distance and to the notion of a curve as an infinilateral polygon.

> We have to keep in mind that to find a tangent means to draw a line that connects two points of the curve at an infinitely small distance, or the continued side of a polygon with an infinite number of angles, which for us takes the place of a curve.[12]

This is not the place to study the intricacies of the Leibnizian calculus. But concerning the complex issue of the progression of variables,[13] we have already remarked that, when thinking of the curve as an infinitary polygon, we also think of the abscissae as lying infinitely close to one another. The variable x is then intended to range over progressions of abscissae. This progression might be constant (as in our earlier example) but it might instead be more useful to fix another progression as being constant, for example, the ordinates. Bos (1974) has amply demonstrated that (a) this indeterminacy was productive and instrumental for the development of the calculus; and (b) that in some cases the results of the differential calculus are independent of the progression selected (for example, all the differential rules given in Leibniz 1684). What is relevant here is to remark that dx is also a variable, a variable that ranges over differences. Thus we can apply to it the operator d to obtain ddx, a variable that ranges over differences of differences. And in general for any $d^n x$ we can reapply the operator d to obtain $d^{n+1} x = dd^n x$. These are the so called nth order differentials. When dx is constant—when the abscissae lie equally apart—then ddx will be zero. But dx need not be constant, and this shows that it is in essence a variable to which the differential operator d might be applied. This completes the technical details required for this chapter.

6.2 Early Debates with Clüver and Nieuwentijt

After the publications of Leibniz (1684, 1686) the Bernoulli brothers and other mathematicians made themselves familiar with the techniques of the calculus and began to extend its range.[14] The following years witnessed an ever growing elaboration of its techniques and applications. A little later the first objections to the new algorithm were raised. Leibniz mentioned Clüver and Nieuwentijt as the earliest opponents to his calculus. Writing to Varignon in 1702 he said:

I ... think that in order solidly to establish the foundations of sciences it is very important that there be such critics; it is in this way that the Skeptics fought the principles of geometry with much reason; that Father Gottignes, a learned Jesuit, wanted to provide better foundations for Algebra, and that Clüver and Nieuwentijt have recently fought, although in different ways, our infinitesimal Analysis ... we must not regret the effort which is needed to justify our Analysis against all kinds of persons capable of understanding it.[15]

Dethleff Clüver's criticisms of the calculus[16] appeared in an obscure paper entitled "Monitum ad Geometras" published in the *Acta Eruditorum* of 1687. His earlier paper "Quadratura circuli infinitis modis demonstrata" (1686) had announced a forthcoming work on a method of "similar infinities." This announcement had aroused the interest of Leibniz and Jakob Bernoulli, who thought there might be something very interesting hidden behind Clüver's promise. But the 1687 paper did not fulfill this promise, although it gave a general criticism of classical quadratures, presented as a consequence of his new method of similar infinities. Clüver claimed that all mathematicians since Archimedes had been wrong about the quadratures of the parabola and other curves.

All the squaring procedures usually followed go against the first law of homogeneous quantities when they assume [the existence of] elements of things as small as one chooses and [the existence of] very small quantities [*quantillae*].[17]

Moreover, he also attacked more specifically the assumption used in the summation of series followed by the new analysts, claiming they

suppose at each step two chimerical principles which have not been demonstrated by anyone. First, that there is a last term in an infinite series; second, that because of the continuously increasing smallness this term is a non-quantity [*non-quantum*], that is, a non-entity or nothing [*non-ens aut nihil*].[18]

This is all that could be found in print of Clüver's criticisms of the calculus. In the first quote Clüver criticizes the use of infinitely small quantities as used in the Leibnizian calculus. Although there was an extensive correspondence between Leibniz, Jakob Bernoulli, and Clüver on the issues raised by Clüver in his 1687 paper, it was only in 1700 that Jakob Hermann devoted a few sections of his essay against Nieuwentijt *Responsio ad considerationes secundas Cl. Viri Bern. Nieuwentiit* to dispose of Clüver's objections in print. The discussion of Clüver's objection occurs in chapter VI, in the scholium to proposition I. From Hermann's discussion it becomes clear why Clüver's claim about the summation of infinitely decreasing series could be seen as a criticism of the Leibnizian calculus. After having shown in proposition 1 that $y + dy$ can be taken as equal to y, Hermann continued:

From this proposition depend the rules for the investigation of the sum of an infinitely decreasing geometrical series. In fact, the sum of every geometrical progression is found by dividing the product obtained from the multiplication of the difference between the first and the last term times the first term, by the difference between the first and the second term and then adding the last term to this quotient. Consequently, the sum of an infinitely decreasing series is equal to the square of the first term divided by the difference between the first and the second term. This derives from the fact that the difference between the first and the last term is the same as the first term because we suppose the last term to be that which is inassignable with respect to the first term of the series. This rule is recognized by all geometers, with the single exception of Clüver, as legitimate.[19]

The following should clarify Hermann's rules. Consider the finite geometric series $t_1, t_2, \ldots, t_n$. Hermann's first rule holds that the sum s_n is obtainable by the following computation: $s_n = \{[(t_1 - t_n) \cdot t_1]/(t_1 - t_2)\} + t_n$. Hermann's second rule can now be easily understood from the first by noting that when t_n decreases indefinitely, one obtains $s_n = t_1^2/(t_1 - t_2)$. Moreover, Hermann clarifies that one does not assume, as Clüver claimed, a "last" t_n but simply operates with a t_n whose size "is inassignable with respect to the first term of the series."[20] We will come back to the centrality of the notion of inassignable or incomparable in the context of the Leibnizian calculus.

Hermann also addressed the issue of the quadrature of the parabola and other curves raised by Clüver. Contrary to most geometers Clüver had claimed that the ratio of the area contained between a segment of a parabola and the circumscribed parallelogram is not as that of 1 to 2 but rather as $(2N^2 + 1)$ to $(4N^2 - 1)$, where "N is a number of similar infinities [*infinitorum similium*] out of which the parabola is constituted."[21] Whereas the Leibnizians would have claimed that the expression, under the assumption of N infinite, was actually equal to $\frac{1}{2}$, Clüver refused the assumption that would allow such a conclusion—that $1/N$ or $1/N^2$ for N infinite can be treated as being zero. Indeed, this might be seen as Clüver's central objection to Leibniz's calculus. In a letter to Leibniz in 1694, Clüver expressed this as follows:

> Allow me the freedom to express my opinion: I think that your method in the differential calculus is not sufficient to obtain the ultimate precision in Geometry. The source of every imperfection is that you take the ratio between the unity and an infinite number to be equal to nothing, i.e. $1/N = 0$, which is ... an impossible supposition.[22]

There is no need to follow here in detail the exchange between Leibniz, Bernoulli, and Clüver. It should only be emphasized that Clüver's criticisms concentrated upon the notion of the elimination of differentials. For Clüver this implied they were treated as zero; the Leibnizians insisted on the notion of incomparability.

The debate with Clüver turned out to be rather unsatisfactory. Although Leibniz and Jakob Bernoulli had put great effort in trying to open a dialogue, it also turned out that Clüver simply did not have the technical skills and intellectual honesty required for such an exchange. A much more interesting discussion was that occasioned by the criticisms of the calculus brought forth by the Dutch theologian, Bernard Nieuwentijt.[23] Let us fix the chronology of the debate. In 1694 Nieuwentijt published a booklet entitled *Considerationes circa analyseos ad quantitates infinite parvas applicatae principia, et calculi differentialis usum in resolvendis problematibus geometricis.* This essay forced Leibniz to answer in an article published in the *Acta Eruditorum* in 1695. In 1696 Nieuwentijt replied with the *Considerationes secundae*, and finally in 1700 Hermann replied for the Leibnizian camp with the *Responsio ad Clariβimi Viri Bernh. Nieuwentiit Considerationes Secundas.*

Nieuwentijt's point of view on the Leibnizian calculus was dictated by his previous mathematical work, which aimed to bring order in the area of late seventeenth-century infinitesimal analysis. This mathematical work is embodied in the *Analysis Infinitorum*, published in 1695 but written over a number of years as an introduction to the area of infinitesimal analysis. As Vermij has remarked, the context of the text bears witness to the fact that it was written for the most part without knowledge of the Leibnizian calculus, a discussion of which appears only in the late chapters of the book. It is there we must look to find out from which standpoint stem the objections of Nieuwentijt to the Leibnizian algorithm.

The work opens in Euclidian manner with a number of definitions and axioms. Nieuwentijt calls a quantity infinitesimal when it is smaller than any arbitrarily given (i.e., finite) quantity, and infinite when its is greater than any arbitrarily given quantity. According to its central axiom, anything that when multiplied, however many times, cannot equal another given quantity, however small, cannot be considered a quantity—geometrically it is a mere nothing.[24] The second axiom states that any arbitrarily given (i.e., finite) quantity can be divided in arbitrarily many equal or unequal parts less than any given quantity. In a number of subsequent *lemmata* it becomes clear that the class of quantities is partioned in given quantities, infinitesimals, and infinite quantities (lemma 1). And since to every quantity corresponds a number, we have the same partition in the field of numbers (lemma 2). Thus, any given quantity is divisible by an arbitrary number (lemma 3). The division of a given quantity b by an infinite number m gives rise to an infinitesimal quantity (lemma 6). Of great importance is lemma 10, which represents the main peculiarity of Nieuwentijt's approach. If one considers b/m and multiplies it by itself or by another infinitesimal quantity c/m then the product bb/mm or bc/mm is zero or nothing.[25] This follows from axiom 1. If we multiply any of the two quantities by m (the largest possible number) then we obtain bb/m or bc/m which is still an infinitesimal—it cannot be equal to any given (finite) quantity. Therefore bb/mm and bc/mm must be equal to zero. In further lemmata (culminating in lemma 25) Nieuwentijt "proves" that, for an infinitesimal increment of the abscissa, the hypotenuse of the differential triangle coincides with the segment of the curve between x and $x + e$, that is, a curve is really an infinilateral polygon.

On the basis of the above results, Nieuwentijt had been able to make some sense of a number of infinitesimal procedures that called for the elimination of quantities involving products of infinitesimal quantities. Consider the determination of the subtangent to the parabola (see Fig. 34). Let e denote an infinitesimal increment ($e = b/m$ for some finite b and m infinite) on the axis of the abscissae and TP the subtangent. Let the increment of the ordinates correspond to the point $x + e$ be y^*. Then, the triangles TPM and the infinitesimal triangle mRM are similar and hence y^*: $e = y$: PT. Thus, $y^* = ey/\text{PT}$. Now the point $(x + e, y + y^*)$ must satisfy the original equation. So $x + e = (y + y^*)^2 = y^2 + 2y^*y + y^{*2}$. Since y^* is an infinitesimal $y^{*2} = 0$, by lemma 10, and thus subtracting the original equation we obtain $e = 2y^*y$ in terms of which we can write $y^* = e/2y$. Notice that the elimination of y^{*2} is justified by the explicit postulation of $y^{*2} = 0$ and not, as in the Leibnizian calculus, by the fact that y^{*2} is incomparably small in comparison with $2y^*y$. Now, from the above, PT $= ey/y^*$ and therefore PT $= ey/(e/2y) = 2y^2$. But $x = y^2$ and thus PT $= 2x$.

Let us stress some of the differences between Nieuwentijt and Leibniz. Nieuwentijt holds there is an infinite number m; the infinitesimals are generated dividing a finite number by m. Moreover, m is the largest number. Leibniz always held that the existence of a largest number is contradictory.[26] Nieuwentijt's notion of infinitesimal b/m is that of an infinitesimal constant, whereas we have seen how the Leibnizian dx is a variable that ranges over progressions of abscissae. Thus, whereas we can apply the operator d to the variable dx, there is no correspondent notion in Nieuwentijt's system. Finally, b/m cannot be eliminated from the computations because it differs from zero, but the Leibnizian dx's can be eliminated when they are infinitely small with respect to the other terms of the equation. Conversely, squares of infinitesimals are always to be considered equal to zero in Nieuwentijt's system, but this is not generally the case with the Leibnizian algorithm. We are now well placed to understand the exchange between Nieuwentijt and Leibniz.

In the *Considerationes* (1694) Nieuwentijt proposed a foundational analysis of some of the major infinitesimalist methods of the later seventeenth century, those of Barrow, Newton, and Leibniz. I will concentrate on his criticism of the Leibnizian differential calculus. Nieuwentijt begins by giving a number of lemmas proper to the Leibnizian calculus, obtained from several articles by Leibniz and Johann Bernoulli. He then claimed that from these principles one can obtain a contradiction—curves behave like straight lines. Leibniz's answer to the "paradox" will show that Nieuwentijt had made a simple mistake in applying a rule by Bernoulli, and thus I will omit the example. However, I will discuss later an improved form of the "paradox" which appeared in the *Considerationes secundae*.

Besides its initial objection, Leibniz rightly individuated three main points in Nieuwentijt's attack. The first is that the differential calculus, as well as Barrow's and Newton's methods, commits a mistake in treating infinitely small quantities as zero. Second, Leibniz's calculus cannot be applied to exponential functions, say functions of the form $x = y^z$. Finally, although Nieuwentijt accepts first-order differentials, he rejects higher-order differentials. Whereas the second challenge is simply a technical one, the first and the third objections are dictated to Nieuwentijt by the obvious inconsistency between those principles and the principles at the basis of his *Analysis Infinitorum*.

Leibniz's answer to the first objection shows the deep conflict between the two mathematical systems. Whereas Nieuwentijt starts with the assumption that two quantities are equal if their difference is zero, Leibniz claims that two quantities are equal not only when their difference is absolutely zero, but also when their difference is incomparably small with respect to those quantities of which it is the difference. Thus, infinitesimal quantities have no ratio in the Euclidian sense to finite quantities. Although in practice it is always more direct to operate with the elimination of infinitesimal quantities, one can always use an Archimedean reductio ad absurdum to prove the validity of the claims so obtained. We see here stated one of the major strategies used by Leibniz for the foundation of the infinitesimal calculus, a reduction to the reductio ad absurdum of the ancients. We are already familiar with this strategy from chapter 5. Leibniz then adds a remark concerning his principle of equality in order to anticipate a possible objection. His definition of equality should be upheld because it has proved its mettle by providing all the results that are delivered by the other method (i.e., by exhaustion), which is only apparently more rigorous. Here we can see a sort of inductive justification of the calculus; the heuristic fruitfulness of the Leibnizian algorithm "justifies" the adoption of a new definition of equality.

The same sort of fruitfulness leads Leibniz to accept, unlike Nieuwentijt, products of differentials of first order as different from zero and thus as real quantities. Moreover, he objects to Nieuwentijt that it is rather strange to posit that a segment dx is different from zero and at the same time that the area of the square with side dx is equal to zero. It is true that $dx\,dx$ cannot be made greater than any finite quantity by multiplcation even of an infinite number, but, Leibniz objects, it can be made so by multiplying it for an infinitely infinite number. And, Leibniz claims, once one admits an infinite number m, one cannot refuse to admit the existence of m^2, obtained multiplying m by itself.

Concerning the second objection, related to the impossibility of dealing with the differentiation of expressions such as y^x in terms of the Leibnizian algorithm, Leibniz used the opportunity to publish some new results.[27]

Finally, concerning the third objection, Leibniz notices how it stems from the same grounds as the first—a ddx multiplied by an infinite number does not make a finite quantity and is therefore a zero. Consequently, the reply to the first objection—the appeal to infinitely infinite numbers—can also be applied here. And Leibniz also provides another argument. Nieuwentijt would agree that if a and b are quantities then the quantity c such that $a: b = b: c$ should also be a quantity. Letting $a = x$ and $b = dx$ he shows that in the logarithmic curve the ddx progress as the squares of dx. This is supposed to show the existence of the differentials of higher order.

A few months after the *Responsio*, Leibniz sent an additional two-page clarification to the *Acta Eruditorum*. There he proposed to interpret differentials of any order by finite quantities that are proportional to them. In essence, this strategy for dealing with higher-order differentials is a generalization of that presented in the *Nova Methodus*, where first-order differentials were introduced as finite segments. However, Leibniz does not show how the strategy is supposed to be carried out in detail. Bos has devoted great attention to this suggestion by Leibniz and has reconstructed the main lines of how the argument should work. He points out that if, on the one hand, this approach seems to push the calculus in the direction of the later notion of derivative and a predominance of the concept of function, on the other hand, it does so only at the cost of limiting the generality of the Leibnizian calculus by forcing the choice of "one variable as independent variable whose differential must then implicitly be supposed constant."[28]

Leibniz's answers did not satisfy Nieuwentijt who replied in 1696 with his *Considerationes secundae*, divided into five sections. The first section deals with the elimination of infinitely small quantities in the Leibnizian calculus. The second attempts to show that in problems of infinitesimal analysis one can always get by with only first-order differentials. The third contains a reply to Leibniz's answer to the objections that Nieuwentijt had raised in the *Considerationes*. The fourth deals with Nieuwentijt's own method of infinitesimal analysis. And, the fifth concerns the exponential calculus. From this table of contents we see that the *Considerationes secundae* are quite a substantial work, as is Jakob Hermann's *Responsio as Clarißimi Viri Bernh. Niuwentiit* (1700). Hermann's *Responsio* follows the structure of the *Considerationes secundae* and gives an almost point-by-point commentary of the latter work. Inevitably, I will have to be selective.

Section 1 of the *Considerationes secundae* accuses Leibniz of using an ambiguous definition of equality; Nieuwentijt insists on the necessity of not eliminating differentials of first order and of considering their products as zeros. To this effect he provides an example aimed at showing that, if products of differentials are not considered to be zero, we can derive absurd conclusions from the differential calculus. The example is as follows. Consider the equilateral hyperbola given by the equation

$$2rx + xx = yy. \tag{6.1}$$

Substituting $x + dx$ and $y + dy$ for x and y respectively we obtain

$$2rx + 2r\,dx + xx + 2x\,dx + dx\,dx = yy + 2y\,dy + dy\,dy. \tag{6.2}$$

Since $2rx + xx = yy$ we get

$$2r\,dx + 2x\,dx + dx\,dx = 2y\,dy + dy\,dy. \tag{6.3}$$

According to the Leibnizian calculus, the differential equation of the equilateral hyperbola is

$$2r\,dx + 2x\,dx = 2y\,dy. \tag{6.4}$$

Thus we obtain $dx\,dx = dy\,dy$ and by taking roots $dx = dy$. In other words, the hyperbola turns out to behave like a straight line. Nieuwentijt concluded that the only way to get out of the paradox was to consider products of first-order differentials as equal to zero. In his commentary on these passages, Hermann points out that Nieuwentijt's alleged paradox relies on the principle at stake between Nieuwentijt and the Leibnizians. In order to obtain $dx\,dx = dy\,dy$ from (6.3) and (6.4), Nieuwentijt applies the reasoning that if equals are subtracted from equals the remaining quantities are equal. This stems from the principle that two quantities are equal only if their difference is absolutely zero. But according to Hermann, that is exactly what is at stake. In the remaining part of the first section (§§8–9), Nieuwentijt discussed Leibniz's assertion that the calculus could be seen as dealing with incomparable quantities, according to a number of lemmas published in *Acta Eruditorum* of 1689. The reference is to the *Tentamen de motuum coelestium causis*, where Leibniz had claimed that one could have avoided reference to infinitely small quantities by using quantities as small as one likes, so that the error produced would be less than any given error. In order to make himself clear, he also added a metaphor: the diameter of the earth is an infinitely small line in comparison with the universe. The metaphor allowed Nieuwentijt to infer that the quantities at stake are thus finite quantities and therefore comparable. Thus he concluded that in the Leibnizian calculus one ascribes to infinitely small quantities the properties of finite quantities, and to incomparable quantities those of comparable quantities.

Section 2 of the *Considerationes secundae* proposed another paradox, which follows from the rules of the differential calculus, to show that differentials of higher order must be equal to zero. I omit the example because its approach is similar to those we have covered already. Hermann's discussion of the example reiterates his rejection of the principle that $dx\,dx = 0$ and emphasizes that differentials are to be considered insignificant only in the context of equations containing terms that are incomparably greater than those differentials. An interesting claim is made by Nieuwentijt in section 15, where he asserts that giving up higher-order differentials does not mutilate mathematical analysis because everything that can be obtained through higher-order differentials can be obtained by using first-order differentials.[29] However, Hermann showed in his reply that Nieuwentijt's proof of the claim made an implicit use of higher-order differentials.

Section 3 of the *Considerationes secundae* contains a reply to Leibniz's *Responsio*. Hermann remarks that Nieuwentijt wrongly applied Bernoulli's statement in the "paradox" he devised, so Leibniz was right to make his objection.

Section 4 of the *Considerationes secundae* and Hermann's discussion of it are perhaps the most significant of the exchange. Nieuwentijt is forced by Leibniz's criticism of his infinitesimal procedures to attempt a clear grounding of his own approach and must now play a defensive role. This allows Hermann to give a devastating overview of the principles of his adversary. The issue between the two revolves around the central problem of whether there can be powers "potestates" of infinity. Indeed, if there are such powers then Leibniz is right in asserting that b/mm is also a quantity different from zero, since multiplied by mm it gives b; but if mm does not exist then Nieuwentijt has the upper hand. Whereas Nieuwentijt attempts a demonstration in Euclidian style that there are no powers of the infinite, Hermann attempts to show the existence of arbitrary degrees of infinity, thereby showing the weakness of the principles of his adversary. Nieuwentijt takes as an evident proposition 'whatever can be augmented, or of which there can be something greater, is finite'. Hermann is quite right in objecting that this is exactly what is at stake—whether the infinite is also subject to increase. Thus Hermann concludes that the other propositions put forth by Nieuwentijt, such as proposition 4 to the effect that an infinite number is the greatest number, fall with the first one.[30] By contrast, Hermann proposes a geometrical example to show how there are degrees of the infinite. He uses the fact that there exists an infinite sequence of nested hyperbolic spaces contained betwen the same asymptotes such that each of their areas is infinite. Since the hyperbolas are nested, the areas provide us with a hierarchy of infinities. Another interesting objection raised by Hermann is that, if one follows Nieuwentijt's principle, all the differentials of first order must be equal. It is certainly not easy to judge exactly what follows from Nieuwentijt's principle; the number m or an infinitesimal b/m are subject to algebraic operations, but it is not clear what they are. However, if an infinitesimal can be multiplied by a finite number, Hermann is right to point out the following. Let a, b, e, f be finite, and consider the quantities ab/em and ab/fm with $ab/em > ab/fm$. But then $fm > bm$ and thus we end up with degrees of infinity.

Section 5 of the *Considerationes secundae* goes back to the issue of exponential functions and Hermann's discussion of it relies on Bernoulli (1697). Finally, chapter 6 of the *Responsio* proposes an axiomatic treatment of the principles on which the calculus relies. I will not rehearse Hermann's axiomatization.

Nieuwentijt's *Considerationes secundae* and Hermann's *Responsio* represent the last stage of the Leibniz–Nieuwentijt debate. Leibniz had not answered directly to the *Considerationes secundae*, but Hermann, at that time a student of Jakob Bernoulli, had rebuked Nieuwentijt point by point. The exchange with Clüver and with Nieuwentijt had put great emphasis on the notion of a hierarchy of infinite numbers. Leibniz had clearly asserted the existence of a hierarchy of infinitely small and infinitely great quantities (in the 1696 issue of *Acta Eruditorum*). Notwithstanding, infinite numbers occur rather rarely in the practice of the Leibnizian calculus.[31] Nieuwentijt did not publish anything else on the foundations of the calculus, and in later works admitted to have been wrong in his criticisms. The exchange between Leibniz, Nieuwentijt, and Hermann had, however, highlighted the foundational difficulties that the calculus had to face. Leibniz's strategies of justification were never fully carried out in print, and a certain amount of confusion was bound to arise from the fragmentary and often alternative suggestions given by Leibniz as to the fundamental concepts of his calculus. Indeed, Leibniz's calculus had to face an even more radical challenge in the heated debate within the Paris Academy of Sciences from 1700 to 1705, a debate to which we now turn.

6.3   The Foundational Debate in the Paris Academy of Sciences

6.3.1   The Rolle-Varignon Debate (1700–1701)

Through the teaching of Johann I Bernoulli a group of French mathematicians, centered around the charismatic figure, Malebranche, came in contact with the new calculus around 1690. This group included L'Hôpital, Varignon, Montmort, Carré, Reyneau, and other less famous mathematicians. In the winter of 1691–92 Johann I Bernoulli initiated the Marquis de L'Hôpital in the most remote secrets of the differential and integral calculus. Bernoulli's lectures were instrumental in later enabling L'Hôpital to write the *Analyse des infiniment petits*. This textbook had a remarkable success and for quite a long time it represented the only accessible road to the differential calculus.

Various French scholars have documented the intense activity and collective effort of the group led by Malebranche to come to a full understanding of the new infinitesimal techniques.[32] Malebranche himself had studied the calculus deeply and was, in effect, the main patron of the "infinitesimalist revolution" in the Academy of Sciences. When the academy was renewed in 1699, a number of new places were opened and Malebranche was elected an honorary member. In the following few years the academy came to include a compact group of "infinitesimalists," among them Carré, Saurin, Guisnée, and Montmort. This group was under the technical guidance of L'Hôpital and Varignon, who were older academicians.[33]

The presence within the academy of a group of mathematicians (including Rolle, Ph. de la Hire, and Galloys), who were decidedly adverse to the new calculus, created an explosive situation.[34] From 1700 to 1706 the academy was divided over the admissibility of the new techniques: on one side stood the infinitesimalist group characterized by its total adherence to the new Leibnizian calculus in the version codified by L'Hôpital and in general by a commitment to the existence of infinitesimal quantities; on the other side, the finitist faction characterized by a refusal to give a rigorous status to infinitesimal considerations and by a general adherence to classical techniques.[35]

The most outspoken adversary of the recognition of the infinitesimal calculus as a subject in rigorous mathematics was the algebraist Michel Rolle (1652–1719), who opened his memoir "Du Nouveau Système de l'Infini" as follows:

Geometry had always been considered as an exact science, and indeed as the source of the exactness which is widespread among the other parts of mathematics. Among its principles one could only find true axioms and all the theorems and problems proposed were either soundly demonstrated or capable of a sound demonstration. And if any false or uncertain propositions were slipped into it they would immediately be banned from this science. But it seems that this feature of exactness does not reign anymore in geometry since the new system of infinitely small quantities has been mixed to it. I do not see that this system has produced anything for the truth and it would seem to me that it often conceals mistakes.[36]

We see that Rolle formulated three distinct attacks: the calculus is not rigorous, it leads to mistakes, and it has not produced any new truth. The first two lines of attack were used by Rolle in the first part of the debate that began in July 1700 and lasted until the end of 1701. The last claim was made in a much stronger way in the second part of the debate (1702–1705). The first part of the debate consisted of fight within the academy between Pierre Varignon and Rolle. Varignon (1654–1722), who had been working on applications of the calculus to mechanics, took the task of defending the new calculus.[37] Although several memoirs were produced, the only published outcome of this part of the debate was the later "Du Nouveau Système de l'Infini." The other sources available to us are the correspondence between Leibniz, Johann I Bernoulli, and Varignon (see Leibniz 1843–63, vol. III; and Bernoulli 1988), the *Registres des Procès verbaux des séances de l'Académie Royale des Sciences*, and a manuscript entitled "Extrait des Réponses faites par Mr. Varignon, en 1700 et 1701 aux objections que Mr. Rolle avait faites contre le calcul différentiel," which has been ascribed by Costabel (1965) to the mathematician Charles Reyneau (1656–1728).[38] From Reyneau's summary it is clear that this first part of the debate can be further divided into two phases. The first phase was primarily of a foundational nature (i.e., concerned with the logical and metaphysical admissibility of the new calculus). The second and later phase was of a more technical nature.

The first half of Reyneau's manuscript provides valuable insight into the foundational part of the debate and gives a careful abstract of Varignon's answers to Rolle. However, as Rolle's position is only summarized in short statements, I will also use 'Du Nouveau Système de l'Infini" as a source for Rolle's arguments.

Rolle articulated his foundational attack in three main objections: (a) the differential calculus postulates a hierarchy of arbitrarily large and arbitrarily small orders of infinities; (b) a quantity $+$ or $-$ its differential is made equal to the very same quantity, which is the same as saying that the part is equal to the whole; and (c) sometimes the differentials are used as nonzero quantities and sometimes as absolute zeros.[39]

Note that objections (a) and (b) were grounded in the denial of the existence of quantities not satisfying the Archimedean axiom and in the refusal to accept a negation of common notion 5 in Euclid and that in (c) Rolle attacked the manipulations of the infinitesimal calculus because the denotation of the differential was shifted at will during the computation. For each of the previous points I will expose Rolle's objections and Varignon's answers.

In the arguments for the first objection Rolle made two related claims. The first claim was that (despite L'Hôpital's claims) the infinitesimalists had given no proof of the existence of these various orders of infinities. What bothered Rolle here was L'Hôpital's claim, made in the preface of *Analyse des infiniment petits*, to be able to give a proof of the existence of infinitesimal quantities by the way of the ancients (i.e., the method of exhaustion). In the paradigm of the period, had the above been carried through, this would have meant a truth-status for statements about infinitesimal quantities and not just the status of an arbitrary mathematical hypothesis.

In his second claim Rolle asserted, apparently without an argument, that talking about differentials was nonsense, because it could be proved that differentials were absolute zeros. In Rolle (1703a, 318) he provided an argument by using the equation $y^2 = ax$ as an example. Using L'Hôpital's rules he obtained the differential equality $a\,dx = 2y\,dy$. Finally, under the assumption that the point, $(x + dx, y + dy)$, lies on the parabola, using the definition of the parabola he got $ax + a\,dx = y^2 + 2y\,dy + dy^2$. Putting the three equations together and solving the system, using the ordinary algebraic law that subtracting equals from equals yields equals (whose validity Rolle took for granted), he arrived at $dy^2 = 0$ and hence $dy = 0$. Finally, substitution of $dy = 0$ in the equation $a\,dx = 2y\,dy$ yielded $dx = 0$. Therefore, Rolle concluded, infinitesimals could not be real quantities. They were, in fact, absolute zeros. (The example works only if we systematically anchor our interpretation to a domain that has only zero and finite quantities).

Rolle's involved argument can be made clear as follows: under the assumption that the same algebraic manipulations rule finite quantities and infinitesimals, from the equation $x + dx = x$, one can infer $dx = 0$. Rolle concluded:

> In the first place one sees that since all these infinites of first sort [*genres*] such a dx or dy have no real extension then all the infinites of the other sorts will also be nothing but absolute zeros in the calculus. All these infinite sequences of infinites, provided by the system, will only be nothings that are supposed to be infinitely contained within other nothings.[40]

Trying to respond to Rolle's first objection, Varignon provided "proofs" of the existence of infinitesimally small quantities. A representative sample is the following "proof" reported by Reyneau. We can divide an interval of time indefinitely, and so this interval of time can be divided into parts infinitely small, called moments. Consider now a body A that moves with constant speed for a time T. The spaces traversed by this body are proportional to the times, so the space described in each moment is to the totality of the space S as an instant t is T. Therefore the space described (on the line) in each instant is a differential.

Rolle's second objection expressed his refusal to identify the whole with the part as in letting $x + dx = x$. Once again Varignon's answer was an attempt to clarify the nature of infinitesimal quantities. It is interesting that Varignon appealed to Newton's *Principia* as the source of rigorous foundation of the calculus. Throughout his answer to Rolle, Varignon quoted verbatim Newton's scholium to lemma XI in book I of the *Principia*. Rolle became confused, said Varignon, because he had not mastered the nature of differentials, which consisted in being variable and not fixed quantities and in decreasing continually until they reached zero, "in fluxu continuo." These quantities were considered only in the moment of their evanescence. This was after all, he continued, the same notion as Newton's "fluxiones," namely, "incrementa vel decrementa momentanea." Being considered in the moment of their evanescence they were therefore neither something nor absolute zeros. Reyneau summarized: "Mr Varignon explains that being *evanescentia divisibilia*, the differentials are always real and subdivisible to infinity until they finally cease to exist; and that is the only point where they change in absolute nothing."[41]

Varignon did not deny that a differential was considered nothing with respect to its integral and he offered a proof of the statement using the techniques of the ancients (i.e., exhaustion):

> Since the nature of differentials. . . . consists in being infinitely small and infinitely changing until zero, in being nothing but *quantitates evanescentes, evanscentia divisibilia*, they will always be smaller than any arbitrary given quantity. Indeed, whatever difference can be assigned between two magnitudes which differ only by a differential it will always be possible, on account of the continual and indefinite variability of this infinitely small differential, and as on the verge of being zero, to find a differential less than the given difference. Which shows, in the way of the ancients, that notwithstanding their difference these two quantities can be taken to be equal.[42]

This justified, concluded Varignon, the manipulations used in the calculus. Insofar as they were manipulated during the computations the differentials were something on the verge of being zero and only at the end did they become zero, in the sense that they were considered in the moments of their evanescence, namely, "non antequam evanescunt, non postea sed cum evanescunt." This also provided an answer to Rolle's third objection.

Rolle and Varignon were unable to find common ground on which to resolve their difficulties. Despite the claims of his ability to prove the existence of infinitesimally small quantities by the way of the ancients (the paradigm of rigor), Varignon managed only to give us his inner perception of mathematical reality: a universe made of variable quantities, essentially dynamic, where fixed quantities were just a special case of the former. To the finitist, Rolle, this was pure nonsense. Only by reducing differentials to zeros could he make sense of Varignon's claims. Rolle's universe was made up to finite quantities of zero: there was no place in it for amphibians. He thus stressed that the problems solved by the calculus could be solved by the common methods, such as those of Fermat and Hudde.

The stress on the methods of Fermat and Hudde led Rolle to challenge his adversary on very specific mathematical examples. In outline Rolle claimed that the differential calculus led to mistakes. His general approach to the problem was to concoct examples of specific curves in which the individuation of maxima and minima carried through with the differential calculus was at odds with the results given by Hudde's rule.[43] Varignon painstakingly interpreted all of Rolle's alleged counterexamples and managed to show that Rolle had made several mistakes as to the nature of Hudde's rule and the applications of the differential algorithm. This explains the reason for Rolle's mistakes in sketching the curves he proposed. Two examples reported by Reyneau will suffice.

On 12 March 1701, Rolle proposed the curve

$$a^{1/3}(y - b) = (x^2 - 2ax + a^2 - b^2)^{2/3}.$$

He claimed that the infinitesimal method did not give all the maxima and

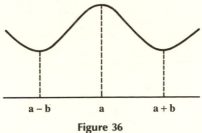

$a - b$ a $a + b$

Figure 36

minima provided by Hudde's rule, and sketched the curve as in Figure 36. Hudde's rule actually gave three ordinates that corresponded to the abscissae, a, $a - b$, $a + b$, respectively. Rolle had applied the differential calculus by putting $dy = 0$, and that gave him a maximum at a, but he had not put $dx = 0$, which is also required for a complete application of the algorithm. Varignon showed how the application of the differential calculus had not been correct and then gave a correct treatment of the curve (whose graph is shown in Figure 37).

On 2 July 1701, Rolle proposed the curve $y = 2 + \sqrt{4x} + \sqrt{4 + 2x}$. He claimed that using the differential calculus one got an imaginary maximum for $x = -4$, whereas by rationalizing the equation and applying Hudde's rule, one got the maximum at $x = 2$. The quartic obtained through the elimination of radicals is $y^4 - 8y^3 + 16y^2 - 12xy^2 + 48yx - 64x + 4x^2 = 0$ (see Fig. 38). The sketch given by Rolle is in Figure 39. Varignon showed that the point D was only the intersection of two branches of the curve and that the correct application of Hudde's rule would yield both the real value and the imaginary one.[44] Rolle had believed that Hudde's rule provided only maxima and minima without realizing that the rule also gave any point in which the curve has double roots hence all points of intersection.

These unfortunate examples constructed by Rolle were one of the reasons for Montucla's aversion toward him. But Rolle's attacks had the merit of raising the question of the criteria for individuating maxima and minima as opposed to simple points of intersection. It was only in 1706 that Guisnée proposed a criterion for distinguishing intersection points from maxima and minima.[45] Furthermore, Rolle's objections stimulated reflection on the nature of Hudde's rule, and its relationship to the methods given in *Analyse des infiniment petits*, as is witnessed by the several letters exchanged by Leibniz and Johann I

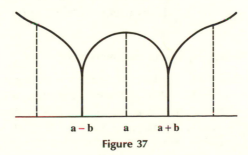

$a - b$ a $a + b$

Figure 37

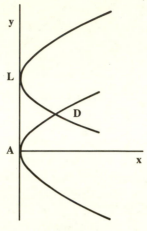

Figure 38

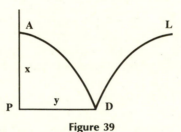

Figure 39

Bernoulli (Leibniz 1843–63, vol. III, pp. 660–672) and also by the work of
Guisnée.

Let us summarize how the problem of the foundations was seen by
Varignon and Rolle. Varignon tried to show that infinitesimals existed. This
belief in the existence of infinitesimals was common to all French infinitesimalists; they shared it with, and probably got it from, Johann I Bernoulli.
Their position can be analyzed as an attempt to provide a semantic referent to
the formal notion of differential. From this point of view, Rolle and Varignon
were closer than we may think. They both shared the assumption that the
foundational problem consisted in making sense of a "realistic ontology."
Moreover, we see that both opponents agreed on the paradigm of rigor; in fact,
Varignon tried to "prove" his claims using the technique of exhaustion.

6.3.2 The Public Debate: Explaining and Intervening

Until then, the debate had raged only within the academy, which explicitly
forbade its members to make public statements about it, in spite of Varignon's
request "to have also the public as judge."[46] The unwillingness of some
members to take a public stand, and perhaps a real concern with the
public image of the newly reorganized academy, contributed to this decision.

Nonetheless, Varignon had sent the memoirs concerning the debate to Johann I Bernoulli and to Leibniz, asking them not to make any public mention of the fight. At the end of 1701 the academy silenced Rolle and Varignon, and the Abbé Bignon, its president, nominated an adjudicatory commission, composed of Gouye, Cassini, and Ph. de la Hire, to judge the claims made by the contenders, the academy's usual procedure. This commission was very favorable to Rolle (Gouye and Ph. de la Hire were in fact on his side) but it never gave a judgment, partly because the situation had become extremely fluid. Some people were becoming less hostile to the infinitesimalist position and were slowly changing their attitudes. This was the case, for example, with the Abbé Gouye, who had anonymously attacked the new calculus in an issue of the *Journal de Trévoux* of May 1701. Reviewing an article by Johann I Bernoulli, Gouye attacked the analysis of the various orders of infinity and ended by saying: "Il ne suffit pas en Géométrie de conclure vray, il faut voir evidemment qu'on le conclut bien."[47] There was no mention in Gouye's article of the ongoing debate inside the Academy. As an academician, Gouye was compelled to stay silent on that point. Leibniz answered Gouye in the famous letter to M. Pinson written on 29 August 1701, parts of which were published in December by the *Journal de Trévoux*. Replying to the attacks of Gouye, Leibniz stated:

> There is no need to take the infinite in a rigorous way, but only in the way in which one says in optics that the rays of the sun come from an infinitely distant point and therefore taken to be parallel. And when there are several degrees of infinity, or infinitely small, this is like as when the globe of the earth is taken to be a point in comparison to the distance of the fixed stars, and a ball that we handle is still a point in comparison to the radius of the globe of the earth. So that the distance of the fixed stars is an infinitely infinite or infinite of the infinite in relation to the diameter of the ball. For, in place of the infinite or of the infinitely small, one can take quantities as great or as small as one needs so that the error be less than the given error. So that one does not differ from Archimedes' style but for the expressions which in our method are more direct and more in accordance with the art of discovery.[48]

The claim of being able to recast any proof involving infinitesimals into a proof in the style of Archimedes—a proof using the method of exhaustion—was extremely suggestive, but it was never developed in print in a completely convincing way. In any case, this last part of Leibniz's letter was ignored by the anti-infinitesimalists, who emphasized a literal reading of the first part of the letter.

This declaration by Leibniz did not help the infinitesimalists fighting inside the academy at all. In fact, as Leibniz stated, if a differential was to its variable as a pebble of sand to the earth, then the differential was still a finite quantity, therefore, the calculus could be granted only the status of an approximation method, not that of a rigorous science. That this conclusion was drawn by others is confirmed by the first letter of Varignon to Leibniz (28 November 1701), who having identified the Abbé Galloys as the sponsor of the anti-infinitesimalist position, asked Leibniz to make a precise statement on what should be understood by "infinitesimal quantity." This was absolutely necessary since "the enemies of your calculus do not stop rejoicing and spread it [the letter to Pinson] as a clear and precise statement of your thought on this issue. Thus, I beg you, Sir, to send us as soon as possible a clear and precise statement of your thought on this matter."[49]

The disciples were asking the master to lead them through the conceptual maze in which they were caught. Leibniz answered Varignon's letter on 2 February 1702. Parts of this letter were published by the *Journal des Sçavans* the same year. The position held by Leibniz in the letter may be summarized in three points. (a) There is no need to base mathematical analysis on metaphysical assumptions. (b) We can nonetheless admit infinitesimal quantities, if not as real, as well-founded fictitious entities, as one does in algebra with square roots of negative numbers. Arguments for this position depended on a form of the metaphysical principle of continuity. Or (c) one could organize the proofs so that the error will be always less than any assigned error.

Leibniz ended by pointing out the positive nature of debates in helping sciences acquire better foundations. This having been the case for algebra and geometry, both of which had survived the attacks of their opponents, Leibniz hoped it would also be the case for "nostre Science des infinis." Leibniz did not think that the calculus was to be justified by its "metaphysics." Consequently for Leibniz, the problem was not, Do infinitely small quantities exist? but, Is the use of infinitely small quantities in the calculus reliable? (Bos 1980a, 87). By this time, the use of negative square roots in algebra was a well-established and accepted practice, although the soundness of its foundations was still largely unresolved. Yet Leibniz in (b) appealed to this accepted practice as a justification for his own. In his letter he merged two different foundational approaches. The first was related to the classical methods of proof by exhaustion; the second was based on a metaphysical principle of continuity.[50]

We are interested here in the consequences of this intervention by Leibniz. If we are to trust Varignon's comments in a letter to Johann I Bernoulli (Leibniz 1843–63, vol. IV, p. 97), Leibniz's letter had the welcome effect of answering the Abbé Gouye's doubts. These were important moves within the academy. The debate had yet to be settled and the infinitesimalists needed to modify an atmosphere that was not in their favor. Even if the letter did have this positive outcome, the infinitesimalists were quite unsatisfied with it. Leibniz had not expressed any commitment to infinitesimal quantities and L'Hôpital got to the point of asking Leibniz not to write anything more on the matter. This is how Leibniz, in a letter of 1716, recalled the events:

> When our friends debated in France with the Abbé Gallois, Father Gouye and others, I told them that I did not believe at all in the existence of truly infinite magnitudes or truly infinitesimal magnitudes. . . . But as the Marquis *de L'Hospital* believed that in saying so I betrayed the cause they begged me not to say anything.[51]

We can conclude, therefore, that the infinitesimalists were deeply dissatisfied with the master. They had looked for a light to follow and they found that Leibniz had no definitive truth to give them concerning infinitesimals.[52] The attacks by Rolle had split the infinitesimalists on the problem of the foundations.

I want to consider for a moment the deep difference between Leibniz's position (as perceived by the French) and the French infinitesimalists' position on the problem of foundations. We have seen that the French took very seriously the notion of "different orders of infinity." In their view this was the foundation of the building. They read Leibniz as insisting on the notion of incomparability. For Leibniz, they thought, it was enough to claim that a quantity and its differential were incomparable. The French considered this a fatal mistake. They argued that if two quantities were only incomparable then their difference was a finite quantity, hence a finite mistake was introduced in the calculus. This was not the case if dx was an infinitely small quantity, where in fact the mistake would be less than any finite quantity. This was a very narrow way to read Leibniz's claims, which were attempting to define a more subtle position by considering the infinitesimals as well-founded fictions. Their literal reading of the sand and globe metaphor meant the French mathematicians were unable to understand Leibniz's more complex position. In effect, Leibniz was proposing a sophisticated "formalistic" foundation for his algorithm. However, by considering the infinitesimals as well-founded fictions, he was introducing a gap between the formal apparatus and the referents. We can say that Leibniz's system was based on a "subversion" of the semantics in favor of a consistent formalism. This could somehow justify his claims that, linguistically, the opposition finite/infinite could be easily relativized.[53] The Parisian mathematicians tried to provide a concrete reference to Leibniz's formalism, however, the state of their art left them open to misunderstandings. Finite quantities and infinitesimals were assumed to be ruled by the same algebraic laws, so nothing could prevent the inference from $x + dx = x$ to $dx = 0$.[54]

6.3.3 Rolle–Saurin (1702–1705): The Peace of the Infinitely Small

The second part of the debate was fought publicly in the *Journal des Sçavans*, which had always been very open to the academicians. On 3 April 1702, the *Journal des Sçavans* published Rolle's article, "Regles et remarques, pour le problème general des tangentes," which proposed some new rules for solving tangent problems. According to Rolle, the existing methods were insufficient to discover all the tangents to geometric curves. Rolle proposed his own rules, emphasizing their origin in ordinary analysis (as opposed to the new analysis). The article ended with a challenge, clearly addressed to the infinitesimalists. Rolle used various examples showing, he claimed, that when we have more than one tangent at a given point on a curve (corresponding, for example, to a point of self intersection of the curve), the "most-used" methods were no longer sufficient. One of Rolle's examples was again the curve

$$y^4 - 8y^3 - 12xy^2 + 48xy + 4x^2 - 64x + 16y^2 = 0. \qquad \text{(A)}$$

Although Rolle never mentioned Varignon or *Analyse des infiniment petits*, the article was a clear challenge to the infinitesimalists. The reply to Rolle was written by a protégé of L'Hôpital, Joseph Saurin (1658–1737), who was not yet an academician. He interpreted Rolle's article as a direct attack against the infinitesimal calculus. Rolle had claimed (we are already familiar with his strategy) that in the case of multiple points the new analysis would not give the classical results. It was true that, for example, in (A) dy/dx becomes indeterminate for $x = 2$. Saurin, using L'Hôpital's rule, was able to show for some of the cases how the methods given by L'Hôpital's book were perfectly fine. He then accused Rolle of plagiarizing L'Hôpital's methods by using notational variants of them, and attacked Rolle with a purely ad hominem arguments.[55] Finally, Saurin challenged Rolle to apply his methods to mechanical curves. Once again the successful applications of the infinitesimal calculus were playing a major role in its acceptance as a rigorous method.

From this point, the debate became more personal and political. Each faction used any means at its disposal to create the conditions for its victory. So, for example, the debate went on in the *Journal de Sçavans*, which Gouye and Bignon directed in 1702. Whereas Rolle's article was published without cuts, Bignon had cut Saurin's answer.[56] We can see, therefore, that the editorial policy of the directors of the *Journal* had favored Rolle over Saurin.

Rolle attacked again in 1703 and 1704 (see Rolle 1703b, 1704) with another memoir on the inverse of tangents. Although Saurin did not immediately answer these attacks, the cause was taken up by Fontenelle, another devoted infinitesimalist and the perpetual secretary of the academy.

Fontenelle had been elected perpetual secretary of the academy in 1697. Among his duties was the yearly compilation of the *Histoire et Mémoires de l'Académie Royale des Sciences*. He also delivered public speeches representing the academy, including the eulogies of the deceased academicians. Since 1694, he had been very close to the group led by Malebranche.

Until this point, Fontenelle, although on the side of the infinitesimalists, had publicly spoken of the debate only in a small note published in the *Histoire* of the academy for the year 1701. One may question the editorial policy of Fontenelle on the subject; his short note did not do justice to a debate that occupied the academy for two years—the *Registres des Procès Verbaux* of the Academy for 1700 and 1701 are almost entirely filled with these debates (see Blay 1986 for extensive quotations from the *Registres*). Still, the note at least gave a hint of the existence of a true problem concerning the foundations of the infinitesimal calculus.[57] But on the whole the note was very flattering to the new system proposed by L'Hôpital. In particular, L'Hôpital's silence during the debate was carefully explained to avoid the impression that L'Hôpital had any fears concerning his calculus. Fontenelle himself had not yet taken an official stand.

In 1704 the debate was at its peak. On 2 February L'Hôpital died, and on 2 April Fontenelle read the "Eloge de M. le Marquis de L'Hôpital." In this eulogy, the differential calculus was described as the "sublime géométrie." L'Hôpital was emphatically described as possessing a map to the "Pays de l'Infini," and as knowing its most remote paths.[58] Given these words it is hard to imagine that the very foundations of this building were still under violent attack within the academy. But Fontenelle, addressing the opposition, went even further by claiming that those who criticized the differential calculus did not understand it. The reference to Rolle and Galloys was very explicit in the comparison made between those who were devoted to the ancients and those who were devoted to learning, regardless of modern or ancient methods.[59] We see how easily Fontenelle skipped over the fundamental issue of the foundations of the new algorithm. This problem had not been settled and Fontenelle knew this all too well. He himself was working on a book that would have provided "La vrai metaphysique" of the infinitesimal calculus.

Nevertheless, the need to destroy the anti-infinitesimalist opposition was too important. No mention was made here of any foundational problem. Reducing the critiques of the noninfinitesimalists to pure ignorance, Fontenelle was taking a very definite stand on the ongoing debate within the academy,[60] and his eulogy of L'Hôpital was perceived as an open declaration of partisanship. Not only did he use his lofty position to make public statements concerning the truth or falsity of the anti-infinitesimalists' claims—a practice that one may clearly question—he went further. The first page of the *Histoire et Mémoires de l'Académie des Sciences* for 1704 had the following foreword:

> In the Mémoires for 1703, p. 312, we have published an essay by M. Rolle entitled 'On the New System of the Infinite'. The considerations that several people have made on this essay, on the principles that are put forth in it, and on the consequences that one could draw, force us to declare that although this essay is found among the other works destined to be printed by the Academy, its intention has never been to adopt anything that can be found in it.[61]

This official condemnation of Rolle's memoir, a flagrant contradiction of the spirit of the academy, raised several doubts concerning the alleged impartiality of this institution. For us the condemnation is important because it showed that Fontenelle (and Bignon) had already made a decision on the debate. This sheds light on the composition of the two groups and, as we shall see, on the composition of the adjudicatory commission nominated in 1705.

Saurin had not responded to the attacks made by Rolle in 1703 and 1704. Rolle's flush of papers and his boasts could have given the impression that he had silenced his adversaries. However, on 23 April 1705, Saurin attacked Rolle again. By then the debate had completely degenerated into mere invective. Some short quotations will give an idea of the level of these last articles. In the aforementioned article Saurin wrote: 'Qui s'imagineroit, qu'avec cette assurance, il ne va qu'à tâtons, & ne parle qu'au hazard?' (Saurin 1705a, 252). Replying on 2 June, Rolle called Saurin "un pitoyable géomètre" (Rolle 1705a, 318). The final article in this long debate was written by Rolle and published on 30 July 1705 (see Rolle 1705b). Rolle kept accusing L'Hôpital of plagiarizing the classical algebraic methods in his *Analyse des infiniment petits* but, on the whole, there was little new theoretical or philosophical content to this last part of the debate. Meanwhile, Saurin was repeatedly imploring the academy to give a final judgment. The feeling that the academy would soon heed his calls and nominate a commission for this purpose only added urgency to the exchange. Leibniz was very annoyed about the whole situation. He thought it important to get a favorable judgment from the academy and a public condemnation of Rolle.[62] At the end of 1705 the Abbé Bignon nominated a commission, including himself, Ph. de la Hire, Galloys, Fontenelle, and Cassini, to provide an official judgment on the whole affair.[63]

The academy made its decision public in January 1706. Rolle was asked to conform better to the regulations of the academy and Saurin was "renvoyé a son bon coeur." Fontenelle referred in 1719 to this decision as the "paix des infiniment petits." Leibniz and Johann I Bernoulli were of course dissatisfied; Leibniz considered the judgment "magis morale quam mathematicum" (Leibniz 1843–63, vol. III, p. 794). But it is clear that, given the composition of forces within the academy, no other verdict would have been possible. The judgment stopped Rolle's attacks, and the death of Galloys in 1707 put an end to the opposition. Varignon wrote to Johann I Bernoulli (10 November 1706) that Rolle, finally converted, was now claiming he had been pressed by others to do what he had done against the infinitely small.[64] We can speculate about Rolle's change. He had alienated himself from the rest of the mathematical community. He probably thought it best to excuse himself and accept a dignified peace. What is certain, however, is that Rolle never did convince himself of the soundness of the infinitesimal calculus. Writing to Leibniz in 1708, Varignon mentioned that Rolle was still making adverse comments.[65]

The death of Galloys and the withdrawal of Rolle marked the final victory of the infinitesimal calculus on the continent. In his preface to the *Élémens de la géométrie de l'infini*, Fontenelle could finally boast: "Despite all of this the Infinite has won and has got a hold of all the lofty speculations of the geometers. The Infinities or Infinitely small of all orders are today equally established and there are no more two parties in the Academy."[66] The battle had not yet been an easy one.

6.3.4 Conclusion

I have devoted a great deal of attention to "political" as well as to theoretical aspects of the debate within the academy because I believe it was an essential step in the proselytizing policy of the Leibnizians. This policy had already been tried on Clüver and Nieuwentijt but it was the debate with Rolle that defeated the dangerous "institutional opposition" to the Leibnizian calculus. There is no doubt that the withdrawal of Rolle and the death of Galloys marked the complete victory of the infinitesimal calculus in France, a victory sought with constant appeal to the authority of the most famous geometers and created by the increasing success of the differential algorithm in solving problems hitherto inaccessible using only algebraic techniques. We must be amazed at the effort spent by the infinitesimalists on winning their battle. The foundational issue remained unclear but the analysts pushed ahead, as Kline would say, "with vigor but without rigor."

Let me also add something concerning the philosophical and mathematical significance of Rolle's objections. As to the mathematical significance, although flawed by several mistakes, Rolle's attacks had the merit of pushing research toward areas not yet completely understood; witness the work by Saurin in the next two decades on singularities on curves, and Guisnées's work on the rules of Hudde and Fermat. As to the philosohical significance, the opposition between finite and infinite is one of the long-standing issues in the philosophy of mathematics. Rolle addressed problems of rigor and the acceptability of infinitary mathematics. This forced the infinitesimalists to look explicitly at the foundational problem and, as we have seen, their answers were far from conclusive.

Rolle's criticisms also foreshadowed Bishop Berkeley's more famous attacks against the fluxional and the differential calculus. Several questions could be asked about the relationship between the early criticisms of the infinitesimal calculus (of Rolle, Nieuwentijt, Clüver, etc.) and the later criticisms. I will limit myself to some brief remarks about the similarities and dissimilarities between Rolle's criticisms and Berkeley's *Analyst*, referring the reader to Blay (1986) for a more thorough analysis. It is quite interesting to find that Rolle's three main objections are raised in the *Analyst*. In particular, paragraphs 6 and 7 of the *Analyst* contain a critique of the existence and conceivability of differentials, and paragraph 18 contains an attack on the use of dx both as a quantity and as an absolute zero. Although the motivations for Rolle's attacks and Berkeley's criticisms differed, the two agreed on a number of points and on an explicit finitism. For Rolle, this finitism was embedded in the Cartesian refusal to admit infinitary mathematics as a rigorous discipline; for Berkeley, more explicit epistemological considerations accounted for the finitist commitment.

Rolle and Berkeley employ different logic in their strategies. Rolle thought that the wrong principles of the analysis were bound to produce falsities; Berkeley never questioned the results of the calculus and proposed his theory of double mistakes to explain how one could, through several errors, arrive "though not at science yet at truth" (Berkeley 1734, 78). Finally, it is my opinion that Rolle's position within the academy made his attacks much more dangerous for the French infinitesimalists than Berkeley's attacks on the British mathematicians. As Fontenelle points out, Rolle's challenge had been extremely radical: "Il y a certainement encore des difficultés à éclaircir dans le Système de la nouvelle Géometrie; mais on parloit de renverser le Systême total" (Fontenelle 1719, 98). And although the foundational problems of the calculus were to haunt mathematics and philosophy for the next two centuries, the victory of the Leibnizians remains an important event in their history.

APPENDIX

I present a translation of Biancani's work *De Mathematicarum Natura Disser-tatio*. This work is an appendix to the *Aristotelis Loca Mathematica* (Bologna, 1615), a commentary on the passages in the Aristotelian corpus dealing with mathematics. The text is here translated in its entirety with the exception of the dedication to Pietro Francesco Malaspina. The translation and the notes are by Gyula Klima. I wish to thank the Griswold Faculty Research Fund (Yale University) for a generous grant which helped cover the costs of the translation.

A TREATISE ON THE NATURE OF MATHEMATICS
ALONG WITH A CHRONOLOGY OF OUTSTANDING
MATHEMATICIANS
BY JOSEPHUS BLANCANUS SJ,
PROFESSOR OF MATHEMATICS IN PARMA,
PRINTED IN THE PRINTING HOUSE OF
BARTHOLOMEUS COCHIUS,
IN BOLOGNA, 1615

SUPPLEMENT ON THE NATURE OF MATHEMATICAL SCIENCES

Translated by Gyula Klima
Dept. of Philosophy, Yale University
Institute of Philosophy of the Hungarian Academy

As in this work[1] we have made several scattered remarks concerning the nature of mathematical sciences, I deemed it neither foreign to the subject, nor unwelcome to the reader to gather here those considerations which seem to be necessary for the adequate perception of their nature. Especially since some recent authors, who touched upon them far too lightly, took on the habit of chattering about this subject, just like blind people about colors, hardly ever considering their intrinsic nature. So, to render our discussion clear, we are going to divide it as follows:

First, we discuss the subject matter of these disciplines.

Second, the medium of geometrical demonstrations, that is to say, whether these are perfect [*potissimae*] demonstrations.[2]

Third, the excellence of the knowledge they supply us.

Fourth, we dispel some calumnies.

Fifth, applied mathematical sciences.

CHAPTER 1   On the Subject of Geometry and Arithmetic, which is called Intelligible Matter

First we are going to discuss pure mathematics, i.e., geometry and arithmetic, which differs in kind from applied mathematics, namely, astronomy, optics [*perspectiva*], mechanics, and music. Quantity abstracted from sensible matter is usually considered in two ways. For it is considered by the natural scientist and the metaphysician[3] in itself, that is, absolutely, insofar as it is quantity, whether it is delimited [*terminata*] or not; and in this way its properties are divisibility, locatability, figurability, etc. But the geometer and the arithmetician consider [quantity] not absolutely, but insofar as it is delimited, as are the finite straight or curved lines in continuous quantity; and the delimited surfaces from which there result various figures, like circle, triangle, etc.; and, finally, the solids, again delimited, which constitute the various species of solid figures, like pyramid, cube, cone, cylinder, etc., which pertain to the geometer. And the same can be observed analogically also in discrete quantity, i.e., in numbers, which the arithmetician considers only insofar as they are delimited [*terminatos*]. However, that it is these genera of delimited quantity that form the subject matter of geometry and arithmetic is clear from the fact that they define only these quantities, and they demonstrate only their various properties, which are entirely different from those that the natural scientist and the metaphysician consider in quantity absolutely. So it is obvious that these properties which the mathematician considers emanate from this quantity insofar as it is delimited, such as equality, inequality, such and such division, transfiguration, various proportions, commensurability, incommensurability, construction of figures, etc. Obviously, these properties do not flow from the intrinsic nature of quantity, for if it is taken to be undelimited [*interminata*], the aforementioned properties do not follow, as nothing, taken to be like this, is equal or unequal, etc., but when delimitation [*terminatio*] is added to quantity, they flow from it by emanation. So it is correct to say that the formal aspect [*formalis ratio*] of mathematical consideration is delimitation, and that its total adequate object is delimited quantity, insofar as it is delimited. For from this delimitation there result the various figures and numbers which the mathematician defines and of which he demonstrates various theorems. But this is the quantity that is usually called intelligible matter, in contradistinction to sensible matter, which concerns the natural scientist, for the former is separated by the intellect from the latter and it is perceived by the intellect alone. So continuous and discrete [quantity], both delimited, are intelligible matter, the one [being the intelligible matter] of geometry, while the other [being the intelligible matter] of arithmetic. And from this it is also clear why the mathematician is said to consider finite quantity, for he considers delimited quantity, which is finite. For what has delimitation, i.e., limits [*terminus, seu fines*], is finite. But if there could be some delimited quantity which is at the same time infinite, Euclid's demonstrations could apply to it as well; for if there were an infinite triangle, it could be shown in the same manner that it has [the] three angles equal to two right angles. However, those who attacked geometrical demonstrations scarcely recognized this delimited quantity as being the subject matter of geometry and arithmetic, which is easily seen in their writings, and this is the primary cause of their error.

Furthermore, as a result of mathematical abstraction from sensible matter, this abstract matter acquires a certain perfection, which is called mathematical perfection. For example, an abstract triangle is an absolutely plane [figure] constituted by three perfectly straight lines, by three angles, and by three absolutely indivisible points which, I think, could hardly be found in the nature of things (excepting, perhaps, celestial things). Hence many [people] object to mathematicians that mathematical entities do not exist, except only by the intellect. However, we should know that even if these mathematical entities do not exist in that perfection, this is merely accidental, for it is well known that both nature and art intend to imitate primarily those mathematical figures, although because of the grossness [*ruditatem*] and imperfection of sensible matter, which is incapable of receiving perfect figures, they do not achieve their end. For nature in the trunks of trees strives after the figure of cylinder, in apples and grapes after spherical or spheroid figure, in the cornea of the eye after circle, indeed, the eye itself is most spherical. The sun and other stars are agreed on all hands to be entirely spherical; the surface of water is globular, and also the earth itself, were it not for the coarseness [*crassities*] and diversity of its matter, would obviously take on a round shape. And isn't it manifest that in marine shells conic spirals are inscribed, while in several herbs cylindrical and plane spirals? But art even more obviously follows these figures; since craftsmen endow almost all their artifacts with quadrangular or round figures, or with circles or ellipses. Indeed, art itself, not unlike nature which it imitates, is [also] defrauded of its proper end by the coarseness of matter. Therefore, even though these [perfect mathematical figures] do not exist in the nature of things, since in the mind of the Author of Nature, as well as in the human mind, their ideas do exist as the exact archetypes of all things, indeed, as exact mathematical entities, the mathematician investigates their ideas, which are primarily intended per se, and which are [the] true entities. For this reason we should hold that these geometrical entities which are perfect in all respects are per se and true beings; whereas natural as well as artificial figures, which exist in the nature of things, as they are not intended [per se] by any efficient cause, are beings *per accidens*, and are imperfect and false. For example, a triangle depicted in a chart is not a true triangle, but the true triangle is that which is in the divine mind. And from these considerations we can easily understand why Plato said that God was doing geometry [*Deum geometrizare*], that is, that just like a true geometer, God contemplates only the perfect ideas of things. Again, poets, who ought to imitate perfect things, at least quite often depict things in their poems not as they are, but conjure them up and represent them to their readers or spectators as they ought to be. Finally, we can also say that these entities are [at least] possible; and who would deny that God or an angel could produce them [in reality]? But for an object of science it is enough to be possible, for science abstracts from the existence of the subject.

Again, with respect to this intelligible matter we distinguish matter even in a further sense, namely, when we speak about parts as being the matter of the whole. For example, when two triangles make up a quadrilateral of any sort, the two triangles are the matter of this quadrilateral. In a similar manner, sometimes several partial angles make up a total angle as its matter. And the same holds for other similar cases: the half, the third, the double, or the remainder of any sort of whole refer to real material causes, as is asserted by Aristotle in tex. 31.2 and tex. 3.5 of the *Metaphysics* and by all philosophers. And this interpretation of matter [in mathematics] is similar to the interpretation of matter in physics, of which the whole composite [substance] is constituted as of a part. For the whole composite [substance] is constituted of matter and form as its parts. However, this interpretation of matter is different from the interpretation sometimes used by physicists, when they consider matter in which, or around which [*in qua, aut circa quam*], as they say, [something is generated]. But this should cause no difficulty, for this interpretation of 'matter' does not belong to the true concept of material cause. On the other hand, those who attack geometrical demonstrations appear scarcely ever to have taken this into consideration, which is the second cause of their error.

Finally, we should pay attention to the momentous fact that geometrical as well as arithmetical definitions are entirely essential definitions, namely, definitions which explicate the whole nature [*quidditatem*] of the thing, and that they are not in the least only explications of names, as the same persons wrongly assume, which is their third error. But that this was also Aristotle's opinion is obvious, for whenever in the *Analytics* he discusses the principles of sciences, he always includes among them geometrical and arithmetical definitions, which he could hardly have done, if these were only explications of names. It is true, nevertheless, that they frequently are explications both of things and of names at the same time. This is quite often the case, namely, when the names are perfect and entirely in agreement with the thing, for "names are quite often well suited to the things they name."

Names of this sort are most often those that have a perfect etymology, when the explication of the name itself is at the same time the essential definition of the thing. Geometrical names and definitions are often of this kind. For example, such is the definition of square; for when I say: a square is a plane figure consisting of four [equal] straight lines and four right angles, I explicate both the concept of the name and the concept of the thing at the same time; for it is called a square [*quadratum*] on account of those four lines, and I explicate its total essence when I say that it consists of four [equal] straight lines and four right angles. For these two taken together constitute the total essence of a square, as they are its constitutive difference, while its genus is quadrilateral plane figure; for which reason this is the most perfect definition, since it manifests not only the essence of the name, but also the total essence of the thing. For as soon as we learn that a square consists of the said things, the soul does not desire to learn anything more about its essence, but comes to rest, whence it is obvious that this definition is of the best kind. Such is also the definition of oblong [*figurae altera parti longioris*]. For when it is said that it is a quadrilateral plane figure, which is rectangular, but which is not equilateral, from this it is obvious why it is called "longer on one side," which is its etymology. But [from this] also its essence becomes known in such a manner that nothing further remains to be asked about it. Again, when it is said that an equilateral triangle is one having three equal sides, at once you see the cause [*causa*] both of the name and of the thing. But such is also the 6th definition of the 1st book [of the *Elements*]: those rectilinear figures are similar which have equal respective angles and equally proportional sides. For there both the etymology and the nature of the thing are made manifest. Again, the 10th definition of the 1st book is of the same kind: commensurable magnitudes are those that are measured by the same measure. I pass over innumerable other examples which one can find in other geometers, lest I linger too long on such an obvious point. However, let us consider those that are in no way definitions of names, but only of things. Euclid's definition of the point is bipartite, in accordance with the nature of point; since it is partly absolute, and partly relative. When the 1st definition states that a point is what has no parts, it is defined insofar as it is absolute, but when later in the 3d definition it is said that the ends of lines are points, it is defined as something belonging to something else. Now by these [definitions] the whole nature of point [*punctum*] is made manifest, but the etymology is not in the least. For a point is so named after the act of piercing [*pungendo*], as if it were a sort of puncture [*punctura*], which notion is not even touched upon in Euclid's definition. Again, when it is said that a line is a length lacking width, where is here the explication of the name? For a line is so named after linen [*a lino*], as if it were a linen string; for in ancient times strings which craftsmen used for measuring were made of linen, just like nowadays they are made of hemp; but it would be ridiculous to look for this explanation in Euclid's definition, by which, however, the essence of line is made perfectly clear.

In a similar manner, when he defines surface as [a quantity] having only length and width, the nature of the thing is manifest, but where is the definition of the name, according to which we call something a surface [*superficiem*] as it were the outer face [*quasi supremam faciem*]? And when it is said that an angle is the inclination of two lines touching each other, where is the notion of the word?—however, the nature, or quiddity of the thing is made manifest. The same point is even more obvious in the case of the perpendicular line, which is doubtless so called after the plumb line [*a perpendiculo*], but this fact does not show up at all in the definition, by which, however, what the thing is

is perfectly explicated. Furthermore, the definition of circle appears to be given
not by intrinsic features, but it is equivalent to the intrinsic definition: for when
it is said that circle is a plane figure contained by a unique line such that all
the [straight] lines drawn to it from a given point inside the figure are equal;
this is like saying that a circle is a plane figure whose center [*medium*] is
equidistant from its boundary points [*extrema*], which is essential, for given
this equidistance, a circle is necessarily given. On the other hand, to hold that
the definition of center [*centrum*] is only an explication of the name is absurd,
for this is a Greek word meaning originally a goad or a spike by which herdsmen
drive cattle.

Again, to think that the definition of rhombus contains only the explication
of the name is equally ridiculous. For a rhombus is so named after some sort
of fish, or a weaver's instrument because of its shape; but its nature is revealed
by its definition, namely, that a rhombus is a quadrilateral, equilateral, but not
rectangular plane figure. The same can be observed in the definitions of bodies,
the first of which is that a solid is [something] that has length, width and
thickness [*crassitudo*], by which the whole nature of the thing is disclosed.

But, to avoid prolixity, I pass over innumerable other entirely essential
definitions, which one can find in [the works of] all geometers. And the same
goes for arithmetical definitions as well, which is immediately evident to anyone
considering them. However, if someone were to concede that these mathematical definitions are essential, but he still denied that these are causal
definitions, which is required by a demonstration, he should listen to Aristotle
rebutting him, who in *De Anima* (tex. 12.2) says that squaring has two
definitions, the one is formal or essential, according to which squaring is the
construction of a square which is equal to a given quadrilateral; while the other
is causal, according to which quadrature is the finding of the middle proportional, for the line of the middle proportional is the cause of the square
equal to the given figure—see our explication of this passage.[4] So it is necessary
for him to concede that geometrical definitions are not only nominal, but also
formal and causal definitions. For which reason it should now be clear that
mathematical definitions surpass [in perfection] the definitions of other sciences,
for all philosophers concede that the ultimate differences of things, without
which there is no true definition, are hidden from us, indeed, so much so that
the same philosophers doubt even whether "rational animal" is the true
definition of man.

Perhaps, it is objected further that these mathematical definitions are often
definitions of a subject; but in a perfect [*potissima*] demonstration, which we
are striving for, it is the causal definitions of properties [*passiones*] that are
primarily and *per se* required, while the definition of the subject is required
only incidentally [*per accidens*], e.g., when something deriving immediately
from the subject is to be demonstrated of it. I think we should respond, firstly,
that since the causal definition of a property is not different from its cause, if
in the definition of the subject the cause of the property is contained, then by
assuming the defintion of the subject, the causal definition of the property is
also assumed. Secondly, in mathematics, the definitions of subjects often come

out as definitions of properties, as it will be obvious below, namely, when the subject itself, say, square, is demonstrated of a figure as its property, or when it is shown that a certain construction correctly yields a square, a triangle, a perpendicular line, and the like. Thirdly, concerning the previous difficulty we said that in Aristotle's opinion there are causal definitions in mathematics, which we confirmed by the example of squaring. Now on the basis of what we have said about scientific definitions we should take note of a certain disparity between the ways mathematics and the other sciences proceed in the cognition of their proper subjects. For in demonstrations from signs [*a signo*], from which other sciences frequently start, only the cognition of the name of the subject is required, but not the essential definition, for its essence, which is hidden, is investigated by its accidents and its properties, from what is posterior [*a posteriori*]; and then, once the essence is detected, we return to the distinct and scientific demonstrations of the properties. However, if the perfect cognition of the object were given in the first place, as is the case with mathematical objects on account of their perfect definitions, we would proceed according to the most beautiful order of nature, from the essence of the object to the demonstration of its properties, as it happens in demonstrations from the cause [*a causa*], as are almost all geometrical and arithmetical demonstrations, except for demonstrations from the impossible [*ab impossibili*]. But here [in mathematical demonstrations not *ab impossibili*] from the premised definitions the entire nature of the subject is primarily given to us, from which, then, we always proceed from what is prior [*a priori*] to the investigation of properties. And in this process the definition of the subject is always to be premised, and its quiddity is to be assumed. So it follows that the mathematical sciences proceed from what is better known to us as well as from what is better known by nature, as is held by Averroës indeed, almost by everybody else, and more recently especially by our Toletus in q.4, bk. 2 of the *Physics*. From what is better known to us, because by the definition of a figure its essence is known before anything else, even when its properties are still ignored. On the other hand, from what is better known by nature, for the essence of the subject is naturally prior to its properties that derive from it, and which are demonstrated of it. And this is the reason why geometrical demonstrations are always so efficient and possess the highest degree of certitude.

CHAPTER 2   On the Medium of Geometrical and Arithmetical Demonstrations, i.e., Whether They Are Perfect Demonstrations

The mathematicians of our age are compelled to guard by every effort what was so far their safe, ancient, and rightful possession from some recent thinkers who strive to take it away. For was there ever a philosopher of stature before Alessandro Piccolomini who attempted to rob geometers of perfect demonstrations? None, indeed! He himself confesses that among recent thinkers he was the first to have caught smell of this "truth"; but in fact he was the first from antiquity, for the two or three ancient thinkers whom he tries to bring up in support of his opinion do not support him at all, as we shall see.

First, therefore, we invoke the authorities of antiquity, especially Aristotle, for the affirmative answer [to the question whether geometrical demonstrations are perfect]. Well, in fact I find it unworthy and superfluous to dispute about Aristotle's opinion with anyone who has perused his *Posterior Analytics*, and to quibble in vain over some passages to determine his mind, for throughout these two books he appears to do nothing else, but to delineate the idea of perfect demonstration on the basis of geometrical demonstrations. Indeed, he attributes all conditions and everything else required for a perfect demonstration everywhere to geometrical demonstrations, and this he always confirms, not only in his precepts but also by his examples. And I take it that Aristotle never expressed anything more clearly, and he proved nothing more amply, than the fact that geometrical demonstrations are perfect in all respects, so that it would appear entirely unworthy of a Philosopher to distort his absolutely clear position [on this point]. In my view, it would be more proper to give up the name "peripatetic" at this point rather than to use the peripatetic doctrine, like many do, as a disguise, or to give it such a perverted interpretation. Even if it would be sufficient, therefore, to refer the reader to the books of the *Analytics* and their commentators, nevertheless, I am not reluctant to put forward some selected passages, which are indeed so manifest that one just wonders how the authors of the contrary opinion could interpret them at their caprice. The first is tex. 23, bk. 1, *Posterior Analytics*: "We know anything not incidentally [*non secundum accidens*], when we know it by that on account of which it is such, from its principles, and insofar as it is such, as when we know that [the triangle] has [three angles] equal to two right angles, which is such by itself and from its principles." Where, as you see, Aristotle explicitly asserts that the demonstration by which the geometer shows that the triangle has three angles equal to two right angles proceeds from what are first, immediate, per se, and insofar as it is what it is; and by no means from what are incidental [*per accidens*]. Just as if he stated that it is the most powerful and perfect [demonstration] in every respect. But of this demonstration we shall have more to say below; meanwhile, see our explication of the cited passage above in our mathematical quotations.

Again, in tex. 29 of the first book of the *Posterior Analytics*, [we read]: "And those [propositions] are more properly converted which are [used] in mathematics, for they [involve] no accident (and it is in this that they differ from dialectical [propositions]), but [are] definitions," where you see that mathematicians do not use any accident, or what is contingent, but definitions, that is, [they do not demonstrate] by something contingent, but by the formal cause. In tex. 31 [we read]: "Of the [syllogistic] figures the most scientific is the first figure, for it is by this figure that mathematical sciences, like arithmetic, geometry, and optics present their demonstrations, but I could as well enumerate all other sciences which consider the why [*propter quid*]." Furthermore, in the *Posterior Analytics*, in tex. 11, bk. 2, he asserts that the demonstration by which the geometer proves that the angle drawn in a semicircle is a right angle is a proof from the material cause, indeed, he presents this as the best example of a demonstration of this kind. But of this demonstration we shall also have more to say below; meanwhile see again the explication of this locus in the mathematical quotations. Let this much suffice from logic, unless more should be inserted here later. In the second book of the *Physics*, tex. 68, we read: "For the question 'for what reason?' [*propter quid*] is ultimately reduced to what something is [*ipsum quid est*, i.e., quiddity] in the case of immobile things, as in mathematics it is reduced ultimately to the definition of right angle or commensurability or something like this." Again, we see the [role of] formal cause in mathematical demonstrations. See the explanation of this passage given by us above. In the sixth book of the *Metaphysics*, tex. 1, we can read: "Also mathematical entities have their principles, elements, and causes." In *Metaphysics*, 11, c. 1., s. 3: "So it is obvious that there are three genera of speculative sciences, namely, Physics, Mathematics, and Theology"; from all this you can see how clear Aristotle's position is.

As to Plato's authority, it is certain that he recognized material and formal causes in mathematics, for, as Aristotle testifies in the first book of the *Metaphysics*, c. 7, he did not believe that philosophical speculations should deal much with other causes than the formal and the material, treated of by the mathematicians, as he never explicated the efficient and final causes, for the reason that these are never discussed by mathematicians. Again, Proclus, c. 10, bk. 7 in [his commentary on] Euclid, says that Plato calls mathematics a science entirely of sempiternal things. And somewhat later [he adds] that we should not say therefore that Plato banishes mathematics from among the sciences. Also, at the end of the chapter he says: "Mathematics, however, is a science not without suppositions, but one cognizing the proper concepts of the soul, giving the causes of conclusions." Note what he says: "giving the causes of conclusions." And he concludes later by adding that all this was said concerning Plato's position on mathematics.

But that he [Plato] regarded mathematical sciences as the most perfect ones is justly believed also on the basis of his own words. For why should he have said that God was doing geometry, unless for the reason of the excellence of geometry? Why did he ban from his school all those who were ignorant of geometry? Why did he put it before natural philosophy in the [process of] ascent to the consideration of the supreme Good? But how unworthily others try to drag him over to their own side will be evident later, when we shall dispel their calumnies.

Let there follow in the third place the authority of Proclus himself, who in the first and second books of his commentary on Euclid is full of praises of mathematical sciences and especially geometry, and that they are perfect sciences he not only affirms, but also demonstrates. He takes up the topic in chapter 10 of the first book, where he amply demonstrates from Plato that they are sciences that give the causes of their conclusions, i.e., which provide perfect demonstrations. Again, in c. 5 of bk. 2, speaking about Euclid, he says: "Concerning his teaching of the elements of geometry, anyone will admire him especially for the order and [careful] selection of the things that he shows by these elements: for he did not take up all those things that he could have said, but only those that he could teach in an elementary order. Still, [he presents] syllogistic modes of all kinds, some taking credit from causes, others from perfectly certain signs, but all invincible and certain, and suitable to a science." Here we should note the phrase: "taking credit from causes," by which he clearly indicates the he acknowledges causes in Euclidian demonstrations.

Furthermore, in book 3, in his comments on Euclid's first proposition he says: "When geometers construct a syllogism *per impossibile*, then they only wish to discover the symptom, but when they use a perfect demonstration, then, if it is carried out in a particular case, the cause is still not manifest, but if it is universal, covering all similar cases, then also the reason why [*propter quid*] [such a symptom occurs] will be manifest." Again, you can see [the role of] the reason why [*propter quid*] in geometry. Also, somewhat later in the same commentary: "What we call [here] demonstration sometimes does indeed have the proper characteristics of a demonstration, namely, proving the conclusion by definitions as their media, for this is what renders a demonstration perfect." Where we should note that according to Proclus geometers use definitions as media, which is required for the most exact demonstration, as he himself says. And he illustrates this on the example of Euclid's first demonstration, saying: "When by drawing circles it is shown that the constructed triangle is equilateral, the recognition is from the cause, for we say that the equality of these circles is the cause of the equality of the sides of the triangle." What else could Proclus say more clearly than this? This, nevertheless, escaped the busy eyes of our opponents. For otherwise it is obvious from Piccolomini's work that he perused Proclus carefully precisely for this point; how it could then happen that he did not see this [is a miracle]. But many of us nowadays do philosophy not to find the truth but to find what we like.

We decided to bring up in support of our claim only these three philosophers from among the ancients, namely, Plato, Aristotle, and Proclus, for they are the ones whom our opponents try to join to their ranks despite all reason, as should already be clear from the foregoing discussion. I omit the citation of the opinions of other Greek, Arab, and Latin philosophers, for they all unanimously praise geometrical demonstrations as the most exact of all, indeed by the testimony of Piccolomini himself, who, in the beginning of his booklet on mathematical certainty says: "Almost all Latin authors, like St. Albert, St. Thomas, Marsilius, Aegidius, Zimara, and many others interpreted Averroës in the same way, saying that mathematics is of the highest degree of certitude, and that mathematics demonstrates from what is better known both to us and by nature, indeed, that it is almost the only science which uses the kind of demonstration that is called perfect, namely, the one by which we can clearly get to know at the same time not only that the effect is, but also why it is." Indeed, [Piccolomini] himself can be said to be absolutely the first [to hold this view] for nobody before him whose works are extant said the same, even if he cunningly strives to join Proclus, Plato, and Aristotle to himself. After him, on the other hand, almost only two followed in his footsteps, namely, Pererius and the Conimbricenses. But almost everybody else after him embraced the contrary opinion, from among whose ranks it will be enough to refer to only two, who are the most excellent philosophers of our time, Toletus and Zabarella. For Toletus in q. 4, bk. 2, concl. 3, writes thus: "The physicist and the mathematician differ in their method of demonstration. For the physicist often uses demonstrations from signs and effects, for the causes he considers are frequently hidden [*occultae*], and imperceptible in themselves, while their effects are perceptible, like death, motion, etc., which are evident to the senses, but whose causes are removed from the senses. But the mathematician often proceeds from what is prior, for the causes he considers are better known than their effects, for he abstracts from the senses, and that which is prior is better known by the intellect." Observe, dear reader, how sincerely a professor of natural philosophy tells the truth about mathematics, so that he even puts it before physics [in certainty]. As to Iacobus Zabarella, he always acknowledges mathematical demonstrations in his logical work as the most perfect, and he expounds Aristotle's geometrical examples as being true, and completely appropriate to the things [considered] themselves; wherefore there is no reason why we should quote here one rather than another of his dicta. I would not, however, omit mentioning that he confessed to have assiduously perused the whole Euclid two or three times, so that he could properly follow Aristotle on the nature of demonstrations, when he observed that Aristotle had tested everything that he had prescribed about demonstrations, like against a touchstone, against the norms of geometry. I forgot where he says this, but I am sure I read this somewhere in his work. Finally, in the fourth place, we confirm the same point by the common authority of all ancient authors, who always call geometrical proofs demonstrations by appropriation [*per antonomasiam*], and not reasons, or opinions, or tenets [*sententiae*], as it happens in other parts of philosophy. But let us turn from authority to reason.

First. A true and perfect demonstration, according to Averroës, should proceed from what are better known both to us and to nature. Such are geometrical demonstrations, as we could see a little earlier, so they are the most perfect demonstrations.

Second. From Themistius, in c. 2, bk. 2 of his paraphrase of the *Posterior Analytics*, we have it that the most perfect demonstration should show both what [is the case] and why [it is the case] [*& quod & propter quid*], which is indeed rather exhibited by geometrical and arithmetical demonstrations, than by any others. For example, demonstration 32.3 [in Euclid's *Elements*] shows that the angle drawn in a semicircle is a right angle, which was entirely unknown, and gives also the cause for this, which was equally unknown. But almost the same is the case with all the rest. But in applied mathematics, in Physics and Metaphysics, the effects are often well known, but their causes are hidden; we should say, therefore, with Averroës and Themistius, that geometrical demonstrations are most excellent [*praestantissimas*].

The third argument, which is the most evident, is taken from the analysis of some demonstrations. For what is the use in carrying on this disputation in terms of extrinsic features, when we can go, as it were, inside the very thing, and by a certain anatomy of these demonstrations we can see with our own eyes their core, their media [*earum media*]? But first we have to recall that a most perfect demonstration is not only one that gives the proper and adequate cause of [the property of] the thing to be demonstrated, but also one that evidently shows that this property [*passio*] proceeds from that cause, so—as Aristotle says—that the thing could not be otherwise; which is, in fact, characteristic par excellence of mathematical demonstrations. Now this cause in geometry and arithmetic is either a material cause, namely, when they use parts of some whole as their media, or it is a formal cause, namely, when the medium is the definition of the subject or of the property. I am also aware of the fact, however, that some say that a perfect demonstration proceeds from a formal cause in a different sense, because it contains the causal definition of the property, which exhibits its cause and so it is like its form, which constitutes a thing in [its] being.

We should note secondly that all demonstrations are ultimately resolved into something which is either self-evident [*per se notum*] or confirmed from what is posterior [*a posteriori comprobatum*]. For it is enough if the cause is manifested, howsoever this is achieved. I say this because of some people, who upon noticing in geometrical demonstrations some lines or divisions which are not intrinsic to the thing under consideration think at once that such demonstrations are by something extrinsic to this thing. But they are mistaken, for they do not recognize that those lines or partitions are not the media of these demonstrations, but are provided for the finding of the medium [*ad medij inventionem*] and its connection to the property [to be proved]. And that their doubts are entirely misguided is shown by the fact that many demonstrations proceed without any construction of lines or any divisions, as do demonstrations 15, 33, 34, 42, and 36 only in the first book of the *Elements*. But this is the main source of their error.

These things having been premised, first we shall show that there are formal causes in geometrical demonstrations, and then that there are material causes as well. And [we show] this first by the analysis of Euclid's first demonstration, which proceeds from the formal cause. And since this demonstration is not [the proof of] a threorem, but is [the solution of] a problem, we should know that our opponents completely ignored the fact that in every problem something is taught by the construction of some lines. For example, in the present one Euclid teaches why by the drawing of certain circles around a given line and by drawing certain lines as prescribed we get an equilateral triangle, as is obvious to anyone considering the thing. So those lines, as the radii of those circles, are by no means extrinsic to the thing which the demonstration is about, on the contrary, they are its subject. But since given this construction it is obvious that what is constructed is a triangle,[5] he does not care to demonstrate that it is a triangle, but as it is not known whether it is equilateral, the whole demonstration is devoted to proving the equality of those three lines.

Although it is obvious in itself that this demonstration contains [reference to] a cause, as we shall see this soon, we do not lack the authority of Proclus for this point either, which is so clear that I am absolutely puzzled why Piccolomini, this avid reader of Proclus, did not see it. For Proclus, commenting on this demonstration, says the following: "When by the drawing of circles it is shown that the triangle constructed is equilateral the cognition is achieved by the cause, for we say that the equality of the circles is the cause of the equality of the sides of that triangle." And these words contain not only the authority, but also the best reason why this demonstration proceeds from the cause, for it plainly shows that the cause of the equality of the sides is that they are the radii of equal circles. This reasoning proceeds from the definition of the subject, which is the circle, although not the whole definition is supplied, only as much of it as is needed, namely, the definition of radii, which suffices for drawing the conclusion, as Zabarella correctly remarks, speaking about this demonstration. Since, therefore, the medium is the definition of the subject, it is obvious that this is a perfect demonstration, which provides the proper and adequate cause of the property [*passio*] demonstrated, namely, the nature of circle. And is this way Euclid perfectly demonstrated that the construction he prescribed yields an equilateral triangle. So, the subject is the configuration of these lines and circles, the medium is the definition of circle and the property [*passio*] is that [the figure constructed] is an equilateral triangle. From this demonstration we can even glean the causal definition of this property, namely, that an equilateral triangle is one arising from such a construction. So this demonstration lacks nothing for being a perfect demonstration. From which you can see how unjustly it was attacked by some people, who thought it was a demonstration by extrinsic features. The cause of their error was that they believed that it demonstrated that the triangle is equilateral in an absolute sense. But they were mistaken, for in this, and in all other problems, what is demonstrated is that such and such a construction yields a triangle or a square or something else, as should be clear to anyone taking even a cursory look at Euclid.

I find it befitting to consider yet another [proof] proceeding from the formal cause. It is the 46th of the first book of the *Elements*. And this is again a problem, by which Euclid teaches how a square is constructed upon a given straight line. So he gives us a certain construction of lines, of which he demonstrates later that it yields a square, so that this construction plays the role of the subject, of which it is demonstrated that it is a square. And so he did not intend, as some people falsely believe, to demonstrate absolutely that that [arrangement of four lines] is a square, but that what results from such a construction is a square. There are two essential features of a square: the first is that it should have four equal sides, and the second that it should have four right angles, as is clear from its definition. But neither of these suffices without the other. For a rhombus has four equal sides, while an oblong has four right angles, but neither of these is a square. But if these two belong to any figure at the same time, they necessarily make it a square. So Euclid proved that both of these are present in the [constructed] figure as a result of this construction and that consequently it satisfies the definition of the square. Therefore, this is a perfect demonstration, because it provides the intrinsic, proper, and adequate cause, on account of which the thing is. And we should note that the effect is really distinct here from the cause. For to be a square (which is the effect) is not only to have four right angles, and neither is it only to have four equal sides, but to have both at the same time in the same thing; so there results here a certain whole, or composite, which is something different from the parts taken separately. But in this demonstration the cause is the parts taken separately, while the effect is the composite resulting from their union. We should also note that the demonstration proceeds from the defintion of the subject, for those two essential features of the square are taken from the definition of those things that are in the construction, which, as I indicated above, serves here as the subject. Also, from this definition of the parts of the subject contained in the demonstration we can glean the causal definition of the property [*passio*] [to be proven] itself, which is: a square is a figure having four right angles and four equal sides produced by such a construction. We should note finally that howsoever it is shown that these two are present here, either from the cause or from the effect, it does not make any difference in the perfection of this demonstration. For it is enough if we have the proper cause of the thing so that it cannot be otherwise. You will encounter hundreds of similar [demonstrations] by the formal cause in the works of Euclid, Archimedes, Apollonius, and other geometers. See the Appendix at the end of this work, in which you will find all demonstrations of the first book of the Elements analyzed, many of which are from the formal cause.

But let us turn now to the material cause, following the lead of Aristotle. Let us take therefore the celebrated 32d [proposition] of the first book of the Elements, which our opponents often bring up against mathematicians. And since commenting on tex. 23 of the first book of the *Posterior Analytics* we showed that it proceeded by the material cause, to avoid useless repetition, it is sufficient now to reread that explication. Here, however, I will examine its first part, namely, the one showing that an external angle of any triangle is equal to the two internal angles opposite to it. The medium of this proof, if it is put into the rigorous form of a demonstration, is this: the external angle is divisible into two angles which are equal to the two internal angles of the triangle [opposed to it], respectively, therefore also the total angle will be equal to the two taken together. But that the external angle is divisible into two parts equal to the internal angles he proves by dividing it by a line parallel to the opposite side of the triangle, wherefore at once from the nature of parallel lines it appears that the partial angles constituting the external angle are equal to the internal angles of the triangle; from which it follows that the whole external angle is equal to the two internal angles taken together. But this kind of argumentation, from the potential parts to the whole, is regarded by all philosophers as proceeding from the material cause, and Aristotle himself asserts the same in tex. 3 of bk. 5 of the *Metaphysics* too. Also, in tex. 11 of bk. 2 of the *Posterior Analytics* he uses a similar example to explicate [the notion of] material cause. On the other hand, the geometers do not [explicitly] say that such an angle or figure is divisible into parts that are equal to some others, but they divide it at once, for the sake of brevity, using actuality for potentiality, for actuality presupposes potentiality. As Aristotle rightly remarked in tex. 20 of bk. 9 of the *Metaphysics*: "Also diagrams [*descriptiones*] are actually understood, for making the [appropriate] divisions we understand [them at once], and if they were divided, they would be manifest, but now they [the divisions] are present only potentially," etc., you already have our explication of this passage above. By diagrams here he means the geometrical demonstrations, as we frequently pointed this out in the body of this work above. There are countless demonstrations in the works of geometers that proceed by such divisions, and which, therefore are from the material cause. There are several in the first book of the *Elements*, as is clear from the Appendix given at the end of this work. We should also note that the cause by its nature is distinct from the effect, just like potentiality differs from actuality; for it is from some whole's being divisible into certain parts that are equal to others that it follows that the whole is actually equal to something else. And [this demonstration] is a priori, for the parts are naturally prior to the whole, as they are its cause. Note also that the parallel line by which the [external] angle is divided is drawn in order to find the medium of the demonstration, but it is by no means the medium itself. Therefore this demonstration is not by extrinsic features, unless you want to say that the minor premise is proved by such extrinsic features, which I willingly concede, as it does not derogate from he demonstration itself. So it is by the intrinsic, proper, and adequate cause of that equality, for parts with respect to the whole are such [a cause]. It is therefore a perfect demonstration, which was to be demonstrated.

Having demonstrated this first part of this proposition, Euclid proves the other part, namely, that every triangle has three angles etc., since the parts of two right angles are equal to these three. And this medium is [taken] equally from the material cause, [leading] from the parts to the whole. See the explication of this in tex. 23, bk. 1, *Posterior Analytics* where you can even see that this can be demonstrated in the Pythagorean manner as well, without any division, but by actually existing part. I say this for those who fear that [otherwise] the medium would not be found a priori. But to get rid of this scruple they should know that in the case of demonstrations of this kind, in which something is shown to be equal to something else by providing a division, it often happens that only one of these equal things is divided, wherefore their equality is caused on the part of the undivided thing by parts which actually precede and constitute the whole. And this is the case in both parts of the 32d, according to Euclid, and also in the 47th of bk. 1 of the *Elements*, and in many others. But Piccolomini objects first from Proclus by [quoting] the following: "When it is shown that a triangle has three angles equal to two right angles, from the fact that its external angle is equal to the two opposite internal angles, how is this a demonstration from the cause? Isn't the medium [rather] a certain sign here? For the internal angles are equal to two right angles even when the external angle does not exist, since the triangle exists even when its side is not extended." After this Proclus sets about demonstrating that Euclid's first demonstration is by the cause and is therefore a true demonstration, about which Piccolomini in his own quotation cunningly remains silent.

To the objection I reply first that the external angle in the Euclidian demonstration is by no means extrinsic, for in this second part it is taken as the subject of the demonstration, namely, as the part of two right angles, since with the angle next to it it makes two right angles to which the three angles of the triangle are proven to be equal, which seems to have escaped Proclus' attention. Secondly, if this Euclidian [proof] is not a demonstration for him, he should take the Pythagorean proof of the same, which proves what is intended without an external angle, and without any division; and this will dispel all doubts [on this score]. Thirdly, if our opponents could prove, which they will never do, that this demonstration is not a priori, does it follow from this that all others are similar [in this respect], as they are compelled to infer? Not, by any means. By what sort of logical "ius gentium" do they want to infer a universal from a single particular?

Secondly, you may object that this property, namely, having three angles etc. is not convertible with the property of being a triangle, i.e., it is not a property of the thing pertaining to it in virtue of what the thing is [*non esse secundum quod ipsum*], as the logicians say. For there is some figure besides triangles, as we can see in Proclus, that has the same property [*proprietas*]. My reply to this is that having three rectilinear angles (for it is with these that Euclid is dealing with) equal, etc. is convertible with being a triangle, for [even] Proclus converts them. But that figure which has three angles equal to two right angles is not rectilinear, as we can see in Proclus, therefore it is irrelevant to Euclid's or Pythagoras' idea. But then we can conclude with Proclus: "For we have to say also that the property of having three angles equal to two right angles is present per se and in virtue of what it is [*secundum quod ipsum*] in the triangle; whence Aristotle has this example at hand in his tract on demonstration, when considering [what belongs to something] insofar as what it is."

We considered another proof which according to Aristotle proceeds by the material cause, in tex. 11, bk. 2, *Posterior Analytics*, where he says that the angle inscribed in a semicircle is a right angle, as it is the half of two right angles, the medium of which is from the material cause, for to be the half is to be a part. The cause, therefore, which causes that angle to be a right angle is the quantity constituting [this angle], which is the half of two right angles, but perhaps we can say even more correctly that it is a right angle because it is divisible into two parts which taken together are equal to the half of two right angles, i.e., to a right angle. However, the line by which it is divided is not the medium, but what manifests the medium. In the subsequent Appendix at the end of this work you will see many more proofs from the material cause only from the first book of the *Elements*.

I do not find it necessary to examine any demonstration from arithmetic, as it is well known that it demonstrates in the same way as geometry does, as you can clearly see this in books 7, 8, and 9 of the *Elements*. Indeed, whatever we said so far about the one, we want it to be understood as concerning both, since according to Eutocius in the commentary of Apollonius, "these doctrines appear to be twins."[6]

Some General Objections to the Foregoing

First, these geometrical causes do not appear to be real causes, for they do not seem to be sufficiently distinct from their effects. For in the case of the formal cause the parts of the definition are identical with what is defined, and in the case of the material cause the parts are identical with the whole, and so they are not real causes, and hence nor real demonstrations. I respond first that when the parts are taken separately, not insofar as they constitute the whole, they are distinct from the whole, which means the parts in their union and the form of the composite, and this distinction is not only a distinction of reason [*quae distinctio non est solius rationis*].[7]

Secondly, although there does not appear to be here a distinction as great as in applied mathematics, or in physics, it is great enough to suffice for the perfect demonstration, which is obvious by the authority of Aristotle, Plato, Proclus, and all the Greeks, Arabs and Latins (except for two or three recent ones), who all agree that these demonstrations are most perfect, as we said above.

Thirdly, however little this distinction may be, it is certainly not only a distinction of reason, which is clear primarily according to the opinion of those who hold that a relation is distinct from its foundation, as they say, really, or modally, or formally. But secondly, the same is clear also according to the opinion of all others, especially more recent thinkers, referring variously to the same [distinction]. For some call it a formal [distinction], others call it real, others modal, others [one flowing] from the nature of the thing [*ex natura rei*], others real modal, and still others name it by other formalities, but by each one of these they mean something real to be present in it, which suffices for the perfect demonstration. For it is sufficient for a demonstration to be perfect, if it reveals the proper and adequate cause of the effect in accordance with the nature of the thing, for in this way it suffices for our intellect so that it can come to a rest and intuit the truth, which is the end of the perfect demonstration. And a greater or lesser distinction does not make a more or less true cause, but that is the true cause which truly causes the effect which is distinct from it not only by a distinction of reason, and hence that is a true demonstration which demonstrates by this cause.

Fourthly, this however little distinction, on the other hand, is greatly conducive to the perfection of the demonstration. For it is owing to this [smallness of the distinction] that in the demonstration it becomes obvious that this cause is the true and proper cause of the demonstrated property [*affectio*], so that it cannot proceed from a more proximate cause, which does not appear so clearly in any other science.

Second objection. The geometer proves that same conclusion by several demonstrations, and therefore by several media, but of one effect there is only one proper and adequate cause.

I respond first that it is possible to demonstrate the same thing by several demonstrations of which one may be a priori, while another a posteriori.

Secondly, if all of these are a priori, then they are essentially one and the same, while they are many only accidentally, for in all of these the principal medium is going to be the same, but the construction, by which it is found will be different, as is clear in the case of the 32d [proposition] of the first book, which is demonstrated differently by Euclid, by Pythagoras, and by Proclus, but in which all there is the same medium, namely, the material cause, although the construction is different.

Third objection. Geometrical demonstrations do not consist of what are proper and per se, for the geometer does not consider the essence of quantity, nor its properties, insofar as they emanate from its essence, wherefore he has to proceed from some common and merely extrinsic considerations. I respond that by what was said in the first chapter about intelligible matter and geometrical definitions this objection is more than sufficiently refuted. For the subject matter of geometry is not quantity per se, but insofar as it is delimited, the whole essence of which is known by the geometer from essential definitions. But both of these points were missed by our opponents.

Furthermore, it is false that the geometer proceeds from considerations common to many sciences, which [procedure] Aristotle forbids in bk. 1 of *Posterior Analytics*. For the geometer proceeds from the common principles of delimited quantity, i.e., of figures and numbers, which is not only permitted, but also has to be the case according to tex. 20 and 25 in bk. 1 of *Posterior Analytics*. And he does not even take up the same principle again, except where there is a formal effect of it, and even then only by restricting it to that particular case.

CHAPTER 3   The Calumnies of Some Recent Thinkers against Mathematics are Dispelled

The first [calumny] is [that] by which Alessandro Piccolomini and his followers maliciously bring in Proclus against the mathematicians. In order that you can clearly see this, I quote this from Proclus' full passage which he [Piccolomini] cites mutilated, and even in Greek, so that its real point will be more easily missed. So Proclus in the third book of his commentary on Euclid writes as follows: "It appeared to many that geometry does not consider causes and the reason why [something is the case] [*propter quid*]. This is the opinion of Amphonimus, taking his lead from Aristotle." It is this much that is quoted by Piccolomini in Greek, to which he adds: "What more do we need for this opinion?" But let it not miss your attention, dear reader, that this opinion is not that of Proclus, but that of Amphonimus, some philosopher of no name, who under the sham protection of Aristotle tries to take causes away from geometry, while this opinion is presented by Piccolomini as if it were the opinion of Proclus himself. But let us see what Piccolomini omitted. For Proclus continues as follows: "One can encounter—says Geminus—also this kind of investigation in geometry, in which way it is not the geometer's task to investigate the cause why [something is the case]; but in a circle one can inscribe an infinity of polygons, while in a sphere it is impossible to inscribe an infinity of polyhedrons of equal sides and angles, constructed of similar planes; to whom does it belong to investigate this besides the geometer?" This is Geminus' point cited by Proclus for the refutation of the opinion of Amphonimus. After this Proclus goes on to expound his own opinion as follows: "When geometers construct a syllogism per impossibile, then they only wish to discover the symptom, but when they use a perfect demonstration, then, if it is carried out in a particular case, the cause is still not manifest, however, if it is universal, covering all similar cases, then also the reason by [*propter quid*] [such a symptom occurs] will be manifest." This is the whole, intact context of this locus, brought up mutilated by our opponent, from which you can clearly see Proclus' opinion about geometry.

The second calumny is [that] by which they interpret (a however reluctant) Aristotle. But it is not only his transparent passages from the *Analytics*, *Physics*, and *Metaphysics* quoted above that they distort to a perverted interpretation, but besides these they bring up a unique passage which explicitly appears to be opposed to mathematics, and which they falsely believe to be in their favour. This passage is in some hidden corner of his works, namely, in the second book of the *Eudemian Ethics*, c. 7: "In the case of immobile things, like in mathematics, something is called a principle not per se, but on account of some similarity." But the germane interpretation of this passage is not against, but in favour of mathematicians. For Aristotle is speaking here about the efficient principle from which human actions come forth by motion, so that he can teach that in man there are some principles of some actions which are proper to human beings and which are free. But such principles are denied to be in immobile things, for these are necessary beings, lacking liberty. On the other hand, [it is asserted that] there are some principles even in this case, by a certain similarity, that is, just as free principles are to free actions, so are necessary principles to necessary actions. From which it follows that just as free principles are the adequate causes of those actions, so are mathematical principles the adequate causes of mathematical properties, which even Aristotle confirms somewhat later by the following: "For if given that the triangle has two right angles it is necessary that a quadrangle has four right angles, then it is clear that the triangle's having two right angles is the cause of this."And in order that we understand that he is speaking about the proper cause which is the medium of the demonstration, he adds: "And that this is necessarily the case is clear from the *Analytics*." Therefore this passage is absolutely in favour of the mathematicians against whom our opponents brought it up. So there is no passage in Aristotle left that would not clearly support our position.

The third point is [that] by which they strive to invoke Plato, an excellent supporter and scholar of mathematics himself, against the mathematicians. For they state that in bk. 7 of the *Republic* he said that mathematicians dream about quantity. But, lest deception should occur, here is what Plato says, faithfully translated from the Greek: "And the others, of which we said that in a way they have their share in true things, namely, geometry and its companions, somehow dream about essence itself. But nothing can be genuinely learned from them, insofar as they adhere to suppositions, and they regard them as so valid and unchangeable that they are unable to give their reason." Notice here first that Plato does not say absolutely that the geometer is dreaming but that he is dreaming somehow. Furthermore, he does not say that the geometer is dreaming about quantity, but about essence, so if we wished to enter into a tug of war with our opponents and stick to the letter, as they do, they would have nothing against the mathematicians. But let us grant them that Plato means here quantity itself, and let us see then what his point is. In order to see this we should know that the whole of bk. 7 of the *Republic* deals with the education of the guard and governor of the Republic, whom he wants to be first of all most competent by nature both in action and in speculation, and he wants him to be wise, that is, to be expert in theology, which he also calls dialectics, by which, without any discursive reasoning, he can contemplate the essences of things, but especially that of the supreme Good. But, Plato says, in order to arrive at this divine contemplation, first he has to devote himself to some human disciplines. Plato here divides philosophy into three parts. Into dialectics or theology, which he attributes to the intellect without any supposition and discursive reasoning, and it is only this part that he regards as being worthy of the name of science. Secondly, into mathematics, which he locates in cogitation[8] or reasoning, and which, therefore presupposes certain principles. Thirdly, and finally, into opinion, which deals with natural things, and which he locates in the imagination. Concerning this threefold division in Plato's text, Marsilio Ficino writes the following in his conspectus of bk. 7 of the *Republic*: "Divine things appear to be represented in three domains [*tribus aquis*], first, though obscurely, in physical considerations, secondly, and more distinctly, in mathematics and thirdly, and most clearly, in metaphysics." And somewhat later: "Plato regarded the divine forms as entirely immortal and as being the truly real things, of which mathematical forms are images, while natural things are their shadows." And after this: "When he realized that Thales, Democritus, and Anaxagoras just as much neglected divine things as they were interested in natural things; while, on the other hand, he saw that Pherecides, Pythagoras, and the Pythagoreans, indeed, all leading mathematicians were equally excellent theologians, and godly in their morals, he correctly concluded, partly from experience, partly from reasoning, that curiosity in natural studies often turns the soul away from divine things." And somewhat later: "Wherefore this 7th book of the *Republic*—where he leads the soul through appropriate degrees to the supreme Good, the Sun, that is, to God, and to the divine ideas, the stars, as it were—does not make mention of natural science in this ascension, but presents some degrees leading more conveniently to divine things, namely, mathematical [sciences], among which two are pure, namely, arithmetic and geometry, etc.; later on, Plato enumerates the rest of the mathematical sciences, recommends them one by one, and admits them into the republic." Several paragraphs later Ficino continues as follows: "So when he says that the soul is elevated from the night-light to the Moon and from the Moon to the Sun, Plato by this indicates the ascent of the soul from the natural to the mathematical, and from these to the divine forms." And passing over a few [points], he finally places theology, which he calls metaphysics and dialectics, before all others, as one governing all, and using the services of each one of them for its own proper end. And its own proper end is to embrace the totality of being, and to define what is anything, giving the reason for its essence, and to demonstrate whatever follows from any essence. But he regards the other faculties as menial in comparison to the nobility of this one. For they either decline to the opinions of human beings, or, even if they elevate themselves to the consideration of incorporeal things to the extent their capacity permits, still, they only dream about them in a way, and he says that mathematics is of this kind. From this you can clearly see that Plato asserted that mathematics dreams about the essence of things not absolutely, but in comparison to theology. So you can understand why he did not want to call mathematics a science, since it was only theology that he considered worthy of this name. And for this reason he considered physics even less worthy of this name, for he calls it opinion, while mathematics he calls cogitation [*cogitatio*] or reasoning. And it is on account of the same comparison that he calls mathematics less certain than theology, for the latter does not presuppose anything, and it is not discursive, but intuitive, while the former, having laid down some principles which they are unable to prove, proceeds discursively, and so some error may crop up in the discursive reasoning itself. You can see the explication of the same passage in Proclus c. 10, bk. 1 in [his commentary on] Euclid, as follows: "Let me briefly explain what Plato meant when in the *Republic* he took away the name of science from mathematics." And somewhat later: "Having distinguished science from arts, he divides science into one that he deems to be without any presuppositions, and another one gushing forth from presuppositions." And somewhat later: "And it is in this way that he says that mathematics, which uses presuppositions, is inferior to the perfect science which does not have any presuppositions; for this one is truly a science by which we can comprehend everything that there is." So you can clearly see by the authority of these philosophers that Plato said all these things not absolutely, but by comparison.

After these, Ficino continues to expound Plato's position as follows: "If argumentative skills are imparted to adolescents, this debilitates their sense of honesty, whence they become immoderate, indeed, supercilious and impious, as is said also in the *Philebus* and in the *Laws*, therefore, they are to be instructed in mathematics before the age of thirty and are to be equally exercized in public service by turns." Let us finally conclude with a beautiful passage from the same 7th book of the *Republic*, which Proclus renders almost verbatim in the following manner: "Therefore Socrates rightly said in the *Republic* that while the mind's eye is blinded, indeed, is gouged by other pursuits, the mathematical disciplines restore it and elevate it to the contemplation of Who Is, and from the imitations to the true things, for the beauty and order of mathematical reasonings, and the firmness and stability of contemplation join us and perfectly attach us to the intellects, which always remain the same, shine together with divine beauty, observing their mutual order." You [certainly] noticed, [my dear] reader, [even] in these few [quotations], how many praises Plato amasses for mathematics in this 7th book of the *Republic*, so that almost the whole appears to be its encomium. So it is a miracle that our opponents could dig up a passage against mathematics from the same 7th book, among so many of its praises, giving it a perverted interpretation, thereby joining themselves to spiders, who, from the nectar-dripping flowers, wherefrom bees collect honey, collect poison.

Indeed, who could ever doubt Plato's opinion about mathematics, given the fact that he banished from his Academy everyone ignorant of geometry [*ageometretos*], and that, as Piccolomini himself reports from Philoponus, he presented his audience daily with some mathematical problem. Again, he was the one who, in bks. 6 and 7 of the *Laws*, legislated about eduction in every single mathematical science, where he praises geometry so highly that he asserts that to ignore the incommensurability of quantities is not human ignorance, but the ignorance of pigs and cattle. Finally, [consider] how worthily and honourably he speaks about astronomy, and arithmetic and geometry that lead to it, in the *Epinomis*. It is here that you can find the most outstanding eulogy of astronomy, for the reason that among all sciences this is the one that elevates the soul to heavenly things, and from there to the cognition and love of the supreme Good, of which Plato divinely asserts here many times that it is the true wisdom. For the sake of brevity I pass over many other passages from Plato, for who would not clearly see, even by taking a casual look, that he, above all philosophers, is the most excellent advocate of mathematics?

The fourth [calumny] is that mathematics, and especially geometry, consists rather in imagination than in reasoning, and therefore is a science requiring the talents of a child, for even children have imagination. To which there assists the authority of Aristotle, who, in c. 8, bk. 6 of the *Ethics*, asks: "How does it come about that a child can be a mathematician, but cannot be wise or a natural scientist?" Also, there is the further point that in ancient times mathematics was taught to children before other sciences.

I respond that, as we said in the preceding response following Plato's opinion, it is not imagination, but reasoning, or cogitation that is used in mathematics, while imagination is used in natural science. But listen to Plato himself in the same 7th book: "Let us call then—he says—the first of these knowledge [*scientia*], the second one cognition, the third one belief, and the last one imagination." But we know that he places the last two in natural science. We also have Proclus' authority, who in ch. 5 of bk. 1 writes as follows: "So we said, following Plato's opinion, that the adequate instrument for judging all mathematical things is cogitation, which is superior to opinion, but which is inferior to understanding." And by cogitation we should understand some movement of the mind, that is, discursive reasoning, which is evident from the literal meaning of both the Greek "noematos"[9] and the Latin word, for "cogitatio" is said quasi "coagitatio," i.e., a certain agitation of the mind, which is the same as discursive reasoning. So it is obvious from the authority of these philosophers that reasoning is used in mathematics, while imagination is used in natural science, which our opponents contested. But why rely on authority, when the thing in itself can be seen? Anyone who considers geometrical demonstrations will clearly see that they work not by flimsy imagination, but by very complicated reasonings, for there are many in which fifty to sixty inferences are connected to one another. But why am I speaking about many, when Euclid's whole work is but an admirable continuous chain of inferences, so that his last demonstrations contain myriads of consequences, if they are resolved [into their first principles]; but imagination lacks any inferences. But if we consider their invention, they will appear to be entirely admirable, partly because they prove so abstruse and esoteric things, partly because the media by which they prove them require the acumen of a divine ingenuity for their investigation, wherefore their authors immortalized their names. So theorem 5 of bk. 1 is still celebrated under the name of Thales the Milesian, its inventor, theorem 11 [bears] the name of Oenipodes, theorem 32 the name of the Pythagoreans, and 47 that of Pythagoras himself. And how much glory did it yield for Hippocrates that he squared the lunula, and how much for Archimedes to have squared the parabola? The *Conics* of Apollonius Pergeus prepared him the name of a great geometer. It is not only puerile imagination, but every virile understanding that seems to be surpassed by far by these and many other things. But the reason why Aristotle said that a child can be a mathematician but not a wise person or a natural scientist is given by himself, namely, because for both of these experience is required, which the child lacks, for it is provided only in a long time; on the other hand, a child understands more easily moral, than geometrical matters, for it is easier to understand what virtue or vice is, etc., than to understand the fifth or the seventh theorem of the first book [of the *Elements*], but the child will not thereby become prudent, for prudence is not a speculative, but a practical virtue. Therefore that a child cannot be wise, or a natural scientist, is not due to a lack of intelligence, but to a lack of experience. Nor is mathematics to be called puerile on account of the fact that in antiquity it was first taught to children, as even Plato says, since they devoted to mathematics also the vigor and bloom of their full adulthood, as they were involved in it to the age of thirty. It could be rightly called puerile only if they had dealt with it only in their childhood. I can sincerely say, on the basis of many years' experience in teaching mathematics, that whomever I found to have mathematical talents, he was equally excellent in other subjects. For this study requires all sorts of [intellectual] skills [*omnes ingenii partes*], imagination, [aptitude in] reasoning and [good] memory. This is why the ancients tested children's talents by mathematics, as by a touchstone, and banished from other studies those who were incompetent in mathematics. Listen to Plato in bk. 7 of the *Republic*: "And have you noticed that those people who have natural talents for mathematics appear to be smart, so to speak, also in all other subjects?" And later in conclusion he says: "For all these reasons that we have considered, mathematics is scarcely negligible, but should be taught especially to those who are particularly talented."

Fifthly, geometry is censured for its many demonstrations carried out by superposition, which, as a method of demonstration appears to our opponents very defective and almost ridiculous. But we should know first that in the whole Euclidian corpus there are only three demonstrations by superposition. Secondly, [we should realize] that those are as perfect and as evident as are the others, for they are mistaken who think that superposition here is the medium of the demonstration, for it is there in place of a construction. And what are to be proved to be equal are not even the superposed things, as they think, for this would be a reason of no moment, and not even a geometrical, but rather a physical one, for it would rely on the senses; but some things which are equal are superposed here, so that from their superposition there will be apparent the equality of those that are not superposed. Consider 4 of bk. 1 and you will see that here two equal sides of two triangles are superposed, and then their bases, which are not superposed are inferred to be equal. And the reason by which they are proved to be equal is their congruence, and not that they are superposed, as our opponents think, not understanding what is the medium of this demonstration.

The sixth, ridiculous calumny is of someone who reprehends geometers because they often use circles, as is clear, he says, from 6, 4, and 8 of bk. 1 of the *Elements*. For if he is speaking about the circle which is a geometrical figure, then it is found only in the first of these, as is obvious even to one who just looks at the figures alone like children, but if he is speaking about the circle which is a fault in demonstration, then this is even more false, and that kind of circle is not found in any of these demonstrations.

The seventh is [that] by which they claim that geometers do not have a true and proper matter, for that is physical matter, and that therefore they do not have material cause either. But we should say that although geometers lack physical matter, they do not lack mathematical matter, which is intelligible matter, of which we spoke in c. 1.

The eighth is of someone saying that it is a common opinion that mathematics is not a science; but this is manifestly false, for from among so many Greek, Arab, and Latin philosophers he is able to come up with only two or three who are of this opinion, namely, Piccolomini, who is followed by Pererius.

The ninth is of someone else's, who reproaches geometers because they reduce so many things to the universal axiom that those which are identical with a third one are identical themselves. But this person has little knowledge of the principles of geometers, for that axiom never appears in mathematics, indeed, it cannot, for it does not involve quantity.

The tenth is [that] by which they claim that mathematical entities do not exist. But this smear is readily removed by what we said in the beginning about intelligible matter.

The eleventh is that abstraction from [sensible] matter damages the perfection of mathematical demonstrations. To this responds the most erudite Toletus; in q. 4 bk. 2 of the *Physics* he says the following: "The physicist often uses demonstrations from effects or signs, for the causes he considers are frequently hidden and are not per se sensible, while the mathematician more often proceeds from what are prior, for the causes he considers are better known than the effects, for he abstracts from the senses, and in the intellect it is better known what is prior." Afterwards, in concl. 4 he says the following: "All imperfection of physics derives from matter, whence Aristotle, giving the reason for this inexactitude, says in tex. 16, bk. 2 of the *Metaphysics*: "Nature has matter," and somewhat later: "But mathematical things for they are separated from this matter, are absolutely necessary, for a triangle always has three angles equal to two right ones." From which it is obvious that the perfection of mathematics derives from abstraction, contrary to the opponents' opinion.

The twelfth is that mathematics abstracts from the good. But Aristotle acquits mathematics from this charge, when in bk. 13 of the *Metaphysics* he says: "Those who claim that mathematics says nothing about the good or the beautiful speak falsely, for it does say, and it does show especially a great deal about them; for even if it does not mention them by name, by showing the works [of good] and reasons [of beauty], does it not say anything about them? For the species of beauty are order, symmetry [*commensuratio*] and shapeliness [*definitum*], which are shown especially by mathematical sciences."

The thirteenth is that geometry and arithmetic, since they are speculative sciences, are useless and boring. But this objection applies to all speculative sciences which are not [cultivated] for the sake of some use, but for the sake of themselves. And this objection is made usually by those who commercialize science, as he himself complains, i.e. by those who want to make them profitable. These merchants rather than philosophers in soul we refer to chapters 8, 9, and 10 of bk. 1 of Proclus, where he amply discusses the utility of these sciences. But if it is a philosopher who is making this objection, let him suffice the utility that, by the help of mathematics, all mathematical passages of Aristotle, which are almost four hundred, are easily understood, and so a perfect understanding of the whole corpus of Aristotle can be reached.

As regards the enjoyment, they will find in Proclus at the same locus the following: "Those who contempt the cognition of mathematical sciences, have no taste for the pleasures in them, and those who ignore mathematics grasp only vulgar pleasures." It is for this reason that noble men and princes, who dedicated themselves to learning, not to profit, but for the sake of philosophy, found much pleasure especially in mathematical studies. Among whom the most famous where in antiquity Archimedes, a relative of the king of Sicily, Boethius the consul, Alfonso king of Spain, while in our times, Marquis Guidobaldus, prince Tycho Brahe, Franciscus Candalla, and many others, whose enduring monuments the world will marvel in all ages.

In the fourteenth place, they reproach mathematics for the ignobility of its subject, namely, that it is an accident. But to this we respond first that even if it is an accident, it is nevertheless immaterial and abstract, for which reason it is placed between the subjects of physics and metaphysics.[10] Secondly, it is better to get to know innumerable, marvelous truths about an accident, than always to be cast from one side to the other, by the whirlpool of a thousand of opinions and dissensions, especially concerning material substance, and hence never to arrive at the cognition of any substance at all. Thirdly, in applied mathematics the case is different, where it is not bare quantity, but either the heavenly bodies, or musical sounds, or the modes of vision and deception, or the powers of machines are studied, with the same ends in mind and with the same scope as in other subjects studied by other philosophers.

The fifteenth is [that] which they add either as a joke, or from sheer ignorance, namely, that mathematicians were often proscribed and condemned by both secular and sacred law, and that they were expelled more than once [*olim non raro*] from the Empire by the edicts of Roman Emperors. In fact, we should never respond to this, for nobody can be so much lacking in erudition, as not to know that these pseudomathematicians were those called more aptly astrologers [*Genethliaci*], or fortune-tellers [*Chaldaei*] or soothsayers [*Iudiciarii*], whose teaching nobody can prove to me by any means, as it relies neither on experience, nor on reasons, but it is sheer deception and fraud, and often just superstition. Therefore it is to be wondered why these arts are never abolished once and for all, but, as Cornelius Tacitus says in bk. 1 of *Histories*: "This kind of people, infidel to the powerful, and treacherous to the hopeful, in our society will always be condemned, and will always be kept." Read the twelve books of Pico della Mirandola against the astrologers. For further assistance there are Tycho and Kepler, who, although astronomers themselves, many times condemned this kind of astronomy. But those act cantankerously who seek to shift the blame from these rascals to all mathematicians. I only wanted to say all this lest the more simpleminded should be deceived by these slanderers.

The sixteenth is [that] which they put forward by asking [first] in general whether mathematics has perfect demonstrations, then later in the discussion they bring up several points against mathematics, and at the end of the treatise they claim that these concern only geometry and arithmetic. Wherefore, unless the reader peruses everything to the end, which rarely happens, he will be deceived, for he will think that all mathematical sciences were concerned, while the authors themselves acknowledge that they have never spoken about applied mathematics, i.e., astronomy, music, optics, and mechanics, which they readily admit to be true demonstrative sciences.

The seventeenth is the calumny of some very recent philosopher, who, having deployed several points against mathematics, contrary to custom, does not raise objections to his own position, but disregarding many passages from Aristotle and other ancient philosophers speaking against him, finally concludes, which nobody dared so far, that mathematics is not a part of philosophy at all, despite the fact that nothing else is more frequently stated by Aristotle and by other peripatetics than that philosophy has three parts, namely, physics, mathematics, and metaphysics. Furthermore, he frequently states that the certitude of mathematics derives from its showing everything to the senses, i.e., from its truths being perceived by the senses. But this we have proved above several times to be entirely false, on the basis that the subject matter of mathematics is entirely intelligible, but not sensible, and there is nobody with at least a superficial acquaintance with mathematics who would not admit this.

Finally you should know, my dear reader, that I said all the above sincerely and out of love of truth alone, which you can ascertain yourself, if you turn to the authors whom I cited, which I request that you do, for there you will find even more than what I said here. On the other hand, you could see how zealously others, whose duty would be to foster and guard them, persecute these beautiful disciplines, I do not know upon what counsel.

CHAPTER 4   On the Excellence of the Knowledge that Geometry and Arithmetic Provide for Us

The nobility and excellence of a science should be considered not only on the basis of its subject and its medium, but also, and even more, on the basis of the cognition that it yields for us, which is their end, for the more excellent and noble this cognition is, the more excellent the science is to be deemed. For, as Aristotle says in the beginning of bk. 2 of the *Metaphysics*, "the end of science is truth." This is also confirmed by Plato, who in the *Symposium* asserts that truth is the soul's nourishment. But geometry and arithmetic, as they always provide perspicuity, always follow the truth, wherefore Aristotle in c.7 bk. 1 of the *Ethics* calls geometry the explorer of truth. For the other sciences, except for applied mathematics, rarely produce perspicuity, and also rarely follow the truth, but they almost always generate opinions, and so Plato did not want to call them sciences, but opinions. From which it follows that we should assert without qualification that mathematics is the most excellent among sciences, as even among opinions the most excellent is the truth.

But it is not only from its truth, but also from its admirability that the excellence of such a cognition derives. For mathematical conclusions, with few exceptions, are admirable truths, which can be admired in the way Cicero admires them, who in bk. 1 of *De Oratore* says: "Who would ignore how arcane a subject and how recondite, complex and subtle art is cultivated by the people called mathematicians?" Indeed, who would not be amazed when he understands that every triangle has three angles equal to two right angles? And that every rectilinear figure has external angles, even if they are a thousand, equal only to four right angles? Again, that two parallelograms constructed on the same base and within the same pair of parallel lines are equal, however much either of them is elongated? How admirable is 47 of bk. 1, so that upon its discovery Pythagoras sacrificed a hecatomb to the Muses? And how subtle is 14 of bk. 2 of the *Elements*, which provides an equal square for any rectilinear figure? Furthermore, in the third book, how many and how great miracles are contained by that angle of contact, which, however great it may be, still, cannot be divided by a straight line! But, to make a long story short, who would not be totally stupefied considering the incommensurability of so many magnitudes, treated of in book 10 of the *Elements*, and the incommensurability of the diagonal with the side; and who would not assert with Plato that the ignorance of this is not human ignorance, but the ignorance of swines and cattle? And how much are we astounded by the inscription of the five regular solids in the same sphere? And when we realize that there can be only five regular solids in the whole nature of things? So Cardanus rightly says in bk. 16 of *De Subtilitate*: "Euclid deserves praise especially for two reasons: the unshakable firmness of the teachings of the *Elements*, and such an absolute perfection that you may not rightfully dare to compare another work to it; and hence it comes about that it shines so much with the light of truth that in arduous questions only those who are familiar with Euclid appear to be able to discern truth from falsity."

But if we turn to the works of Archimedes, how often do they stupefy us? As when he shows that a certain triangle is equal to a given circle. Or when he squares parabolas, or investigates the center of gravity of planes, or when he calculates the number of the grains of sand filling the whole universe, or when he demonstrates that the whole machinery of the world could be moved out of its place even by an ant, although these last two belong to applied mathematics. But the book on spirals, and the other one on bodies floating in water, how admirable are they? And then demonstrating various things about the sphere and the cylinder, how much he surpasses others, and indeed himself by far, when among other things he shows that the surface of any sphere is four times [the area of] its main circle! Again, if a cylinder, a sphere, and a cone have the same height, and their bases are the main circle of the sphere, their proportion is as that of 3, 2, and 1, respectively. So, as a monument to this outstanding genius, a marble sphere and a marble cylinder were placed on his tomb, as Cicero reports in bk. 5 of *Tusculanae Disputationes*. Here he also boasts that when he was a quaestor in Sicily, he discovered this tomb, neglected by the Syracusans, fenced on all sides and covered by briars and thornbushes. So in bk. 16 of *De Subtilitate* Cardanus rightly extols Archimedes as the phoenix of geniuses, placing him above all men excelling in subtlety, even above Aristotle, for two reasons: "Archimedes was the first not only on account of his achievements just presented, but also because of his mechanics, by which he frequently defeated the Roman forces." Again, Apollonius of Perga, also known as the Great Geometer, by no means inferior to Archimedes, how wonderful and how abstruse things did he bring to light in his *Conics*? But among others the most admirable is that he discovered those lines, which he calls asymptotes, which, if extended to infinity, always approach, but never reach each other. I omit Hipsicles, Theodosius Tripolites, Menelaus, Serenus, Pappus, and others, whose works surpass all admiration, and which are put forth with such wonderful consistency and certainty that there is nobody who would not believe to the ingenuity of these ancient geometers. Wherefore we conclude this part with Cardanus, bk. 16, *De Subtilitate*: "No wonder that geometry is the subtlest of all sciences, for although it starts from the most manifest principles, whereby it gave good reason for its having been taught first even to children, it is a miracle how quickly it takes us from the most obvious to the most abstruse, and elevates us from the humblest to the highest things."

But let us now consider the fruits of arithmetic, in which, beyond the magnificient discoveries of Euclid, Iordanus, and Maurolicus, how wonderful is that supernatural monster of all sciences, called algebra? There is perhaps nothing more sophisticated, and more profound, in the whole encyclopedia of learning. It equals no human ingenuity, but what you would rather call heavenly revelation. It adds, subtracts, multiplies, and divides numbers, called surds [*surdos*], which cannot be expressed by any means, but which it handles just like ordinary numbers. And those that are smaller than nothing, what is more abstruse than them? But by both of these it solved such admirable questions and enigmas that those people who are expert in this subject do not fear anything obscure or arduous in the infinite realm of numbers, so that you will consider them not people, but some sorts of angels or wizards.

To conclude this discussion of geometry and arithmetic we sum up what they can lay claim to as follows.

The first is that they have all the distinct parts of a science, namely, essential definitions in the first place; secondly, postulates; and thirdly, axioms, which are the three genera of principles from which a science is deduced. Therefore, in the fourth place, there follow propositions with their demonstrations which are either problems or theorems. And this is the most beautiful order of doctrine, which even Aristotle taught, and which outside of mathematics, especially pure mathematics, is never found.

The second is that from the certainty of the aforementioned principles it derives that mathematics proceeds from what is better known both to us and by nature.

The third is that all their arguments are demonstrations, partly a priori, partly a posteriori, where nothing is merely probable, and where there is no conflict of opinions, but the whole is discerned as clear, consistent, and true.

The fourth is that a priori demonstrations proceed only from intrinsic causes, namely, matter and form.

The fifth is that their demonstrations in most cases show both what is the case [*quid*] and why it is the case [*propter quid*] at the same time.

The sixth is the wonderful, perpetual interweaving and interdependence of demonstrations.

CHAPTER 5   On Applied Mathematics, Astronomy, Optics, Mechanics, and Music

Regarding the subject matter of these sciences, as there is agreement on this among all philosophers, we have no reason to say anything about it. And that they present us with perfect demonstrations, by which they show us wonderful truths, which are a pleasure to know, we shall briefly demonstrate at once. But we do not lack Aristotle's authority either, who in tex. 30, bk. 1, *Posterior Analytics* asserts that they have demonstrations of causes as follows: "For here the 'what' is to be known by those who perceive, but the 'why' by the mathematicians, for they have the demonstrations of the causes." And here Aristotle is speaking about these applied mathematical sciences. See our explication of this passage or, if you prefer, of others above, but now let us turn our attention to the thing itself.

To begin with astronomy, isn't the demonstration of the eclipse of the moon (even by the testimony of Aristotle and his commentators, especially Zabarella) a perfect demonstration? For it renders evident the proper and adequate cause of the property [*affectio*] in question, i.e., the eclipse, namely, the interposition of the Earth. But we should say the same of the solar eclipse, the cause of which is shown to be the interposition of the Moon. And that these demonstrations were discovered by the astronomers is known from their books, as well as the fact that they use geometrical media, namely, circle, diameter, and diametric opposition, and that therefore how certain they are is obvious from the infallible prediction of eclipses.

Secondly, why is the Sun more days in the Zodiac in summer than it is in winter? They give the apogee as the cause.

Thirdly, why is the moon illuminated successively? Because it is spherical.

Fourthly, why are the tropics curved in a solar horologium, while the equator is a straight line? Because those are conic sections, but the equator is the intersection of two planes.

Fifthly, why is it that the Sun does not illuminate the whole Earth simultaneously, but successively? Because the earth is spherical.

How wonderful and gratifying are those pursuits of which even the sacred scriptures speak with awe? To scrutinize the height of the sky and the depths of the abyss with extreme daring? To teach us clearly the magnitude and distances of the Earth, the Moon, and the Sun with plainly divine acumen. So this powerful philosophy manifests the structure and symmetry of the whole world, than which nothing is worthier of cognition, so one can rightly sing:

Happy are the souls who first strived to cognize these
And to ascend to the upper realm.
Who took the distant stars to our eyes
And replaced theirs by ethereal ingenuity.

An equally happy and wonderful part of astronomy is geography, by which, either on a globe or on a map, all continents and all the seas, as if they were present, can be studied. Also you can learn with great pleasure where anything is, in which zone and in what climate.

Again, in optics we do not lack perfect demonstrations either. For example, why is the eye spherical? So that perpendicular lines can fall on it from every direction. But why perpendicular lines? In order to produce distinct sight. Here you have the final causes! Why does a concave mirror scorch something here? Because the reflected sun-rays are collected here. Why does a stick appear broken in water? Because it is seen by refracted lines. Why is the rainbow circular? Because it is seen only under a determinate angle, which can be located only on an arch. Where you see at once how worthy are these insights.

Again, in mechanics. Why does a wedge have so much power? Because it consists of two levers. Where does the *cochlea*'s mighty power come from? It consists of a wedge and a lever. Indeed, what is more amazing than the fact that any weight, or even the whole universe could be moved by the force of an ant? To master, as Aristotle says, the recalcitrant nature? How subtle are the things that once Archimedes, and recently Commandinus and Luca Valerius demonstrated about the center of gravity?

Finally, music has its own demonstrations. For example, a tone consists of two minor semitones and a comma because a sesquioctave proportion[11] consists of two minor semitones and a comma; and a tone consists in the sesquioctave proportion. Again, the diapentes consists of three tones, and a minor semitone, for if from the interval of one and a half, which is the diapentes, you take away a sesquithird, there remains a sesquioctave. The sesquithird contains two tones with a minor semitone. And here you have the material causes! Why is it that twice the diapentes or twice the diatessaron cannot be harmoniously composed? You have the explanation above sect. 19 problem 34. But how wonderful is it that Pythagoras divided sounds into proportions as if they were some permanent quantities?

What remains would be to speak about practical mathematics, in which all causes are manifestly present. For on account of the fact that they are practical they necessarily involve the final cause. And they often give the efficient, material, or formal cause to prove their premises, which they assume to conclude to what they principally intend. Indeed, among all practical sciences the most excellent is geodesy [*geometria practica*]. For who would not be amazed that surveyors measure by sight alone any magnitudes, like towers or mountains, without even going there?

From these it manifestly appears that mathematical sciences have perfect demonstrations, whose causes are so distinct from their effects that no calumnies can do any harm to them. Therefore, even if our opponents could prove, which they never can, that geometry and arithmetic lacks them, they would have to admit this concerning the other [disciplines] mentioned above that they reason by all genera of causes, and that they excel with such clarity that they leave nothing in ambiguity or controversy. For mathematics, as Aristotle says in bk. 1 of the *Sophistical Refutations*, is not argumentative. Thence, it comes about that this whole wonderful and worthy cognition is sheer truth, which is the end of all sciences and the nourishment of our souls.

PRAISE BE TO GOD.

APPENDIX

Finally, in order to render the nature of mathematical sciences even more manifest, and that Aristotle's mathematical passages will be better illuminated, we consider the demonstrations of the first book of Euclid's *Elements* and relate each one of them to its proper class of demonstrations.

By the first demonstration Euclid shows that the triangle constructed in the given manner is equilateral by the proximate medium, namely, by the fact that it has three equal sides, which is the definition of the subject of this demonstration, namely, of the equilateral triangle itself, wherefore this demonstration is from the formal cause.

By the second demonstration he shows that two lines are equal, because they both are equal to a third one, which reasoning relies on the axiom that what are equal to a third one are equal themselves. And this is an ostensive demonstration, not from a cause but from a sign [*a signo*]; for their being equal to a third one is the sign of their equality.

The third demonstration uses the same medium as the second.

The fourth shows, first of those two triangles that they have equal bases, for those bases are mutually congruent. Secondly, it shows that their two angles are equal, respectively, and both for the same reason, namely, because they are mutually congruent. If you say, therefore, that the definition of equality is mutual congruence, then this demonstration will be by the formal cause; but if you say that it is only a sign of equality, then this demonstration is from a sign and a posteriori.

The fifth shows, first of all, of an isosceles triangle that the angles on its base are equal, for the reason that if from equals you take away equals, what remain will be equal. And this reasoning, even by the testimony of Aristotle, is by the material cause, for to be the half, the third, the double or the remainder or the like of some whole is nothing but to be parts of that whole; but parts are matter, as Aristotle explicitly teaches in tex. 3, bk. 5 of *Metaphysics*, which you find explained above, along with other passages. Secondly, it demonstrates of the same isosceles [triangle] that the angles under its base are equal, because they are opposite the two sides proven to be equal by the fourth above, which seems to be some sign of their equality.

The sixth proves that those two sides of that triangle are equal *ab impossibili*, because otherwise it would follow that the part is equal to the whole.

The seventh demonstrates that the two latter lines necessarily coincide with the two former, for otherwise it would follow either that the part is equal to the whole or that the angles under the base or even those that are above the base of the isosceles [triangle] are unequal, the opposite of which was shown by the fifth.

The eighth shows that congruent angles are equal, namely, by axiom 8. This appears to be from a sign.

The ninth proves that divided angle to be halved, by means of the preceding eighth [proposition]; so it is of the same kind.

The tenth proves that line to be divided in two equal lines, because those two are the bases of the triangles of the fourth [demonstration]; but this seems to be the definition of being the bases of such triangles, wherefore this demonstration should be from the definition of the subject and by the formal cause.

The eleventh proves that that line makes right angles, for it makes equal angles with the subjected line [i.e., on which it is erected]. For according to definition 10, if the angles produced by such a line are equal, then they are also right angles. So the demonstration proceeds from the defintion.

The twelfth proves that this line is perpendicular from the definition of perpendicular line, for it makes equal, right angles with the subjected line. Therefore this demonstration is from the definition, is a priori, and by the formal cause.

The thirteenth proves that two angles are equal to two right angles because they are equal to a third one; for which reason this is from a sign.

The fourteenth proves what is intended on the basis that otherwise it would follow that the part is equal to the whole.

The fifteenth proves that the angles [joined] at the vertex are equal, for if from equals you take away equals the rest remain or are equal. So this is a demonstration by the material cause, as was said of the fifth.

The sixteenth proves that the external angle is greater than the internal, because it is greater than another, which is equal to the internal angle. This is from a sign.

The seventeenth proves that two angles are smaller than two other angles from axiom 4, namely, that if to two unequals you add two equals, then the two resulting wholes will be unequal; where the cause of the inequality of the wholes is what is added, the addition of which yields the two wholes. So what is added is a part, which is the matter of the whole. Therefore this demonstrates by the material cause.

The eighteenth proves that an angle is greater than another, because the former is like a whole, while the latter is like its part. This is reduced to the material cause.

The nineteenth proves what it intends *ab impossibili.*

The twentienth proves that those two sides are greater than the third, because they are equal to a line which is greater than that third side. This is from a sign.

The twenty-first proves that those two straight lines are shorter than the two others on the basis that they are shorter than a given quantity which is shorter than the other two lines. From a sign. Secondly, it proves that that angle is greater than the other, because it is greater than a certain angle that is greater than that other. Equally from a sign.

The twenty-second uses the axiom that what are equal to a third one, etc.

The twenty-third proves that two angles are equal, because they are opposite the bases of the triangles of the eight demonstration. Seems to proceed from the definition of these angles.

The twenty-fourth proves that that side is longer than the other side because it is equal to another side which is also greater than that side.

The twenty-fifth proves the proposition by reductio ad absurdum [*deducens ad absurdum*].

The twenty-sixth demonstrates by reductio ad absurdum [*deducendo ad inconveniens*].

The twenty-seventh proves that those lines are parallel because they can never meet. This is from the definition of parallels.

The twenty-eighth I take to proceed from the cause, for it shows that two straight lines are equidistant because their alternate angles are equal, and those angles are the cause of the equidistance of these lines. The same holds for the second part of the demonstration.

The first part of the twenty-ninth is proven *ab impossibili.* The second part from a sign, on the basis that those that are equal to a third etc. The same holds for the third part.

The thirtieth proves that these lines are parallel from the twenty-seventh, therefore this is of the same kind.

The thirty-first is of the same kind as the twenty-seventh, so it is by the formal cause.

The thirty-second proves that the external angle is equal to the two opposing[12] internal angles, on the basis that the parts of the external angle are equal to the parts of those [taken together], i.e., from the equality of the parts it infers the equality of the wholes, which is a demonstration by the material cause. Secondly, it proves the celebrated proposition that every triangle has three, etc., which I most amply discussed above in connection with tex. 23, bk. 1, *Posterior Analytics*, where Aristotle brings it up as an example of the perfect demonstration.

The thirty-third demonstrates partly on the basis of the fourth, partly on the basis of the twenty-seventh. Therefore these parts are to be classified with those.

The thirty-fourth proves three points. The first point it proves by the twenty-sixth. The second it proves by the axiom that if to equals you add equals then the resulting wholes are equal, which it applies to two angles, and so this demonstration is from the parts to the wholes, i.e., from the material cause. It concludes to the third point by the fourth demonstration.

The thirty-fifth proceeds by the material cause, for in each case it proves that those two parallelograms are equal, because if equals are added to equals the resulting wholes are equal, as we said in the preceding.

The thirty-sixth proves that two things are equal because they are equal to a third, so this proves from a sign, a posteriori.

The thirty-seventh proves that two triangles are equal, because they are the halves of those equal parallelograms, and so this is from the material cause.

The thirty-eighth demonstrates on the same basis as the previous one.

The thirty-ninth proves the proposition by reducing its opposite ad absurdum.

The fortieth demonstrates in a similar fashion as the preceding thirty-ninth [proposition].

The forty-first proves of one thing that it is the double of another, because it is the double of something else equal to this other. Seems to be from a sign.

The forty-second proves that a parallelogram and a triangle are equal because they are the double of the same triangle, i.e., by the material cause.

The forty-third proves that two parallelograms are equal because they are the remainder after taking away equals from equals. This is the material cause.

The forty-fourth proves that a parallelogram is equal to a triangle because they are both equal to a third, i.e., from a sign.

The forty-fifth proves that a whole parallelogram is equal to a whole rectilinear figure because their parts are equal. This is evidently the material cause.

The forty-sixth proves that a quadrilateral is a square from the definition of square, namely, because it has four right angles and four equal sides. So this is from the formal cause.

The forty-seventh proves that the square constructed on the side opposite its right angle is equal to the two squares on the other two sides of the same right-angled triangle. The reason is taken from the parts, namely, because the parts of the aforementioned square are equal to the other two squares, respectively, and therefore the whole square is equal to those taken together. This is evidently the material cause.

The forty-eighth proves of some angle that it is a right angle, on the basis that it is equal to a right angle. The demonstration is from a sign.

Let these few points suffice so that all philosophers have something from which they can judge geometrical demonstrations. But nobody should judge the other mathematical sciences in the same way, for astronomy, optics, and the others make use also of the other kinds of causes in their demonstrations, as was shown in c. 5 of [this work] *The Nature of Mathematics*. And although these often demonstrate from the effects, they yield such evidence that, as Themistius says, they have no counterinstance.

Many people urged me to prepare a work of the same kind about Plato's mathematical passages. But when I intended to comply with this request I found that Theon, a Greek author of Smirna, already carried this out a long time ago, and his work is still preserved in the Vatican Library, as Iosephus Auria says in his preface to Theodosius' *Tripolita*, where he promises that he will translate it from the Greek soon, but I do not know whether he fulfilled this promise. So it is the task of contemporary Platonists, lest what is done should be done again, finally to prepare a Latin edition.

PRAISE BE TO GOD.

NOTES

Introduction

1. On the application of the mathematical method in philosophy, theology, and natural philosophy see bibliography quoted in note 39 of chapter IV.

2. In this book I have limited myself to the analysis of the disciplines of pure mathematics and thus the question of the relationship between mathematics and physics will not be addressed.

3. The reference is to Brunschvicg (1912). My work has in common with Brunschvicg's book the emphasis on mathematical practice although my approach differs from his on a number of substantial issues. Brunschvicg puts more emphasis on the study of the systems of mathematical philosophy of authors like Descartes, Spinoza, and Leibniz whereas I tend to remain closer to the foundational issues; my choice of topics is consequently quite different.

4. Attention to mathematical mysticism is found for instance in Strong (1936).

5. I use this term rather like Becker (1954), although in a much wider acception.

6. For general introductions to the history of mathematics in the seventeenth century see Boyer (1968), Cantor (1900–1901), Kline (1972), Montucla (1799–1802), Whiteside (1960–61), and Zeuthen (1966). For the rediscovery of Greek mathematical texts, see Rose (1975).

Chapter 1

1. Jardine (1988, 686–693) gives an overview of the debates on demonstrative regress (*regressus demonstrativus*), defined as "a procedure which combines an inference from an observed effect to its proximate cause with an inference from the proximate cause to the observed effect" (p. 686).

2. Randall (1961, 62–63).

3. See E. McMullin (1962, 52–66), B. S. Eastwood (1992, 84–99), and Jardine (1988).

4. The best general sources for seventeenth-century mathematics are Boyer (1968), Cantor (1900–1901), Kline (1972), Montucla (1799–1802), Whiteside (1960–61), and Zeuthen (1966). Further references will be given elsewhere.

5. I have discussed the issue in connection with whether or not Descartes' *Géométrie* constitutes a revolution in mathematics in Mancosu (1992b).

6. For summary introduction to the debate the reader is referred to Jardine (1988) especially pp. 693–697 and Schüling (1969, II.9). For bibliographical information, further references, and a detailed analysis of the authors involved in the Renaissance part of

the debate see de Pace (1993) and Giacobbe (1972a, 1972b, 1973, 1976, 1977). See also the articles in Olivieri (1983), Galluzzi (1973), and Crombie (1977). The following are some of the primary sources: Piccolomini (1547), Barozzi (1560), Catena (1556, 1561, 1563), Pereyra (1576), Collegium Conimbricense (1594), Biancani (1615).

7. Aristotle, *Posterior Analytics* (1941, 111).

8. J. Barnes (1975, 96) uses "explanation" to render the Greek *aitia*. He motivates his choice as follows: "'Explanation' and its cognates render *aitia* and its cognates; the traditional translation is 'cause.' Aristotle's synonyms for *aitia* are *to dioti* and *to dia ti* (literally, 'the wherefore' and 'the because of what'—I translate 'the reason why'); thus to give the *aitia* of something is to say why it is the case, and X is *aiton* of Y just in case Y is because of X (cf. Bonitz, 177a50–2). Hence 'cause', as it is used in colloquial English, is a fairly good translation of *aitia* (cf. the conjunction 'because'). Philosophical usage, however, seems generally to base itself on a Humean analysis of causation; and an *aitia* is not a Humean cause. For this reason it is probably advisable to adopt a different translation; 'explanation' seems better than 'reason'."

9. Aristotle, *Posterior Analytics* (1941, 111–112).

10. Aristotle, *Posterior Analytics* (1941, 131).

11.. Randall (1961, 27).

12. Translation modified from Crombie (1977, 67). Here is the complete text from Pereyra (1576, 24): "Mea opinio est, Mathematicas disciplinas non esse propriè scientias: in quam opinionem adducor tum alijs tum hoc uno maximè argumento. Scire est rem per caussam cognoscere propter quam res est; & scientia est demonstrationis effectus; demonstratio autem (loquor de perfectissimo demonstrationis genere) constare debet ex his quae sunt per se & propria eius quod demonstratur; quae verò sunt per accidens, & communia, excluduntur a perfectis demonstrationibus, sed Mathematicus, neque considerat essentiam quantitatis, neque affectiones eius tractat prout manant ex tali essentia, neque declarat eas per proprias caussas, propter quam insunt quantitati, neque conficit demonstrationes suas ex praedicatis proprijs & per se, sed ex communibus, & per accidens, ergo doctrina Mathematica non est propriè scientia." Later it will be useful to refer to the text immediately following the quote just given "ergo doctrina Mathematica non est propriè scientia: Maior huius syllogismi non eget probatione, etenim apertè elicitur ex his quae scripta sunt ab Arist. I. Post. Confirmatio Minoris ducitur ex his, quae scribit Plato in 7. lib. de Republ. dicens Mathematicos somniare circa quantitatem, & in tractandis suis demonstrationibus non scientificè sed ex quibusdam suppositionibus procedere. quamobrem non vult doctrinam eorum appellare intelligentiam aut scientiam, sed tantum cogitationem: in quam sententiam multa scribit Proclus in I. lib. suorum Commentariorum in Euclidem. Verum, tametsi neque Platonem neque Proclum neque alios Philosophos graves, haberemus auctores huius sententiae, tamen id per se manifestum fit cuivis qui vel leviter modo attigerit eruditum illum Mathematicorum pulverem. Nam si quis secum reputet atque diligenter consideret demonstrationes geometricas, quae continentur libris Elementorum Euclid. planè intelliget eas sic esse affectas ut ante diximus: ac ut de multis unum aut alterum proferam exemplum, Geometer demonstrat triangulum habere tres angulos aequales duobus rectis, propterea quod angulus externus, qui efficitur ex latere illius trianguli producto, sit aequalis duobus angulis eiusdem trianguli sibi oppositis: Quis non videt hoc medium non esse caussam illius passionis quae demonstratur? cum prius natura sit triangulum esse, & habere tres angulos aequales duobus rectis, quàm vel produci latus illius, vel ab eo latere fieri angulum aequalem duobus rectis, quàm vel produci latus illius vel ab eo latere fieri angulum aequalem duobus internis? Praeterea, tale medium habet se omnino per accidens ad illam passionem; nam sive latus producatur, & fiat angulus externus,

sive non, immo tametsi fingamus productionem illius lateris; effectionemque anguli externi esse impossibilem, nihilominus tamen illa passio inesset triangulo; at, quid aliud definitur esse accidens quàm quod potest adesse & abesse rei praeter eius corruptionem? Ad haec, illas propositiones, Totum est maius sua parte, aequales esse lineas quae ducuntur a centro ad circumferentiam, illud latus esse maius, quod opponitur maiori angulo, & id genus alia, quàm crebro usurpat in demonstrando? in quàm multis demonstrationibus eas pro medio adhibet & inculcat Mathematicus? ut necesse sit ex his demonstrationibus quae constant praedicatis communibus, non gigne perfectam scientiam" (Pereyra 1576, 24–25). This passage contains many of the themes that characterized the *Quaestio*: (a) the scientificalness of mathematics; (b) the causal nature of the syllogism; (c) the use of proposition I.32 from Euclid's *Elements*.

13. *Exercitationes*, in Gassendi (1658, vol. III, p. 209). English translation in Gassendi (1972, 107).

14. On Barozzi and Biancani see note 6 and Rose (1975); on Wallis and Barrow see below and Mancosu (1992a); on Clavius and the mathematical sciences see Crombie (1977) and Wallace (1984, 136–141).

15. In *Monumenta Paedagogica Soc. Jesus* (1901, 473). The translation is from Crombie (1977, 66).

16. See Wallace (1984) for a list of the teachers at the Collegium and the courses they held; see Galluzzi (1973) and Crombie (1977) for more information on Clavius and his role in the revival of Platonism in the late Renaissance.

17. For the latin see note 12.

18. Sections 1.2.2 and 1.3.1 originate from my previous articles Mancosu (1991, 1992a). Section 1.3.2 is taken from Mancosu (1995).

19. On Biancani see Giacobbe (1976), Galluzzi (1973, 56–65), Dear (1987, 146–152; 1988, 67–68), and Wallace (1984, 141–148).

20. Biancani (1615, 5).

21. Biancani (1615, 7).

22. Dear (1988, 67).

23. Biancani (1615, 14).

24. Dear (1988, 72).

25. See Barrow (1683). Translations from Barrow (1970).

26. Barrow (1970, 66; 1683, 76).

27. "And here by the Way we may take notice of their Opinion who will have Mathematical Figures to have no other Existence in the Nature of Things than in the Mind alone. And it is wonderful to me that this Opinion should be embraced by Persons, who are otherwise most excellently skilled in the Mathematics: Among whom we may reckon ... Blancanus, whose Words are these; Though Mathematical Beings have no real Existence, yet because their Ideas do exist both in the Divine and Human Mind, as the most exact Types of Things, therefore the Mathematician treats of those Ideas which of themselves are primarily intended, and are true Beings [*Libro de Natura Mathem.*, p. 7]" (Barrow 1970, 76; 1683, 84).

28. "Which Sentiment notwithstanding is absolutely false, and easy to be refuted from the foregoing Discursus, and what is most Opposite to it seems, in my opinion, to be most true; viz. That all imaginable Geometrical Figures are really inherent in every Particle of Matter, I say really inherent in Fact and to the utmost Perfection, though not apparent to the Sense.... Moreover if it be supposed (viz.) that Mathematical Things cannot exist, there will also be an End of those Ideas or Types formed in the Mind, which will be no more than mere Dreams or the Idols of Things no where existing" (Barrow 1970, 76–77; 1683, 84–85).

29. Barrow (1970, 80; 1683, 87).

30. Barrow (1970, 80; 1683, 88).

31. "Lastly, he [Aristotle] demands them to be the Causes of their Conclusions; which last Condition may be accepted two Ways: Either first only as they contain the Reason which necessarily causes the Conclusions to be believed as true, and produces a certain Assent, i.e. as the mean Term assumed obtains a necessary Connection with the Terms entering the Conclusion; whence arises that which is called a demonstration τοῦ ὅτι that a thing is: or secondly more strictly, as the mean Term applied is more than a necessary Effect and certain Sign, i.e. as it is a proper Cause of the Attribute or Property, which is predicated of the Subject in the conclusion; and hence is that called a Causal Demonstration, or a Demonstration τοῦ διότι why a thing is. But there is no Reason to doubt, but the last Condition understood in the former Sense agrees with the Premisses of every Mathematical Syllogisms, since there are no such Syllogisms, which do not most strongly compel the Assent; nor does this follow because the Premisses are necessarily true (for otherwise they are not admitted by Mathematicians), but this Necessity argues that there is an essential Connection and Causal Dependence of the Terms between themselves in which it is founded, because the Accidents may be separated, and consequently the accidental Predicates are only attributed to the Subject contingently. [I. Post. c.6] Things Essential (says Aristotle) are necessarily in every Genus, but Things Accidental are not necessary: And every such kind of Argumentation begetting a lesser Degree of Science is reckoned a more low and ignoble Demonstration, because it shews a Thing to be so only from its Effect or Sign, not from its Cause; but yet this more clearly convinces the Mind, and most validly confirms the Truth. There is therefore no Mathematical Discursus which proceeds not thus far. But that the foresaid Condition taken in the latter Sense does also agree with many Mathematical Ratiocinations, i.e. that the mean Term assumed in them has the Force of a Cause in Respect of the Property attributed to the Subject, Aristotle is our first author" (Barrow 1970, 81–82; 1683, 88–89).

32. Barrow (1970, 83; 1683, 89–90).

33. It is all one, as to the Nature of the Thing, from which the Discursus takes its rise, for which soever Link of the Chain you take hold of, the Whole will follow" (Barrow 1970, 88; 1683, 93).

34. Barrow (1970, 88; 1683, 93).

35. Barrow does not consider material causes, which had, however, played a certain role in the *Quaestio*.

36. Barrow (1970, 88–90; 1683, 94).

37. Barrow (1970, 90; 1683, 95).

38. Barrow (1970, 97; 1683, 101).

39. Barrow (1970, 99; 1683, 102–103). This is inconsistent with a number of statements made by Barrow in lectures 21 and 22 on the lower dignity of proofs by reductio as absurdum.

40. See Rochot (1957); also Mancosu and Vailati (1991).

41. "Concludo ergo, quaecumque est certitudo & evidentia in disciplinis Mathematicis eas pertinere ad apparentiam; nullo modo ad causas germanas vel naturas etiam rerum intimas" *Exercitationes*, in Gassendi (1658, vol. III, p. 209). English translation from Gassendi (1972, 107).

42. Such attacks by proxy were a common strategy in the period.

43. Popkin (1979, 85) called attention to Langius' work: "With regard to mathematics the sceptical atmosphere of the seventeenth century was apparently strong enough to require that some defence be given for this 'queen of the sciences'. There is a

work by Wilhelm Langius, of 1656, on the truth of geometry, against sceptics and Sextus Empiricus." The full quote by Langius is the following: "Equidem non me fugit, multa à Petro Ramo viro doctissimo atq; insigni Geometra contra methodum Euclideam fuisse proposita: quae tamen ideo tacitus praetereo, quod illum vitium, non ipsas veritates concernat, nec tam Geometricum sit, quam Logicum. Fuere alii qui de natura demonstrationum Mathematicarum, varia disputarunt; quibus egregiè satisfecit Franciscus Barocius patritius Venetus in celeberrima Pataviensi Academia Mathematum Professor Publicus, qui in illa Oratione, quam publice habuit, tum cum primum Mathemata profiteri inciperet, variis argumentis tam ex auctoritate, quam ex solida ratione petitis, pererudite ac solide comprobavit demonstrationes Mathematicas non modo vere & proprie demonstrationes appellari, secus quam aliqui sentirent, sed & omnium primas esse ac certissimas. Qui ergo haec plenius cognita habere cupit illum adeat. Neq; enim his diutius immorari libet, cum ipsa prima principia totaq; Geometrica materia à cavillis malevolorum satis sit vindicata" (Langius 1656, 156–157). Weigel (1658, 6) also quotes Soner and Picart as excluding the mathematical proofs from the realm of true demonstrations. Soner's and Picart's statements are contained in Scherbius, Sonerus, and Picartus (1644).

44. Piccolomini (1547, 105r).

45. Barozzi (1560, 26r, 27r-v).

46. Pereyra (1576, 72).

47. Biancani (1615, 10).

48. Rivaltus (1615, iiij) verso of the mentioned *Prolegomena*. Rivaltus' edition of Archimedes' works was, together with that of Commandino, one of the standard reference works in mathematics in the early part of the seventeenth century.

49. Rivaltus (1615, iiij) verso of the *Prolegomena*.

50. "Unde rursus animadvertere est Geometras non causis rei uti, sed causis quibus rei cognoscitur. Satis enim illis est, si rem ita esse demonstrarint, nec quo pacto res sit quaerunt" (Rivaltus 1615, Scholium to the Quadrature of the Parabola).

51. Guldin (1635–41, 287). The title of the fourth book is *De Centro Gravitatis liber quartus, de Gloria, ab Usu Centri Gravitatis . . . Sive Archimedes Illustratus.*

52. Guldin (1635–41, 287).

53. On Euclid's notion of superposition see Goldstein (1972), Mueller (1981), von Fritz (1959), Inhetveen (1981), Russell (1903, 405–407), and Wagner (1983). Russell says: "The fourth proposition is the first in which Euclid employs the method of superposition—a method which, since he will make any *détour* to avoid it, he evidently dislikes, and rightly, since it has no logical validity, and strikes every intelligent child as a juggle." I refer the reader to the remaining discussion in Russell for a clarification of how motion should be intended in geometry—as a "class of one-one relations." See also Couturat (1905, 188–195) for an interesting overview and further references on the issue of movement and congruency in elementary geometry.

54. Euclid (1956, vol. I, pp. 247–248).

55. See Euclid (1956, vol. I, p. 225) and Murdoch (1966, 421).

56. Barrow (1970, 187; 1683, 167).

57. "Applicatio verò quanvis superpositiones sit tolerabilior, tamen in Geometria repudiatur: immò ne lineam quidem transportare licet" (Peletier 1557, 15). On the topic of motion in geometry see chapter 4.

58. Candalla (1566, 5).

59. Some Aristotelian philosophers would deny causality to mathematics on account of its not relying on motion, and at the same time explain away the mathematician's talk of motion as an abstract one. For example, Pereyra in

De communibus (1603) says "Sed nullum genus caussae proprie tractari in disciplinis mathematicis potest etiam confirmari ratione et testimonio Arist. Ratio sit
haec: res mathematicae abstractae sunt a motu, ergo ab omni generae caussae"
(p. 70). Also: "Res Mathematicae abstractae sunt a motu, ergo ab omni generae causae"
(p. 116). And "Mathematicus usurpat multa vocabula, ut lineas . . . concurrere, quae
significant motum non quidem verum et naturalem, sed tantummodo imaginarium et
intellegibilem" (p. 118).

Molland (1991, 183) discussing ancient geometry states: "But first we turn to more
general considerations concerning the place of motion in geometry. The Platonic
quotation above [Republic 527A] would seem to make discussions of motion in-
appropriate to geometry, and Aristotle also, although he does not have a separate world
of mathematicals, but considers geometrical objects as abstracted from sensible ones,
still seems rather uneasy about motion." Molland proceeds to discuss some Aristotelian
passages and the dispute between the followers of Speusippus and those of Menaechmus
concerning the role of constructions in geometry. This latter debate is also analyzed in
Lachterman (1989); see also Killing (1898, vol. II, sect. V, §2).

60. This debate played a large role in the foundational reflection of the seventeenth
century and, in particular, as to the validity of the axiom that the whole is greater than
the part. The historical and foundational significance of this debate is well described in
Maierù (1990) and de Olaso (1990).

61. Clavius (1589, 121).

62. Clavius (1589, 121).

63. Savile (1621, 196).

64. Savile (1621, 198).

65. Although these debates are by now almost entirely forgotten, they might have
played an important role in later periods. I mentioned that Bolzano in his 1804 work
Betrachtungen über einige Gegenstände der Elementargeometrie criticizes, as remarked
by Russ, congruency in terms remarkably similar to those of Peletier: " But the concept
of congruence itself is both empirical and superfluous. *Empirical*: for if I say A is
congruent to B, I think of A as an *object* which I *distinguish* from B by the *space* which
it occupies. *Superfluous*: one uses the concept of covering to deduce the equality of two
things if they are shown to cover each other in a certain position, according to the axiom
'spatial things which cover each other are equal to each other' (In this way, one actually
proves identity when only equality had to be shown). Now one could never conclude
that two things are congruent, i.e. that their boundaries are identical, until one had
shown that all their determining pieces are identical. But if one proves this one can also
deduce without covering that these determining things are identical. Therefore Schultz
omitted the concept of covering throughout his *Anfangsgründe* without needing to alter
much on this account" (Russ 1980a, A51–A52).

Whether or not Bolzano was aware of his predecessors in 1804 there is evidence
that he became familiar with them soon after. In the *Miscellanea Mathematica*
(1808–1811) published in the *Gesamtausgabe* we read: "*V*.[on] Euklids *Ausg*[a]*be*
d[urc]*h* J. *Peletarius* sagt Kästner (G[e]sch.[ichte] d[e]r M[a]th.[emat*i*k]|I B[and]
S.326) "Ueb[e]r e[in]e b[e]k[ann]te Einw[e]nd[un]g, d[ie] *m*[an] auch w[o]h1
neuerl[*i*]ch|g.[egen] d[ie] B[e]w[ei]se a.[us] d.[em] *Deck*[en] g[e]m[a]cht hat° (Hier
zielt K.[ästner] ohne Zw[e*i*]f[e]l|auf *Schultz*en)° erklärt er °(Peletarius)° sich s[e]hr
r[ic]ht[*i*]g: Figur[en]|*auf* e[inan]d[e]r *leg*[en] ist *mechanisch*, ab[e]r sie auf ein.[ander]
g[e]l[e]gt *denk*[en], ||mathematisch.-°(?)°-" (Bolzano 1979, 102).

I do not want to enter here into the problem of whether and how Schultz avoided
congruency in his *Anfangsgründe*. It was enough to show that the early criticisms of

proofs by superposition were in nature very similar to later ones, and that the former might indeed have influenced the latter directly. Let me add that Arnauld in the preface to his *Nouveau Elemens de Géométrie* also criticizes the use of congruency in geometrical proofs; see Arnauld (1775–81, vol. 42, p. 140). Gottignies excludes it from theoretical geometry; see Gottignies (1686, book III, pp. 42–43). On Gottignies' work see Bosmans (1928a). More on the issue of congruency is also found in the debate between Barrow, Hobbes, and Wallis and in the exchange between Cavalieri and Guldin.

66. Biancani (1615, 24).

67. See the introduction to Huet (1680).

Chapter 2

1. Knorr (1986, 1); compare Knorr (1982).

2. After the works of Andersen and Giusti this approach to Cavalieri's work is becoming standard. See, for example, de Gandt (1991), Jesseph (1989; 1993a, ch. IV).

3. The translations are from Heath's edition of Euclid's *Elements*. Later on I will also refer to the definition of equality of ratio given in definition 5: "Magnitudes are said to be in the same ratio, the first to the second and the third to the fourth, when, if any equimultiples whatever be taken of the first and the third, and any equimultiples whatever of the second and fourth, the former equimultiples alike exceed, are equal to, or alike fall short of, the latter equimultiples respectively taken in corresponding order" (Euclid 1956, vol. II, p. 114).

4. For the variety of extensions of the exhaustion method in the seventeenth century see Whiteside (1960–61). For Valerio see Bosmans (1913) and Divizia (1983).

5. For a more complete technical treatment see Andersen (1985, sect. V).

6. See the preface to Cavalieri (1635).

7. Cavalieri (1635, book II, pp. 8–9).

8. Cavalieri (1635, book II, p.13).

9. Andersen (1985) provides a detailed analysis of the implicit assumptions found in Cavalieri's proofs. Some of them will be mentioned later on.

10. Giusti (1980, 36).

11. Giusti (1980, 38).

12. Giusti (1980, 38–39).

13. Cavalieri (1635, book II, p. 78).

14. Cavalieri (1635, book II, p. 102).

15. Struik's translation is somewhat clearer than the original text: "Figurae planae quaecunque in eisdem parallelis constitutae, in quibus, ductis quibuscunque eisdem parallelis aequidistantibus rectis lineis, conceptae cuiuscumque rectae lineae portiones sunt aequales, etiam inter se aequales erunt. Et figurae solidae quaecumque in eisdem planis parallelis constitutae, in quibus, ductis quibuscunque planis eisdem planis parallelis aequidistantibus, conceptae cuiuscumque sic ducti plani in ipsis solidis figurae planae sunt aequales, pariter inter se aequales erunt. Dicatur autem figurae aequaliter analogae, tum planae, tum ipsae solidae inter se comparatae, ac etiam iuxta regulas lineas, seu plana parallela, in quibus esse supponuntur, cum hoc fuerit opus explicare" (Cavalieri 1635, book VII, p. 4).

16. Cavalieri (1635, book VII, pp. 7–8); Struik (1969, 210). The English translation uses a different labeling for the figures: ABC for BZ& and XYZ for CβΛ.

17. See Cavalieri (1966, 723–769).

18. To these open attacks one should however add the general hostility of the Jesuits to Cavalieri's indivisibles. Festa (1990, 1992) provides archival evidence to show

that the teaching of indivisibilist techniques in geometry, as well as the use of the atomistic theory in physics, was forbidden in the Jesuit schools by means of decrees, the first dated 1632, issued by the 'revision' fathers of the Collegium Romanum. Festa argues that the hostility to atoms and indivisibles was motivated by theological concerns about the dogma of transubstantiation. Of course, the whole issue is relevant to the role played by the Jesuits in Galileo's trial and to the exact nature of the accusations raised against Galileo, an issue that has been central to Redondi (1983) and the debates on Redondi's claims. Notice that the authors who ostracized the use of indivisibles were in turn strongly opposed by the supporters of the indivisibilist approach. The reviewer of Tacquet's *Opera Mathematica* in the *Philosophical Transactions* of 1668–69 writes: "Follow his [Tacquet's] *Annularia & Cylindrica*; the first 4 Books whereof were first published in 1651, and are common enough to be had here; which may make the Reader wonder at their being reprinted; especially considering, that though they have deservedly received much applause, yet they have likewise been censur'd for opposing and neglecting other Methods, whereby the Author might have rendered, what he delivers, more universally and briefly" (p. 873). Moreover Angeli, quoted in the same review, in his *De Infinitorum Spiralium Spatiorum Mensura* (1660) says of Guldin: "P. Guldinis, Centro-barycae (anno 1635. & 1640. editae) Author famosus (at Cavalierianorum Indivisibilium contemptor et irrisor, qui dum Indivisibilibus irrisit, seipsum ridiculum praebuit) altius omnibus volatum sumpsit, at conatu irrito, & Icari fine, ut ipsemet fatetur" (p. 874). This review is of great interest because it gives an overview of the spread of indivisibilist approaches among seventeenth-century mathematicians. Contemporary treatments of the fortunes of the indivisibilist method are given in Giusti (1980, 1982) and Andersen (1986). For Tacquet's attack on Cavalieri's work see Bosmans (1923) and chapter 5.

19. For a detailed account of the genesis of the third *Exercitatio* see L. Lombardo Radice in Cavalieri (1966) and Giusti (1980).

20. Cavalieri (1647, 180).

21. See Giusti (1980, 61) for more details and an assessment of Cavalieri's defence.

22. Cavalieri (1635, book I, p. 19). For an analysis of this statement as a precursor of the mean value theorem of the calculus see Andersen (1985, 299).

23. Cavalieri (1635, book I, p. 19).

24. Cavalieri (1647, 189–190).

25. Guldin (1635–41, book IV, p. 340).

26. Cavalieri (1647, 199). For an extensive treatment of the background debates on the nature of the continuum and an extensive bibliography see Giorello (1985, chs. 4–5).

27. Guldin (1635–41, book IV, p. 341).

28. Cavalieri (1647, 202).

29. Cavalieri (1647, 203).

30. Guldin (1635–41, book IV, pp. 342–343).

31. Cavalieri (1647, 212).

32. See Bulmer-Thomas (1984) and Ulivi (1982).

33. "Ex his porro ipsis Primis, ac Puris Scientjs, Arithmetica videlicet & Geometria, Tertia alia componitur, utramque copiose complectens, quae Purarum disciplinarum Mathematicarum omnium nobilissima est, DIVINA nimirum ALGEBRA" (Guldin 1635–41, 2).

34. Guldin (1635–41, p. 23)

35. Guldin (1635–41, book II, p. 143).

36. Guldin (1635–41, p. 147).

37. This line of defence is common to Cavalieri and Guldin. Obtaining results that

agreed with the results of the ancients was used as empirical support for the basic principles of the theory. In this sense one could apply to these authors Lakatos' analysis of empiricism in the foundation of mathematics. For example, Cavalieri says: "Non inutile autem mihi videtur eße animadvertere pro huius confirmatione, hoc pro vero supposito, quam plurima, quae ab Euclide, Archimede, & alijs ostensa sunt, à me pariter fuiße demonstrata, measque conclusiones ad unguem cum illorum conclusionibus concordare, quod evidens signum eße potest, me in principijs vera assumpsisse, licet sciam, & ex falsis principijs sophisticè vera aliquando deduci posse, quod tamen in tot, et tot conclusionibus, methodo geometrica demonstratis mihi accidisse absurdam putarem" (Cavalieri 1635, book II, p. 18).

38. Guldin (1635–41, book IV, p. 297).
39. Guldin (1635–41, book IV, p. 286).
40. Guldin (1635–41, book IV, p. 287).
41. Guldin (1635–41, book IV, p. 288).
42. For the sake of comparison I outline the Archimedean proof.

THEOREM. *The area C of a circle is equal to the area T of a right triangle whose legs are equal to the radius and the circumference of the circle* (see Fig. 40).

PROOF. Assume $C \neq T$. Then either $T < C$ or $C < T$. We show that in both cases we obtain a contradiction. Assume $T < C$. Then $C = T + D$ for some positive quantity D. Inscribe inside the circle a square, then an octagon, . . . , and so on until we obtain a polygon P whose area differs from that of the circle C by less than D. In other words, P is closer to C than is T. Let $C = P + D_1$. Then since $C = T + D$, $C = P + D_1$ and $D_1 < D$ we infer that $T < P$ (*).

Now let AE be any side of the polygon, and ON the perpendicular on AE from the center O. Now $ON < r$ where r is the radius of the circle. Moreover the perimeter of the polygon (Per) is less than the circumference of the circle. It follows that $ON < WY$ and $Per < WZ$. Therefore $P < T$. But this contradicts (*). Thus C cannot be greater than T (+).

By a symmetric argument through the circumscription of regular polygons to the circle we show that C cannot be less than T. $(++)$.

From (+) and $(++)$ we obtain $C = T$. This completes the proof.

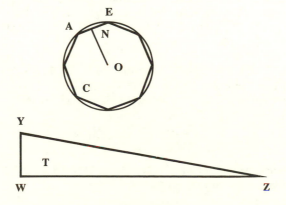

Figure 40

43. "Propositio IV. Omnis trianguli centrum gravitatis est in medio rectae lineae, basi aequidistantis, quae bina latera ita dividit, ut segmenta ad angulum, reliquis dupla sunt. Propositio VI. Omnis parallelogrammi centrum gravitatis est in recta linea, quae opposita latera bisecta sunt" (Guldin 1635–41, book I, pp. 90–91).

44. Ulivi (1982) reproduces the proofs of Cavalieri and Torricelli. The first printed proof of Guldin's theorem was published in 1659 by Tacquet in *Cylindrica et Annularia*.

45. Cavalieri (1647, 235).

46. Cavalieri (1647, 238).

47. Cavalieri (1647, 52). This had already been noted by the mathematician Lombardo Radice in his Italian translation and commentary of Cavalieri (1966). See his note 23, p. 256. The opposition between ostensive proofs and proofs by reductio is often stressed by Cavalieri. Consider, for example, this passage taken from a letter to Galileo dated 30 April 1627: "Ed ho anche trovato la demonstrazione ostensiva che il cilindro sia triplo del cono, che non avevo trovata se non ad impossibile, cioé nella mia maniera provando che tutti i quadrati del parallelogrammo siano tripli di tutti i quadrati" (Cavalieri 1966, 747). But Cavalieri often appeals to classical theorems that are, in fact, proved by contradiction (as for instance in book VI, theorem II, proposition II).

48. Wallis (1685, 3). Descartes, Torricelli, and others make similar statements. Klausing (1701) extremised these positions by claiming that the so-called new mathematics of the seventeenth century was not new at all.

49. Torricelli (1644b, vol. I, p. 173).

50. The call number of the manuscript, called *Scene*, is Mss. Galil. vol. 130. I have not been able to consult it directly. My quotes are taken from Belloni (1987).

51. Belloni (1987, 32).

52. Belloni (1987, 32).

53. Belloni (1987, 34).

Chapter 3

1. (G 297). Quotations from the *Géométrie* are from the Smith and Latham edition (Descartes 1952). I use the following abbreviations: (G 54) indicates Descartes (1952, 54) and (A-T 30) stands for the Adam and Tannery edition, Descartes (1897–1910, 30). I have sometimes modified Smith and Latham's translation. Apart from more general histories of mathematics, there are several introductions specifically to the *Géométrie*; among them are Bos (1981), Giusti (1987), Grosholz (1991a), Itard (1956), Krämer (1989), Lachterman (1989), Milhaud (1921), Scott (1952), and Vuillemin (1960). All of section 3.1 is taken from Mancosu (1992b).

2. (G 297).

3. On the relationship between Viète and Descartes see Giusti (1987), Klein (1968), Milhaud (1921), and Tamborini (1987).

4. The problem can be stated in an inessential variant by introducing a factor of proportionality λ:

$$CB \cdot CF = \lambda \cdot CD \cdot CH.$$

In the solution I assume that the lines are positioned exactly as shown in Figure 18, so as to avoid needless complications with signs.

5. (G 307).

6. (G 313).

7. Pappus says: "If there be more than six lines, it is no longer permissible to say 'If the ratio be given between some figure contained by four of them to some figure contained by the remainder,' since no figure can be contained in more than three dimensions. It is true that some recent writers have agreed among themselves to use such expressions, but they have no clear meaning when they multiply the rectangle contained by these straight lines with the square on that or the rectangle contained by those" (Thomas 1967, 601–603).

8. "The ancients have very rightly remarked . . . " (G 315).

9. Pappus (1933, 38).

10. (G 315).

11. The descriptions of these curves are easily found in any good history of mathematics, such as Boyer (1968), Kline (1972) and especially Heath (1921). The reader should keep in mind that the spiral and the quadratrix are transcendental curves, whereas the conchoid and the cissoid are algebraic curves. See also Lebesgue (1950).

12. (G 316–317).

13. Molland (1976, 35).

14. (G 316).

15. (G 319).

16. "With this Sporus is rightly displeased for these reasons. The very thing for which the construction is thought to serve is actually assumed in the hypothesis. For how it is possible, with two points starting from B, to make one of them move along a straight line to A and the other along a circumference to D in an equal time, unless you first know the ratio of the straight line AB to the circumference BED? In fact this ratio must also be that of the speeds of motion. For, if you employ speeds not definitely adjusted (to this ratio), how can you make the motions end at the same moment, unless this should sometime happen by pure chance? Is not the thing thus shown to be absurd?

"Again, the extremity of the curve which they employ for squaring the circle, I mean the point in which the curve cuts the straight line AD, is not found at all. For if, in the figure, the straight lines CB, BA are made to end their motion together, they will then coincide with AD itself and will not cut one another any more. In fact they cease to intersect before they coincide with AD, and yet it was the intersection of these lines which was supposed to give the extremity of the curve, where it met the straight line AD. Unless indeed any one should assert that the curve is conceived to be produced further, in the same way as we suppose straight lines to be produced, as far as AD. But this does not follow from the assumptions made; the point G can only be found by first assuming (as known) the ratio of the circumference to the straight line." Quoted in Heath (1921, vol. 1, pp. 229–230).

17. This seems to be the rationale for Pappus' construction of the quadratrix by means of the spiral and the cylindrical helix. Molland (1976, 27) says: "It seems clear that Pappus regarded the spiral and the cylindrical helix as having a firmer claim to the status of being geometrical than the quadratrix, which could however receive authentication by being derived from them. The constructions used in the derivation must also have been regarded as having a fairly firm geometrical status." However, these derivations are not pointwise constructions, and the spiral and the cylindrical helix are, from Descartes' point of view, as problematic as the quadratrix. See Pappus (1933, book IV) and Molland (1976, 27) for a description of Pappus' constructions.

18. This appendix is also reproduced with some variants in the *Geometria Practica*, book VII, pp. 189–194. The appendix is not in the first edition of the work (Clavius 1574), which is why I cite the third edition (Clavius 1591, 349–359). In the third edition the first two diagrams are mislabeled, but Figure 21 here is a correctly labeled version.

19. Clavius (1591, 296). And again, after having described the standard construction of the quadratrix by two independent motions: "Sed quia duo isti motus uniformes, quorum unus per circumferentiam DB, sit, & alter per lineas rectas DA, CB, effici non possunt, nisi proportio habeatur circularis lineae ad rectam, merito à Pappo descriptio haec reprehenditur: quippe cum ignota adhuc sit ea proportio, & quae per hanc lineam investiganda proponatur. Quare nos Geometrice eandem lineam Quadratricem descri-bemus hoc modo" (Clavius 1591, 296). This passage seems to attribute the non-geometrical nature of Pappus' decription not to the two movements, but to the rectification of the circumference involved in determining their speeds.

20. "SED quia punctum E, in latere AB, inveniri Geometricè non potest, cum ibi omni sectio rectarum cesset; ut illud sine notabili errore, qui scilicet sub sensum cadat, reperiamus, utemur hoc artificio" (Clavius, 1591, 296).

21. Clavius (1591, 297). An interesting criticism of the pointwise construction of the Quadratrix is found in Biancani's *Sphaera Mundi seu Cosmographia* (1620). Biancani says: "Quartò, fallaciter demonstramus, quando in constructione assumitur aliquid, cuius constructio ignoratur, ut si ad quadrandum circulum dicat quis, sumatur linea recta aequalis periferiae circuli; hoc enim geometricè nondum inventum est; & si mechanicè, vel organicè fiat nititur sensu; similiter peccant omnes demonstrationes in quibus usui sunt lineae punctuales, ut est linea Conchoidis Nicomedis apud Clavium in Geometria pract. li.8 p. 25. & linea Quadratrix apud Clavium ad finem 6. Euclid. huiusmodi enim lineae non sunt quid continuum, cum ex punctis constent, & propterea nequeunt partes ipsarum praecisae haberi, cum incertum sit ubinam sint puncta linea constituentia in Quadratrice praeterea ultimum punctum haberi nequit. Nicomedes paralogizat ducens lineam quandam quae terminatur ad Conchilem punctualem, quia incertum est an ad unum ex punctis illis definat, secus terminari ab ea nequit" (Biancani 1620, 409). An attempt to improve Clavius' construction was made in Lansbergius (1628, 37–52). On Lansbergius see Bosmans (1928b). More work on the quadratrix is found in Guldin's *Centrobaryca* in the 'Digressio de quadratura circuli, Lineaque Quadratrice' (book I, ch. VI).

22. It is interesting to remark that in the *Geometria Practica* Clavius gives a description of the conchoid by points, thus avoiding the use of instruments: "Nicomedes construit prius instrumentum quoddam, quo lineam inflexam describit, quam Con-chilem, vel Conchoideos appellat. sed nos omisse eo instrumento, eandem (quod ad nostrum institutum satis est) per puncta delineamus, hac ratione" (Clavius 1604, 162). I think it would be worthwhile to investigate Clavius' notion of acceptable constructions in geometry.

23. (G 339–340).

24. Bos (1981, 325).

25. (G 340–341). Descartes does not give an example in the *Géométrie* of this type of representation. However, from a passage in a letter to Mersenne dated 27 May 1638, it is clear that the Archimedean procedure for squaring the circle would fall under such a category: "Vous me demandez si ie pense qu'un globe, roulant sur un plan, décrit une ligne égale à sa circonference, à quoy ie répons simplement qu'oüy, par l'une des maximes que i'ay écrites, sçavoir que toutes les choses que nous concevons clairement et distinctement sont vrayes. Car ie conçoy bien aisément une meme ligne pouvoir estre tantost droite & tantost courbée, comme une corde" (A-T, vol. II, pp. 140–141). Descartes has no problems in conceiving of a circumference equal in length to a straight line (as in Archimedes' quadrature of the circle, where we begin by straightening the circumference); nevertheless, since the proportion between the circular and straight lines is unknown to us, this procedure should not be used in geometry.

26. Bos (1981, 314–315).

27. However, it should be remarked that Aristotle in *Physics* (e.g., book VII, 248[a], 10) is worrying more specifically about proportionality between circular and straight lines. For example, talking about circular and rectilinear motions, Aristotle says: "None the less, if the two motions are commensurable, we are confronted with the consequence stated above, viz. that there might be a straight line equal to a circle. But these are not commensurable: and so the corresponding motions are not commensurable either" *Physics*, book VII, 248[b], 5). For a more general analysis of these texts see Heath (1949, 140–142). By the Aristotelian dogma in the text, I mean the strong form of it given in Descartes' text. On the problem of rectification of curves, see Boyer (1964), Hofmann (1974, ch. 8), and Yoder (1988, ch. 7).

28. Here is the original text: "L'invention de Mr Gaudey est tres bonne & tres exacte en prattique; toutesfois affin que vous ne pensiés pas que je me fusse mespris de vous mander que cela ne pouvoit estre Geometrique, ie vous diray que c'est ne pas le cylindre qui est cause de l'effait, comme vous m'aviés fait entendre, et qu'il n'y fait pas plus que le cercle ou la ligne droitte, mais que le tout depend de la ligne helice que vous ne m'aviés point nommee & qui n'est pas une ligne plus receue en Geometrie que celle qu'on appelle *quadratricem*, pource qu'elle sert a quarrer le cercle & mesme a diviser l'angle en toutes sortes des parties esgales, aussy bien que celle cy & a beaucoup d'autres usage que vous pourrés voir dans les elemans d'Euclide commantés par Clavius. Car encore qu'on puisse trouver une infinité de points par ou passe l'helice & la quadratrice, toutefois on ne peut trouver Geometriquement aucun des poins qui sont necessaires pour les effaits desirés tant de l'une que de l'autre; & on ne les peut tracer toutes entieres que par la rencontre de deux mouvemans qui ne dependent point l'un de l'autre, ou bien l'helice par le moyen d'un filet, car tournant un filet de biais autour du cylindre, il decrit iustemant cete ligne la; mais on peut avec le mesme filet quarrer le circle, ci bien que cela ne nous donne rien de nouveau en Geometrie. Ie ne laisse pas d'estimer bien fort l'invention de Mr Gaudey, & ne croy pas qu'il s'en puisse trouver de meilleure pour le mesme effait" (A-T, vol. I, pp. 70–71). The problem solved by Gaudey is mentioned in a letter from Descartes to Mersenne dated 8 October 1629: "De diviser les cercles en 27 & 29, ie le croy, mechaniquement, mais non pas en Geometrie. Il est vray qu'il se peut en 29 par le moyen d'un cylindre, encore que peu de gens en puissent trouver le moyen; mais non pas en 29, ny en tous autres, & si on m'en veut envoyer la pratique, i'ose vous promettre de faire voir qu'elle n'est pas exacte" (A-T, vol. I, p. 25).

29. (A-T, vol. II, p. 91).

30. Mersenne (1634, 275).

31. A careful analysis of this text is given by Costabel (1985). This is the text (see Fig. 41): "CIRCULI QUADRATIO. Ad *quadrandum circulum* nihil aptius invenio quam si dato quadrato *bf* adjungatur rectangulum *cg* comprehensum sub lineis *ac* & *cb*, quod sit aequale quartae parti quadrati *bf*; item rectangulum *dh*, factum ex lineis *da*, *dc* aequale quartae parti praecedentis; & eodem modo rectangulum *ei*, atque alia infinita usque ad *x*: quae omnia simul aequabuntur tertiae parti quadrati *bf*. Et haec linea *ax* erit diameter circuli, cujus circumferentia aequalis est circumferentiae hujus quadrati *bf*: est autem *ac* diameter circuli octogono, quadrato *bf* isoperimetro, inscripti; *ad* diameter circuli inscripti figurae 16 laterum, *ae* diameter circuli inscripti figurae 32 laterum, quadrato *bf* isoperimetrae; & sic in infinitum (A-T, vol. X, pp. 304–305).

32. Indeed, a confirmation of my claim is also provided by the fact that in the debate between Huygens and James Gregory on the possibility of squaring the circle geometrically, which occurred after the first rectifications of curves, both authors agreed that the only allowable solutions were geometrical in the 'Cartesian' sense. On this topic

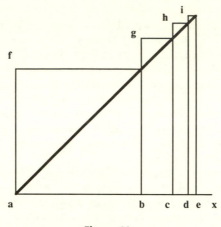

Figure 41

see Breger (1986) and references therein. Breger's article is especially useful for tracing the development and dissolution of the geometrical-mechanical distinction in Leibniz's work.

33. For further details on Descartes' method of tangents and a comparison with that of Fermat, see Mahoney (1973), Milhaud (1921, ch. VII), Vuillemin (1960, 57–65), Galuzzi (1980), and Giusti (1984).

34. (G 369–370).

35. In connection with Descartes' program, Bos says "it contrasted so strongly with earlier approaches that one can speak of a new paradigm" (Bos 1981, 304).

36. (A-T, vol. II, 480).

37. Bos (1981, 323).

38. Giusti (1987, 429).

39. See Vuillemin (1960), Belaval (1960), or Costabel (1985).

40. See Milhaud (1921), Vuillemin (1960), Belaval (1960), Scriba (1960–61), or Costabel (1985).

41. Vuillemin (1960, 9).

42. Costabel (1985, 38).

43. Belaval (1960, 301).

44. Thus in the reply to the objections to the second mediation, he says: "L'analyse montre la vraye voye par laquelle une chose a esté methodiquement inventée, & fait voir comment les effets dépendent des causes. . . . La synthese, au contraire, par une voye tout autre, & comme en examinant les causes par leurs effects (bien que la preuve qu'elle contient soit souvent aussi des effets par les causes), démontre à la verité clairement ce qui est contenu en ses conclusions, & se sert d'une longue suite de definitions, de demandes, d'axiomes, de theoremes et des problemes, afin que, si on luy nie quelques consequences, elle face voir comment elles sont contenuës dans les antecedens et qu'elle arrache le consentement du lecteur, tant obstiné & opiniatre qu'il puisse estre; mais elle ne donne, comme l'autre, une entiere satisfaction aux esprits de ceux qui desirent d'aprendre, parce qu'elle n'enseigne pas la methode par laquelle la chose a esté inventée" (A-T, vol. IX, pp. 121–122). The Latin uses *a priori and a posteriori* instead of 'from causes to effects' and 'from effects to causes' (A-T, vol. VII, pp. 155-156). Attention to these passages has also been drawn, among others, by Vuillemin (1960, 165–166) and

Israel (1990, 444–445). The best analysis of Descartes' philosophical work in relation to the analysis/synthesis opposition is found in Engfer (1982, ch. 3).

45. (A-T, vol. I, pp. 489–490).

46. (A-T, vol. II, p. 274).

47. Mahoney (1980, 141).

48. A very complicated problem, which I will not even attempt to address here, is the relationship between geometry and algebra, and the advantages and disadvantages of the algebraic and geometrical approach in mathematical practice. These topics are discussed at length, among others, by Leibniz and Newton. Leibniz had even planned a dialogue on this subject. A few pages containing the plan of the dialogue are preserved in the Leibniz manuscripts under the call number LH35 VIII, 30f.35. It was clear to Leibniz that the algebraization of mathematics did not mean the loss of significance of the geometrical analysis of problems. In the review of Prestet's book quoted later in the chapter we read: "Les jeunes gens [de nostre temps] d'aujourd'huy n'ont que trop [d'inclination pour se] d'aversion pour la Geometrie et plusieurs se jettent dans l'Algebre [sans] à corps perdu faisant des abstractions en l'air qu'ils ne [peuvent] sçauroient jamais appliquer à ce qu'il y a de reel dans le monde, sçavoir aux figures et aux mouvemens. . . . Il faut considerer que la Geometrie a une analyse à part qui luy est propre, où l'Algebre n'entrevient point [qui]. Cette analyse nous donne souvent des voyes naturelles lors que celles de l'Algebre sont forcées" (Robinet 1955, 62–63). Newton defends similar views in, for example, the introduction to "The geometry of curve lines" (c. 1680) in Newton (1967-81, vol. IV, pp. 422–423).

49. No complete account of these debates has yet been written. A good overview of the debates concerning the relationship between algebra, geometry, and arithmetic is given by Pycior (1987). I also found very useful a survey of the debate given in an unpublished typescript by Siegmund Probst *Die Kontroverse zwischen John Wallis und Thomas Hobbes in den "Philosophical Transactions"* (1990). Some parts of this work have now appeared as Probst (1993). On the controversy see also Cajori (1929) and Scott (1938, ch. 10).

50. On John Wallis' mathematical production see Scott (1938), Scriba (1966), and Prag (1931).

51. On the *Mathesis Universalis* in the late Renaissance see Crapulli (1967). For the seventeenth century see Arndt (1971) and Mittelstraß (1979).

52. A quotation by Barrow shows us that these issues also raised the problem of the exact relationship between algebra and arithmetic: "Now as to what pertains to these *Surd Numbers* (which, as it were by way of Reproach and Calumny, having no Merit of their own are also stiled *Irrational, Irregular,* and *Inexplicable*) they are by many denied to be Numbers properly speaking, and are wont to be banished from Arithmetic to another Science, (which yet is no science) *viz. Algebra.* And by this they demutilate Arithmetic of its noblest and most profitable Member" (Barrow 1683, 59; 1970, 44).

53. Klein (1968, 223). The reader is referred to Klein's classic *Greek Mathematical Thought and the Origin of Algebra* for a thorough analysis of these developments. Klein concentrated his attention in particular on Stevin, Descartes, and Wallis.

54. Barrow's reaction to the analytic mathematics is dealt with in Sasaki (1985). The best account of Barrow's mathematical work is Mahoney (1990).

55. Barrow (1683, lec. III, pp. 60–61; 1970, 46).

56. Besides the literature mentioned in note 2 on Hobbes' philosophy of mathematics one should also consult Breidert (1979), Gargani (1971), Giorello (1990), Mancosu (1992a), Medina (1985), Melis (1973), Sacksteder (1980, 1981), Schuhmann (1985), and Jesseph (1993b).

57. "Hac usus est methodo primus (quantum scio) Diophantus, paucis adhibitis notis (praeter literas) symbolis radicum, quadratorum, cuborum. Nunc autem tota algebra, aucta symbolis ab Oughtredo et Cartesio, et ab his geometriam applicata, nomen obtinuit geometriae symbolicae: infecitque hujus aevi geometras, geometriae verae pestis" (Hobbes 1845b, vol. IV, p. 442).

58. Hobbes (1845a, vol. VI, p. 329).

59. Barrow (1683, lec. XVII, p. 281; 1970, 328). Barrow also reproaches Gregorius à Sancto Vincentio of the same mistake: "That great Man [Gregorius] therefore, as *Tacquet* thinks, did not frame any new Science about Proportions, but only fashioned the old Doctrine in another Model, and that not over apposite, and delivered it in new Words; which yet he has enriched with many Theorems invented by himself. And as we have said, it is common to him with the rest [i.e. Wallis and Mersenne] that embrace this Doctrine (*viz.* concerning the Reasons and Quantities of Reasons), to confound Reasons with numerical Fractions" (Barrow 1683, lec. XX, p. 326; 1970, 378). On Barrow's reaction to the analytic mathematics, with particular reference to the debates on the nature of proportion theory, see Sasaki (1985). On Gregorius see Dhombres (1992, 1994).

60. See Tropfke (1933, 96–103) for a useful list of seventeenth-century texts dealing with the nature of negative numbers.

61. Arnauld (1667, art. 61). Also Leibniz makes some interesting remarks about this rule especially in connection to a debate between Clavius and his opponents. Clavius proved the rule by relying on the analogy between the operation " − " and the negation of a statement, so that to negate a statement twice is to assert it. See Leibniz (1976, 126–127).

62. The text can also be found in Schrecker (1935). The first edition of the *Elémens* was strongly influenced by Malebranche. Therefore the work has received a great amount of attention. On Prestet and his role in the Malebranchist milieu, and on Malebranche's philosophy of mathematics see Brunschvicg (1912) and Robinet (1960a, 1961, 1970). On the role played by Malebranche's philosophy for the "algebraization of mathematics" see Fraser (1990) and Hobart (1988).

63. Schrecker (1935, 85).

64. "Je voudrois donc qu'on ne dît jamais *moins telle grandeur*, que cela n'eût quelque rapport à quelque grandeur positive, dont cette grandeur affectée du signe de moins pût être retranchée" (Schrecker 1935, 86).

65. "Je conclus de tout cèla que moins par moins sans rapport à plus est une fiction, dont on ne se laisse pas de se pouvoir servir utilement" (Schrecker 1935, 86).

66. "Je trouve même qu'il import beaucoup pour bien établir les fondemens des sciences qu'il y ait de tels contredisans; c'est ainsi que les Sceptiques combattaient les principes de la Geometrie, avec tout autant de raison; que le P. Gottignies, Jesuite savant, voulut jetter de meilleurs fondemens de l'Algebre, et que Messieurs Cluver et Nieuwentiit ont combattu depuis peu, quoyque differemment, nostre Analyse infinitesimale" Leibniz to Varignon, 2 February 1702, in Leibniz (1843–63, vol. IV, p. 94). On Gottignies see Bosmans (1928a).

67. On Tacquet's *Arithmetic* see Bosmans (1927). Jesseph (1993a) discusses the importance of this text in the context of Berkeley's foundational work in arithmetic.

68. In particular Bosmans (1928a) conjectures a possible influence of van Roomen (Adrianus Romanus) on Tacquet and Gottignies.

69. Prestet [1675] 1689, 3–4). Also of interest, especially in connection with the issue of finitism is section XXI: "Si le plus d'une grandeur est si grand qu'on ne puisse lui rien ajoûter qu'elle n'ait déja, cette grandeur est infiniment vrai. Et si le moins d'une

grandeur estoit si grand, qu'on ne pust lui rien retrancher dont elle ne manquest déja, cette grandeur seroit infiniment fausse. Mais parceque nostre esprit est resserré dans des bornes tres-étroites, & que si une grandeur estoit vray ou fausse infiniment, elle ne seroit resserrée dans aucunes bornes, nous n'entreprendons point de comprendre ni même de raisonner sur l'infini. Nous entreprendons seulement de raisonner sur des grandeurs finies qui peuvent recevoir le plus & le moins."

70. Gottignies (1687, 18).

71. Gottignies (1687, 25)

72. Leibniz (1712, 388). Leibniz's paper was written in the context of the, discussion of a famous claim by Wallis on the existence of numbers greater than infinity. On the context and the details of Leibniz's text and his position concerning negative numbers see the introduction by Parmentier in Leibniz (1989, 422–432). To the bibliographical references provided by Parmentier one should also add Schrecker (1946) where the history of the debate concerning quantities greater than infinite is followed through the works of Varignon, Grandi, and Fontenelle.

73. Leibniz (1695a, 322). There is no doubt that one of the persons Leibniz is thinking of is his long-time correspondent, Michelangelo Fardella. Gottignies' point of view were, in fact, followed by Fardella in the second volume of his *Utraque Dialectica Rationalis et Mathematica* (1695) where he dealt, among other things, with the meaning of negative quantities. A perusal of the extensive correspondence between Leibniz and Fardella (110 letters from Fardella to Leibniz and 20 letters from Leibniz to Fardella) preserved at the Niedersächsische Bibliothek zu Hanover did not, however, reveal any epistolary discussion about this topic between Leibniz and Fardella. On Fardella's mathematical work see Palladino (1988). On Fardella's role in the defence of Gottignies' *Logistica Universalis* see Bosmans (1928a).

74. Robinet (1955, 62).

Chapter 4

1. In an excellent survey article entitled "Epistemology of the Sciences" Nicholas Jardine (1988) gave an overview of the debates which characterized the Renaissance reflection on the epistemology of mathematics, astronomy, and natural science. Jardine pointed out that the debates on *regressus* in natural science and the issue of the status of astronomical hypotheses have "played a considerable role in the controversy about the question of continuity between the 'new' sciences and the epistemologies of the seventeenth century and earlier developments" (p. 708). He also remarked that in the case of mathematics the situation was rather different: "The sources and fortunes of the sixteenth-century Italian discussions of mathematical demonstrations and the grounds of certainty have been little studied. These debates are, however, reflected in the treatments of the status of mathematics by Christophorus Clavius, Giuseppe Biancani and Galileo's friend and mentor Jacopo Mazzoni, treatments which interestingly combine insistence on the certainty and excellence of mathematics and mathematical demonstration with emphasis on the substantial role for mathematics in the study of nature" (p. 709). A study of the seventeenth century fortunes of the *Quaestio* was given in Mancosu (1992a).

2. McMullin (1992, 53).

3. For an overview of the debates on the nature of definitions in the seventeenth century see de Angelis (1964, 82–99). Section 4.1 is taken from Mancosu (1995).

4. See Lachterman (1989, 87–91) for an analysis of this Euclidian use of motion.

5. Heath (1921, vol. II, p. 64).

6. The interaction between motion and the generation of the continuum has already been dealt with extensively in the literature. In the text I review only the main points of the issue. For more details I refer the reader to the works Cohen (1883), Vivanti (1894), and Moretto (1984). Vivanti dealt with this problem in his *Il concetto d'infinitesimo e la sua applicazione alla matematica*. In chapter 4 of that book he gave an overview of the notion of intensive infinitesimal, defined as an entity that possesses no magnitude but contains a tendency to generate magnitudes (through motion). This is the Pythagorean notion that we have already recalled above in connection with Aristotle's discussion in *On the Soul* and which is found again, in Cusa and Bruno. Cusa, talks about the line as the *explicatio* of the point in several passages of his work. See also Bruno (1889, vol. I, p. 148) and Clavius (1589, 13). Vivanti recalls the important link between motion and the continuum established, among others, in Sover, Guldin, Cavalieri, Barrow, Ceva, Hobbes, and Newton. Sover claims in *Curvi ac Recti Proportio* (1630, 271) that geometry cannot be understood without the idea of motion: "Ajo neque geometriam esse absque motu neque ejus veritatem sine motu intelligi posse." The work by Ceva referred to is *Geometria Motus* of 1692.

7. "L'invention des touchantes de cette ligne, par une méthode qu'il trouva alors, et qu'il divulgua incontinent, laquelle est si générale qu'elle s'étend aux touchantes de toutes les courbes: elle consiste en la composition du mouvements" (Pascal 1963, 118).

8. Roberval (1693, 25).

9. Roberval (1693, 25).

10. For details see, among others, Auger (1962), Zeuthen (1966, 321–325), Baron (1969, 174–177), and Clero and Le Rest (1981, 69–72).

11. "A noi basterà d'aver accennato per qual via Archimede possa esser venuto in cognizione d'una verità tanto astrusa, e per così dire inopinabile come la suddetta. Credo certo che l'Autore a bello studio volesse occultare, e invilupare la dimostrazione del Teorema; tanto che non si potesse conoscere da che origine egli ne aveva derivata la cognizione. Però nel corso di tanti secoli non è stata mai questa passione della spirale capita evidentemente, non per altro, se non per la mancanza della dottrina *de motu*, nota benissimo fino nei suoi tempi ad Archimede, ma pubblicata solo nei nostri dal Galileo. Che i mezzi de i quali l'Autore si serve nella dimostrazione siano per così dire improprii, e che altrettanto appropriati siano gli addoprati da noi, si può scorger dalla definizione stessa, la quale altro non contiene che l'imaginazione di due movimenti dalla mistione dei quali risulta poi un certo viaggio spiralmente incurvato. Perciò chi con le cose poste nella definizione, cioè con la dottrina del moto, cercasse di provare anche i Teoremi dipendenti da quella, mi pare che egli si servirebbe dei mezzi proprii per arrivare alle conclusioni, e che però produrrebbe scienza evidente, e (come dicono) *a priori*. Al contrario dimostrandosi indirettamente tali proprietà, con mezzi alieni alla definizione, oltre l'oscurità e lunghezza nella quale s'incorrerà, si produrrà nel lettore una scienza in certo modo accidentale; di tal sorte, che egli conoscerà bene di non poter contradire a quella proposta, ma non intenderà già come e per qual causa quella conclusions sia vera" (Torricelli 1975, 492–493). The heuristic character of Roberval's method is evidenced by Roberval's attitude vis-à-vis his results; see Clero and Le Rest (1981, 72).

12. Barrow (1670, 159); compare Barrow (1916, 35).

13. Barrow (1916, 47).

14. Barrow (1670, 195). Translation from Barrow (1916, 55–56).

15. "Barrow's proof couples kinematic intuition with an implicit principle of continuity. Take any point K on the tangent to the left of the point of tangency, and

draw KOG parallel to TZ. During the time of uniform motion of TZ over DC (= GM), the point on the tangent traverses KG, and the point on the curve traverses OG. Since KG > OG, the vertical velocity of the point on the tangent is greater than that of the point describing the curve at O; for even while accelerating between O and M the latter does not travel as far as does K uniformly. By contrast, for any point on the right, the point K would travel less far vertically in moving toward M than would point O, even though O would be decelerating. Since the vertical velocity of O is less than the vertical velocity of K for all points above M and greater for all points below, the velocities must be equal at M.

It is worth noting that Barrow's demonstration makes no appeal to infinitesimals or limits. In the style of Fermat's original derivation of his methods of maxima and minima and of tangents, Barrow takes an arbitrary interval GM and derives a relationship that holds for all values within that interval. He takes as given a principle akin to Rolle's theorem that, in going from positive to negative values, a quantity must pass through 0. The validity of such a principle—and how it can be demonstrated—became a staple theme of analysis in the eighteenth and nineteenth centuries, but Barrow apparently thought it self-evident" (Mahoney 1990, 208–209)

16. The centrality of motion to Newton's mathematical work, say *On the Quadrature of Curves*, is well known.

17. Barrow (1683, lec. 4, p. 73; 1970, 61–62).

18. Barrow (1683, lec. 12, p. 197; 1970, 223).

19. Barrow (1683, lec. 5, p. 89; 1970, 83).

20. Wallis (1655, 12–14).

21. "That which you call perplexity in the explication [of geometrical proportion], is your predjudice, arising from the symbols in your fancy. For men that pretend no less to natural philosophy than to geometry, to find fault with bringing motion and time into a definition, when there is no effect in nature which is not produced in time by motion, is a shame. But you swim upon other men's bladders in the superficies of geometry, without being able to endure diving, which is no fault of mine; and therefore I shall, without your leave, be bold to say, I am the first one that hath made the grounds of geometry firm and coherent" (Hobbes 1845a, 242).

22. Hobbes (1962, 84).

23. "Tous les traits par lesquels Spinoza caractérise la géométrie . . . sont ceux que souligne Hobbes. Ainsi, pour Hobbes: (1) Les causes des *universalia* sont connues de soi (*notae per se*). (2) Elles se réduisent à une: le mouvement. (3) De la variété des mouvements naît la variété des figures: 'Causa eorum omnium universalia una est motus; nam et figuram omnium varietatem ex varietate oritur motuum quibus construuntur, nec motus aliam causam habere intelligi potest praeter alium motum' (*De Corpore* (1665), chap. VI, §v, Londres, 1839, *Op. Lat.*, I, p. 62). (4) Le mouvement permet la définition *per generationem* (*generationes seu descriptiones, ibid.*, p. 63), c'est-à-dire par la cause. (5) Par là est possible la science, puisque '*scire est per causam scire*' (*Examinatio, Op. Lat.*, IV, p. 42; *De Corpore*, ch. I, §II, chap. VI, §§I, IV–VI; *De Homine*, 1658, chap. X, §IV, *Op. Lat.*, II, p. 92). (6) Du mouvement du point naît la ligne, du mouvement de la ligne la surface, du mouvement de la surface le corps (*Examinatio*, pp. 31, 33, 58; *De Corpore*, p. 63). (7) Ainsi par le mouvement s'obtiennent toutes les définitions génétiques, par exemple, celle du cercle: 'Circulus est figura descripta per lineae, in piano existentis et cujus unus terminus quiescrit, circumductionem' (*Examinatio*, p. 64, *De Corpore*, pp. 5–6, 72), celles de la sphère, du cône, du cylindre, etc. (*Examinatio, ibid.* et p. 86; *Six Lessons to the Savilian Professors of the Mathematics*, 1656, *Eng. Works*, VII, pp. 215 sqq.). (8) Ces définitions, contrairement aux définitions statiques, rendent compte

de la possibilité de la chose (*Examinatio, ibid., De Corpore*, I, §I, §5). Elles en font connaître toutes les propriétés. 'Ex generatione sola cognoscuntur constructi affectiones' (*Examinatio*, p. 66; *De Corpore*, I, chap. I, §V, VI, §§IV–VI; *De Homine*, chap. X, §§IV–V; *Six Lessons*, pp. 210, 212, 214, etc.)" (Gueroult 1974, 484–485).

Gueroult (1974, 467–487) gives a detailed account of Spinoza's conception of geometry and its relationship to that of Hobbes.

24. The English translation is from Arnauld and Nicole (1874). This section has been taken from Mancosu (1991).

25. These passages are clearly influenced by Pascal (1657–58). On Pascal's *De l'esprit géométrique* see Schobinger (1974).

26. Arnauld and Nicole (1662, 326; 1872, 338).

27. Arnauld and Nicole (1662, 332; 1872, 344).

28. Arnauld and Nicole (1662, 328; 1872, 340).

29. Arnauld and Nicole (1662, 328–329; 1872, 340–341).

30. In Arnauld (1775–81, vol. XLII). For details about the fortune of this work see Arnauld (1775–81, vol. XLII, pp. V–VIII). For an analysis of this work from the mathematical point of view see Bopp (1902). From the Euclidian commentator, Proclus, we learn that already in Greek times there were attempts to develop reconstructions of geometry which were free from the use of proofs by contradiction: "It is a difficult task in any science to select and arrange properly the elements out of which all the matters are produced and into which they can be resolved. Of those who have attempted it [for geometry] some have brought together more theorems, some less; some have used rather short demonstrations, others have extended their treatment to great lengths; some have avoided the reduction to impossibility, others proportion; some have devised defences in advance against attacks upon the starting-points; and in general many ways of constructing elementary expositions have been individually invented" (Proclus 1970, 60). On the role played by proofs by contradiction in the development of ancient geometry see Szabó (1976). An analysis of Greek mathematics with particular emphasis on proofs by contradiction has been given in Gardies (1991).

31. Philosophical Transactions (1670, 2054–2057).

32. Bolzano (1804, A14).

33. Bolzano (1810, 63–64; 1810, A170). This passage contains the nucleus of the theory of *Grund* and *Folge* presented in the later works of Bolzano.

34. Bolzano (1978, 93). For an overview of Bolzano's theory of science see Buhl (1961).

35. Bolzano (1837, §525, p. 261).

36. Bolzano (1837, §525, pp. 261–262).

37. Bolzano (1837, §525, pp. 262–263). Whether or not every direct proof gives the ground (the reason) for the conclusion was a controversial issue. Bolzano (1837, vol. IV, pp. 261–263) lists Jakob, Krug, and Reinhold as holding the thesis that every direct proof gives the ground for the conclusion. By contrast, Bolzano thinks that there are direct proofs that are not a priori. This position is certainly not original with him.

38. Dummett (1991,70).

39. For the pre-Kantian period see de Angelis (1964), Arndt (1971), Schüling (1969), de Vleeschauwer (1961), Risse (1970), Tonelli (1959), and Engfer (1982). In particular, the Kantian distinction between philosophy and mathematics has been the subject of numerous investigations. For a first introduction to Kant's theory of mathematics see Posy (1992) and Friedman (1992).

40. Kant (1965, 577).

41. Kant (1965, 625).

42. The opposition between direct proofs, which most of the time give the *why*, and the indirect proofs, which only give the *that*, is very much alive in the eighteenth century. For example, we read in Crusius: "Ferner (2) ist ein Beweis entweder *a priori*, wenn man die Wahrheit der Conclusion aus ihrem Grunde, welcher machet, daß sie wahr ist, also herleitet, daß man daraus verstehet, nicht nur *daß*, sondern *warum* sie wahr ist. Ein *Beweis a posteriori ist*, da man die Wahrheit der Conclusion aus einem Erkenntnisgrunde, welcher nur anzeiget, daß sie wahr ist, dergestalt herleitet, daß man daraus nur verstehet, daß die Sache also sey, noch nicht aber, warum sie also ist" (Crusius 1747, 82). In §524 Crusius then classifies proof by contradiction as a posteriori. A detailed exposition of Kant's conception of *Beweis* is found in Mellin (1798) *ad vocem.*

43. Kant (1965, 626)

44. Kant (1965, 626).

45. Kant (1965, 627–628).

46. Kant (1965, 628). Descartes, Spinoza, and Wolff are certainly prominent in Kant's mind. On Descartes' extensive use of reductio ad absurdum in metaphysics see Engfer (1982, §16). On Spinoza's use of reductio see Krähe (1874, 8–9) and Gueroult (1968).

47. This Kantian position was held also by several influential followers of Kant. Let me recall here Fries' statement in his *System der Logik* (1819): "Die apagogische Beweisart paßt daher nur für eine Erkenntnißweise, welche Klarheit genug hat, um die Vollständigkeit der vorausgesetzten Disjunktionen sicher übersehen zu lassen. So werden sie z.B. in der reinen Mathematik mit Leichtigkeit gebraucht; in philosophischen Untersuchungen aber müssen sie vermieden werden, weil man da bey sehr allgemeinen Eintheilungsgründen leicht eine nur konträre Entgegensetzung schon für widersprechend nehmen kann" (Fries 1819, 321).

48. Schoenflies (1906, 20)

49. Schoenflies (1906, 20).

50. Schoenflies (1906, 21).

51. Frege (1979, 179–180).

52. Bolzano (1810, 38) and Russ (1980a, A145).

53. Bolzano (1810, 138–139) and Russ (1980a, A246).

54. Bolzano (1837, vol. IV, p. 291).

55. Bolzano (1837, vol. IV, p. 266).

56. Bolzano (1978, 93). The issue of indirect proofs appears also in the *Größenlehre*; see Bolzano (1981, §16, pp. 72–73).

57. Bolzano (1837, vol. IV, p. 269; 1972, 385).

58. Bolzano (1837, vol. IV, p. 271; 1972, 386).

59. Bolzano (1837, vol. IV, p. 271; 1972, 386).

60. Bolzano (1837, vol. IV, p. 277; 1972, 390–391).

61. Bolzano (1837, vol. IV, p. 278).

62. "Ich meines Theils möchte der Meinung des Aristoteles beitreten; . . . so ist es mir doch bisher mit allen Beispielen, mit denen ich einen Versuch gemacht (namentlich mit allen in *Euklids Elementen* vorkommenden Beweisen *per absurdum*) gelungen, sie ostensiv zu machen; vorausgesetzt, daß man jeden Beweis ostensiv nennt, sobald er nur nicht apagogisch ist, und einen Beweis nur dann apagogisch nennt, wenn er sich eines hypothetischen Obersatzes bedienet, der die Verneinung des zu beweisenden Satzes in seinem Vordersatze, und eine Ungereimtheit in seinem Nachsatze enthält. Bei diesen Begriffen bleibt ein Beweis ostensiv auch wenn ein sogennanter Schluss der Umkehrung in ihm vorkommt; es sey der ganz gewöhnliche, wo man aus einem Satze der form:

'Jedes A ist ein B,' den Schlußsatz: 'Was also nicht B ist, ist auch kein A,' ableitet" (Bolzano 1837, vol. IV, pp. 278–279).

63. "Es scheint mir nunmehr wahrscheinlich, daß die gewünschte Umgestaltung des indirekten Beweises immer möglich sein dürfte, obwohl dafür schwerlich eine Begründung gegeben werden kann, und die von Bolzano versuchte Begründung sicher nicht ausreichend ist, wie ich in dem früheren Aufsatz hinreichend gezeigt zu haben glaube. Ich bin also demnach damals insofern zu weit gegangen, als ich glaubte, mit zwei Beispielen aufwarten zu können, die auch nicht in der erwähnten Weise auf den modus tollens hinausgespielt zu werden vermöchten" (Hölder 1930, 97–98).

64. Trendelenburg (1870, ch. XX, pp. 431–442).

65. Hessenberg's attitude towards indirect proofs was expressed clearly in §12: "Darum sollte das Arbeiten mit *problematischen Annahmen* nach Möglichkeit vermieden werden. Denn alle aus ihnen gezogenen Folgerungen sind selbst problematisch, darum keine *Resultate* im mathematischen und keine *Ruhepunkte* in psychologischen Sinne. Die häufigste Form der problematischen Annahme ist die Annahme des Gegenteiles der zu beweisenden Behauptung im indirekten Beweis. Man verwendet sie am besten nur in heuristischem Sinne als Wegweiser für die weitere Ausgestaltung der Betrachtung. *Muß* man dagegen Folgerungen aus ihr ziehen, so geschehe es möglichst gegen Ende des Beweises, damit die Widerlegung in einem Zuge erfolgen kann, der kurz genug ist, um einer Gliederung entraten zu können" (Hessenberg 1912, 6–7).

66. I made some remarks about similarities between intuitionism and Arnauld's theory of science in the conclusion of Mancosu (1991).

67. See Löwenheim (1946), Cauman (1967), and Gardies (1991). It would take me too far to assess their claims thoroughly.

68. Dummett (1991, 25–26).

69. Let me make a little aside. As is well known, there is no evidence that Frege ever read Bolzano, since he never quotes him. However, I must confess that I find the use of the same proposition and of the same reduction strategy to be evidence for Frege's debt to Bolzano's *Wissenschaftslehre*, a debt already conjectured by many scholars (see Kluge 1980, ch. VI). Indeed, it would be quite simple to point to the similarities between Frege's conception and Bolzano's conception of deduction, both in terms of their emphasis on grounds and on their insistence that a proper inference must proceed from truths to truths. I grant that one could explain many of their similarities in terms of a common tradition to which they belong. However, I find it hard to explain away the use of I.19 in Frege's reduction just by appealing to mere coincidence. After all, there are proofs by reductio in Euclid that are easier and occur before I.19, say I.7. Be that as it may, it is evident that Frege's answer to the challenge of proof by contradiction could only be resolved by showing that the appeal to false assumptions in the indirect proof could be eliminated; he did this by employing Bolzano's strategy either by hitting on it independently or by borrowing it directly from the *Wissenschaftslehre*. Of course, there is also the possibility that Frege was influenced by some other work containing Bolzano's reduction or one similar to it. But until I am shown such a text, I will opt for a direct influence of Bolzano on Frege.

Chapter 5

1. "Nicht zwar, wie Kästner sagt, alle, aber gewiß die meisten paradoxen Behauptungen, denen wir auf dem Gebiete der Mathematik begegnen, sind Sätze, die den Begriff des Unendlichen entweder unmittelbar enthalten oder doch bei ihrer versuchten Beweisführung in irgendeiner Weise sich auf ihn stützen" (Bolzano 1975, 1).

2. Guldin (1635–41, book II, p. 4). This did not stop Galileo from making use of indivisibles in *Two New Sciences*.

3. See for instance Mark Smith (1976) and Giorello (1985). Giorello situates Galileo's work in the context of ancient, medieval and early modern debates on the composition of the continuum.

4. Galilei (1974, 39–40).

5. "SALV. I don't see how any other decision can be reached than to say that all the numbers are infinitely many; all squares infinitely many; all their roots infinitely many; that the multitude of squares is not less than that of all numbers, nor is the latter greater than the former. And in final conclusion, the attributes of equal, greater, and less have no place in infinite, but only in bounded quantities. So when Simplicio proposes to me several unequal lines, and asks me how it can be that there are not more points in the greater than in the lesser, I reply to him that there are neither more, nor less, nor the same number [*altrettanti*, just as many], but in each there are infinitely many" (Galilei 1974, 41).

6. Galilei (1974, 36–37).

7. Galilei (1974, 37).

8. The paradox of the wheel has a long history and plays a central role in Galileo's discussion on the nature of the continuum in the *Discorsi*. The discussion is instrumental in addressing the issue of how we can give a satisfactory account of physical phenomena such as expansion and rarefaction of material substances. The paradox of the wheel can be stated, in a simplified form, as follows (Fig. 42). Consider two concentric circles with radii AB and AC. A complete rotation of the greater circle describes a line equal to the circumference, say BF. At the same time, the smaller circle describes a distance CE equal to BF. But, how is this possible, since the smaller circle has also gone through a single rotation and should thus describe a length equal to its circumference?

There are various issues raised by the discussion of this paradox. The first is how is it possible to explain physically what is going on. But the great merit of Galileo, as Drabkin has pointed out, is to have seen that the real paradoxical aspect of the situation described in the paradox of the wheel consists in the one-to-one correspondence between infinite aggregates of different size. In the *Discorsi* Galileo resolved the paradox by analyzing the motion of concentric polygons and then by treating the circle as a polygon with infinitely many sides. His conclusion was that the smaller circle leaps along the way. For an extensive discussion of the paradox see Drabkin (1950) and Costabel (1964).

9. "Ella dice, che se tutte le linee di due superficie eguali sono eguali, diminuendole ugualmente, l'ultime esinanizioni di esse dovriano essere uguali: il che poi non appare nell'esempio della scodella e del cono, restando in quella una circonferenza di cerchio, et in questo un punto, infinitamente minore di quella. Hora io direi che pure in questo

Figure 42

essempio si verifica la magior proposizione, cioè che restano le ultime esinanitioni pure eguali; poiché detraendo parti eguali da interi eguali, è conveniente, s'habbiano da intendere le rimanenti essere eguali, che e le detratte e le lasciate siano del medesimo genere, non essendo comparabili quelle che sono di diverso genere, come ella sa benissimo. Hora, nel suo esempio, gli indivisibili sono piani, e di questi rimangono sempre parti uguali, detrahendone parti uguali dal cono e dalla scodella; e perché per arrivare all'ultima esinanitione di questi, cioé all'annullare i piani (per dir così) basta levargli una dimensione, perciò parmi che con ragione si dica che queste ultime esinanizioni siano eguali (se ben più tosto negativamente che positivamente), essendo noi arrivati al nullo piano tanto nel cono quanto nella scodella, non havendoci che far niente che in uno resti un punto e nell'altro una linea, come che tanto sia niun piano la linea come il ponto" (Cavalieri 1966, 754–755).

10. In the letter dated 2 October 1634, Cavalieri says: "Quanto alle circonferenze de' cerchi concentrici, dico che per liberarmi da questi argomenti che si ponno fare, massime intorno alle linee rette o curve, segate da tutte le linee o da tutti i piani di varie figure, io ho distinto i punti di retto transito e di obliquo transito, sì come anco le linee di retto transito e di obliquo transito, non parendomi che si debbano cambiare quelli di retto transito con quelli di obliquo transito; e per misura de' continui ho assunto, per le linee i punti di retto transito, e per i piani le linee di retto transito; per i solidi poi non vi bisogna tal distinzione (che cosa siano poi i punti o linee di retto transito overo di obliquo transito, vien dichiarato nel libro 2, alla def. prima e nell'appendice seguente). E che importi questa varietà di transito è manifesto, poiché quanto una linea sarà tagliata meno obliquamente dalle parallele, magior spazio comprenderanno le estreme parallele fra loro, et il massimo sarà quando la segaranno perpendicularmente, cioé con retto transito: hora io prendo questo retto transito e lascio l'obliquo, come variabile in infiniti modi. Che poi tanti punti si causino da tutte le parallele, cosi nella perpendicolare come nella obliqua, questo non lo negarò, come anco nelle circonferenze concentriche; ma che perciò dovesse dirsi tanto lunga l'una come l'altra, mentre volessimo compor le linee di punti, dico che la differenza di questi transiti può cagionare questo, potendosi credere che questi punti siano forsi più diradati nell'obliqua che nella perpendiculare. Tuttavia, comunque ciò sia, non mi pare di essere astretto a rispondere a questo, poiché assolutamente io non mi dichiaro di componere il continuo d'indivisibili, ma solo mostro che i continui hanno la proporzione degli aggregati di questi indivisibili, non assumendo io se non le linee o punti di retto transito" (Cavalieri 1966, 756–757).

11. See Fromondus (1631). A discussion of Fromondus is given in Giorello (1985) and Beeley (1995).

12. Cavalieri (1635, book II, p. 4).

13. "Che gli indivisibili tutti sieno eguali fra di loro, cioè i punti alli punti, le linee in larghezza alle linee e le superficie in profondità alle superficie, è opinione a giudizio mio non solo difficile da provarsi, ma anco falsa. Se siano due circoli concentrici, e dal centro s'intendano tirate tutte le linee a tutti i punti della periferia maggiore, non è dubbio che altrettanti punti faranno i transiti delle linee sulla periferia minore, e ciascuno di questi sarà tanto minore di ciascuno di quelli quanto il diametro è minore del diametro" (Torricelli 1975, 505).

14. A full analysis of the Torricellian account is contained in De Gandt (1987).

15. Cavalieri (1647, 239).

16. De Gandt (1987, 177–179).

17. Cavalieri (1647, 239–240).

18. Barrow (1670, lec. III). Many mathematicians were well aware that most paradoxes arose because the distinction between oblique and direct transit was not taken

into account. Giusti (1980, 46–47) quotes a letter from de Sluse to Pascal: "iay eu occasion de voir le livret contre les indivisibles composé par Monsr. Le Blanc [Thomas White] ... L'origine de toutes ces difficultes ne depend que de ce qu'il n'a pas observe dans les examples qu'il oppose le *diversitatem transitus*, ce que toutefois Cavallerius a si soigneusement recomande, et lequel bien observe ne permettra iamais que l'on tombe en aucune paralogisme." In the same tone, Arnauld in his brief introduction to the method of indivisibles contained in his *Nouveaux Elémens de de Géométrie* (pp. 306–311) after having explained the notion of transit concludes: "Et c'est proprement delà que depend la verité de cette nouvelle methode (& non que le continu soit composé d'indivisibles) ce qui l'a fait même appeller par quelques uns, la Geometrie de l'infini.

"Il faut donc bien prendre garde que les lignes (par le rapport desquelles on dit qu'une somme des ces lignes paralleles qui remplissent un espace, est égale à une autre somme) les coupent perpendiculairement. Et c'est où il y a plus de danger de ce tromper. Sur ces fondemens voicy les Theoremes que l'on établit" (p. 308).

19. Tacquet (1651, 13–4).

20. "J'ai voulu faire cet avertissement, pour montrer que tout ce qui est démontré par la véritable règle des indivisibles, se démontrera aussi à la rigueur et à la manière des anciens; et ... l'une de ces méthodes ne diffère de l'autre qu'en la manière de parler; ce qui ne peut blesser les personnes raisonnables, quand on les a une fois averyes de ce qu'on entend par là ... Je ne feray aucune difficulté d'user de cette expression: *la somme des ordonnées*, qui semble n'estre pas géométrique à ceux qui n'entendent pas la doctrine des indivisibles, et qui s'imaginent que c'est pécher contre la géométrie que d'exprimer un plan par un nombre indéfiny de lignes; ce qui ne vient que de leur manque d'intelligence, puisqu'on n'entend autre chose par là sinon la somme d'un nombre indéfiny de rectangles faits de chaque ordonnée avec chacune des petites portions égales du diamètre, dont la somme est certainement un plan, qui ne diffère de l'espace du demy circle, que d'une quantité moindre qu'aucune donnée" (Pascal 1904–14, VIII, pp. 352–353.) On Pascal's approach to infinitesimal analysis see Bosmans (1923), Russo (1962), and Clero and Le Rest (1981). In a letter to Torricelli, Roberval (1693) has a similar theory: "Est inter Cavalerii methodum et nostram exigua quedam differentia; ille enim cujusvis superficiei indivisibilia secundum infinitas lineas, solidi autem indivisibilia secundum infinitas superficies considerat. Nostra autem methodus, si non omnia, certe hoc caveat, ne heterogenea comparare videtur: nos enim infinita nostra seu indivisibilia sic consideramus. Lineam quidem tanquam si ex infinitis seu indefinitis numero lineis constet, superficiem ex infinitis seu indefinitis numero superficiebus, solidum ex solidis." On Roberval's theory see Walker (1932) and Auger (1962). For Wallis see the literature quoted in section 3.2.

21. On Leibniz's years in Paris see Hofmann (1974). On the issue of the dates see Knobloch. (1993).

22. For a detailed analysis of the treatise see Knobloch (1989, 1993, 1994) and Scholtz (1934).

23. For instance, Giusti (1980, 48) claims that after Torricelli "only a few figures of second rank remain to ponder over the principles." Scholtz (1934, 7–9) had used Leibniz's treatise to argue the point against Gerhardt, Weißenborn, and Zeuthen. Jesseph (1989) also stresses the importance given to foundations by seventeenth-century mathematicians but does not quote this work by Leibniz.

24. Leibniz (1993, 39).

25. "Demonstratio illud habet singulare, quod rem non per inscripta ac circumscripta simul, sed per sola inscripta absolvit. Equidem fateor nullam hactenus notam esse viam, qua vel unica quadratura perfecte demonstrari possit sine deductione ad

absurdum; imo rationes habeo, cur verear ut id fieri possit per naturam rerum sine quantitatibus fictitiis, infinitis scilicet vel infinite parvis assumptis: ex omnibus tamen ad absurdum deductionibus nullam esse credo simplicem magis et naturalem, ac directae demonstrationi propiorem, quam quae non solum simpliciter ostendit, inter duas quantitates nullam esse differentiam, adeoque eas esse aequales, (cum alioquin alteram altera neque majorem neque minorem esse ratiocinatione duplici probari soleat) sed et quae uno tantum termino medio, inscripto scilicet circumscripto, non vero utroque simul, utitur; adeoque efficit, ut clariores de his rebus comprehensiones habeamus" Leibniz (1993, 35).

26. In Scholium to prop. XXIII he remarks again on such use: "Quae de infinitis atque infinite parvis huc usque diximus, obscura quibusdam videbuntur, ut omnia nova; sed mediocri meditatione ab unoquoque facile percipientur: qui vero perceperit, fructum agnoscet. Nec refert an tales quantitates sint in rerum natura, sufficit enim fictione introduci, cum loquendi cogitandique, ac proinde inveniendi pariter ac demonstrandi compendia praebeant, ne semper inscriptis vel circumscriptis uti, et ad absurdum ducere, et errorem assignabili quovis minorem ostendere necesse sit. Quod tamen ad modum eorum quae prop. 6.7.8. diximus facile fieri posse constat. Imo si quidem possibile est directas de his rebus exhiberi demonstrationes, ausim asserere, non posse eas dari, nisi his quantitatibus fictitiis, infinite parvis, aut infinitis, admissis, adde supra prop. 7 schol." (Leibniz 1993, 69).

27. For instance in the *Nouveaux Essais sur l'Entendement Humain*, book IV, ch. VIII, par. 2 we read: "Ne reconnaissez-vous pas que réduire une proposition à l'absurdité, c'est démontrer sa contradictoire? Je crois bien qu'on n'instruira pas un homme en lui disant qu'il ne doit pas nier et affirmer le même en même temps, mais on l'instruit en lui montrant par la force des conséquences qu'il le fait sans y penser. Il est difficile à mon avis de se passer toujours de ces démonstrationes apagogiques, c'est-à-dire qui réduisent à l'absurdité, et de tout prouver par les ostensives, comme on les appelle."

28. Leibniz (1993, 67). The paradox has been presented in detail in Knobloch (1989, 1990, 1994).

29. On Leibniz and this axiom, especially with reference to Galileo and Saint-Vincent, see Hofmann (1974, 12–14). Bosinelli (1991, 163–164), and Knobloch (1990, 34–35); compare de Olaso (1990).

30. "Car apparement on s'attendoit, & on devoit s'attendre à le trouver infini," (Fontenelle 1727, 457). Fontenelle does not mention Torricelli by name but only gives the description of the acute hyperbolic solid. Section 5.2, with the exception of 5.2.4, is taken from Mancosu and Vailati (1991).

31. Evangelista Torricelli, *Opera Geometrica* (1644a), republished in *Opera di Evangelista Torricelli* (1919–44). The *Opera Geometrica* has been completely translated into Italian by Belloni in *Opere Scelte di Evangelista Torricelli* (1975). Parts of the work *De solido hyperbolico acuto* (1644b), to which we will often refer in this section, have been translated in Struik (1969, 227–231).

32. Torricelli (1919–44, vol. 3, p. 65). Cavalieri's admiration for the infinitely long solid was not momentary, for he mentions the result also in his last work: "Corpus (quod ipse [Torricellius] vocat, Solidum acutum hyperbolicum) infinitae longitudinis, geometricae insolens, sed tamen admirable . . . per indivisibilia tamen curva . . . mensura subiecit" (Cavalieri 1647, 2). Cavalieri also gave a construction of an infinitely long solid of finite volume in his *Exercitationes*, Prop. 38, p. 536. See the free translation of Walker (1932, 68–69).

33. Mersenne (1972, vol. 12, p. 206).

34. Galilei (1975, 63).

35. Itard (1975, 122).

36. Mersenne (1972, vol. 12, p. 257). The statement of the theorem Torricelli sent to the French mathematicans is equivalent to the one he proved in *De solido* . . . .

37. Here we cannot study the technical developments originated by Torricell's theorem. For Torricelli's further work on infinite hyperbolas see Bortolotti (1924, 1925). In particular, pages 212–213 of the first article are on the acute hyperbolic solid.

38. On Torricelli's development of the indivisibilist techniques see de Gandt (1987).

39. *De solido hyperbolico acuto*, in Torricelli (1919–44, vol. 1, p. 173).

40. *De solido. . .*, in Torricelli (1919–44, vol. 1, p. 174). Torricelli seems to defend his originality at all costs, even though Cavalieri mentioned to him in 1641 that he had already made use of curved indivisibles to compare spirals with parabolas. In fact, a few theorems in the *Geometria* make use of curved indivisibles.

41. Andersen has shown that many mathematicians learned the techniques of indivisibles through Torricelli's version rather than through the original texts by Cavalieri. This accounts, in her opinion, for the common misunderstandings about the nature of Cavalieri's method. See Andersen (1986) and de Gandt (1992).

42. *De infinitis parabolis*, in Torricelli (1919–44, vol. 1, p. 321).

43. *De solido. . .*, in Torricelli (1919–44, vol. 1, p. 190).

44. *De solido. . .*, in Torricelli (1919–44, Vol. 1, p. 193).

45. *De solido. . .*, in Torricelli (1919–44, vol. 1, p. 194).

46. Torricelli (1919–44, vol. 1, p. 321). The reference is here to the paradox of the bowl, presented by Galileo in the first day of the *Two New Sciences* (see section 5.1).

47. Before concluding the technical treatment, let me add something about the technical fortune of such results. Torricelli's infinitely long solid was only the first of a flurry of geometric figures, infinite in one or even two dimensions, that were studied by early-modern mathematicians. In a note appended to a proposition on infinitely long figures of his *De Quadratura Arithmetica* (1993, 132). Leibniz gave a detailed overview of such results, mentioning Torricelli, Gregorius, Huygens, and Wallis. And, one should add the names of Fermat and Stefano degli Angeli, perhaps others, too.

48. For Cavalieri's remarks, see note 32.

49. Gassendi, *Rebuttals* (1972, 212).

50. Gassendi, *Rebuttals* (1972, 212).

51. *De dimensione parabolae*, in Torricelli (1919–44, vol. 1, p. 94).

52. *De solido. . .*, in Torricelli (1919–44, vol. 1, p. 173).

53. Galilei (1975, 1–2).

54. *Racconto di alcuni problemi proposti e passati scambievolmente tra gli matematici di Francia et il Torricelli ne i quattro anni prossimamente passati*, in Torricelli (1919–44, vol. 3, pp. 7–432, see p. 13).

55. Gassendi, *Syntagma* (1658, vol. 1, p. 264b). Bayle (1974, under Zenon) used this passage by Gassendi to defend his skeptical views about mathematics. For more on Bayle and Gassendi see Mancosu and Vailati (1991). Also Newton in 1693 draws attention to the paradoxical nature of results about infinitely long geometrical objects: "There are many things concerning numbers and magnitudes which to men not learned in mathematics will appear paradoxical, and yet are entirely true. As that an area of infinite lengh, and solid of infinite length and width, can be measured" (McGuire 1978, 118).

56. Aristotle's dictum occurs in *De Coelo* I, 6, 274a.

57. *De solido. . .*, in Torricelli (1919–44, vol. 1, p. 173). Torricelli was not quite right. For, in criticizing Aristotle's point that an infinite body must be infinite in all three dimensions, Oresme (d. 1378) had not only given examples of solids infinite in one or two dimensions, whose volumes are finite, but had also explained that such results

obtained because the infinite increase of one dimension is countered by the infinite decrease of another. See, among other works, Oresme (1968, 119). However, this in no way diminishes Torricelli's merit because Oresme's results were long forgotten by the early seventeenth century, and mathematicians and philosophers of the caliber of Roberval, Mersenne, Descartes, Huygens, Fermat, Barrow, Wallis, and Leibniz never challenged Torricelli's claim to priority. For a fascinating survey of problems connecting cosmology and infinite bodies in medieval thought see Duhem (1914–59); parts of this work have been translated into English in Duhem (1975). See especially the section on the infinitely large (vol. VII of the French edition, pp. 89-157, and pp. 73-132 of the English translation).

58. Euclid, *Elements*, book XI, def 1. In this connection one should consider the finitistic statements made by Biancani quoted in chapter 1.

59. Mersenne (1644, p. 2, unnumbered). On Mersenne and the infinite see also Field (1994).

60. The translation is partially taken from Koyré (1978, 243).

61. This does not commit me to take any position on the delicate question of Torricelli's "Platonism." Koyré (1978, 243), commenting on Torricelli's conception of geometry, concentrated on the passages from the introduction to the *De dimensione parabolae* to stress Torricelli's emphasis on the freedom of the geometer (and mechanician) to define its objects. "The separation from physical reality, the geometrization of space, the identification of physical space with geometrical space, which had been, according to Torricelli, incompletely achieved by Archimedes, is now accomplished. Physics = mechanics; mechanics = geometry. So Torricelli has no hesitation in transporting his 'corporeal' balance into 'imaginary' space beyond the sphere of the stars, to a really infinite distance. Geometrical space is infinite; and now at last the space of mechanics, and hence of physics—regardless of the actual dimension of the real universe—have become infinite in their turn." Koyré's remark should be integrated by the observations made in Galluzzi (1976, 1979). Galluzzi argues against the possible mistake which Koyré's remark may generate, namely, that of reading Torricelli as a radical "Platonist" whose work in geometry and mechanics is completely removed from physical interests. The reader interested in the debate on the "Platonism" of Torricelli, namely, how the theoretical science of motion agrees with the experimental results, should also consult the introduction by Belloni to the Italian translation of the selected works by Torricelli.

62. Barrow (1683, lec. 16, p. 255).

63. Barrow (1683, lec. 16, p. 255).

64. So, Aristotle argues against an infinite body on the basis that it would be infinitely heavy. See *On the Heavens* I, 6.

65. Barrow held that some axioms are necessary to all reasoning and gave a few; that sense in its own way is an undoubted criterion for truth; that the possibility of a thing is argued from the existence of its like (Barrow 1683, lec. 7, p. 110).

66. Barrow (1683, lec. 7, p. 107).

67. Barrow (1683, lec. 16, p. 256).

68. Barrow (1683, lec. 5, p. 84).

69. Barrow (1683, lec. 5, pp. 84–85).

70. Barrow (1683, lec. 10, p. 160).

71. Barrow (1683, lec. 10, p. 152).

72. Barrow (1683, lec. 7, p. 111).

73. Barrow (1683, lec. 7, p. 110).

74. Barrow (1683, lec. 7, p. 111).

75. Barrow (1683, lec. 7, p. 111).

76. Barrow (1683, lec. 7, p. 111).

77. Barrow (1683, lec. 7, p. 113).

78. Barrow (1683, lec. 16, p. 225). As we saw, Oresme had already pointed out that an infinitely long solid can have a finite volume if, while one dimension increases infinitely, the other decreases infinitely.

79. See Itard (1975, 122).

80. He claimed that our knowledge of infinity shows that our intellect does not need a corporeal organ for its function. He also tried to strengthen a version of the cosmological argument for the existence of God by appealing, albeit obscurely, to asymptotic spaces. See the preface to Pardies (1671).

81. See the preface to Pardies (1671).

82. Arnauld and Nicole (1872, 63, 334).

83. Arnauld and Nicole (1872, 307). This passage was added in the fourth edition (1674).

84. The words he uses are "comprehendere" and "intelligere." See Descartes' *Meditationes de Prima Philosophia* (1897–1910/1972, vol. 7, p. 46). For a discussion of Descartes' views on infinity see, among others, McGuire (1983) and North (1983).

85. Descartes (1897–1910/1972, vol. 3, p. 292). The translation is by Anthony Kenny, editor of *Descartes. Philosophical Letters* (Minneapolis: University of Minnesota Press, 1981), p. 93.

86. Descartes, *Principia Philosophiae* I, 26, in Descartes (1897–1910/1972, vol. 7, p. 15). Descartes heard of Torricelli's result very early. In December 1643 he praised Roberval's proof in a letter to Mersenne (Mersenne 1972, vol. 12, pp. 377–378). But three years later, when his relations with Roberval had become sour, he told Mersenne that Roberval's achievement, compared with Torricelli's was minor (Descartes 1897–1910/1972, vol. 4, p. 553). However, although he held interesting views concerning our knowledge of infinity, and although Torricelli's result bears on them, Descartes did not comment on its philosophical implications. Similarly, in spite of his interest in the notion of infinity, Spinoza mentions Torricelli only in connection with the void.

87. See his letter to Clerselier, June 1646 (Descartes 1972, vol. 4, p. 442). See also Costabel (1985).

88. See Leibniz (1969, 387). It is not my intention to discuss here the complexities of Leibniz's theory of infinity; see the excellent articles of Bosinelli (1991) and Knobloch (1990, 1994) and many of the essays contained in Lamarra (1990a).

89. Leibniz (1969, 584).

90. "Caeterum ingenuitas nostra non patitur ut dissimulemus, non esse ista tam mira, quam hominibus primo aspectu videntur. R.P. Pardies e Societate Jesu, scriptis elegantibus notus eruditis, ac vita longiore dignus, tantum hujusmodi meditationibus tribuebat, ut crederet efficax satis argumentum praebere ad evincendam animae immaterialitatem | quemadmodum in compendii Geometrici praefatione asseruit erg. |. Mihi videtur ipsam per se naturam mentis, et operationes, praesertim quibus in se revertitur, sufficere ut | a corpore, sive erg. | a re duobus tantum | praedita erg. |, extensione scilicet, et massa, | praedita gestr. ‖ id est | a erg. | corpore, erg. u. gestr.. ‖ distinguatur. Quanquam non negem singulares quasdam operationes caeteris, saltem apparere, mirabiliores; quas plus (aaaaaa) ad p (bbbbbb) valere si non ad probandum, certe ad persuadendum, non abnuerim. Quod hanc vero attinet | mentis actionem erg. | qua spatia infinita metimur, (aaaaaaa) ea ex (bbbbbbb) ea nihil extraordinarium continet, cum fictione quadam nitatur, et supposita quadam linea terminata quidem, infinita tamen, nullo negotio (aaaaaaaa) procedit (bbbbbbbb) procedat, (aaaaaaaaa) nec

(bbbbbbbbb) unde non plus habet difficultatis, quam si finitum longitudine spatium metiremur" (Leibniz 1993, 132–133). The letters a and b refer to two different drafts of the manuscript; "erg." stands for "inserted" and "gestr." for "'erased."

91. "Quod hanc vero attinet | mentis actionem erg. | qua spatia infinita metimur, (aaaaaaa) ea ex (bbbbbbb) ea nihil extraordinarium continet, cum fictione quadam nitatur, et supposita quadam *linea terminata quidem, infinita tamen,* nullo negotio (aaaaaaaa) procedit (bbbbbbbb) procedat, (aaaaaaaaa) nec (bbbbbbbbb) unde non plus habet difficultatis, quam si finitum longitudine spatium metiremur " (Leibniz 1993, 133).

92. "Interminatum itaque voco in quo nullum punctum ultimum sumi potest, saltem ab una parte. Infinitum vero, quantitatem sive terminatam, sive interminatam, modo qualibet a nobis assignabili, numerisve designabili, majorem |intelligamus erg.|. An autem hujusmodi quantitates ferat natura rerum Metaphysici est disquirere; Geometrae sufficit, quid ex ipsis positis sequatur, demonstrare. gests.|" (Leibniz 1993, 133). On the issue of the *infinitum terminatum* see the references provided in Knobloch (1994).

93. No complete account of these debates has yet been written. A good overview of the debates concerning the relationship between algebra, geometry, and arithmetic is given by Pycior (1987). I also found very useful a survey of the debate given in an unpublished typescript by Siegmund Probst *Die Kontroverse zwischen John Wallis und Thomas Hobbes in den "Philosophical Transactions"* (1990). Some parts of this work have now appeared as Probst (1993). On the controversy see also Cajori (1929) and Scott (1938, ch. 10).

94. John Wallis, *Arithmetica Infinitorum* (1656–70, vol. I, p. 257).

95. Wallis, *Arithmetica* (1656–70, p. 412).

96. Thomas Hobbes, *Leviathan* (1845a, vol. 3, p. 6).

97. Hobbes, *Leviathan* (1845a, vol. 3, p. 17).

98. Hobbes, *Leviathan* (1845a, vol. 3, p. 17).

99. Hobbes (1845b, vol. 5, p. 213).

100. Hobbes (1845b, vol. 5, p. 213). Hobbes' point was reasonable. Tacquet, in his *Dissertatio phisico-Mathematica de Motu Circuli et Sphaerae* (1650), states as his tenth definition: "Cum *infinitum* dicimus intellige indefinitum, sive quantumvis magnum, aut multum; sic enim loquuntur Geometrae" (Tacquet 1650, p. 146).

101. Hobbes (1845b, vol. 5, p. 154).

102. Wallis (1671, p. 2242).

103. Hobbes (1845b, vol. 5, p. 209). Hobbes got so involved in the issue that he mentioned it in his autobiography in latin verse:

Addidit Oxoniae Praelector Savilianus
Wallisius multo nobile dogma magis:
Nempe infinitae molis finem esse, et habere
Finitum partes et sine fine datas:
Quae duo fecerunt insanos dogmata, quotquot
festinaverunt esse geometrici.

See his *Thomae Hobbes Malmesburiensis vita Carmine expressa authore seipso* (1679) in Hobbes (1845b, vol. 1, p. xcv).

104. Hobbes (1845a, vol. 7, p. 433).

105. Wallis (1671, p. 2243). Indeed, Torricelli's solid has no center of gravity.

106. Hobbes (1845a, vol. 7, p. 445).

107. Hobbes (1845b, vol. 5, p. 213).

108. Hobbes (1845b, vol. 5, p. 213). Hobbes is not very careful here and mistates

the theorem by confusing the height of the cylinder with the diameter of its base. However, the error is trivial and without consequences for what follows.

109. Hobbes (1845b, vol. 5, pp. 155, 157).

110. Hobbes (1845b, vol. 4, p. 58; vol. 5, p. 206).

111. Hobbes (1845b, vol. 4, p. 74).

112. Hobbes (1845b, vol. pp. 173–174).

113. Hobbes (1845b, vol. 4, p. 75).

114. Euclid, *Elements*, Book 5, def. 4.

115. In this, as we saw, he was not far away from what Torricelli himself seems to have thought.

116. Hobbes, *Leviathan*, (1845a, vol. 3, pp. 23–24).

117. John Locke (1975, book 2, ch. 17, sec. 22). For reasons too complex to be discussed here, after the third quarter of the seventeenth century the fortune of Torricelli's solid began to decline. However, the hyperbolic solid found its way into the mathematical dictionaries of the early eighteenth century and even into the *Encyclopedie*. See "Hyperbolicum Acutum" in Harris (1704); "Hyperbolicum Acutum" in Stone (1726) and "Solide Hyperbolique Aigu" in d'Alembert (1751–80). Indeed, it can still be found in contemporary calculus textbooks, sometimes under the colorful name of Gabriel's horn.

Chapter 6

1. For a presentation of the main concepts of the calculus both in its Leibnizian and Newtonian versions see Bos (1980a). For Newton's justifications of his calculus see Kitcher (1973). For the steps that led to the Leibnizian calculus see Hoffman (1974).

2. See Rupert Hall (1980).

3. See Jesseph (1993a).

4. The *Nova Methodus* is translated in Struik (1969). Heinekamp (1986) is a collection of articles devoted to the *Nova Methodus*.

5. For a comparison of the different methods of tangents in the seventeenth century see Giusti (1984).

6. Actually Leibniz speaks in this article of difference rather than differential. However, it is the term *differential* that is used in most of his other publications on the calculus.

7. On L'Hôpital's textbook see Boyer (1946) and Coolidge (1949).

8. L'Hôpital (1696, 1–2) and Struik (1969, 313).

9. L'Hôpital (1696, 2–3) and Struik (1969, 314).

10. "Mihi consideratio Differentiarum et Summarum in seriebus Numerorum primam lucem affuderat, cum animadverterem differentias tangentibus et summas quadraturis respondere" (Leibniz to Wallis, 28 May, 1697, in Leibniz (1843–63, vol. IV, p. 25).

11. See Bos (1974, appendix 1) for a study of the relationship between Leibniz's calculus and Cavalieri's theory of indivisibles.

12. Leibniz (1684, 223) and Struik (1969, 276).

13. The most complete treatment of the technical features of the Leibnizian calculus is given by Bos (1974).

14. See Hess and Nagel (1989) for the development of the calculus by Leibniz and the Bernoullis and for further references.

15. Leibniz to Varignon, 2 February 1702, in Leibniz (1843–63, vol. IV, pp. 94–95).

16. For a much more detailed exposition of Clüver's debate with the Leibnizians see Mancosu and Vailati (1990).

17. Clüver (1687, 587).

18. Clüver (1687, 587).

19. Hermann (1700, 57).

20. Leibniz and Johann I Bernoulli also discussed this issue of the infinieth term of an infinite series. See Johann I Bernoulli to Leibniz, 7 January 1699, in Leibniz (1843–63, vol. III, pp. 561–563).

21. Clüver (1687, 586).

22. Clüver to Leibniz, 4 June 1694; manuscript preserved at the Niedersächsische Bibliothek zu Hanover under the call number LBr 163, fo. 13v.

23. Nieuwentijt's criticisms of the calculus are also dealt with in Giorello (1985), Vermeulen (1985, 1986), Petry (1986), and Vermij (1989).

24. "Quicquid toties sumi, hoc est per tantum numerum multiplicari non potest, ut datam ullam quantitatem, ut ut exiguam, magnitudine suâ aequare valeat, sed in re geometrica merum *nihil*" (Nieuwentijt 1695, 2).

25. "Si pars qualibet datâ minor b/m ducatur in se ipsam, vel aliam qualibet datâ minorem c/m, erit productum bb/mm seu bc/mm aequale nihil seu non quantum" (Nieuwentijt 1695, 4).

26. See Knobloch (1990) and Bosinelli (1991) for the appropriate references.

27. Nieuwentijt's criticisms had a powerful stimulus on the Leibnizians. The Leibniz–Nieuwentijt debate is at the origin of an article on the exponential calculus published by Johann I Bernoulli in 1697 and of some independent researches by Varignon ("De Calculo Exponentiali") which, although written around 1695, were only published posthumously as an appendix to Varignon's *Nouveaux Eclaircissemens sur l'Analyse des Infiniment Petits* (1725).

28. Bos (1974, 66).

29. "Sola aequationum ad infinitesimas reductione (seu primi generis differentiatione) omnia obtineri posse, quae differentiationum gradibus utcunque remotis legitimè inveniri queunt" (Nieuwentijt 1696, 24).

30. It is a curiosity that Nieuwentijt claims there is a difference between 2 times m and m times 2. And although the reasons adduced might be wrong, notice how Nieuwentijt is often willing to play with the idea that the algebraic rules ruling the infinitely large and the infinitely small differ from the algebraic rules for finite quantities.

31. On the issue of the infinitely large in the practice of the Leibnizian calculus see Bos (1974, 78).

32. See Robinet (1960b) and Costabel in Malebranche (1958–68, vol. XVII-2).

33. The reader is referred to Malebranche (1958–68, vol. XX) for detailed biographies of the "Malebranchists."

34. Rolle was an algebraist; Galloys (1632–1707) had done some work on ancient geometry; and Ph. de la Hire (1640–1718) had done important work on conic sections.

35. The most complete accounts of this debate are Blay (1986) and Mancosu (1989). Previous treatments include Costabel (1965), Fleckenstein (1948), Ianovskaia (1947), Montucla (1799–1802), Peiffer (1988, 1990), Sergescu (1938, 1942). On Varignon's relation to Leibniz and Newton see Peiffer (1990). Sections 5.2 and 5.3 are taken from Mancosu (1989).

36. Rolle (1703a, 312). Although published in the proceedings of the Parisian Academy of Sciences for 1703, the memoir represented material used in the early stage of the debate, that is, during 1700–1701.

37. On Varignon's work in mechanics see the fundamental Blay (1992). See also Fleckenstein (1948).

38. The manuscript has been edited by Peiffer in Bernoulli (1988).

39.   See Bernoulli (1988, 352) and letter 55 from Varignon to Johann I Bernoulli in Bernoulli (1988, 255).

40.   Rolle (1703a, 324).

41.   Bernoulli (1988, 356).

42.   Bernoulli (1988, 357).

43.   Descartes, in the *Géométrie*, had given a method for finding the normal at a point of an arbitrary curve. This method rested essentially on the determination of a double root of a suitable equation obtained from the data of the problem. The difficulty remained in finding the double root. It was Johann Hudde (in 1659) who published a rule for determining double roots of an arbitrary polynomial. The generalization to an arbitrary algebraic curve $\sum c_{ij}x^i y^j = 0$ was given by Sluse (published in 1672). The letter by Hudde was published in the second edition of the Latin translation of Descartes' *Géométrie*. The rule can be described as follows. Starting from an arbitrary polynomial $P(x) = \sum a_i x^i$ and an arbitrary arithmetical progression $a, a + k, a + 2k, \ldots, a + nk$, if we multiply $a_0 x^0$ by a, $a_1 x^1$ by $a + k$, and so on, we obtain another polynomial $P^*(x) = \sum a_i(a + ik)x_i$. Hudde asserted that if c is a double root of $P(x) = 0$ then c is a root of $P^*(x) = 0$. Note that for $a = 0$ and $k = 1$ we have $P^*(x) = xP'(x)$ where $P'(x)$ is the derivative of $P(x)$. This rule can be used to determine points of maxima and minima. A maximum or a minimum value M of $P(x)$ occurs, as Fermat had already noticed, at a double root of the equation $P(x) - M = 0$; hence at a root of $(P(x) - M)^* = 0$.

44.   Blay (1986, 237–240) contains an extensive discussion of the first example.

45.   The rule for finding maxima and minima given in the *Analyse des infiniment petits* required one to set $dy = 0$ and $dx = 0$.. Guisnée's criterion stated that when from both these suppositions one obtained the same finite values for x and y (i.e., both conditions determined the same point of the curve) then that point was an intersection point and not a true point of maximum or minimum: "Lorsque dans l'une & dans l'autre supposition de $dx = 0$ (qui est la même chose que $dy = \infty$), & de $dx = \infty$ (qui est la même chose que $dy = 0$), l'on trouvera, pour chacune des deux coordonnées x & y, les mêmes valeurs en termes finis ou nuls; on sera assûré que la Courbe, dont la nature est exprimée par l'équation sur laquelle on opere, a un noeud au point où les coordonnées ont les valeurs trouvées" (Guisnée 1706, 34).

46.   Bernoulli (1988, 254).

47.   Gouye (1701, 234).

48.   Leibniz 1701, 270–271).

49.   Leibniz (1843–63, vol. IV, p. 90).

50.   For a detailed analysis of these two foundational efforts see Bos (1974, 1980a), Horvath (1982, 1986), and Krämer (1991). Recent treatments of Leibniz's conception of infinitesimals are, among others, Costabel (1988), Granger (1981), Robinet (1986, 283–302), Earman (1975), Juškevič (1969), and Wurtz (1989).

51.   Leibniz (1716, 500)

52.   Signs of this deep disappointment were clearly expressed by Fontenelle in his eulogy of Leibniz read in 1716: "Il ne faut pas dissimuler ici une chose assez singuliere. Si M. Leibnitz n'est pas de son côté aussi-bien que M. Neuton l'Inventeur du Sistême des Infiniment petits, il s'en faut infiniment peu. Il a connu cette infinité d'ordres d'Infiniment petits toujours infiniment plus petits les uns que les autres, & cela dans la rigueur géométrique, & les plus grands Géometres ont adopté cette idée dans toute cette rigueur. Il semble cependant qu'il en ait ensuite été effrayé lui-même, & qu'il ait crû que ces différents ordres d'Infiniment petits n'étoient que des grandeurs *incomparables*, à cause de leur extrême inégalité, comme le seroient un grain de sable & le Globe de la

Terre, la Terre & la Sphere qui comprend les Planetes, &c. Or ce ne seroit-là qu'une grande inégalité, mais non pas infinie, telle qu'on l'établit dans ce Sistème. Aussi ceux même qui l'ont pris de lui n'en ont-ils pas pris cet adoucissement, qui gâteroit tout. Un Architecte a fait un Bâtiment si hardi qu'il n'ose lui-même y loger, & il se trouve des gens qui se fient plus que lui à sa solidité, qui y logent sans crainte, &, qui plus est, sans accident. Mais peut-être l'adoucissement n'étoit-il qu'une condescendance pour ceux dont l'imagination se seroit révoltée. S'il faut tempérer la vérité en Géométrie, que sera-ce en d'autres matieres?" (Fontenelle 1716, 114–115).

53. "& il se trouve que les Regles du fini réussissent dans l'infini, comme s'il y avoit des Atomes (c'est-à-dire, des élemens assignables de la matiere,) quoy qu'il n'y en ait point, la matiere étant actuellement sous-divisible sans fin; & que *vice versa* les Regles de l'infini réussissent dans le fini, comme s'il y avoit des infiniment petits Metaphysiques, quoy qu'on n'en ait point besoin, & que la division de la matiere ne parvienne jamais à des parcelles infiniment petites. C'est parce que tout ce gouverne par raison, & qu'autrement il n'y auroit point de science ny de Regle; ce qui ne seroit point conforme avec la nature du souverain Principe" (Leibniz 1702, 186).

54. We have seen that the problem of limiting the validity of the usual algebraic laws in reasoning with infinitesimals was also central in the debate with Nieuwentijt. Jakob Bernoulli had earlier warned against the use of the usual algebraic laws, such as 'if equals are subtracted from equals, the results are equal,' in computations involving infinitesimal quantities. However, by not addressing the problem explicitly, l'Hôpital gave his opponents the opportunity for a strong criticism of the *Analyse des infiniment petits*.

55. "En lisant cet Article, on sent un Auteur, qui chagrin de ne pouvoir se passer du Calcul differentiel qu'il n'aime pas, tâche de profiter ce qu'il peut y avoir de commun entre ce Calcul & la methode de M. de Fermat pour le confondre entierement avec cette methode" (Saurin 1702, 531).

56. Here is the bitter comment of Varignon taken from a letter to Johann I Bernoulli written in the summer of 1702: "Quant à ce que vous luy [L'Hôpital] aviez envoyé pour être publié dans le Journal de Sçavans, je vous diray qu'on n'y met plus du tout de mathematiques depuis la lettre de M. Leibnitz que j'y fis inserer il y a 5 ou 6 mois, le party étant pris de n'y en plus mettre à moins que ce ne soit dans des Journaux extraordinaires, pour lesquels obtenir il faut avoir de quoy les remplir, outre qu'on ne les accorde encore qu'avec peine à cause du peu de gens qui en achetent. C'est pour cela que M. le Marquis de L'Hôpital avec tout son credit a eu touttes les peines du monde à en obtenir un pour publier la Reponse qu'il a fait faire à M. Rolle par un nommé Mr. Saurin; encore M. l'Abbé Bignon (qui a aussi la direction de ce Journal comme Neveu de M. le Chancelier, et qui n'avoit (dit-il) reçu l'Ecrit de M. Rolle que parce qu'il n'y paroissoit aucune contestation) a-t-il voulu qu'on en retranchast tout ce qu'il y avoit de personnel; ce qui a tout à fait défiguré cette Reponse" (Bernoulli 1988, 324).

57. "Il saura bien, si la nouvelle Géometrie n'est pas solide, se retracter de la grande vogue qu'il commence à lui donner, & y démêler, avec le tems les erreurs qu'il n'y a pas encore apperçûes" (Fontenelle 1701, 89).

58. "M. de L'Hôpital résolut de communiquer sans réserve les trésors cachés de la nouvelle Géométrie, & il le fit dans le fameux Livre de *l'Analyse des Infiniment petits*, qu'il publia en 1696. Là, furent dévoilés tous les secrets de l'Infini Géométrique, & de l'Infini de l'Infini; en un mot, de tous ces différens ordres d'Infinis, qui s'élevent les uns au-dessus des autres, & forment l'Edifice le plus étonnant & le plus hardi que l'Esprit humain ait jamais osé imaginer" (Fontenelle 1704a, 131).

59. "Aussi cet Ouvrage a-t-il été reçu avec un applaudissement universel: car l'applaudissement est universel, quand on peut très-facilment compter dans toute l'Europe les suffrages qui manquent, & il doit toujours en manquer quelques-uns aux choses nouvelles & originales, sur-tout quand elles demandent à être bien entendues. Ceux qui remarquent les évenemens de l'Histoire des Sciences, savent avec quelle avidité l'Analyse des Infiniment petits a été saisie par tous les Géometres naissans, à qui l'ancienne & la nouvelle méthode sont indifférentes, & qui n'ont d'autre intérêt que celui d'être instruits. Comme le dessein de l'Auter avoit été principalement de faire des Mathématiciens, & de jetter dans les esprits les semences de la haute Géométrie, il a eu le plaisir de voir qu'elles y fructifoient tous les jours, & que des Problemes réservés autrefois à ceux qui avoient vieilli dans les épines des Mathématiques, devenoient des coups d'essai de jeunes gens. Apparemment la révolution deviendra encore plus grande, & il se seroit trouvé avec le temps autant de Disciples qu'il y eût eu de Mathématiciens" (Fontenelle 1704a, 133).

60. To avoid the suspicion that my reading is a superimposition on the text, I want to quote another source to show that Fontenelle's words had a much clearer and stronger meaning in their original context: "Mr. l'Abbé Bignon en donnant à Mr. de Fontenelle les loüanges qu'il meritoit pour les deux beaux discours qu'il venoit de prononcer, luy dit qu'il avoit fait si hautement l'éloge de la Geometrie des infiniments petits, qu'après cela on ne pouvoit douter qu'il n'en fût le partisan declaré. Que cependant ceux qui n'étoient point initiez dans les mysteres de cette nouvelle Geometrie étoient effrayez d'entendre qu'il y eût des infinis, des infinis d'infinis & des infinis plus grands ou plus petits que d'autres infinis; parce qu'ils ne voyent que le comble de l'édifice sans sçavoir sur quel fondement il étoit appuyé. Il exhorta donc Mr. de Fontenelle qui travaille à des Elemens du calcul differentiel de les donner au plûtôt au public, afin de convaincre tout le monde de la solidité de cette sublime Geometrie à qui il venoit de donner tant d'éloges." (*Journal de Trévoux*, 1704, pp. 1016–1017).

61. Fontenelle (1704b, unnumbered).

62. Writing to Varignon, he said: "J'ay receu enfin le Journal du 13me d'Avril de cette année, qu'un Suedois m'a apporté, et j'ay vû que je n'avois pas besoin d'autre instruction, ny de beaucoup de discussion, pour examiner ce qui est contesté entre M. Saurin et M. Rolle. C'est pourquoy, pour satisfaire à vostre desir, et au sien, quoyque d'ailleurs je n'aime pas les contestations, je vous envoye le papire cyjoint, esperant qu'il sera conforme à vostre intention. La mienne seroit que sans le publier on le communiquat a M. l'Abbé Bignon. . . .

"Peutestre qu'elle le portera à terminer selon la justice une dispute scandaleuse du costé de celuy qui fait des objections les plus frivoles qui se puissent voir, en l'obligeant de reconnoistre qu'on a satisfait sur cet article. Je pense même à en écrire aussi à M. l'Abbé Gallois et à adresser la lettre pour luy à M. l'Abbé Bignon. Si cela ne servira de rien, il faut abandonner la pensée de faire rendre justice à M. Saurin et à nostre calcul par l'Academie, et nous tacherons de ramasser des jugemens des autres" (Leibniz 1843–63, vol. IV, pp. 127–128).

63. Varignon's testimony is important in assessing the political composition of the commission: "Vostre lettre du 26 Julliet dernier me fut rendue sur la fin du même mois. Je fus aussi tost porter à M. l'Abbé Bignon celle que vous m'adressiez pour lui, avec celle que son paquet contenoit aussi pour M. l'Abbé Galloys. M. l'Abbé Bignon lut la sienne sur le champ, et il me dist qu'il ne manqueroit pas de vous faire réponse, et qu'en attendant j'eusse à vous asseurer qu'il avait desja donné des ordres pour terminer la dispute d'entre M. Saurin et M. Rolle; que pour Juges avec luy, il avait nommé M. Cassini, M. de la Hire, M. l'Abbé Galloys et M. de Fontenelle, qui est le seul de ceux

qui sont pour les infiniment petits, qui n'ait pas été récusé. Pour nous, nous n'avons récusé personne, non pas même M. l'Abbé Galloys, tout ennemi déclaré qu'il est de ce calcul, ny M. de la Hire, quelque livré qu'il soit à M. l'Abbé Galloys: M. Saurin a seulement demandé que le jugement de chacun de ces Mrs. fust rendu public, pour retenir les ennemis du calcul par la crainte d'exposer leur réputation." (Leibniz 1843–63, vol. IV, pp. 131–132). It is clear the fight was far from being decided.

64. "J'écris a M. Hermann que M. Rolle est enfin converti: il vous dira comment il m'est l'est venu a marquer et à M. de Fontenelle; il l'a aussi marqué au P. Malebranche, disant qu'on l'avoit poussé a faire ce qu'il a fait contre les infiniment petits, et qu'il en etoit faché" (Malebranche 1958–68, vol. XIX, p. 739).

65. "J'apprend cependant que M. Rolle ne laisse pas de décrier encore sourdament ce calcul par le monde" (Leibniz 1843–63, vol. IV, p. 167).

66. See the preface to Fontenelle (1727).

Appendix

1. A reference to the *Aristotelis Loca Mathematica*. Subsequent reference to this work will not explicitly be marked. In general, Biancani's quotations of and reference to other authors are given here as they appear in the text, not checked against modern editions.

2. "Medium," as will be seen, is not used in the text in the strict sense of the middle term of an Aristotelian syllogism, but it is used more loosely, as referring to anything that "mediates," anything that establishes the connection between the terms of the conclusion. "Potissima" (literally, most powerful) will be translated as "perfect."

3. My correction for "mathematician" of the text.

4. In the proportion $a: x = x: b$: the middle proportional x is the side of the square equal in area to the quadrilateral ab.

5. I deleted "equilaterum" of the text here, as it ruins the sense of the sentence.

6. Quoted in Greek in the text.

7. As opposed to a real distinction, namely, a distinction between things as they are in themselves, no matter how and whether they are considered by the intellect.

8. "Cognitio" is certainly a misprint for "cogitatio" here; see below.

9. In Greek in the text.

10. My correction for "Mathematics."

11. As I am not familiar with the musical theory underlying these examples I only transliterated the technical terminology of the text. Anyhow, the point which they serve to illustrate is clear, even without understanding the relevant theoretical details.

12. My correction for "appositis."

REFERENCES

Andersen, K., 1985. Cavalieri's method of indivisibles. *Archive for the History of Exact Sciences*, 31, pp. 291–367.

———. 1986. The method of indivisibles: Changing understandings, in *300 Jahre "Nova Methodus" von G. W. Leibniz (1684–1984)*, edited by A. Heinekamp. *Studia Leibnitiana*, special issue 14. Franz Steiner Verlag, Stuttgart, pp. 14–25.

Anderson, A., 1616. *Vindiciae Archimedis*. Parisiis.

Aristotle, 1941. *The Basic Works of Aristotle*, edited and translated by R. McKeon. Random House, New York.

Arnauld, A., 1667. *Nouveaux Elémens de Géométrie*. Paris. Reprinted in vol. 42 of Arnauld (1775–81).

———. 1775–81. *Oeuvres de Messire Antoine Arnauld ...*, edited by Du Pac de Bellegarde and Hautefage. Paris.

Arnauld, A., Nicole, P., 1662/1965. *La Logique ou l'Art de Penser*, edited by P. Claire and F. Girbal. Presses Universitaires de France, Paris.

———. 1872. *The Port-Royal Logic*, 7th ed., translated by Thomas Spencer Baynes. Edinburgh.

Arndt, H. W., 1971. *Methodo Scientifica Pertractatum. Mos geometricus und Kalkülbegriff in der philosophischen Theorienbildung des 17. und 18. Jahrhunderts*. Walter de Gruyter, Berlin/New York.

Auger, L., 1962. *Un Savant Méconnu: Gilles Personne de Roberval (1602–1675)*. Blanchard, Paris.

Barnes, J., 1975. *Aristotle's Posterior Analytics*. Oxford University Press, Oxford.

Baron, M., 1969. *The Origins of the Infinitesimal Calculus*. Dover, New York.

Barozzi, F., 1560. *Opusculum, in quo una Oratio, & duae Questiones: altera de certitudine, & altera de medietate Mathematicarum continentur*. Patavii.

Barrow, I., 1670. *Lectiones Geometricae*. Londini, in Barrow (1976).

———. 1683. *Lectiones Mathematicae*. Londini, in Barrow (1976).

———. 1916. *The Geometrical Lectures of Isaac Barrow*, edited by J. M. Child. Open Court.

———. 1970. *The Usefulness of Mathematical Learning being ...*, (London, 1734), translation of Barrow 1683 by J. Kirby; reprint by Cass Publishing Company, London.

———. 1976. *The Mathematical Works*, edited by W. Whewell. Georg Olms Verlag, Hildesheim/New York.

Bayle, P., 1974. *Dictionnaire Historique et Critique*. Editions Sociales, Paris.

Becker, O., 1954/1965. *Grundlagen der Mathematik in geschichtlicher Entwicklung.* Karl Alber Verlag, Freiburg/München. Reprint by Suhrkamp, Frankfurt.

Beeley, P., 1995. *Kontinuität und Mechanismus. Eine Studie zur Philosophie des jungen Leibniz in ihren historischen Beziehungen. Studia Leibnitiana,* supplement 30. Franz Steiner Verlag, Stuttgart.

Belaval, Y., 1960. *Leibniz Critique de Descartes.* Gallimard, Paris.

Belgioioso, G. et al., 1990. *Descartes: il Metodo e i Saggi. Atti del Convegno per il 350o anniversario della pubblicazione del Discours de la Méthode e degli Essais.* Istituto della Enciclopedia Italiana, Rome.

Belloni, L., 1987. Torricelli et son époque (le triumvirat des élèves de Castelli: Magiotti, Nardi et Torricelli), pp. 29–38 in De Gandt (1987).

Berg, J., 1962. *Bolzano's Logic.* Almquist & Wiksell, Stockholm.

Berkeley, G. 1734. The analyst; or a discourse addressed to an infidel mathematician, in *The Works of George Berkeley Bishop of Cloyne,* edited by A. A. Luce and T. E. Jessop, vol. 4, pp. 53–102. Nelson, London/Edinburgh, 1948–57.

Bernoulli, Joh. I, 1697/1968. Principia Calculi Exponentialium seu Percurrentium. *Acta Eruditorum,* pp. 125–133. Also in *Opera Omnia,* edited by N. Cramer, 4 vols., Lausanne/Geneva, 1742; reprinted by Georg Olms, Hildesheim.

————. 1988. *Der Briefwechsel von Johann I Bernoulli. Band 2. Der Briefwechsel mit Pierre Varignon. Erster Teil: 1692–1702.* Bearbeitet und kommentiert von Pierre Costabel und Jeanne Peiffer: unter Benutzung von Vorarbeiten von Joachim Otto Fleckenstein, edited by D. Speiser. Birkhäuser, Basel, Boston, Berlin.

Bettini, M., 1648. *Aerarium Philosophiae Mathematicae.* Bononiae.

Biancani, G., 1615. *De Mathematicarum Natura Dissertatio.* Bononiae.

————. 1620. *Sphaera Mundi seu Cosmographia.* Bononiae.

Blay, M., 1986. Deux moments de la critique du calcul infinitésimal: Michel Rolle et George Berkeley. *Revue d'Histoire des Sciences,* 39/3, pp. 223–253.

————. 1992. *La Naissance de la Mechanique Analytique. La Science du Mouvement au Tournant des XVIIe et XVIIIe Siècles.* Presses Universitaires de France, Paris.

Bolzano, B., 1804. *Betrachtungen über einige Gegenstände der Elementargeometrie,* translated in Russ (1980a).

————. 1810. *Beiträge zu einer begründeteren Darstellung der Mathematik,* translated in Russ (1980a).

————. 1837. *Wissenschaftslehre.* Sulzbach.

————. 1972. *Theory of Science,* edited and translated by R. George. University of California Press, Berkeley.

————. 1975. *Paradoxien des Unendlichen.* Meiner, Hamburg.

————. 1978. *Vermischte Philosophische und Physikalische Schriften,* edited by J. Berg. Part of Bernard-Bolzano *Gesamtausgabe,* edited by E. Winter, J. Berg, F. Kambartel, J. Louzil, and B. van Rootselaar. Frommann Verlag, Stuttgart, 1969–.

————. 1979. *Miscellanea Mathematica 1808–1811,* II:B2(2), edited by Bob van Rootselaar and Anna van der Lugt. Part of Bernard-Bolzano *Gesamtausgabe,* edited by E. Winter, J. Berg, F. Kambartel, J. Louzil, and B. van Rootselaar. Frommann Verlag, Stuttgart, 1969–.

————. 1981. *Von der mathematischen Lehrart,* edited by J. Berg. Frommann-Holzboog, Stuttgart-Bad Cannstatt.

Bopp, K., 1902. Antoine Arnauld, der grosse Arnauld, als Mathematiker. *Abhandlungen zur Geschichte der mathematischen Wissenschaften,* vol. 14. Teubner, Leipzig.

Bortolotti, E., 1924. La scoperta e le successive generalizzazioni di un teorema fondamentale di calcolo integrale. *Archeion,* 5, pp. 205–227.

Bortolotti, E., 1925. La memoria *De infinitis hyperbolis* di Torricelli. *Archeion*, 6, pp. 139–152.

Bos, H. J. M., 1974. Differentials, higher-order differentials and the derivative in the Leibnizian calculus. *Archive for History of Exact Sciences*, 14, pp. 1–90.

———. 1980. Newton, Leibniz and the Leibnizian tradition, pp. 49–93 in Grattan-Guinness (1980).

———. 1981. On the representation of curves in Descartes' *Géométrie*. *Archive for the History of Exact Sciences*, 24, pp. 295–338.

———. 1984. Arguments on motivation in the rise and decline of a mathematical theory: The 'Construction of Equations,' 1637–ca. 1750. *Archive for the History of Exact Sciences*, 30, pp. 731–780.

———. 1990. The structure of Descartes' *Géométrie*, pp. 349–369 in Belgioioso et al. (1990).

Bosinelli, F. C. M., 1991. Über Leibniz' Unendlichkeitstheorie. *Studia Leibnitiana*, XXIII/2, pp. 151–169.

Bosmans, H., 1913. Les démonstrations par l'analyse infinitésimale chez Luc Valerio. *Annales de la Société Scientifique de Bruxelles*, 37, pp. 211–228.

———. 1920. Sur une contradiction reprochée a la théorie des "indivisibles" chez Cavalieri, *Annales de la Société Scientifique de Bruxelles*, 42, pp. 82–89.

———. 1923. La notion des indivisibles chez Blaise Pascal. *Archeion. Achivio di Storia della Scienza*, 4, pp. 369–379.

———. 1927. André Tacquet (S.J.) et son traité d'arithmétique théorique et practique. *Isis*, 9, pp. 64–82.

———. 1928a. La "Logistique" de Gilles-François de Gottignies de la Compagnie de Jésus. *Revue des Questions Scientifiques*, 4(13), pp. 215–244.

———. 1928b. Ph. van Lansberge de Gand (1561–1632). *Mathesis*, 42, pp. 5–9.

Bourbaki, N., 1960. *Éléments d'Histoire des Mathematiques*. Hermann, Paris.

Boyer, C. B., 1946. The first calculus textbooks. *Mathematics Teacher*, 39, pp. 159–167.

———. 1956. *History of Analytic Geometry*. Scripta Mathematica, New York.

———. 1959. *The History of the Calculus and its Conceptual Development*. Dover, New York.

———. 1964. Early rectifications of curves, in *L'Aventure de la Science. Mélanges A. Koyré*. Hermann, Paris, vol. I, pp. 30–39.

———. 1968/1989. *A History of Mathematics*. Wiley, New York. Second edition by C. B. Boyer and U. Merzbach.

Breger, H., 1986. Leibniz' Einführung des Transzendenten, in *300 Jahre "Nova Methodus" von G. W. Leibniz (1684–1984)*, edited by A. Heinekamp. *Studia Leibnitiana*, special issue 14, Franz Steiner Verlag, Stuttgart, pp. 119–132.

———. 1990. Das Kontinuum bei Leibniz, pp. 53–67 in Lamarra (1990a).

———. 1991. Der Mechanistische Denkstil in der Mathematik des 17. Jahrhunderts, in *Leibniz im philosophischen Diskurs über Geometrie und Erfahrung*, edited by H. Hecht. Berlin, pp. 15–46.

Breidert, W., 1979. Les mathématiques et la méthode mathématique chez Hobbes. *Revue Internationale de Philosophie*, 33, pp. 415–431.

Bruno, G., 1889. *Opera latine conscripta*, edited by Tocco e Vitelli, Florence.

Brunschvicg, L., 1912/1981. *Les Étapes de la Philosophie Mathématique*. Paris. Reprinted by Blanchard, Paris.

Bucciantini, M., Torrini, M., eds., 1992. *Geometria e Atomsimo nella Scuola Galileiana*. Leo S. Olschki, Florence.

Buhl, G., 1961. *Ableitbarkeit und Abfolge in der Wissenschaftstheorie Bolzanos*. Cologne.

Bulmer-Thomas, I., 1984. Guldin's Theorem—or Pappus's? *Isis*, 75, pp. 348–352.

Cajori, F., 1929. Controversies on mathematics between Wallis, Hobbes, and Barrow. *Mathematics Teacher*, 22, pp. 146–151.

Candalla, F., 1566. *Euclidis Megarensis Mathematici Clarissimi Elementa Geometrica*. Parisiis.

Cantor, M., 1900–1901/1965. *Vorlesungen über die Geschichte der Mathematik*, vols II and III, Teubner, Leipzig. Reprinted by Johnson Reprint Corporation, New York.

Catena, P., 1556. *Universa loca in logicam Aristotelis in mathematicas disciplinas*. Venetiis.

——. 1561. *Super loca mathematica contenta in Topicis et Elenchis Aristotelis*. Venetiis.

——. 1563. *Oratio pro idea methodi*. Patavii.

Cauman, L., 1967. On indirect proof. *Scripta Mathematica*, XXVIII, pp. 101–115.

Cavalieri, B., 1635. *Geometria indivisibilibus continuorum nova quadam ratione promota*. Bononiae.

——. 1647. *Exercitationes Geometricae Sex*. Bononiae.

——. 1966. *Geometria degli indivisibili*, translated with introduction and notes by L. Lombardo Radice. Utet, Turin.

Cellini, G., 1966a. Gli indivisibili nel pensiero matematico e filosofico di Bonaventura Cavalieri. *Periodico di Matematiche*, vol. 44, pp. 1–21.

——. 1966b. Le dimostrazioni di Cavalieri del suo principio. *Periodico di Matematiche*, vol. 44, pp. 85–105.

Clavius, C., 1589. *Commentaria in Euclidis Elementorum Libri XV*, 2d ed.

——. 1591. *Commentaria in Euclidis Elementorum Libri XV ...*, 3d ed., in vol. I of Clavius (1611–12).

——. 1604. *Geometria Practica*, in vol. II of Clavius (1611–12).

——. 1611–12. *Opera Mathematica*, 5 vols. Moguntiae.

Clero, J. P., Le Rest, E., 1981. *La Naissance du Calcul Infinitesimal au XVIIème Siècle*. CNRS, Paris.

Clüver, D., 1686. Quadratura circuli infinitis modis demonstrata a Dethlevo Clüvero, e Soc. Reg. Anglicana. *Acta Eruditorum*, 5, pp. 369–371.

——. 1687. Dethlevi Clüveri e Soc. Reg. Anglic. Monitum ad Geometras. *Acta Eruditorum*, 6, pp. 585–588.

Cohen, H., 1883/1968. *Das Prinzip der Infinitesimalmethode und seine Geschichte*. Berlin. Reprinted by Suhrkamp, Frankfurt.

Collegium Conimbricense, 1594. *Commentarii ... In octo libros Physicorum Aristotelis*. Coimbra.

Commandino, F., 1565. *Liber de Centro Gravitatis Solidorum*. Bononiae.

Conway, D., Kerszberg, P., eds., 1995. *The Sovereignty of Construction: Studies in the Thought of David Lachterman*. Rodopi, Amsterdam.

Coolidge, J. L., 1949. *The Mathematics of Great Amateurs*. Dover, New York.

Costabel, P., 1964. La roue d'Aristote et les critiques françaises à l'argument de Galilée. *Revue d'Histoire des Sciences*, XVII, pp. 385–396.

——. 1965. *Pierre Varignon (1654–1722) et la Diffusion en France du Calcul Différentiel et intégral*. Conference given at the Palais de la Découverte, 4 December 1965, series D, no. 108, Paris.

——. 1982. *Demarches Originales de Descartes Savant*. Vrin, Paris.

——. 1985. Descartes et la mathématique de l'infini. *Historia Scientiarum*, 26, pp. 37–49.

——. 1988. Leibniz et la notion de "fiction bien fondée," in *Leibniz, Tradition und Aktualität*, V. Internationaler Leibniz-Kongreß, Vorträge, pp. 174–180.

Couturat, L., 1905/1980. *Les Principes des Mathématiques*. Reprinted by Blanchard, Paris.

Crapulli, G., 1969. *Mathesis Universalis: Genesi di un'Idea nel XVI Secolo*. Edizioni dell'Ateneo, Rome.

Crombie, A., 1952. *Augustine to Galileo*. Heinemann, London.

———. 1953. *Robert Grosseteste and the Origins of Experimental Science, 1100–1700*. Clarendon Press, Oxford.

———. 1977. Mathematics and Platonism in the sixteenth-century Italian universities and in Jesuit educational policy, in *Prismata, Naturwissenschaftsgeschichtliche Studien*, edited by Y. Maeyama and W. G. Saltzer. Franz Steiner Verlag, Wiesbaden, pp. 63–94.

Crusius, C. A., 1747. *Weg zur Gewißheit und Zuverläßigkeit der menschlichen Erkenntniß*. Leipzig.

D'Alembert, J., 1751–80/1966. *Encyclopédie ou Dictionnaire Raisonné Des Sciences, Des Arts et Des Metiers*, Lausanne/Berne. Reprinted by Frommann, Stuttgart-Bad Cannstatt.

De Angelis, E., 1964. *Il Metodo Geometrico nella Filosofia del Seicento*. Pisa.

Dear, P., 1987. Jesuit mathematical science and the reconstruction of experience in the early seventeenth century. *Studies in History and Philosophy of Science*, 18/2, pp. 133–175.

———. 1988. *Mersenne and the Learning of the Schools*. Cornell University Press, Ithaca/London.

De Gandt, F., 1987. *L'Oeuvre de Torricelli: Science Galiléenne et Nouvelle Géométrie*. Les Belles Lettres, Paris.

———. 1991. Cavalieri's indivisibles and Euclid's canons, in *Revolution and Continuity: Essays in the History and Philosophy of Early Modern Science*, edited by P. Barker and R. Ariew. Catholic University of America Press, Washington D.C., pp. 157–182.

———. 1992. L'évolution de la théorie des indivisibles et l'apport de Torricelli, pp. 103–118 in Bucciantini and Torrini (1992).

De Olaso, E., 1990. Scepticism and the infinite, pp. 95–118 in Lamarra (1990a).

De Pace, A., 1993. *Le Matematiche e il Mondo*. Franco Angeli, Milan.

Descartes, R., 1637. *Discours de la Méthode pour bien conduire sa raison, et chercher la verité dans les sciences. Plus la Dioptrique, les Météores et la Géométrie, qui sont des esseis de cete Méthode*. Leyde.

———. 1649. *Geometria ... cum notis Florimondi de Beaune ... Opera atque studio Francisci à Schooten*. Leyde.

———. 1659–61. *Geometria. Editio secunda*. Amstelodami.

———. 1897–1910/1972. *Oeuvres*, edited by C. Adam and P. Tannery, Cerf New Edition, 12 vols. Vrin, Paris.

———. 1952. *The Geometry of René Descartes*, edited by D. E. Smith and M. L. Latham. Open Court.

De Vleeschauwer, H. J., 1961. *More seu ordine geometrico demonstratum*. Communications of the University of South Africa, Pretoria.

Dhombres, J., 1992. Le continu baroque, ou comment ne pas jouer discret, in *Le Labyrinthe du Continu*, edited by J.-M. Salanskis and H. Sinaceur. Springer Verlag, Paris, pp. 47–60.

———. 1994. La culture mathématique au temps de la formation de Desargues: le monde des coniques, in *Desargues en son Temps*, edited by J. Dhombres and J. Sakarovitch. Blanchard, Paris, pp. 55–85.

Divizia, F., 1983. Osservazioni sul *De centro gravitatis solidorum* di Luca Valerio. *Physis*, 25/2, pp. 227–249.

Drabkin, I. E., 1950. Aristotle's wheel: Notes on the history of a paradox. *Osiris*, IX, pp. 162–198.

Duhem, P., 1914–59. *Le Système du Monde. Histoire des Doctrines Cosmologiques de Platon à Copernic*, 10 vols. Hermann, Paris.

———. 1975. *Medieval Cosmology*, edited by R. Ariew. The University of Chicago Press, Chicago.

Dummett, M., 1991. *Frege: Philosophy of Mathematics*. Duckworth, London.

Earman, J., 1975. Infinities, infinitesimals, and indivisibles: The Leibnizian labyrinth. *Studia Leibnitiana*, VII/2, pp. 236–251.

Eastwood, B. S., 1992. A second look on the continuity of western science from the Middle Ages. *Isis*. 1992, pp. 84–99.

Engfer, H.-J., 1982. *Philosophie als Analysis*. Studien zur Entwicklung philosophischer Analysiskonzeptionen unter dem Einfluß mathematischer Methodenmodelle im 17. und frühen 18. Jahrhundert. Frommann-Holzboog, Stuttgart-Bad Cannstatt.

Euclid, 1956. *Elements*, edited by T. Heath. Dover, New York.

Fabri, H., 1669. *Synopsis Geometrica*. Lugduni Gallorum.

Festa, E., 1990. La querelle de l'atomisme: Galilée, Cavalieri et les jésuites. *La Recherche*, 224, pp. 1038–1047.

———. 1992. Quelques aspects de la controverse sur les indivisibles, pp. 193–207 in Bucciantini and Torrini (1992).

Field, J. V., 1994. The infinitely great and the infinitely small in the work of Girard Desargues, in *Desargues en son Temps*, edited by J. Dhombres and J. Sakarovitch. Blanchard, Paris, pp. 219–230.

Fleckenstein, J. O., 1948. Pierre Varignon und die mathematischen Wissenschaften im Zeitalter des Cartesianismus. *Archives Internationales d'Histoire des Sciences*, 2, pp. 76–138.

Fontenelle, B., 1701. *Histoire et Mémoires de l'Académie Royale des Sciences*, note, pp. 87–89.

———. 1704a. *Histoire et Mémoires de l'Académie Royale des Sciences*, Eloge de M. le Marquis de L'Hôpital, pp. 125–136.

———. 1704b. *Histoire et Mémoires de l'Académie Royale des Sciences*, foreword p. i.

———. 1716. *Histoire et Mémoires de l'Académie Royale des Sciences*, Eloge de M. Leibniz, pp. 94–128.

———. 1719. *Histoire et Mémoires de l'Académie Royale des Sciences*, Eloge de M. Rolle, pp. 94–100.

———. 1727. Elemens de la geometrie de l'infini, in *Suite de Memoires de l'Acadèmie Royale des Sciences, 1725*. Paris.

Fraser, C. G., 1990. Lagrange's analytical mathematics, its cartesian origins and reception in Comte's positive philosophy. *Studies in History and Philosophy of Science*, 21/2, pp. 243–256.

Frege, G., 1979. *Posthumous Writings*. Basic Blackwell, Oxford.

Friedman, M., 1992. *Kant and the Exact Sciences*. Harvard University Press, Cambridge, Mass.

Fries, J. F., 1819. *System der Logik*. Heidelberg.

Fromondus, L., 1631. *Labyrinthus sive de compositione continui*. Antverpiae.

Galilei, G., 1974. *Two New Sciences*, translated and edited by Stillman Drake. University of Wisconsin Press, Madison.

———. 1975. *Opere dei discepoli di Galileo, Carteggio (1642–1648)*, edited by P. Galluzzi and M. Torrini. Giunti Barbera, Florence.

Galluzzi, P., 1973. Il "Platonismo" del tardo cinquecento e la filosofia di Galileo, in *Ricerche sulla Cultura dell'Italia Moderna*, edited by P. Zambelli. Laterza, Bari, pp. 39–79.

———. 1976. Evangelista Torricelli. Concezione della matematica e problema degli occhiali. *Annali dell'Istituto e Museo di Storia della Scienza di Firenze*, 1/1, pp. 71–95.

———. 1979. Vecchie e nuove prospettive torricelliane, in *La Scuola Galileiana*. Prospettive di Ricerca. La Nuova Italia, Florence, pp. 13–51.

Galuzzi, M., 1980. Il problema delle tangenti nella *Géométrie* di Descartes. *Archive for the History of Exact Sciences*, 22, pp. 37–51.

Gardies, J.-L., 1991. *Le Raisonnement par l'Absurde*. Presses Universitaires de France, Paris.

Gargani, A., 1971. *Hobbes e la Scienza*. Einaudi, Turin.

Gassendi, P., 1658/1964. *Petri Gassendi Opera Omnia*, 6 vols. Lyon. Reprinted by Frommann Verlag, Stuttgart-Bad Cannstatt.

———. 1972. *The Selected Works of Pierre Gassendi*, edited by C. B. Brush. Johnson Reprint Corporation, New York.

Gaukroger, S., ed., 1980. *Descartes: Philosophy, Mathematics and Physics*. Harvester Press, Hassocks (Sussex).

Gentzen, G., 1969. Investigations into logical deduction, in *The Collected Papers of G. Gentzen*, edited by M. E. Szabo. North Holland, Amsterdam.

Giacobbe, G. C., 1972a. Il commentarium de certitudine mathematicarum disciplinarum di Alessandro Piccolomini. *Physis* XIV, 2, pp. 162–193.

———. 1972b. Francesco Barozzi e la Quaestio de certitudine mathematicarum. *Physis*, XIV/4, pp. 357–374.

———. 1973. La riflessione metamatematica di Pietro Catena. *Physis* XV, 2, pp. 178–196.

———. 1976. Epigoni nel seicento della "Quaestio de certitudine mathematicarum": Giuseppe Biancani. *Physis*, XVIII, 1, pp. 5–40.

———. 1977. Un gesuita progressista nella "Quaestio de certitudine mathematicarum" rinascimentale: Benito Pereyra. *Physis*, XIX, pp. 51–86.

Gilbert, N. W., 1963. Galileo and the School of Padua. *Journal of the History of Philosophy*, I, pp. 223–231.

Gillies, D., ed., 1992. *Revolutions in Mathematics*. Oxford University Press, Oxford.

Giorello, G., 1985. *Lo Spettro e il Libertino*. Mondadori, Milan.

———. 1990. Pratica geometrica e immagine della matematica in Thomas Hobbes, in *Hobbes oggi*, edited by A. Napoli. Franco Angeli, Milan, pp. 215–244.

Giusti, E., 1980. *Bonaventura Cavalieri and the Theory of Indivisibles*. Cremonese, Rome.

———. 1982. Dopo Cavalieri. La discussione sugli indivisibili, in *Atti del Colloquio "La Storia della matematica in Italia,"* edited by L. Grugnetti and O. Montaldo. Cagliari.

———. 1984. A tre secoli dal calcolo: la questione delle origini. *Bollettino UMI*, 6(3A), pp. 1–55.

———. 1987. La *Géométrie* di Descartes tra numeri e grandezze. *Giornale Critico della Filosofia Italiana*, VI, 409–432. Also in Belgioioso et al. (1990, pp. 419–439).

———. 1990. Immagini del continuo, pp. 3–32, in Lemarra (1990a).

Goldstein, M., 1972. The historical development of group theoretical ideas in connection with Euclid's axiom of congruence. *Notre Dame Journal of Formal Logic*, XII, pp. 331–349.

Gottignies, G. F. de, 1669. *Elementa Geometriae Planae*. Angeli Bernado, Romae.

———. 1687. *Logistica Universalis*. Novelli de Bonis, Neapoli.

Gouye, T., 1701. Nouvelle méthode pour déterminer aisément les rayons de a développée dans toute sorte de courbe algébraique. *Journal de Trévoux*, pp. 422–430.

Granger, G. G., 1981. Philosophie et mathématique Leibniziennes. *Revue de Métaphysique et de Morale*, 86, pp. 1–37.

Grattan-Guinness, I., ed., 1980. *From the Calculus to Set Theory, 1630–1910: An Introductory History*. Duckworth, London.

Grimaldi, N., Marion, J. L., eds., 1987. *Le Discours et sa Méthode*. Presses Universitaires de France, Paris.

Grosholz, E. R., 1980. Descartes' unification of algebra and geometry, pp. 157–168 in Gaukroger (1980).

———. 1991a. *Cartesian Method and the Problem of Reduction*. Clarendon Press, Oxford.

———. 1991b. Descartes' *Geometry* and the classical tradition, in *Revolution and Continuity: Essays in the History and Philosophy of Early Modern Science*, edited by P. Barker and R. Ariew. Catholic University of America Press, Washington D.C., pp. 183–196.

Gueroult, M., 1968. *Spinoza, Dieu*, vol. I. Georg Olms Verlag, Hildesheim.

———. 1974. *Spinoza, L'âme*, vol. II. Georg Olms Verlag, Hildesheim.

Guisnée, 1706. Observations sur les methodes de maximis et minimis, où l'on fait voir l'identité & la difference de celle de l'analyse des infiniment petits avec celle de Mrs Fermat & Hude. *Histoire et Mémoires de l'Académie Royale des Sciences*, pp. 24–51.

Guldin, P., 1635–41. *Centrobaryca*. Viennae.

Hall, A. Rupert, 1980. *Philosophers at War. The Quarrel between Newton and Leibniz*. Cambridge University Press, Cambridge.

Harris, J., 1704. *Lexicon Technicum*. London.

Heath, T., 1921/1981. *A History of Greek Mathematics*, 2 vols. Reprinted by Dover, New York.

———. 1949. *Mathematics in Aristotle*. Clarendon Press, Oxford.

Heinekamp, A., ed., 1986. *300 Jahre "Nova Methodus" von G. W. Leibniz (1684–1984)*. *Studia Leibnitiana*, special issue 14. Franz Steiner Verlag, Stuttgart.

Hermann, J., 1700. *Jacobi Hermanni responsio ad considerationes secundas Cl. Viri Bern. Nieuventiit*. Basel.

Hess, H.-J., Nagel, F., eds., 1989. *Der Ausbau des calculus durch Leibniz und die Brüder Bernoulli. Studia Leibnitiana*, special issue 17, Franz Steiner Verlag, Stuttgart.

Hessenberg, G., 1912/1965. *Transzendenz von e and π. Ein Beitrag zur Höheren Mathematik vom elementaren Standpunkt aus*. Teubner. Reprinted by Johnson Reprint Corporation.

Hobart, M. E., 1988. Malebranche, mathematics, and natural theology. *International Studies in Philosophy*, XX/1, pp. 11–25.

Hobbes, T., 1845a/1966. *The English Works*, edited by W. Molesworth. London. Reprinted by Scientia Verlag, Darmstadt.

———. 1845b/1966. *Opera Philosophica quae Latine Scripsit*, edited by W. Molesworth. London. Reprinted by Scientia Verlag, Darmstadt.

———. 1962. *Body, Man, and Citizen*, edited by R. S. Peters. Colliers Books.

Hofmann, J. H., 1974. *Leibniz in Paris 1672–1676*. Cambridge University Press, Cambridge.

Hölder, O., 1929. Der indirekte Beweis in der Mathematik. *Berichte der Sächsischen Akademie der Wissenschaften zu Leipzig*, 81, pp. 201–216.

Hölder, O., 1930. Nachtrag zu meinen Aufsatz über den indirekten Beweis. *Berichte der Sächsischen Akademie der Wissenschaften zu Leipzig*, 82, pp. 97–104.

Horvath, M., 1982. The problem of infinitesimal small quantities in the Leibnizian mathematics. *Studia Leibnitiana*, supplement 22, pp. 149–157.

———. 1986. On the attempts made by Leibniz to justify his calculus. *Studia Leibnitiana* 18/1, pp. 60–71.

Houzel, C., Ovaert, J.-L., Raymond, P., and Sensuc, J.-J., 1976. *Philosophie et Calcul de l'Infini*. Maspero, Paris.

Huet, P. D., 1680. *Demonstratio Evangelica*. Amstelodami.

Ianovskaia, S. A., 1947. Michel Rolle as critic of the analysis of the infinitely small (in Russian). *Works of the Institute of History of the Soviet Academy of Sciences*, I, pp. 327–346.

Inhetveen, R., 1981. Können die Gegenstände der Geometrie bewegt werden? in *Vernunft, Handlung und Erfahrung*, edited by Oswald Schwemmer. Verlag C. H. Beck, Munich, pp. 64–68.

Itard, J., 1956. *La Géométrie de Descartes*. Les conférences du Palais de la Découvert, series D, no. 39.

———. 1975. La lettre de Torricelli à Roberval d'octobre 1643. *Revue d'Histoire des Science*, 28/2, pp. 113–124.

Israel, G., 1990. Dalle *Regulae* alla *Géométrie*, pp. 441–474 in Belgioioso et al. (1990).

Jardine, N., 1976. Galileo's road to truth and the demonstrative regress. *Studies in History and Philosophy of Science*, 7(4), pp. 277–318.

———. 1988. The epistemology of the sciences, in *The Cambridge History of Renaissance Philosophy*, edited by C. B. Schmitt, Q. R. D. Skinner, and E. Kessler. Cambridge University Press, Cambridge, pp. 685–711.

Jesseph, D., 1989. Philosophical theory and mathematical practice in the seventeenth century. *Studies in History and Philosophy of Science*, 20, pp. 215–244.

———. 1993a. *Berkeley's Philosophy of Mathematics*. University of Chicago Press, Chicago/London.

———. 1993b. Of analytics and indivisibles: Hobbes on the methods of modern mathematics. *Revue d'Histoire des Sciences*, XLVI-2/3, pp. 153–193.

Juškevič, A. P., 1969. Gottfried Wilhelm Leibniz und die Grundlagen der Infinitesimal-rechnung. *Studia Leibnitiana*, supplement II, pp. 1–19.

Kant, I., 1965. *Critique of Pure Reason*, translated by Norman Kemp Smith. St. Martin's Press, New York.

Kepler, J., 1615. *Nova Stereometria Doliorum*. Lincii.

Killing, W., 1898. *Einführung in die Grundlagen der Geometrie*, vol. II. Paderborn.

Kitcher, P., 1973. Fluxions, limits and infinite littleness: A study of Newton's presentation of the calculus. *Isis*, 64, pp. 33–49.

Klausing, M. H., 1701. *De Mathesi Nova non Nova*. Vitembergae Saxonum.

Klein, J., 1968. *Greek Mathematical Thought and the Origin of Algebra*. MIT Press, Cambridge, Mass.

Kline, M., 1972. *Mathematical Thought from Ancient to Modern Times*. Oxford University Press, Oxford.

Kluge, E.-H. W., 1980. *The Metaphysics of Gottlob Frege*. Martinus Nijhoff, The Hague, Boston, London.

Knabe, K. A. F., 1885. *Die Formen des indirecten Beweises*. Cassell.

Knobloch, E., 1989. Leibniz et son manuscrit inédité sur la quadrature des sections coniques, in *Proceedings of the Leibniz Renaissance International Workshop, Florence, 2–5 June 1986*, pp. 127–151.

Knobloch, E., 1990. L'infini dans les mathématiques de Leibniz, pp. 33–51 in Lamarra (1990a).

———. 1993. Introduction, in Leibniz (1993, pp. 9–23).

———. 1994. The infinite in Leibniz's mathematics: The historiographical method of comprehension in context, in *Trends in the Historiography of Science*, edited by K. Gavroglu et al. Kluver, Dordrecht, pp. 265–278.

Knorr, W., 1982. Infinity and continuity: The interaction of mathematics and philosophy in antiquity, in *Infinity and Continuity in Ancient and Medieval thought*, edited by N. Kretzmann. Cornell University Press, Ithaca, N.Y., pp. 112–145.

———. 1986. Before and after Cavalieri: the method of indivisibles in ancient geometry, unpublished typescript.

Koyré, A., 1954. Bonaventura Cavalieri et la géométrie des continus, in *Hommage à Lucien Fèvre*. Colin, Paris. Also in *Etudes d'Histoire de la Pensée Scientifiques*, PUF, 1966, pp. 297–324.

———. 1978. *Galileo Studies*. Humanities Press, Atlantic Highlands, N.J.

Krähe, E., 1874. *Ueber den indirecten Beweis*. Berlin.

Krämer, S., 1989. Über das Verhältnis von Algebra und Geometrie in Descartes' "Geometrie," *Philosophia Naturalis*, 26, pp. 19–40.

———. 1991. Zur Begründung des Infinitesimalkalküls durch Leibniz. *Philosophia Naturalis*, 28, pp. 117–146.

Lachterman, D. R., 1989. *The Ethics of Geometry. A Genealogy of Modernity*. Routledge, New York.

Lamarra, A., ed., 1990a. *L'Infinito in Leibniz. Problemi e Terminologia*. Edizioni dell'Ateneo, Rome.

———. 1990b. Leibniz on Locke on infinity, pp. 173–191 in Lamarra (1990a).

Langius, W., 1656. *De Veritatibus Geometricis Libri II. Prior contra Scepticos & Sextum Empiricum & c. Posterior, contra Marcum Meibomium*. Hafniæ.

Lansbergius, P., 1628. *Cyclometria Nova*. Middelburgi.

Laz, J., 1993. *Bolzano Critique de Kant*. Paris, Vrin.

Lebesgue, H., 1950. *Leçons sur les Constructions Géométriques*. Gauthier-Villars, Paris.

Leibniz, G. W., 1684. Nova Methodus . . . , pp. 220–226 in vol. V of Leibniz (1843–1863).

———. 1686. De Geometria Recondita . . . , pp. 226–233 in vol. V of Leibniz (1843–1863).

———. 1695a. Responsio ad nonnullas difficultates a Dn. Bernardo Niewentiit circa methodum differentialem seu infinitesimalem mota, pp. 320–326 in vol. V of Leibniz (1843–1863).

———. 1695b. Additio ad hoc Schediasma, pp. 327–328 in vol. V of Leibniz (1843–1863).

———. 1701. Mémoire de Mr. Leibniz touchant son sentiment sur le calcul différentiel. *Journal de Trévoux*, pp. 270–272. Reprinted in Leibniz (1843–63, vol. IV, pp. 95–96).

———. 1702. Extrait d'une lettre de M. Leibniz à M. Varignon, contenant l'explication de ce qu'on a rapporté de luy, dans les Mémoires de Trévoux des mois de novembre et décembre derniers. *Journal des Sçavans*, pp. 183–186. Reprinted in Leibniz (1843–63, vol. IV, pp. 91–95).

———. 1712. Observatio quod rationes sive proportiones non habeant locum circa quantitates nihilo minores, et de vero sensu methodi infinitesimalis, pp. 387–389 in vol. V of Leibniz (1843–1863).

———. 1716. Lettre à M. Dangicourt, September 1716, pp. 499–502 in vol. III of Leibniz (1768).

———. 1768. *Opera Omnia*. edited by L. Dutens, 6 vols. Genevae.

Leibniz, G. W., 1843–63/1962. *Mathematische Schriften*, vols. I–VII, edited by C. I. Gerhardt. Berlin und Halle. Reprinted by Georg Olms Verlag, Hildesheim/ New York.

———. 1969. *Philosophical Papers and Letters*, edited by L. Loemker. Reidel, Dordrecht.

———. 1976. *Ein Dialog zur Einführung in die Arithmetik und Algebra*, the original manuscript edited, translated and annotated by Eberhard Knobloch. Frommann-Holzboog, Stuttgart-Bad Cannstatt.

———. 1989. *La Naissance du Calcul Différentiel*, translated with notes and introduction by Marc Parmentier. Vrin, Paris.

———. 1993. *De Quadratura Arithmetica Circuli Ellipseos et Hyperbolae cujus Corollarium est Trigonometria sine Tabulis*, critically edited and annotated by Eberhard Knobloch. Vandenhoeck & Ruprecht, Göttingen.

Lenoir, T. J., 1974. The Social and Intellectual Roots of Discovery in Seventeenth Century Mathematics. Ph.D. Thesis, Indiana University.

———. 1979. Descartes and the geometrization of thought: The methodological background of Descartes' *Géométrie*. *Historia Mathematica*, 6, pp. 355–379.

L'Hôpital, G. F. de, 1696. *Analyse des infiniment petits pour l'intelligence des lignes courbes*. Paris.

Locke, J., 1975. *An Essay Concerning Human Understanding*, edited by P. Nidditch. Clarendon Press, Oxford.

Löwenheim, L., 1946. On making indirect proofs direct. *Scripta Mathematica*, XII, pp. 125–139.

McGuire, J. E., 1978. Newton on place, time, and God: An unpublished source. *The British Journal for the History Of Science*, 11, pp. 114–29.

———. 1983. Space, geometrical objects and infinity: Newton and Descartes on extension, in *Nature Mathematized*, edited by W. R. Shea. Reidel, Dordrecht/ Boston, vol. I, pp. 69–112.

McMullin, E., 1965. Medieval and modern science: Continuity or discontinuity? *International Philosophical Quarterly*, 5, pp. 103–129.

———. 1992. *The Inference that Makes Science*. Marquette University Press, Milwaukee.

Mahoney, M. S., 1973. *The Mathematical Career of Pierre de Fermat, 1601–1665*. Princeton University Press, Princeton.

———. 1980. The beginnings of algebraic thought in the seventeenth century, pp. 141–155 in Gaukroger (1980).

———. 1984. Changing canons of mathematical and physical intelligibility in the later 17th century. *Historia Mathematica*, 11, pp. 417–423.

———. 1990. Barrow's mathematics: Between ancients and moderns, in *Before Newton. The Life and Times of Isaac Barrow*, edited by M. Feingold. Cambridge University Press, Cambridge, pp. 179–249.

Maierù, L., 1990. "... in Christophorum Clavium de Contactu Linearum Apologia": Considerazioni attorno alla polemica tra Peletier e Clavio circa l'angolo di contatto (1579–1589). *Archive for the History of Exact Sciences*, 41/1, pp. 115–137.

Malebranche, N., 1958–68. *Oeuvres Complètes*, edited by A. Robinet, 20 vols. Vrin, Paris.

Mancosu, P., 1989. The metaphysics of the calculus: A foundational debate in the Paris Academy of Sciences, 1700–1706. *Historia Mathematica*, 16, pp. 224–248.

———. 1991. On the status of proofs by contradiction in the seventeenth century. *Synthese*, 88, pp. 15–41.

———. 1992a. Aristotelian Logic and Euclidean mathematics: Seventeenth-century developments of the Quaestio de certitudine mathematicarum. *Studies in History and Philosophy of Science*, 23, pp. 241–265.

Mancosu, P., 1992b. Descartes's *Géométrie* and revolutions in mathematics, pp. 83–116 in Gillies (1992).

———. 1995. Motion and the foundations of mathematics from Peletier to Bolzano, in Conway and Kerszberg (1995).

Mancosu, P., Vailati, E., 1990. Detleff Clüver: An early opponent of the infinitesimal calculus. *Centaurus*, 33, pp. 325–344.

———. 1991. Torricelli's infinitely long solid and its philosophical reception in the seventeenth century. *Isis*, 82, pp. 50–70.

Méchoulan, H., ed., 1988. *Problématique et Réception du Discours de la Méthode et des Essais.* Vrin, Paris.

Medina, J., 1985. Les mathématiques chez Spinoza et Hobbes. *Revue Philosophique*, 2, pp. 177–188.

Melis, P., 1978. Studi sulla matematica di Hobbes. *Annali delle Facoltà di Lettere Filosofia e Magistero dell'Università di Cagliari*, XXXVI, pp. 171–247.

Mellin, G. S. A., 1798. *Encyclopädisches Wörterbuch der Kritischen Philosophie.* Friedrich Frommann, Züllichan/Leipzig, entry *Beweis*, pp. 654–686.

Mersenne, M., 1634/1985. *Les Questions Théologiques, Physiques, Morales et Mathématiques*, Henry Guenon. Reprinted in *Questions Inouyes . . . .* Fayard, Paris.

———. 1644. *Universae Geometriae Mixtaeque Mathematicae Synopsis.* Paris.

———. 1972. *Correspondence du P. Marin Mersenne*, edited by C. De Waard and B. Rochot. CNRS, Paris.

Milhaud, G., 1921. *Descartes Savant.* Alcan, Paris.

Mittelstraß, J., 1979. The philosopher's conception of Mathesis Universalis from Descartes to Leibniz. *Annals of Science*, 36, pp. 593–610.

Molland, A. G., 1976. Shifting the foundations: Descartes's transformation of ancient geometry. *Historia Mathematica*, 3, pp. 21–49.

———. 1991. Implicit versus explicit geometrical methodologies: The case of construction, in *Mathématiques et Philosophie de l'Antiquité à l'Age Classique*, edited by R. Rashed. CNRS, Paris, pp. 181–196.

Montucla, E., 1799–1802. *Histoire des Mathématiques*, 4 vols. Agasse, Paris.

Moretto, A., 1984. *Hegel e la "Matematica dell'Infinito,"* Pubblicazioni di Verifiche. Trento.

Mueller, I., 1981. *Philosophy of Mathematics and Deductive Structure in Euclid's Elements.* MIT Press, Cambridge, Mass.

Murdoch, J. E., 1966. Superposition, congruence and continuity in the Middle Ages, in *Melanges Alexandre Koyré.* Hermann, Paris, vol. II, pp. 416–441.

Newton, I., 1967–81. *The Mathematical Papers of Isaac Newton*, edited by D. T. Whiteside, 8 vols. Cambridge University Press, Cambridge.

Nieuwentijt, B., 1694. *Considerations circa analyseos ad quantitates infinitè parvas applicatae principia et calculi differentialis usum in resolvendis problematibus geometricis.* Amstelædami.

———. 1695. *Analysis Infinitorum, seu curvilineorum proprietates ex polygonorum natura deductæ.* Amstelædami.

———. 1696. *Considerationes secundæ circa calculi differentialis principia; et responsio ad Virum Nobilissimum G. G. Leibnitium.* Amstelædami.

North, J. D., 1983. Finite and otherwise: Aristotle and some seventeenth century views, in *Nature Mathematized*, edited by W. R. Shea. Reidel, Dordrecht/Boston, vol. I, pp. 113–148.

Olivieri, L., ed., 1983. *Aristotelismo Veneto e scienza moderna.* Antenore, Padua.

Oresme, 1968. *Le livre du ciel et du monde*, edited by A. D. Menut and A. J. Denomy. University of Wisconsin Press, Madison.

Palladino, F., 1988. Critica dei Princìpi e metodo logistico nell'opera matematica del cartesiano Michelangelo Fardella. *Nouvelles de la Republique des Lettres*, 1, pp. 51–85.

Pappus, 1933. *La collection mathématique*, translated by P. Ver Eecke, 2 vols. Blanchard, Paris.

Pardies, G. I., 1671. *Élements de Géométrie*. Paris. Second edition 1673.

Pascal, B., 1904–14. *Oeuvres*, edited by L. Brunschvicg, P. Boutroux, and F. Gazier. 14 vols, Paris.

———. 1963. *Oeuvres Complètes*. Seuil, Paris.

Pedersen, K. M., 1980. Techniques of the calculus, 1630–1660, pp. 49–93 in Grattan-Guinness (1980).

Peiffer, J., 1988. La conception de l'infiniment petit chez Pierre Varignon lecteur de Leibniz et de Newton, in *Leibniz, Tradition und Aktualität*, V. Internationaler Leibniz-Kongreß, Vorträge, pp. 710–717.

———. 1990. Pierre Varignon lecteur de Leibniz et de Newton, in *Leibniz' Auseinandersetzung mit Vorgängern und Zeitgenossen*. edited by I. Marchlewitz and A. Heinekamp, *Studia Leibnitiana*, supplement XXVII. Franz Steiner Verlag, Stuttgart, pp. 244–266.

Peletier, J., 1557. *In Euclidis Elementa Geometrica Demonstrationum Libri XV*. Basileae.

Pereyra, B., 1576. *De communibus omnium rerum naturalium principiis et affectionibus libri quindecim*. Romae.

Petry, M. J., 1986. The early reception of the calculus in the Netherlands, in *300 Jahre "Nova Methodus" von G. W. Leibniz (1684–1984)*, edited by A. Heinekamp. *Studia Leibnitiana*, special issue 14. Franz Steiner Verlag, Stuttgart, pp. 202–231.

Philosophical Transactions, 1668–69/1963. Vol. 3–4, pp. 869–876, London. Reprinted by Johnson Reprint Corporation and Kraus Reprint Corporation, New York.

———. 1670/1963. Vol. 5, pp. 2054–2057, London. Reprinted by Johnson Reprint Corporation and Kraus Reprint Corporation, New York.

Piccolomini, A., 1547. *Commentarium de Certitudine Mathematicarum Disciplinarum*. Romae.

Popkin, R., 1979. *The History of Scepticism from Erasmus to Spinoza*. University of California Press, Berkeley.

Posy, C. J., 1992. *Kant's Philosophy of Mathematics: Modern Essays*. Kluwer, Dordrecht.

Prag, A., 1931. John Wallis (1616–1703) zur Ideengeschichte der Mathematik im 17. Jahrhundert. *Quellen und Studien zur Geschichte der Mathematik, Astronomie und Physik*, Abteilung B: Studien 1, pp. 382–412.

Prestet, J., 1689, *Elémens des Mathématiques*. 2d ed., Paris.

Probst, S., 1990. Die Kontroverse zwischen John Wallis und Thomas Hobbes in den "Philosophical Transactions." Unpublished typescript.

———. 1993. Infinity and creation: The origin of the controversy between Thomas Hobbes and the Savilian professors, Seth Ward and John Wallis. *Studies in History and Philosophy of Science*, 26, pp. 271–279.

Proclus, 1970. *A Commentary on the First Book of Euclid's Elements*, translated with an introduction and notes by Glenn R. Morrow. Princeton University Press, Princeton.

Pycior, H. M., 1987. Mathematics and philosophy: Wallis, Hobbes, Barrow, and Berkeley. *Journal of the History of Ideas*, 48, pp. 265–286.

Randall, J. H., 1961. *The School of Padua and the Emergence of Modern Science.* Antenore, Padua.

Redondi, P., 1983. *Galileo Eretico.* Einaudi, Turin.

Reyneau, C., Extrait des réponses faites par Mr. Varignon, en 1700 et 1701 aux objections que Mr. Rolle avait faites contre le calcul différentiel. Manuscript, Bibliothèque Nationale, Fds Fr. 25302 fol. 144–155, edited by J. Peiffer in Bernoulli (1988, Annexe IV, pp. 351–376).

Risse, W., 1970. *Die Logik der Neuzeit,* vol. II, 1640–1780. Frommann-Holzboog, Stuttgart-Bad Cannstatt.

Rivaltus, D., 1615. *Archimedis Opera quae extant novis demonstrationibus commentarisque illustrata per Davidem Rivaltum in Flurantia . . . .* Parisiis.

Roberval, G., 1693. Observations sur la composition des mouvements et sur le moyen de trouver les touchantes des lignes courbes, pp. 1–67 in Roberval (1730).

———. 1730. *Mémoires de l'Académie Royale des Sciences depuis 1666 jusqu'à 1699,* vol. 6. Paris.

Robinet, A., 1955. *Malebranche et Leibniz. Relations Personnelles.* Vrin, Paris.

———. 1960a. Jean Prestet ou la bonne foi cartésienne (1648–1691). *Revue d'Histoire des Sciences,* 13, pp. 95–104.

———. 1960b. Le group malebranchiste introducteur du calcul infinitésimal en France. *Revue d'Histoire des Sciences* 13, pp. 287–308.

———. 1961. La philosophie malebranchiste des mathématiques, *Revue d'Histoire des Sciences,* 14, pp. 205–254.

———. 1970. *Malebranche de l'Académie des Sciences. L'Oeuvre Scientifique, 1674–1715.* Vrin, Paris.

———. 1986. *Architectonique Disjonctive, Automates Systémiques et Idéalité Transcendantale dans l'Oeuvre de G. W. Leibniz.* Vrin, Paris.

Rochot, B., 1957. Gassendi et les mathématiques. *Revue d'Histoire des Sciences,* 10, pp. 69–78.

Rolle, M., 1702. Regle et remarques pour le problème general des tangentes. *Journal des Sçavans* 16, pp. 239–254.

———. 1703a. Du nouveau systême de l'infini. *Histoire et Mémoires de l'Académie Royale des Sciences,* pp. 312–336.

———. 1703b. Remarques de M. Rolle, de l'Académie Royale des Sciences, touchant le problême general des tangentes: Pour servir de replique à la réponse qu'on a inserée, sous le nom de M. Saurin, dans le *Journal des Sçavans* du 3 aoust 1702. *Journal des Sçavans* 30, pp. 478–480.

———. 1703c. Remarques sur les lignes geometriques. *Histoire et Mémoires de l'Académie Royale des Sciences,* pp. 132–139.

———. 1704. Extraits d'une lettre de M. Rolle de l'Académie Royale des Sciences, au sujet de l'inverse des tangentes. *Journal des Sçavans,* 34, pp. 511–515.

———. 1705a. Réponse de M. Rolle de l'Académie Royale des Sciences à l'écrit publié par M. Saurin dans le journal du 23 avril 1705. *Journal des Sçavans* 20, pp. 311–318.

———. 1705b. Extrait d'une lettre de M. Rolle de l'Académie Royale des Sciences, à M. B* touchant l'analyse des infiniment petits: Où il répond à un ecrit que M. Saurin a publié dans le journal du 11 juin dernier. *Journal des Sçavans,* 32, pp. 495–510.

Rose, P. L., 1975. *The Italian Renaissance of Mathematics.* Droz, Geneva.

Russ, S. B., 1980a. The Mathematical Works of Bernard Bolzano Published between 1804 and 1817. Dissertation, Open University.

Russ, S. B., 1980b. A translation of Bolzano's paper on the intermediate value theorem. *Historia Mathematica*, 7, pp. 156–185.

Russell, B., 1903. *Principles of Mathematics*. Cambridge University Press, Cambridge.

Russo, F., 1962. Pascal et l'analyse infinitésimale. *Revue d'Histoire des Sciences*, XV, pp. 303–320.

Sacksteder, W., 1980. Hobbes: The art of the geometricians. *Journal of the History of Philosophy*, 18, pp. 131–146.

———. 1981. Hobbes: Geometrical objects. *Philosophy of Science*, 48, pp. 573–590.

Sasaki, C., 1985. The acceptance of the theory of proportion in the sixteenth and seventeenth centuries: Barrow's reaction to the analytic mathematics. *Historia Scientiarum*, 29, pp. 83–116.

Saurin, J., 1702. Réponse à l'écrit de M. Rolle de l'Académie Royale des Sciences inseré dans le journal du 13 avril 1702 sous le titre "Regle et remarques pour le probleme general des tangentes." *Journal des Sçavans* 33, pp. 519–534.

———. 1705a. Defence de la réponse à M. Rolle de l'Académie Royale des Sciences contenuë dans le *Journal des Sçavans* du 3 aoust 1702 contre la replique de cet auteur publiée en 1703 sous le titre de "Remarques touchant le problême général des tangentes & c." *Journal des Sçavans*, 16, pp. 241–256.

———. 1705b. Refutation de la réponse de M. Rolle inserée dans le *Journal des Sçavans* du 18 mai 1705. *Journal des Sçavans*, 24, pp. 367–382.

Savile, H., 1621. *Praelectiones Tresdecim in Principium Elementorum Euclidis*. Oxonii.

Scaliger, J., 1594. *Cyclometrica elementa duo*. Luduni Batavorum.

Scherbius, P., Soner, E., Picartus, M., 1644. *Philosophia Altdorphina*. Norimbergae.

Schobinger, J. P., 1974. *Kommentar zu Pascals Reflexionen über die Geometrie im Allgemeinen: "De l'esprit géométrique" und "De l'art de persuader."* Schwabe & Co., Basel/Stuttgart.

Schoenflies, A., 1906. Über die logischen Paradoxien der Mengenlehre. *Jahresbericht der deutschen Mathematiker-Vereinigung*, 50, pp. 19–25.

Scholtz, L., 1934. *Die exakte Grundlegung der Infinitesimalrechnung bei Leibniz*. (Teildruck), Marburg. (Inaugural-Dissertation).

Schrecker, P., 1935. Arnauld, Malebranche, Prestet et la théorie des nombres négatives. *Thalès*, II, pp. 82–90.

———. 1946/1969. On the infinite number of infinite orders, in *Studies and Essays in the History of Science and Learning offered in Homage to George Sarton*, edited by M. F. Ashley Montagu. Schuman, New York, pp. 359–373. Reprinted by Kraus Reprint Corporation, New York.

Schuhmann, K., 1985. Geometrie und Philosophie bei Thomas Hobbes. *Philosophisches Jahrbuch*, 92, pp. 161–177.

Schüling, H., 1969. *Die Geschichte der Axiomatischen Methode im 16. und Beginnenden 17. Jahrhundert*. Georg Olms Verlag, Hildesheim/New York.

Scott, J. F., 1938/1981. *The Mathematical Work of John Wallis, D.D., F.R.S. (1616–1703)*. London. Reprinted by Chelsea Publishing Company, New York.

———. 1952. *The Scientific Work of René Descartes*. Taylor and Francis, London.

Scriba, C. J., 1960–61. Zur Lösung des 2. Debeauneschen Problems durch Descartes, *Archive for the History of Exact Sciences*, 1, pp. 406–419.

———. 1966. *Studien zur Mathematik des John Wallis (1606–1703)*. Franz Steiner Verlag, Wiesbaden.

Sergescu, P., 1938. Dernières batailles pour le triomphe du calcul infinitésimal. *Sphinx: Revue Mensuelle des Questions Récréatives*, 8, pp. 125–129.

Sergescu, P., 1942/1944. Un episod din batalia pentru triumful calcului diferential: Polemica Rolle-Saurin 1702–1705. Bucharest. Republished in *Essais Scientifiques*, Timisoara.

Smith, Mark A., 1976. Galileo's theory of indivisibles: Revolution or compromise? *Journal of the History of Ideas*, 37, pp. 571–588.

Sover, B., 1630. *Curvi ac Recti Proportio*. Bononiae.

Stone, E., 1726. *A New Mathematical Dictionary*. Senex, London.

Strong, E., 1936. *Procedures and Metaphysics*. University of California Press, Berkeley.

Struik, D. J., 1969. *A Source Book in Mathematics, 1200–1800*. Princeton University Press, Princeton.

Szabó, A. K., 1976. *The Beginnings of Greek Mathematics*. Reidel, Dordrecht.

Tacquet, A., 1650. Dissertatio phisico-mathematica de motu circuli et sphaerae, in *Opera Mathematica*, vol. 2. Antverpiae, 1669.

———. 1651. Annularia et cylindrica, in *Opera Mathematica*, vol. 1. Antverpiae, 1669.

Tamborini, M., 1987. Tematiche algebriche Vietane nelle regulae e nel libro primo della *Géométrie* di Descartes, in *Miscellanea Secentesca. Saggi su Descartes, Fabri, White*. Cisalpino Goliardica, Milan, pp. 51–84.

Thomas, I., 1967. *Greek Mathematical Works*, 2 vols. Loeb Library.

Tonelli, G., 1959. Der Streit über die mathematische Methode in der Philosophie in der ersten Hälfte des 18. Jahrhunderts und die Entstehung von Kants Schrift über die 'Deutlichkeit'. *Archiv für Philosophie*, IX, pp. 37–66.

Torricelli, E., 1644a. *Opera Geometrica*. Florentaie.

———. 1644b, 1919–44. De solido hyperbolico acuto, in *Opera Geometrica*, Florentiae. Reprinted in *Opere di Evangelista Torricelli*, edited by G. Loria and G. Vassura. Stabilimento Tipografico Montanari, Faenza.

———. 1975. *Opere Scelte di Evangelista Torricelli*. Utet, Turin.

Trendelenburg, A., 1870/1964. *Logische Untersuchungen*, vol. II. Reprinted by Georg Olms, Hildesheim.

Tropfke, J., 1933, *Geschichte der Elementar-Mathematik*, 3d ed., vol. II. Walter de Gruyter & Co., Berlin/Leipzig.

Ulivi, E., 1982. Il teorema di Pappo-Guldino: Dimostrazioni ed attribuzioni. *Bollettino di Storia delle Scienze Matematiche*, vol. II, pp. 179–208.

———. 1990. Il tracciamento delle curve prima di Descartes, pp. 517–541 in Belgioioso et al. (1990).

Valerio, L., 1604. *De Centro Gravitatis Solidorum*. Romae.

Varignon, P., 1703a. Remarques sur les courbes des deux premiers examples proposés par M. Rolle dans le journal du jeudi 13 avril 1702. *Journal des Sçavans*, 3, pp. 41–46.

———. 1703b. Suite des remarques sur les courbes des deux premiers examples proposés par M. Rolle, dans le journal du jeudi 13 avril 1702. *Journal des Sçavans* 4, pp. 49–52.

———. 1725. *Nouveaux Eclaircissemens sur l'Analyse des Infiniment Petits*. Paris.

Vermeulen, B. P., 1985. Berkeley and Nieuwentijt on infinitesimals. *Berkeley Newsletter*, 8, pp. 1–15.

———. 1986. The metaphysical presuppositions of Nieuwentijt's criticism of Leibniz's higher-order differentials, in *300 Jahre "Nova Methodus" von G. W. Leibniz (1684–1984). Studia Leibnitiana*, special issue 14. Franz Steiner Verlag, Stuttgart, pp. 178–184.

Vermij, R. H., 1989. Bernard Nieuwentijt and the Leibnizian calculus. *Studia Leibnitiana*, XXI/1, pp. 69–86.

Vivanti, G., 1894. *Il concetto d'infinitesimo e la sua applicazione alla matematica.* Mantua.

von Fritz, K., 1959. Gleichheit, Kongruenz und Ähnlichkeit in der Antiken Mathematik bis auf Euklid. *Archiv für Begriffsgeschichte,* 4, pp. 7–81.

Vuillemin, J., 1960. *Mathématiques et Metaphysique chez Descartes.* Presses Universitaires de France, Paris.

Wagner, R. J., 1983. Euclid's intended interpretation of superposition. *Historia Mathematica,* 10, pp. 63–89.

Walker, E., 1932. *A Study of the Traité des Indivisibles of Gilles Persone de Roberval.* Teachers College, New York.

Wallace, W., 1984. *Galileo and his Sources: the Heritage of the Collegio Romano in Galileo's Theory of Science.* Princeton University Press, Princeton.

Wallis, J., 1655a. *Elenchus Geometriae Hobbianae.* Oxonii.

———. 1655b. *Arithmetica Infinitorum.* London. Reprinted in vol. 1 of Wallis (1696–99).

———. 1656–70. *Opera Mathematica,* 2 vols. Oxonii.

———. 1665. *Mathesis Universalis: sive arithmeticum opus integrum.* London. Reprinted in vol. 1 of Wallis (1696–99).

———. 1671. Answer to four papers of Mr. Hobs [*sic*], lately published in the month of August, and this present September, 1671. *Philosophical Transactions,* 75, pp. 2241–2250.

———. 1685. *A Treatise of Algebra.* London. Reprinted in vol. 2 of Wallis (1696–99).

———. 1696–99/1972. *Opera Mathematica,* 3 vols. Oxonii. Reprinted by Georg Olms Verlag, Hildesheim/New York.

Weigel, E., 1658. *Analysis Aristotelica ex Euclide Restituta.* Jenae.

Whiteside, D. T., 1960–61. Patterns of mathematical thought in the later seventeenth century. *Archive for the History of Exact Sciences,* 1, pp. 179–388.

Wurtz, J.-P., 1989. La naissance du calcul différential et le problème du statut des infiniment petits: Leibniz et Guillame de l'Hospital, in *La Mathématique non Standard,* edited by H. Barré and J. Harthong. CNRS, Paris, pp. 13–41.

Yoder, J. G., 1988. *Unrolling Time: Christiaan Huygens and the Mathematization of Nature.* Cambridge University Press, Cambridge.

Zeuthen, H. G., 1966. *Geschichte der Mathematik im 16. und 17. Jahrhundert.* Johnson Reprint Corporation, New York.

INDEX